Insurance Management

Fundamental Concepts, Procedures & Practices

INSURANCE MANAGEMENT

Fundamental Concepts, Procedures & Practices

K.C. SHARMA

and

KIYANOUSH GHALAVAND

REGAL PUBLICATIONS

New Delhi - 110 027

INSURANCE MANAGEMENT
Fundamental Concepts, Procedures & Practices

ISBN 978-81-8484-369-9

Typeset by
THE LASER PRINTERS
8/15, 3rd Floor, Subhash Nagar, New Delhi-110027

Printed in India at
MAYUR ENTERPRISES,
WZ Plot No. 3, Gujjar Market, Tihar Village, New Delhi-110018

Published by
REGAL PUBLICATIONS
F-159, Rajouri Garden, New Delhi-110027
Phones : 45546396, 25435369
E-mail : regalbookspub@yahoo.com, regaldeepbooks@yahoo.com

Contents

Preface

All individuals and business organizations increasingly recognize that high levels of professional knowledge and skills are essential to their success. Both of them are increasingly spending on professional education as knowledge and processes change fast in today's scenario due to technology changes as a result of new breakthroughs in science and new dimensions added by research. Expenditure on research and development is considered an investment into a collective future. Investment in human resource, truly called human capital, has thus acquired position in the centre stage of strategies in all the countries to promote economic well-being, better skilled labour forces, social cohesion, team spirit and other positive individual and social benefits. However, investment in professional education is not adequate due to limited public and private resources as identified by 'UNESCO Millennium Goals'. There is a challenge in regard to desired rather needed expansion in professional educational opportunities. The challenge is that of maintaining their quality and ensuring their equitable distribution. This is linked to the questions of harnessing finances in competition with various equally pressing demands on this critical resource.

Reforms have been ushered in the insurance sector and the sector has been opened to foreign competition. We can see that one of the significant gains of insurance sector reforms has been the tremendous increase in the awareness levels of general public about the insurance terms, conditions, privileges of the policyholder, and obligations of the insurer. Deficiency of service can be brought to judicial system to claim damage and compensation. Insurance is sunrise industry; it has tremendous employment opportunities that are growing manifold. A lot of youngsters are coming forward to learn more and more about the insurance subject. Their aim is not only to get a foothold in the employment market but also to improve their knowledge to make informed decisions when they go in for buying insurance and also guide their friends, relatives and kin.

The aim of bringing out this book is to help students, insurance teachers and others interested in the subject to:

(a) become self-reliant, so that they acquire the expertise to determine their own priorities to interpret and use insurance concept effectively;
(b) undertake research, problem-solving and problem formulation; and
(c) sustain capacities to create insurance consciousness.

It has been observed the world over that the Insurers are engaged in a battle to create and maintain high skilled talent in their workforces. There is relentless competition that has led insurers to monitor skills, in particular the training skills, in their executives. This seeks to empower such insurance executives to handle insurance business confidently and to the satisfaction of the insured.

This book would be found surely as a gateway enabling individuals to learn new skills in both the classroom and the workplace, while imbibing their learning rights and execution responsibilities.

While life insurance has taken roots and is becoming a need in many literate persons, the business of general insurance is still on a rapid growth path and has to spread to embrace all spheres concerned. General insurers are contributing to corporate risk management and protection of underlying assets of financing banks. There are increased litigations and consumer activism. General insurance is assisting in liability or casualty management of individuals and corporates. Major lines of general insurance are fire, marine, and miscellaneous including motor insurance. General insurance risks are usually managed on an annual basis. Life Insurance insures lives of individuals, key business functionaries, business partners and groups of workers. Although aspects such as marketing, asset management, survey and adjustment are other technical areas of general insurance yet underwriting and claims management are critical areas for insurance. This book is also an effort to integrate the insurance concepts and practices to present a business model that would possibly work.

This book deals with Insurance Management as regards Fundamental Concepts, Procedures and Practices only. We most gratefully acknowledge the debt due from us to our colleagues and friends for their contribution in the completion of the present work. Our special gratitude goes to Mrs. Vidya Sharma and her daughters, Anjana and Anupama and grandchildren (Mrikula, Kushagara, Abhimanyu and Utkarsh). While Mrs. Vidya Sharma, wife of Dr. K.C. Sharma encouraged us, Anjana and Anupama contributed their ideas; Abhimanyu helped with the computer and Utkarsh fiddled with the computer, as usual, reminding Dr. Sharma of the work awaiting his consistent attention.

We are particularly thankful to Regal Publications, New Delhi, for bringing out this book within a reasonably short time and in a nice get-up.

K.C. SHARMA
KIYANOUSH GHALAVAND

Acknowledgements

Writing book needs good health, academic interest, access to library, facility of Internet, a reasonably good command over the language which, to good measure the author's possess. It has been God-send in Mr. Kiyanoush Ghalavand, an Iranian national that brought experience and maturity to the first author's aid which is hereby thankfully acknowledged.

There have been fairly good number of friends, professors, practitioners and writers who discussed the subject sparing slices of their time not once each but a number of times the authors approached them, without any frown on their forehead rather displayed spontaneous interest in making suggestions, comments and showing the right path, as they considered appropriate. We express our gratitude to them, and do not like to mention each one by name as the list will be very lengthy. We feel that a few names may be given though others are no less important. They are Professor Jai Narain Sharma, Dr. (Miss) Ashu Pasricha, Dr. Sunanda Ghosh, Prof. (Dr.) N.K. Sahni, Dr. (Mrs.) Anupama S. Pathak, Dr. Poonam Sharma, Prof. A.K. Vashisht, Dr. Bimal Anjum, Professor P. Parkash Arya, Dr. (Mrs.) Geetanjali Bhatnagar, Mrs. Anjana Sharma, Dr. Amit Mohindroo and Dr. Deeksha.

Our apologies to many others left out from being mentioned by name but who have made their contribution and enriched the knowledge of the authors; we thank them without mentioning their names.

K.C. SHARMA
KIYANOUSH GHALAVAND

1

Genesis of Insurance

HISTORICAL BACKGROUND

Insurance in the modern sense originated as a formal business in the late seventeenth Century. It is seen that Insurance assumed sophistication in post-Renaissance Europe. In the late 1680s, Mr. Edward Lloyd opened a coffee house that became a popular haunt of ship owners, merchants, and ship-captains. As reliable source of the latest shipping news, Lloyd's became the meeting place for parties wishing to insure cargoes and ships. Lloyd's of London remains the market leader for marine and other special types of insurance.

Indian scholars observe that the Sanskrit term 'yogakshema' or well-being of the society (or insurance) is found in the Rig Veda. The 'Joint Family System' practised in India is a form of micro-insurance to take care of calamitous situations. In day-to-day transactions, too, individuals have been standing guarantee for the debts raised from the money-lenders by their friends and relatives. This guarantee was a kind of insurance, though in a crude manner.

In 1934, the Government of India appointed S.C. Sen, a well-known solicitor, to study and report on the amendments to insurance legislation. The government set-up an Informal Advisory Committee of leading insurance men, headed by N.N. Sircar, the then Law Member in the Council of the Governor-General and Viceroy. This committee submitted a Bill to the Legislative Assembly in 1937. At last, the Insurance Act, 1938 was enacted. The Insurance Act became the corner-stone of Indian insurance legislation.

On May 13, 1971, an ordinance was promulgated by the President of India to take over the management of 107 general insurance companies by the Government of India. General Insurance Business (Nationalization) Act, 1972 or GIBNA became the guiding Act of General Insurance till the IRDA Act was passed in 1999.

The process or method of evaluating an insurer's promises to perform certain obligations under certain specified future situations is not an easy task for the customers of insurance (the insured). The degree of standardization of general insurance products varies from country to country, from rigidly controlled tariff markets to open markets with minimal controls.

Past observations regarding the working of the insurers brought to sharp focus the intensive and unregulated competition in marketing general insurance products can produce inadequate rates and insolvency. It also breeds sharp loss adjusting practices, abortive policy language and tendencies towards monopolization. These are recognized to be against public interest.

There is no economic activity where profit is given a go-by. All businesses and industries aim at profits for their survival and sustenance. Therefore, the insurers need to enter into different types of reinsurance contracts as part of their business. The regulator has to ensure that foreign exchange is not unduly drained-off through reckless reinsurance programmes of the insurers. Many regulators specify that the insurers shall cede a certain percentage of the sum insured on each policy for different classes of insurance written in the country to national reinsure(s) registered in the country.

Rates of premium should be such as to ensure the survival of the insurance company, achieving optimum strategic positioning, providing quality and value for the service, contributing to the society's well-being and optimizing the returns for a given type of risk.

Any circumstance of characteristic or factor that is within the knowledge of the insuring person and is likely to influence the insurer in deciding whether he will accept or refuse the risk, or influence him in assessing the premium that he will charge, must be fully disclosed to the insurer before the contract is concluded. The action of the proposer in withholding these vital details from the insurer is not in keeping with the principle of utmost good faith in insurance. Such behaviour smacks of undesirable business ethics.

The common man knows that insurable interest denotes such an interest in the object insured, whereby any loss or damage to the object would seriously prejudice the interests of the insured. Insurance thrives on theory of large numbers; insurance covers only the pure loss, not the speculative loss. Only losses covered by insurance are paid as claim by the insurers not all losses; this is the principle of nearest cause in insurance.

Indians have not considered insurance as necessary; they are fatalists and take any loss or damage as the will of God. It is this reason why insurance industry in India is lagging behind its counterparts in the developed countries in the fields like risk management and loss prevention techniques as well as the non-life actuarial studies and arbitration. The industry also lacks credible data for insurance product development by loss modelling.

Business of general insurance is still in its movement in rapid growth mode. General insurers are contributing to the corporate risk management and protection of underlying assets of financing banks. With litigations and consumer activism, general insurance is also assisting in liability or casualty management of individuals and corporate bodies. Fire, marine and miscellaneous including motor insurance are presently the major lines of general insurance.

EVOLUTION OF CONCEPT OF INSURANCE

It is a historical fact that the relatively modern societies that built up economies with money and financial instruments evolved other forms of insurance down the centuries. In the money economy context, Chinese and Babylonian traders evolved some methods of transferring or distributing risk as long ago as the 3rd and 2nd millennia BC, respectively. Chinese merchants travelling treacherous river rapids would redistribute their risks across many vessels to limit the loss due to any single vessel being capsized. As recorded in the famous code of Hammurabi, the Babylonians developed a system around 1750 BC that was practised by early Mediterranean sailing merchants. It meant if a merchant received a loan to fund his shipment, he would pay the lender an additional sum in exchange for the lender's guarantee to cancel the loan should the shipment be stolen. The Code of Hammurabi indicates that ancient Babylon had government insurances for theft and crop as well as for adoption of annuity plan. Personal insurance on contribution principle has been found in the Thiasoi of the ancient Greece.

It is believed that Achaemenian monarchs were the first to insure their people through an official process by registering donations to the monarch in governmental notary offices. Each year, in Norouz (beginning of the Iranian New year), the heads of different ethnic groups as well as others who were willing to take part in the process, presented gifts to the monarch. When a gift was worth more than 10,000 Derrik (Achaemenian gold coin weighing 8.35-8.42g), it was registered in a special office so that whenever the person who presented the gift was in trouble, the monarch and the court would help him. As per Jahez, a historian and writer, whenever the donor of the present was in trouble or wanted to construct a building, set-up a fest or have his children married, the court would check the registration and the donor would receive double the amount. The ancient inhabitants of Rhodes invented the concept of the 'general average' whereby merchants whose goods were being shipped together would pay a proportionally divided premium which would be used to reimburse any merchant whose goods were jettisoned (thrownout of a ship to save the ship, lives or other goods) during storm or sinking.

It is believed that the Greeks and the Romans introduced the origins of health and life insurance around 600 AD when they organized guilds called benevolent societies that cared for the families and paid funeral expenses of members upon death. Rome evolved the Fund of Collegia of the soldiery. Funds of the Collegia Tenuiorum were used to meet the unexpected expenses, burial expenses and needs of the soldiers' families; guilds in the middle ages served a similar purpose.

What we now understand about the concept of Insurance, we may like to find how it worked in a different manner before insurance was established in the late 17th century in the modern, systemic and scientific sense. Friendly societies existed in England in which people donated amounts of money to a general pool that could be used for overcoming emergent situations. Stand alone insurance contracts or insurance policies, as we find today, not bundled with loans or other kinds of contracts, are believed to have been invented in Genoa in the 14th century. Insurance pools were formed and backed by pledges of landed estates. These new insurance contracts allowed insurance to be separated from investment. It is interesting to know that Insurance became far more sophisticated in post-renaissance Europe, and its specialized varieties developed.

As England had acquired hegemony over three-fourths of the world countries, either as colonies or under suzerainty, London's growing importance as a centre for trade by the end of the seventeenth century created a sudden spurt in demand for marine insurance. In the late 1680s, Mr. Edward Lloyd opened a coffee house that became a popular haunt of ship owners, merchants, and ship-captains, and thereby the coffee house became a reliable source of the latest shipping news. It became the meeting place for parties wishing to insure cargoes and ships, and also for those willing to underwrite such ventures. Today, Lloyd's of London remains the leading market insurer (note that it is not an insurance company) for marine and other specialized types of insurance, but it works rather differently than the more familiar kinds of insurance that we know.

Regarding regulating Insurance through legal provisions, the earliest version of insurance law relates to marine insurance for which the English are indebted to the Lombards, who, driven away from their native states in Northern and Central Italy about the middle of the 13th century, settled in every maritime country in Europe. It appears that laws issued by the magistrates of Barcelona, laws published in Venice in 1468 and other regulations were familiar to the Lombards. Those laws and regulations formed the basis upon which the Lombards effected insurance on English merchandise from their residences in Lombard Street in London. The power of the Lombards was broken by a decree in 1597. Keate and Gurney state that the most important laws came from an unknown French source in a set of regulations published probably at Rouen in the 17th century. In British statute books, we find no mention of Marine insurance untill 1601 when an Act was passed "concerning matters of assurance amongst Merchants". The Act of Parliament promulgated in 1720 vested monopoly rights of marine insurance in the two companies, Royal Exchange and London Assurance, and Lloyds, until the Act was repealed in 1824. However, there was no marked development in the British Laws until 1756, untill Lord Mansfield became Lord Chief Justice and devoted himself earnestly to the study of the principles of marine insurance and their application in other countries. From Lord Mansfield's times, till the Marine Insurance Act of 1906, the law of marine insurance was administered by an appeal to precedent.

One of the most momentous events of the century happened in London in June 1861 having had unfavourable bearing on the insurance front; it triggered deep thinking and wise theorizing by the finance experts. It was the Great Fire (the greatest since 1666 when insurance was born in rudiments) at Tooley Street, Southward. The devastating and menacing fire apparently started in stored hemp, spread furiously all around the store; it could not be fully extinguished for a fortnight. The fire offices sustained an enormous loss estimated between pound sterling 1 and 2 million. The companies noted and learnt a bitter lesson and concluded that the situation had gone out of hand due to the high loss and low premiums due excessive competition among the insurance firms. In the aftermath of this 'Great Fire of London', that destroyed/devoured 13,200 houses, Nicholas Barbon opened an office to insure buildings. In 1680, he established England's fire insurance company, the Fire Office, to insure brick and frame homes. Insurers came together and to ensure that a repeat of this 'Great

Fire of London' would not happen in the future, a new institution, the Fire Offices Committee (FOC), a voluntary and autonomous association, was formally created by the various fire insurance offices (called those days as simply Fire Offices) in 1868. Under the broad understanding and comprehensive arrangement that was worked out, the companies transacting fire insurance agreed to adhere to certain minimum rates (cartel of insurers established with unanimity). Thus born, the FOC ushered in a new era of cooperation among British insurers. Taking a cue from this development, such organizational framework was adopted by Accident Offices Association (AOA), Engineering Offices Association (EOA) and Aviation Offices Insurance Association (AOIA). It was through this entire process that insurance evolved and established as an independent subject and profession, distinctly different from other branches of financial transitions.

Learning from the United Kingdom's experience, though indirectly, the concept of insurance was given shape in the United States. The first insurance company that underwrote the fire insurance was formed in Charles Town (modern day Charleston) in South Carolina, in 1732. Benjamin Franklin helped to popularize the concept; he also helped to standardise the practice of insurance, particularly that against fire, in the form of perpetual insurance. In 1752, he founded the 'Philadelphia Contributionship' for the insurance of Houses from Loss by Fire. Franklin's company was the first in the US to make contributions towards fire prevention pool. Besides, his company warned against certain fire hazards. In case of certain buildings where the risk of fire was too great, such as all wooden houses, his company refused insurance.

CURRENT INDIAN INSURANCE SCENARIO

The concept of insurance was not absolutely new in India; it was still new in the organized form as witnessed in the West. The fundamental insurance principle of a group sharing the losses of a few had been appreciated in India in some way or other from very ancient times. Hinduism, like other ancient religions, exhorts man to help his fellow men in distress; this attitude was the result of internalization of values and extended from personal life to the field of commerce in some way or the other. Scholars observe that the Sanskrit term 'Yogakshema' (well-being of the society at large) is found in the Rig Veda and that some kind of community insurance was practised by the Aryan tribes of India nearly 3000 years ago. Manu Smriti speaks of a system of collective co-operation. Yajnavalkya, an author and theoretician of the ancient times in India, mentions some transactions akin to insurance. In its earliest and crude form, insurance was probably perceived as a function of the State. In the ninth chapter of the *magnum opus*, Shrimad Bhagavad Gita, Lord Krishna (Lord Vishnu incarnate) promises Yogakshema to devotees. The kings were expected to look after their people and *praja ranjan* (welfare of the subjects) alone could justify their existence according to ancient Sanskrit literature. The 'Joint Family System' practised in India is seen by many as a form of micro-insurance to take care of calamitous situations, including death and sickness within the extended family. In course of time, many monarchs turned despotic and the functions of the State in even advanced countries were limited to the protection of subjects against foreign attacks and maintenance of law and order within the country. In the Indian religious and philosophical contexts (economic transactions included), religion and 'other worldliness' dominated the economic institutions. This state continued until the arrival of the Europeans on the Indian soil and organization of economic activity by them in the fashion/design, as we see it in the modern world that took shape.

We may give credit to the British who started modern life insurance in India through their influence. Many English companies extended their branches to India for underwriting European lives and later Parsee and Indian lives too. Sir John Child, who was the Governor of Bombay Presidency between 1681 and 1690, was instructed by the Court of Directors of East India Company to constitute an insurance office on the Bombay Island. It is not known what came of this organization. The Bombay Insurance Society was set-up in 1793 on Bombay Island by a few well-known European merchants. Life Insurance in its present form came to India from the United Kingdom with the establishment of a British firm, Oriental Life Insurance Company, in Calcutta (now named Kolkata) in 1818 to help the widows of the European community. This was followed by the formation of the Bombay Life Assurance Company in 1829, and the Oriental Government Security Life Insurance Company in 1874. It has been documented that as early as 1822, when Indian social reformers were opposing the prevalent practice of Sati, Raja Ram Mohan Roy appealed through the Calcutta Journal to the good sense of the rich to start a fund for widows and orphans. Round about the decade beginning from 1850, considerable pressure seems to have been brought to bear upon the then British Government of India to operate life insurance business under government control through a department of the State. History tells us that the proposal was turned down as the government did not possess sufficient data on Indian lives and that the insurance consciousness was not present to an adequate degree among the masses. The Princely State of Travancore (part of present Kerala State) was issuing life insurance policies in the late 19th century, and policies of 1896 are still preserved by the Kerala State Insurance Department, Thiruvananthapuram (old name Trivandrum).

There is evidence in India of the earliest known policy in English (dated 1555). It is expressed as on the good ship Santa Cruz 'from any port in the isles of Indes or Calicut unto Lixborne'. It is known that members of the East India Company handled Bottomry Bond transactions as they were allowed to do business or engage in any occupation or pursuit of choice while also being in the service of Company. The first general insurance company, the Triton Insurance Company Limited, was established in Kolkata in 1850; it transacted selected business. The Indian Mercantile Insurance Company Limited, which was set-up in Bombay in 1907, was the first Indian company to transact all classes of general insurance business.

We can rely upon the documented information on non-life insurance operations in the country, as available from the early 20th century. The Royal Exchange Assurance opened shop in India in 1900, and by 1907 almost 10 per cent of its accident insurance business came from India and six other foreign agencies. Royal Exchange Assurance's net marine premium from India for the year 1914 is recorded as pound sterling 40,000 as against pound sterling 17,000 from Australia and pound sterling 10,000 from South Africa. Thus, Indian businessmen, Europeans included, availed of insurance facility.

Bombay (now Mumbai) emerged from the First World War as the Centre of

Indian trade. Inspired by the growth of Indian trade and industry, and encouraged by the undercurrent of nationalism, leading businessmen in Mumbai rose to give concrete shape to proposals for meeting the insurance needs of Indian trade. Five Indian owned insurance offices were established in 1919, almost simultaneously, for transacting general insurance business. The newly formed insurance companies received support from the growth of nationalism in India.

Mahatma Gandhi stated, "The keynote of all our Swaraj is in placing all our insurance with our Indian companies". Jawahar Lal Nehru said, "I hope Indians will realize the importance of patronizing only Indian insurance institutions".

A few years after 1922 were critical for Indian insurance when six new Indian offices were pitted against nearly 150 foreign offices, including some of the largest insurance groups in the world. The general economic conditions were against the Indian offices and political agitation was at its zenith. Simultaneously, a powerful combination of American Offices began their operations followed by a number of French companies a year later. To make matters worse for Indian companies, an all round reduction in rates was enforced in 1928, depression set in a year later, volume and value of foreign trade fell immediately, farm prices came down and purchasing power fell, and internal economy collapsed, while serious fire losses in Karachi (now in Pakistan) and heavy riot losses in Mumbai were incurred

However, the Indian industry came to the rescue of Indian insures and hundreds of Indian businessmen signed a pledge to insure only with Indian offices. By this time, Indian industries such as sugar, paper, matches, paint and cement had gradually begun to take root, aided by a protective tariff system. Indian insurers' share of the total business written in India rose from a mere 11 per cent in 1928 to 22 per cent in 1935 and 32 per cent in 1939, largely at the expense of foreign offices, while the total business itself had registered an increase of only 5 per cent during the period. This tells encouraging story of the success of Indian insurance companies/offices.

DEVELOPMENT OF INDIAN INSURANCE MARKET

So far, we have discussed the evolution of the market prior to the passing of the Insurance Act, 1938. The second phase of evolution of insurance started from the middle of the 1930s. Here, we should know that physical or service product has a life cycle—introduction, adolescence, adult, maturity, decline and finally extinct (or exit). On this analogy, during this period, the Indian market came out of its adolescence and stared addressing problems similar to those faced by the more nature markets. The market and the government were seized by the gravity of the situation, and concerted efforts were made leading to the enactment of the Insurance Act, 1938. The introduction of this Act of 1938 is generally regarded as the turning point for insurance regulation in India and the beginning of the insurance market as it existed in recent times. It would be beneficial at this stage to have a peep into the provisions of this Act.

THE BEGINNINGS: LANDMARKS IN INSURANCE

Indian Insurance Act, 1938

The British government appointed, in 1934, S.C. Sen, a well-known solicitor, as

Officer on Special Duty in the Department of Commerce to study the insurance subject and report on the desired amendments to insurance legislation which could streamline Insurance in India and serve the public purpose as expected by the insured and prospects. Insurance legislation by then was based on the decrees of the Governor-General and Viceroy in Council. Sen studied the British model. He propounded the British ideal of minimum statutory control with maximum publicity and put up his proposal. The government set-up an informal Advisory Committee of leading insurance men, headed by N.N. Sircar, the then Law Member in the Viceroy's Executive Council, with some modifications to the proposal put up by Sen. This Committee elicited views and suggestions from many stakeholders and submitted a Bill to the Legislative Assembly in 1937. The Bill stirred up intense public interest in the country, trade associations submitted memoranda, insurance associations pressed for amendments and a Lloyd's representative flew over from London to watch their interest. Over a thousand amendments were suggested from various quarters and at last the Insurance Act, 1938 was enacted.

However, soon the market started criticizing the Act for its drafting mistakes, contradictions and impractical clauses. It may widely be conceded that the Act wrote a fresh chapter into the history of Indian insurance by attempting to prevent the formation and continuation of mushrooming companies and by introducing sound insurance business practices, some authors commented that it became the most controversial law among Indian statutes.

In quick response to the criticism of various provisions of the Act, the government made two amendments to the Act in 1939. Not only these amendments, but also the Act was again amended in 1940 to remove certain difficulties in administration of the Act. The market situation that came up with World War II and the insurers' experience of working with the Act necessitated further changes and so, further amendments were made in 1941, 1942, 1944, 1946 and 1948.

Despite the flaws that were pointed out by the concerned, the 1938 Act gave the Indian market a regulatory foundation and among other things, provided for the establishment/constitution of a Department of Insurance, compulsory registration of insurance companies, provision for mobilizing deposits by the insurance companies, control on investment of funds, filing of returns on investments and financial condition, licensing of agents, control on commission, prohibition of rebates, filing of policy conditions and premium rates duly certified by an actuary (in the case of life business), periodical valuation of liabilities, and provision for policy-holders' directors on the Boards of the companies. The Act granted very wide powers to the Controller of Insurance in the matter of insurance regulation. The government visualized that the Controller of Insurance should be a person of extraordinary calibre, be actuarially qualified, having human considerations and broad outlook to administer law tactfully and even-handedly. The Indian insurance legislation turned into a good piece of legislation; it was lauded by contemporary commentators as an excellent attempt to penalize the corrupt directors and executive officers, check wild cat schemes and scandals, and to stop acquisition of insurance companies by designing financiers.

The insurance Act became the corner-stone of Indian insurance legislation and along with the insurance Rules framed under it, still remains the most comprehensive legislation on the subject.

2

General Insurance: Concept and Development

In the beginning, it was General insurance which was thought for risk management in trade. Later, it was extended to cover properties and other goods. When we trace the history of Insurance, we find that Insurance is neither very old nor so modern concept; it originated as a formal business in the late 17th Century. Insurance assumed sophistication in post-Renaissance Europe. In the late 1680s, Mr. Edward Lloyd opened a coffee house that became a popular haunt of ship owners, merchants, and ship-captains. A reliable source of the latest shipping news, Lloyd's, became the meeting place for parties wishing to insure cargoes and ships. Lloyd's of London remains the leading market for marine and other specialist types of insurance.

Indian scholars, more particularly those having knowledge of Indian scriptures, observe that the Sanskrit term 'yogakshema' or well-being of the society or insurance is found in the Rig Veda. The 'Joint Family System' practised in India is a form of micro-insurance to take care of calamitous situations.

In 1934, the then British Government appointed S.C. Sen, a well-known solicitor in India, to study and report on the amendments to insurance legislation. The government set-up an Informal Advisory committee of leading insurance men, headed by N.N. Sircar, the then Law Member, in the British India government. This committee submitted a bill to the Legislative Assembly in 1937. At last, the Insurance Act, 1938 was enacted. The Insurance Act became the corner-stone of Indian insurance legislation.

May 13, 1971 was historic date when an ordinance was promulgated by the President of India to take over the ownership and management of 107 general insurance companies then operating in India, by the Government of India. General insurance Business (Nationalization) Act, 1972 or GIBNA became the guiding act of General Insurance till the IRDA Act was passed in 1999.

Evaluating an insurer's promises to perform certain obligations under certain specified future situations is not an easy task for the customers of insurance. The degree of standardization of general insurance products varies from country to country, from rigidly controlled tariff markets to open markets with minimal controls, compatible with the type of government or state of economy.

Intensive or cut-throat and unregulated competition in marketing general insurance products can produce inadequate rates and insolvency. It also breeds sharp loss adjusting practices, abortive policy language and tendencies towards monopolization. These are recognized to be against public interest.

In answering to the requirements of clients, the insurers need to enter into different types of reinsurance contracts as part of their business. The regulator has to ensure that foreign exchange is not unduly drained-off through reckless re-insurance programmes of the insurers. Many regulators specify that the insurers shall cede such percentage of the sum insured on each policy for different classes of insurance written in the country to a national reinsurer(s) registered in the country.

Premium rates are crucial to insurance business; these should ensure the survival of the insurance company, achieving optimum strategy positioning, providing quality and value for the service, contributing to the society's well-being and optimizing the returns for a given type of risk.

As the insurance contract is based on utmost faith, any circumstance that is within the knowledge of the insuring person and is likely to influence the insurer in deciding whether he will accept or refuse the risk, or influence him in assessing the premium that he will charge, must be fully disclosed to the insured before the contract is concluded. The action of the proposer in withholding these vital details from the insurer is not in keeping with the principle of utmost good faith in insurance.

Insurable interest denotes such an interest to the common man, in the object insured, whereby any loss or damage to the object would seriously prejudice the interests of the insured. Insurance thrives on theory of large numbers; insurance covers only the pure risk/loss, not the speculative loss. Only losses covered by insurance are paid as claim by the insurers not all losses; this is the principle of nearest cause in insurance.

Due to lack of innovation, Insurance industry in India is lagging behind its counterparts in the developed countries in such fields as risk management, loss prevention techniques, non-life actuarial studies and arbitration. The industry also lacks credible data for insurance product development by loss modeling.

Indians being conservative, business of general insurance is still in its rapid growth path. Still, the general insurers are contributing to corporate risk management and protection of underlying assets of financing banks. With litigations and consumer activism, general insurance is also assisting in liability or casualty management of individuals and corporates. Fire, marine and miscellaneous including motor insurance are major lines of general insurance.

EVOLUTION OF CONCEPT OF INSURANCE

It is the relatively modern societies that built up economies with money and financial instruments and evolved other forms of insurance down the centuries. In the money economy context, Chinese and Babylonian traders evolved some methods of transferring or distributing risk as long ago as the 3rd and 2nd millennia BC, respectively. Chinese merchants traveling treacherous river rapids would redistribute their wares across many vessels to limit the loss due to any single vessel being incidentally capsized. As recorded in the famous code of Hammurabi, the Babylonians developed a system around 1750 BC that was practised by early Mediterranean sailing merchants. Thereby, if a merchant received a loan to fund his shipment, he would pay the lender an additional sum in exchange for the lender's guarantee to cancel the loan should the shipment be stolen. The Code of Hammurabi indicates that ancient Babylon had government insurances for theft and crop as well as an adoption annuity plan. Personal insurance on contribution principle has been found in the Thiasoi of ancient Greece.

Achaemenian monarchs were believed to have been the first to insure their people through an official process by registering donations to the monarch in governmental notary offices. Each year, in Norouz (beginning of the Iranian New year), the heads of different ethnic groups as well as others who were willing to take part in the process, presented gifts to the monarch. When a gift was worth more than 10,000 Derrik (Achaemenian gold coin weighing 8.35-8.42g), it was registered in a special office so that whenever the person who presented the gift was in trouble, the monarch and the court would help him. As per Jahez, a historian and writer, whenever the donor of the present was in trouble or wanted to construct a building, set-up a fest or have his children married, the court would check the registration and the donor would receive double the amount. The ancient inhabitants of Rhodes invented the concept of the 'general average' whereby merchants whose goods were being shipped together would pay a proportionally divided premium which would be used to reimburse any merchant whose goods were jettisoned (thrown out of a ship to save the ship, lives or other goods) during storm or sinkage.

It is believed that the Greeks and the Romans introduced the origins of health and life insurance around 600 AD when they organized guilds called benevolent societies that cared for the families and paid funeral expenses of members upon death. Rome evolved the Fund of Collegia of the soldiery. Funds of the Collegia Tenuiorum were used to meet the unexpected expenses, burial expenses and needs of the soldiers' families, guilds in the middle ages served a similar purpose.

Friendly societies existed in England in which people donated amounts of money to a general sum that could be used for emergencies; this arrangement worked before insurance was established in the late 17th century. Stand alone insurance contracts or insurance policies not bundled with loans or other kinds of contracts are believed to have been invented in Genoa in the 14th century. Insurance pools were formed and backed by pledges of landed estates. These new insurance contracts allowed insurance to be separated from investment. Insurance became far more sophisticated in post-renaissance Europe, and specialized varieties of insurance developed.

Commercial activity/hub brought London to the centre stage. London's growing importance as a centre for trade by the end of the seventeenth century created a sudden spurt in demand for marine insurance. In the late 1680s, Mr. Edward Lloyd opened a coffee house that became a popular haunt of ship owners, merchants, and ship-captains, and thereby a reliable source of the latest shipping news. It became the meeting place for parties wishing to insure cargoes and ships, and those willing to underwrite such ventures. Today, Lloyd's of London remains the leading market (note that it is not an insurance company) for marine and other specialised types of insurance, but it works rather differently than the more familiar kinds of insurance.

Regarding insurance legislation, the earliest version of insurance law relates to marine insurance for which the English are indebted to the Lombards, who, driven away from their native states in Northern and Central Italy about the middle of the 13th century, settled in every maritime country in Europe. It appears that laws issued by the magistrates of Barcelona, laws published in Venice in 1468 and other regulations were familiar to the Lombards, and those laws/regulations formed the basis upon which the Lombards effected insurance on English merchandise from their residences in Lombard Street. The power of the Lombards was broken by a decree in 1597. Keate and Gurney state that the most important laws came from an unknown French source in a set of regulations published probably at Rouen in the 17th century, and that in British statute books, we find no mention of Marine insurance until 1601 when an act was passed "concerning matters of assurance amongst Merchants." An Act of Parliament passed/enforced in 1720 vested monopoly rights of marine insurance in the two companies, Royal Exchange and London Assurance, and Lloyds until repealed in 1824. There was no marked development in British laws until 1756. Lord Mansfield became Lord Chief Justice and devoted himself earnestly to the study of the principles of marine insurance and its application in other countries. From Lord Mansfield's times, till the passage of Marine Insurance Act of 1906, the law of marine insurance was administered by an appeal to precedent.

Concerning the insurance sector, one of the most momentous events of the century happened in London in June 1861 with the Great Fire (the greatest since 1666) at Tooley Street, Southward. The fire apparently started in stored hemp, spread furiously, could not be fully extinguished for a fortnight, and the fire offices sustained an enormous loss of between pound 1 and 2 million. The companies noted that the situation had gone out of hand due to the high loss and low premiums due to excessive competition. In the aftermath of this Great fire of London, that devoured 13,200 houses, Nicholas Barbon opened an office to insure buildings. In 1680, he established England's fire insurance company, the Fire Office, to insure brick and frame homes. Insurers came together and to ensure that a repeat of this would not happen in the future, a new institution, the Fire Offices Committee (FOC), a voluntary, autonomous association, was formally created by the various fire (insurance) offices in 1868. Those companies transacting fire insurance agreed to adhere to certain minimum rates. FOC ushered in a new era of cooperation among British insurers and was followed by Accident Offices Association (AOA), Engineering Offices Association (EOA) and Aviation Offices Insurance Association (AOIA). Through this entire process, insurance evolved and established as a subject and profession distinctly different from other branches of financial transactions.

In the United States of America, the first insurance company that underwrote the fire insurance risk was formed in Charles Town (modern day Charleston), South Carolina, in 1732. Benjamin Franklin helped to popularize and make standard the practice of insurance, particularly against fire, in the form of perpetual insurance. In 1752, he founded the Philadelphia Contributionship for the insurance of houses from loss by fire. Franklin's company was the first to make contributions toward fire prevention. His company warned against certain fire hazards. In case of certain buildings where the risk of fire was too great, such as all wooden houses, his company refused insurance.

INDIAN INSURANCE SCENARIO TODAY

The fundamental principle of insurance, that is a group sharing the losses of a few, had been appreciated in India in some way or other from the very ancient times. Hinduism, like other religions, exhorts man to help his fellow men in distress in the field of commerce in some way or the other. Scholars observe that the Sanskrit term 'Yogakshema' (well-being of the society of which insurance is a tool) is found in the Rig Veda and that some kind of community insurance was practised by the Aryan tribes of India nearly 3000 years ago. Manu Smriti speaks of a system of 'collective co-operation'. Yajnavalkya mentions some transactions akin to insurance. In its earliest and crude forms, insurance was probably perceived as a function of the State. In the ninth chapter of the Magnum Opus, Shrimad Bhagavad Gita, Lord Krishna promises Yogakshema to devotees. The kings were expected to look after their people, and *praja ranjan* (welfare of the subjects) alone could justify their existence according to ancient Sanskrit literature. The 'Joint Family System' practised in India is seen by many as a form of micro-insurance to take care of calamitous situations, including death and sickness within the extended family. In course of time, many monarchs turned despotic and the functions of the State in even advanced countries were limited to the protection of subjects against foreign attacks and maintenance of law and order within. In the Indian context, religion and 'other worldliness' dominated the economic institutions; insurance was intertwined within the warp and well of the special fabric. This state continued until the arrival of the Europeans on the Indian soil and organization of economic activity, as we see it in the modern world, took shape.

In India, life insurance in modern context, started with the British influence. Many English companies extended their branches to India for underwriting European lives and later Parsee and Indian lives too. Sir John Child, who was the Governor of Bombay (now called Mumbai) between 1681 and 1690, was instructed by the Court of Directors to constitute an insurance office on the Mumbai Island, but it is not known what came of this organization. The Bombay Insurance Society was set-up in 1793 on Bombay Island by a few well-known European Merchants. Life Insurance in its present form came to India from the United Kingdom with the establishment of a British firm, Oriental Life Insurance Company in Kolkata in 1818 to help the widows of the European community. This was followed by the formation of the Bombay Life Assurance Company in 1829, and the Oriental Government Security Life Insurance Company in 1874. It has been documented that as early as 1822, when Indian social reformers were opposing the practice of Sati, Raja Ram Mohan Roy appealed through the Calcutta Journal to the good sense of the rich to start a fund for widows and orphans. Round about the decade beginning from 1850, considerable pressure seems to have been brought to bear upon the then Government of India to operate life insurance business under government control through a department of the State. History tells us that the proposal was turned down as the Government did not possess sufficient data on Indian lives, and as the insurance consciousness was not present to an adequate degree. The Princely State of Travancore (part of present Kerala State) was issuing life insurance policies in the late 19th century, and policies of 1896 are still preserved by the Kerala State Insurance Department, Thiruvananthapuram.

In India, the earliest known policy in English (dated 1555) is expressed as on the good ship Santa Crux "from any port in the isles of Indies of Calicut unto lixborne". It is known that members of the East India Company handled Bottomry Bond transactions. The first general insurance company, the Triton Insurance Company Limited, was established in Kolkata in 1850. The Indian Mercantile Insurance Company Limited, which was set-up in Mumbai in 1907, was the first Indian company to transact all classes of general insurance business.

Documented information on non-life insurance operations in the country is available from the early 20th century. The Royal Exchange Assurance opened shop in India in 1900, and by 1907, almost 10 per cent of its accident business came from India and 6 other foreign agencies. Royal Exchange Assurance's net marine premium from India for the year 1914 is recorded as pound 40,000 as against pound 17,000 from Australia and pound 10,000 from South Africa.

When Mumbai emerged from World War I as the centre of Indian trade, inspired by the growth of Indian trade and industry, and encouraged by the undercurrent of nationalism, leading businessmen in Mumbai rose to give concrete shape to proposals for meeting the insurance needs of Indian trade. Five offices were established in 1919, almost simultaneously, for transacting general insurance business. The newly formed insurance companies received support from the growth of nationalism in India.

Mahatma Gandhi stated, "The keynote of all our Swaraj is in placing all our insurance with our Indian companies", while Nehru said, "I hope Indians will realize the importance of patronizing only Indian insurance institutions".

The few years after 1922 were critical for Indian insurance when six new Indian offices were pitted against nearly 150 foreign offices, including those of some of the largest insurance groups in the world. The general economic conditions were against them and political agitation was at its zenith. Simultaneously, a powerful combination of American offices began their operations to be followed by a number of French companies a year later. To make matters worse for the Indian companies, an all round reduction in rates was enforced in 1928, depression set in a year later, foreign trade fell immediately, farm prices came down and purchasing power fell, and internal economy collapsed, while serious fire losses in Karachi and heavy riot losses in Mumbai were incurred.

However, the industry came to the rescue of Indian insurers and hundreds of Indian businessmen signed a pledge to insure only with Indian offices. By this time, Indian industries such as sugar, paper, matches, paint and cement had gradually begun to take root, aided by a protective tariff system. Indian insurers' share of the total business written in India rose from a mere 11 per cent in 1928 to 22 per cent in 1935 and 32 per cent in 1939, largely at the expense of foreign offices, while the total business itself had registered an increase of only 5 per cent during the period.

EVOLUTION OF INDIAN INSURANCE MARKET

The evolution of the market prior to the Insurance Act, 1938 has just been discussed. The second phase of evolution started from the middle of the 1930s.

During this period, the Indian market came out of its adolescence and stared addressing problems similar to those faced by the more nature markets. The market and the government were seized by the gravity of the situation, and concerted efforts were made leading to the enactment of the Insurance Act, 1938. The introduction of this Act of 1938 is generally regarded as the turning point for insurance regulation in India and the beginning of the insurance market as it currently exists, and existed some time back too.

BEGINNING: THE INSURANCE ACT, 1938

This Act has been discussed in Chapter 1 briefly; here it is discussed with more details as the evolution of Insurance in India can not omit, by any design, a reference to this Act. This Act is considered the bed-rock legislation in India as far as the insurance business is concerned. The Government appointed S.C. Sen, a well-known Solicitor, in 1934, as Officer on Special Duty in the Department of Commerce to study and report on the amendments to insurance legislation. Sen propounded the British ideal of minimum statutory control with maximum autonomy. With some modifications, the government set-up an informal Advisory Committee of leading insurance men, headed by N.N. Sircar, the then Law Member. This committee elicited views and suggestions from many stakeholders and submitted a bill to the Legislative Assembly in 1937. The bill stirred up intense public interest in the country. The trade associations submitted memoranda, insurance associations pressed for amendments and a Lloyd's representative flew over from London to watch their interest. Over a thousand amendments were suggested from various quarters and at last the Insurance Act, 1938 was enacted.

However, soon the market started criticizing the Act for its drafting mistakes, contradictions and impractical clauses. Though it was widely conceded that the act wrote a fresh chapter into the history of Indian insurance by attempting to prevent the formation and continuation of mushroom companies and by introducing sound insurance business practices, some authors commented that it became the most controversial law among Indian statutes.

In quick response to the criticism, the government made two amendments to the Act in 1939. To remove certain difficulties in administration, the Act was again amended in 1940. The market situation that came up with World War II and the insurers' experience of working with the Act necessitated further changes. Further amendments were made in 1941, 1942, 1944, 1946 and 1948.

Despite the flaws, the 1938 Act gave the Indian market a regulatory foundation and amongst other things, provided for the constitution of a Department of Insurance, compulsory registration of insurance companies, provision for deposits, control on investment of funds, filing of returns on investments and financial condition, licensing of agents, control on commission, prohibition of rebates, filing of policy conditions and premium rates duly certified by an actuary (in the case of life business), periodical, valuation of liabilities, and provision for policyholders' directors. The Act granted very wide powers to the Controller of Insurance in the matter of insurance regulation. The government visualized that the Controller of Insurance should be a person of extraordinary calibre, be actuarially qualified, having human considerations and broad outlook to administer law tactfully and even handedly. The Indian insurance legislation was lauded by contemporary commentator as an excellent attempt to penalize the corrupt directors and executive officers, check wild cat schemes and scandals, and to stop acquisition of insurance companies by designing financiers.

The Insurance Act, 1938, became the corner stone of Indian insurance legislation and along with the insurance Rules formed under it, the Act still remains the most comprehensive legislation on the subject. However, need was felt for amendments and so, the Act of 1950 was passed.

THE INSURANCE AMENDMENT ACT, 1950

The introduction of this comprehensive legislation, however, did not prevent the large-scale increase of new companies and the failures of existing companies. In response to the situation, in April 1945 a committee under the chairmanship of Sir Gowasji Jehangir was appointed to enquire into the undesirable developments in the management of the insurance companies and recommend suitable remedial measures. On the basis of this committee's recommendations, a bill was introduced. The bill was thrice referred to a Select committee and thrice withdrawn on account of various reasons. Again, a Committee under the chairmanship of S. Ranganathan was appointed to report on the working of the Indian Insurance Act and to give suggestions for further legislation. The Bill was redrafted, incorporating the suggestions of the committee and passed as the Insurance Amendment Act, 1950.

The salient features of this Act are the requirement of minimum capital, stricter control on investment and submission of periodical returns on investments, ceiling on expenses of management and agency commission, and appointment of administrators for mismanaged companies. The amendment created a statutory Association called the General Insurance Council. The existing Insurance Associations at Bombay, Calcutta and Madras were converted into the Bombay. Calcutta and Madras Regional Councils under the General Insurance Council with powers to frame and enforce tariff rates and regulations. Another statutory body called the Tariff Committee was constituted under the General Insurance Council and vested with powers to control and regulate the rates, advantages, terms and conditions that might be offered by its members and associate members in respect of general insurance business. The Tariff Committee was an All India body controlling and exercising powers over all Regional Council. Although the actual rates were framed by the Rating committees of Regional Councils, the Tariff Committee had the power to decide all major outstanding issues and, if necessary, override the Regional Councils. Changes in the economic environment made it incumbent upon the government to pass further legislation to take care of the deficiencies or lack of adequate coping provisions for effective conduct of business of Insurance and to do public good.

THE INSURANCE AMENDMENT ACT, 1968

Even after the enactment of the amendment to the Insurance Act, the failure of companies did not stop. As per published reports, during the ten-year period from 1945 (when the Jehangir Committee was constituted) to 1954, 533 valuation reports of insurance companies were submitted to the Controller of Insurance. Of these, 86 valuations showed a deficit, which was not covered by the free paid-up capital. Of these, 25 insurers went into liquidation and another 25 insurers had to transfer their business to other companies. This situation created an increased focus on the social security angle of insurance and the hardships that the common people would suffer if an insurance company became bankrupt. In response to the situation, the Insurance Act of 1938 was again amended in 1968 in order to provide for better social control over general insurance business. This amendment is popularly referred to in insurance circles as the 'introduction of social control measures of 1968 or as Social control amendments.

The amendment provided for regulation of investments, minimum solvency margin regulations, payment of premium before commencement of risk, licensing of surveyors, empowered the controller to carry out inspection, investigation and search, and seizure of books. These amendments, which came into force in June, 1969, renamed the Tariff Committee of the General Insurance Council as the 'Tariff Advisory Committee' and established it as a body corporate with perpetual succession and made the Controller of Insurance its Chairman.

NATIONALISATION OF LIFE INSURANCE

On January 19, 1956, the Central Government took over the 154 Indian Life insurance companies, 75 provident societies and 16 non-Indian insurance companies then operating in India. These were nationalized and the Life Insurance Corporation of India (LIC) was formed on September 1, 1956 by the enactment of the life Insurance corporation of India Act, 1956. The persistent problem of insolvency of life insurers was possibly the most compelling reason leading to the nationalization of the life insurance business. Corresponding changes on the general insurance side were also being contemplated by the government.

GENERAL INSURANCE BUSINESS (NATIONALIZATION) ACT, 1972 (GIBNA)

On May 13, 1971, an ordinance was promulgated by the President of India to take over the management of the existing 107 general insurance companies by the Government of India. Vide the General Insurance Business (nationalization) Act, 1972, the General Insurance Corporation of India (GIC) and its four nationalized subsidiaries were formed with effect from January 1, 1973 and all the existing 107 general insurance companies were merged with these four companies. The four nationalized general insurance companies thus formed were the National Insurance Company Limited with its head office at Kolkata, the New India Assurance Company Limited, headquartered at Mumbai, the Oriental Insurance Company with New Delhi as it head office, and the Untied India Insurance Company Limited with its headquarters at Chennai. A small segment comprising a few state government Insurance Departments insuring properties owned by the respective states had substantial financial interests, Crop Insurance Departments of State Governments, the Calcutta Hospital and Nursing Home Benefits Association Limited, Export Credit and Guarantee Corporation Limited (ECGC), and the Deposit Insurance Corporation were excepted from the scope of the take over. These insurance entities are referred to as exempted insurers in the market. The cumulative effect of all these successive developments was that the Indian general insurance industry was changed into a state monopoly from January 1, 1973. (As explained earlier, the life insurance industry had already become a state monopoly).

The general insurance market was thus left with four public sector insurers who sold the same products at the same rates, either under tariffs formed by the Tariff Advisory Committee or under market agreement entered among the four companies and competition was limited only to the quality of service. Nationalization was generally successful in generating more confidence in the insured, as contracts signed with government owned companies were perceived as backed by a sovereign assurance. The new public sector companies inherited a diversified portfolio, talented personnel and strategic business connections on which they could build on. Insurance penetration increased, ancillary services got organized and employment opportunities grew rather consistently for 15 to 20 years.

Nationalization, however, had its own share of weaknesses. Problems arose due to overstaffing, governmental interference in management, lack of freedom in decision-making, inability of the management to nurture feelings of company loyalty, as well as deficiencies in the system, which could neither provide enough motivation for meritorious employees nor effectively penalize employees for non-performance or lethargy. Professionalism started waning and market penetration stagnated. Growth in the balance sheet was largely limited to the country's inflation and the returns that companies could earn by investing their surplus funds. The report of the Advisory Group on Insurance Regulation (AGIR) of the Standing Committee on International Financial Standards and Codes set-up by the Reserve Bank of India describe the national market situation with one holding company and four subsidiaries as follows:

The "phased" globalization of the Indian economy that started in the early nineties began having its impact on this monopolistic structure. Further, the liberalization of insurance markets was among the objectives of the Uruguay round negotiations conducted under the auspices of GATT. These negotiations included trade in services; insurance had been included in the context of financial services (Para 59 of UNCTAD Report, January 19, 1993)

MACHINERY OF THE INSURANCE SYSTEM

The legal entity (company) that assumes the risk is the insurer. An entity seeking to transfer risk (an individual, corporation, association of any type, etc.) becomes the insured party, once the risk is assumed by an insurer, (the insuring party) by means of a contract called as insurance policy. The fee paid by the insured to the insurer for assuming the risk is called the premium. Generally, an insurance contract includes, at a minimum, some elements like the parties (the insurer, the insured, and the beneficiaries), the premium, the period of coverage, the particular loss event covered and the amount of coverage (i.e. the amount to be paid to the insured or beneficiary in the event of a loss). The policy also states the kind of loss events (perils) that it covers either as an active statement or by a set of exclusions (events not covered).

When insured parties experience a loss for a specified peril, the coverage entitles the policyholders to make a claim against the insurer for the covered amount of loss as specified by the policy. When an insurer makes a payment on the claim, the insured is said to be indemnified against the loss events covered in the policy. The insurance premiums from many insured are used to fund accounts reserved for later payment of claims, theoretically, for a relatively few claimants and for over head costs. An insurer has to set aside and maintain adequate funds for anticipated losses (i.e. reserves) and for the expenses in running the establishment and servicing the insured. The remaining margin (surplus) is an insurer's profit.

Agents (now called Counsellers or Advisors)

Apart from the above, there are insurance agents who represent the insurer to the insured and procure the business on behalf of their principals. Agents are given a commission on the business that they bring in. Agents are sometimes referred to as insurance advisors.

Brokers (Intermediaries)

Insurance Brokers form another component of the insurance system. As the agent represents the insurer to the insured, the broker represents his client, someone in need of insurance, to one or more insurance houses. An insurance broker shops around amongst many companies for the best insurance policy.

However, with insurance brokers, the fee is usually paid in the form of commission from the insurer that is selected for insurance, rather than directly from the client. There are also companies known as insurance consultants. Similar to an insurance broker, an insurance consultant also shops around amongst many companies for the best insurance policy. However, in this context, the customers cause these consultants to shop around amongst many companies for the best of the insurance policies. Neither insurance consultants nor insurance brokers are representatives (authorised to commit or remit or compromise, etc.) of insurance companies and no risks are transferred to them during insurance transactions.

Third Party Administrators

Third party administrators are certain expert companies in particular field that are contracted by insurance companies to perform claims handling service for a group or category of clients. These companies often have special expertise that the insurance companies do not have.

Co-insurance

Cases do exist where the insurers do not want to keep (or retain) the entire risk with them. In such cases, the insurers agree to share the risk and the premium proportionately. This arrangement is referred to as co-insurance.

Re-insurance

In many cases, the insurers may feel that retaining a particular risk or group of risks could be too risky for them. In other words, they may not like over-exposure to a particular risk or types of risks. Often, they retain a part of the risk up to the level at which they feel comfortable, and transfer the remaining risk to another insurer called reinsurer. Thus, reinsurers provide insurance to insurance companies. Reinsurance is a means by which an insurance company can protect itself against the risk of losses by transferring their risk to other entities.

To sum-up, reinsurance companies are insurance companies that sell policies to other insurance companies, allowing them to reduce their risk and protect them selves from very large losses. The reinsurance market is dominated by a few very large companies with huge reserves. A reinsurer may also be a direct writer of insurance risks as well.

Insurance surveyors and claims adjusters are terms used to describe someone who evaluates the damage caused to property of people when an insurance related accident occurs. In both the United Kingdom and the Republic of Ireland the term Loss Adjuster is used. They verify the extent of loss, examine the loss *vis-à-vis* the coverage of the insurance policy, investigate liability for the damages caused, and assess the liability under the policy. These professionals handle properly the claims involving damage to buildings and structures, or liability claims involving personal injuries or third person property damage from liability situations, such as motor vehicle accidents, or damage to ships or cargo on board, as the case may be. Some specialize in a particular type of claims, while some surveyors and adjusters handle multiple types of claims and are known as Multi-Line adjusters.

REGULATION OF INSURANCE BUSINESS

Insurers (Insurance Companies) are regulated in different countries through different systems and procedures. However, there are some fundamental philosophies that form the basis of most of the insurance regulatory regimes among various countries. Some of the fundamental philosophies are discussed in this section.

Insurance companies are broadly classified into two: (a) Life insurance companies that sell life insurance, annuities and pension products, and (b) Non-life or General Insurance companies that sell other types of insurance. The main reason for the distinction between the two types of companies is that life, annuity and pension business is long-term in nature, coverage for life assurance or a pension can cover risks over many decades. By contrast, non-life insurance usually covers a shorter period, such as one year. These companies typically insure automobiles, buildings, household items, business, travel risks, merchandise in transit, ships, airplanes, accident risks and the like.

Insurance regulation is distinctly different from regulation in other branches of finance or economics. By virtue of the contract between the insured and the insurer, the premium paid to the insurer stays with him in return for a promise of indemnification in the event of a loss. The insurer needs to act as per his promise only if the fortuitous event happens. Theoretically, this situation arises only for a small number of policies issued by the insurer. Statistically, as the number of policies increase, the proportion of the number of losses to the number of policies actually decreases.

The uniqueness of insurance necessitates that it regulations have to be laid down in an intricate manner. Regulations need to be rigid enough to prevent fraudulent fly-by-night operators, flexible enough to promote genuine business decisions, and delicate enough to foster creative ideas. In contrast to the *laissez faire* or 'let the people do as they choose' philosophy in many other area so business, concepts of responsible underwriting, clarity of contract terms, transparency of dealings, prudent investments and policyholders protection have been matters of regulatory concern.

Watch on Funds in Public Interest

The insurer thus has large amounts of public funds under his control and a much larger amount of promises to keep. Because of this unique position, insurance companies hold huge funds in the market. That is the reason why insurers should serve the society through employment of those funds for growth and development. The insurers should be ready to serve the desired social objectives. The insurance mechanism has not only been accepted but also encouraged by the insurance business as well as by the customers.

Ensuring Long-term Financial Solvency of Insurers

The insurers have to guarantee performance of a financial obligation in the event of certain contingencies that might affect the insured at various degrees of probability. When such situations arise, if an insurer fails to hold the safety net, the particular insured's trust is betrayed. The larger issue is that the feeling of comfort and confidence that the general public responses in the insurance industry gets shattered. Financial solvency is the foundation of public confidence in the private insurance mechanism and historically has been the primary objective of regulation. Here, the insurance regulator uses macro-level controls, such as prescribing a high capital base for issuing licenses and ensuring healthy solvency margins so that only deep pocketed players enter the insurance market.

Steps Towards Standardizing Insurance Products

Standardisation brings about uniformity. In its absence, discrimination creeps in as customized products can have different/specific terms. When insurance products are standardised, the customers of tangible goods and services can easily evaluate the product and promises made by sellers. However, for customers of insurance, evaluating an insurer's promises to perform certain obligations under certain specified future situations is not an easy task. In contrast to consumable commodities and many financial services, insurance products are not subject to easy evaluation by the customers at the purchase point. One often finds that many insurance products are purchased merely to fulfil conditions set by banks or other financing institutions when loans are sanctioned. Many of the contract conditions are sometimes not comprehensible to the common man. Here, the insurance regulator ensures a considerable degree of standardization of insurance products.

The degree of standardization of products varies from country to country, from rigidly controlled tariff markets, such as India, Taiwan, Thailand, Sri Lanka at one end of the spectrum to open markets with minimal controls, such as Singapore, United Kingdom and many States of USA at the other extreme where insurance products are by and large controlled by the market forces of demand and supply. Self-explanatory terms of standardization, such as 'Prior Approval', 'Modified Prior Approval', 'Flex Rating', 'File and Use', 'Use and File', 'State Prescribed', etc. are internationally used to denote the degree of control exercised by the regulator on insurance products.

Preventing Fraud and Speculation by Insurers

Because of the fiduciary nature of the policyholder insurer relationship and the resulting opportunity for fraud and financial speculation, complete freedom of entry of new insurance firms into the market is not desirable. The situation of a large amount of public money getting pooled up in a few hands for long periods allows the possibility of the insurers mismanaging public funds through imprudent speculative investments, risky money management decisions or even sheer complacency, unless the market is well regulated. On the other hand, unless regulations allow sufficient flexibility, the insurers will not be able to make prudent innovative decisions to ensure a healthy growth of the funds entrusted to their care and custody. The insurance regulator has to decide how much freedom the insurers should enjoy while managing public funds. Strict norms for investment, transparency in balance sheets, and audit of accounts are some methods that regulators employ for enforcing discipline in financial management.

Creating a Level-playing Ground for Insurers inter-se

Economists concur that intensive unregulated competition in marketing insurance products can produce inadequate rates and insolvency, sharp loss adjusting practices, abortive policy language, and possible tendencies towards monopolization, all of which are recognized to be against public interest. Here, the regulator has to create a level playing ground for all insurers. Ensuring an equitable and congenial environment for business houses well entrenched in the market, government guaranteed insurers, multinational corporate houses, novice insurers and local tender feet insurers is a daunting task for a regulator, apart from attempts towards standardizing insurance product, regulators try to ensure a level playing ground by drawing uniform norms for drawing balance sheets, valuation of assets, actuarial vetting of rates, etc. also, norms are laid down for ensuring policyholders' protection and fairness in dealings. Standards of ethics are insisted upon in advertising as well as in correctly conveying policy terms to the insured through trained agents. The regulator has to maintain uniform yardsticks of strictness with all insurers whether dealing with violations of regulations or grievances relating to deficiencies in services.

Monitoring of Re-insurance

In order to reduce liabilities, Insurers enter into agreements with re-insurers and thereby reduce their risk. The insurers need to enter into different types of reinsurance contracts as part of their business. The regulator has to ensure that foreign exchange is not unduly drained-off through reckless reinsurance programmes of the insurers. Objectives of regulation could include maximizing the country's capacity to retain its insurance business within, or ensuring that local companies do not carry too much of risk, disproportionate to their capacity. Regulations would ensure that the insurers secure the bets possible reinsurance protection, get competitive rates for placing the reinsurance business and simplify the administration of business. Many regulators specify that the insurers shall cede such percentage of the sum insured on each policy for different classes of insurance written in the country to a national reinsurers or reinsures registered in the country.

Other concerns include the financial position of the reinsurers the possibility of the reinsures becoming insolvent when there is a chain of catastrophes, unequal reinsurance arrangements entered into by inexperienced insurance companies and the possibility that insurance companies use reinsurance contract only as a means of cash transfer abroad. Experts in the field argue that having very low reinsurance limits may result in excessive outflow of foreign exchange and thus, it has to be guarded against. On the contrary, high retention limits may result in erosion of the stability of a company in case of large or catastrophic claims. There are instances of general insurance companies in some developing countries ceding hundred per cent of their business to reinsures (i.e. zero retention limit), or acting as 'fronting' companies of reinsurers. Such activities are not regarded healthy for the market.

Pricing of Insurance Products

Proper rate fixing or pricing of an insurance product is an area of concerns for the regulator. Stories of rate cutting are not unheard of even in closed markets where only government companies transact insurance business. Under-pricing of insurance products is malady very common to the relatively free markets of insurance. Cutting of rates below the actual cost of the indemnity weakens the industry. In open competitions, insurance rates are often dependent on the bargaining strength of the insured than the features of the risk as such. Large buyers, therefore, may obtain their insurance too cheaply, as opposed to others who are not in a position to derive sharp bargain. Effective regulation is needed to ensure that insurance products are priced on sound technical reasons.

An insurance policy should be correctly priced for different reasons. While a high price would bring better profits to the insurer, the insured has to bear the brunt of it. Also, potential clients would shy away from the market, thereby limiting the insurers' scope of reaping the advantages of the law of large numbers. A price less than adequate to meet the risk should no doubt bring joy to policyholder at the sales office. However, lesser price would erode the insurers' bottom line and weaken their capacity to meet their obligations in the event of a loss. Historically, insurance law-makers have dreaded this situation. As per the findings of the 'Joint Committee' of the Assembly and Senate of the State of New York as early as 1911, wherever there has been a cutting of rates below the actual cost of the indemnity and the policyholder gets his insurance very cheaply, its effect on all companies is weakening. They observe that "the mutual character of insurance is so strong that nothing that tends to give inferior protection can be for the public good". An insurer's pricing objectives depend on the overall objectives of the insurer and the state of the insurance market. These pricing objectives may be expressed in three main ways to achieve a specified rate of return of capita, to maximize profits, and to maintain or extend market share.

Regulators address the issue of product pricing based on certain operational principle depending upon the degree of regulation each country decides upon. The guidelines issued by the Motor Accidents Authority (MAA) the regulatory body of the New South Wales State of Australia, for the preparation of the rate filing reports are given below as an example.

"Premiums must be sufficient to pay all acquisition and policy administration costs, provide a sum of money to meet the best estimate of the cost of claims (including claims management expense), provide a profit margin representing an adequate return on capital invested and compensation for the risk, and provide for other matters a prudent insurers would make provision for" (Hart, Buchanan, & Howe).

Rates should be so fixed as to ensure that survival of the insurance company, achieving optimum strategic positioning, providing quality and value for the service, contributing to the society's well-being, and optimizing the returns for a given type of risk. Insurance pricing methods can be divided into three major categories (i) individual rating, (ii) class or manual rating, and (iii) modification rating, usually referred to as merit rating. Principal modification rating methods include schedule rating, experience rating, retrospective rating and premium discount plans., the terms of the insurance contract, the conditions under which losses are payable (the insurance cover), and the past experience of losses in the particular type of insurance are taken into reckoning while fixing rates.

Data Repository and Risk Evaluation

Regulators require insurers to maintain their own internal databases and to create national data warehouses so that the products can be priced scientifically based on statistical data. In places, like Japan, New South Wales of Australia and Massachusetts of USA, the concept of Reference Loss Cost Rate (RLCR) is followed. Here, the insurer compares his past loss experience in a particular segment of insurance with the corresponding overall past loss experience in a particular segment of insurance with the corresponding overall past loss experience of the industry from a national data warehouse. Internationally, there are many accepted standards of pricing insurance products and reserving or making provisions for future payment of claims. Premium are the main source of income for the insurers from which all the insurer's expenditure has to be met. An insurer's expenditure includes his management expenses, such as rent, office maintenance salaries, agency commissions, advertisement expense, taxes, etc. on one hand, and pure claims costs, assumed liabilities, incidental expenditure, such as surveyor's fees, legal expense, etc. on the other.

Theory of Large Numbers

When a dice is repeated many times, the average outcome is the expected value. The premium that an insured would pay would be minuscule compared to the magnitude of the loss that the insurer is liable to pay in the event of a claim. However, historically, the actual number (frequency) of loss-making policies are very less in comparison to the number of policies issued, and the total quantum of losses payable (severity) is lesser than the total amount of premium received. Thus, in any given period, the losses of the few are borne by the majority of the policyholders who do not incur losses. Statistically, the insurers know that the probability of incurring losses actually decreases when the number of policies increase. This apparent paradox is referred in insurance parlance as the law or theory of large numbers.

Creating Reserves by Insurers/Re-insurers

Even in the case of yearly policies, the insurer's liabilities go beyond the close of the policy period. The amount of the liability for future claim payments can be very uncertain, particularly for long-term classes of policies and cannot be measured precisely. An insurer's standards for creating reserves or reserving for his liabilities are most important for his security. These liabilities include the insurer's liability to meet payments on claims that have been reported to the insurer (reported claims), payment on claim that have already occurred but have not yet been reported to the insurer called as incurred but not reported (IBNR) claims, payment on claims that have not yet occurred but for which the premium has already been paid, other payments, such as super annotation, long service leave, holiday pay, and so on. These liabilities have to be assessed for creating sufficient reserves. In countries where procedural delays are inherent to the judicial system, liability claims can take many years for a court judgment. The award may consist the liability amount peruse, interest, as well as costs of the claimant. It is important, therefore, for the insurer to estimate his anticipated liabilities accurately and create reserves for setting them. This process, known as reserving is done using actuarial calculations in many developed markets.

PRESENT DAY TRENDS IN INSURANCE

The insurance industry has grown down the years alongside the economy. Modern day economists consider insurance penetration as a yardstick of economic development. Most of the developed and developing countries have been taking significant steps in both economic and insurance reform over the last three decades. The reform process is an ongoing process.

Bodies such as World Trade Organization (WTO), World Bank, Asian Development Bank (ADB), Basel Committee on Banking Supervision (BCBS) and many other international bodies have taken active interest in addressing insurance related problems at intentional forum. The International Association of Insurance Supervisors (IAIS) is a full-time body working for the development of insurance through multi-pronged strategies. It has developed core insurance principles relevant to contemporary markets, promoted discussions on areas of common concern, augmented educational endeavours of the developing countries, and provided a forum of interaction among the insurance supervisors and professionals all over the world.

SUMMARY

This unit has provided an overview of insurance and the basic concept of insurance so that the readers can appreciate the importance of insurance in the society and the economy. A brief history of the evolution of insurance as a separate stream of knowledge over the years has been provided in this unit. The evolution of the Indian market has also been traced. The unit familiarizes you to the insurance mechanism and the players in the insurance field. It also touches upon some common terms in the insurance market. The principles of insurance will be discussed in detail in unit 2. Fundamental aspects of insurance regulation along with its purposes have been discussed. A brief mention of the present day trend in insurance has been given.

(1) Insurance is an arrangement, whereby many other people who also are susceptible to the same type of losses share the financial losses of a few.

(2) The insured and the insurer are the two parties of an insurance contract.

(3) A risk is the uncertainty part of any activity that cannot be reasonably foreseen to happen within a particular time or in a particular manner. In insurance, the chance or likelihood of a loss to occur is the risk covered.

(4) An objective risk is on that exists in nature and is commonly applicable for

all persons or entities facing the same situation. Risks are subjective when it depends on the individual's perception as to how far an objective situation can apply in his particular case.

(5) Risk can be categorized as 'pure' when there is a chance of a loss without any chance of gain. In case there is a possibility of a gain ensuring from the loss, the risk is called a 'speculative' risk.

(6) Risk perception is the subjective Judgement that people make about the characteristics and severity of a risk.

(7) Physical hazards refer to certain physical conditions that create or increase the chance of loss from any peril. Moral hazard denotes the dishonesty of the insured that can increase the probability of a claim. Morale hazards refer to an indifferent or callous attitude of the insured that increases or inflates the quantum of loss.

(8) Personal losses such as death and poor health, losses to ones material possession such as houses and vehicles, loss of expected income from one's business consequential to a property loss, and liabilities to third parties are examples of insurable loses.

(9) Chinese merchants traveling treacherous river raids would redistribute their wares across many vessels to limit the loss due to any single vessel's capsizing. Babylonians developed a system around 1750 BC, whereby if a merchant received a loan to fund his shipment, he would pay the lender an additional sum in exchange for the lender's guarantee to cancel the loan, should the shipment be stolen. In Rhodes, there was a system, whereby, merchants whose goods were being shipped together would pay a proportionally divided premium that would be used to reimburse any merchant whose goods were jettisoned during storm or sinkage.

(10) The Great Fire of London that devoured 13,200 houses and caused losses of about pound 2 million to insurers, created a new awareness about insurance and increased cooperation among insurers that resulted in the creation of the fire (insurance) offices in 1868 and popularized fire insurance.

(11) The insurance principles of a group the losses of a few had been appreciated in India from very ancient times. In ancient India, the concept of 'Yogakshem' or insurance is found in the Rig Veda. Manu Smriti speaks of a system of collative co-operation and Yajnavalkya mentions some transactions akin to insurance. The 'Joint Family System' practised in India is seen by many as a form of micro-insurance to take care of calamitous situation, including death and sickness within the extended family.

(12) In post-World War-I India, encouraged by the spirit of nationalism, businessmen in Mumbai established fire offices to meet the insurance needs of Indian trade. The new insurance companies received support from the growth of nationalism in India, and Mahatma Gandhi and Nehru spoke in favour of Indian insurance institutions. Later on, hundred of Indian businessmen signed a pledge to insure only with Indian offices. As a result, Indian insurers share of a total business written indene rose from a mere 11 per cent in 1928 to 22 per cent in 1935 and to 31 per cent in 1939, largely

at the expense of foreign offices, while the total business itself had increased only by 5 per cent during that period.

(13) The act granted very wide powers to the Controller of insurance in the matter of insurance regulation. The government visualized that the controller of insurance should be a person of extraordinary caliber, qualified, tactful and even handed. Compulsory registration of insurance companies, control on investments of funds, licensing of agents, control on commission, prohibition of rebates, and filing of policy conditions and premium rates duly certified by an actuary (in the case of life business) were made compulsory. The Indian insurance legislation was lauded by contemporary commentators as an excellent attempt to penalize the corrupt directors and executive offices, check wild cat schemes, and to stop acquition of insurance companies by designing financiers.

(14) The Insurance Act became the corner stone of Indian insurance legislation and, along with the Insurance Rules formed under it, remains the most comprehensive legislation on the subject.

(15) The main changes as result of the amendment were as follows:
- (a) Requirement of minimum capital,
- (b) Stricter control on investments,
- (c) Submission of periodical returns on investments,
- (d) Ceiling on expense of management and agency commission,
- (e) Appointment of administrators for mismanaged companies, and
- (f) Creation of Statutory bodies—General Insurance Council and Tariff Committee to frame and enforce tariff rates and regulations.

(16) Sir Gowasji Jehangir, was chairman of the original committee, and S. Ranganathan, was chairman of the review committee.

(17) The amendment provided for:
- (a) Regulation of investments,
- (b) Minimum solvency, margin regulations,
- (c) Payment of premium before commencement of risk, and
- (d) Licensing of surveyors, and powers to the controller to carry out inspection, investigation and search and seizure of books.

Tariff Committee (TC) of the General Insurance Council (GIC) was renamed as Tariff Advisory Committee (TAC) and established as a body corporate with perpetual succession. The controller of Insurance (ToI) was made its chairman.

(18) After enactment of GIBNA, the general insurance market was left with four public sector insurers who sold the same products at the same rates, either under tariffs framed by TAC or under market agreement's and competition was limited only to the quality of service. Nationalization improved the confidence of the insured, as contracts signed with government owned companies were perceived as backed by a sovereign assurance.

(19) The four nationalized general insurance companies formed under GIBNA were the National Insurance Company Limited, the New India Assurance Company Limited, the Oriental Insurance Company, and the United India Insurance Company Limited.

(20) The legal entity that assumes the risk is the insurer. The entity who transfers the risk is the insured party, the fee paid by the insured to the insurer for assuming the risk is called the premium and the evidence of the contract is the insurance policy.

(21) Insurance Agents represent the insurer to the insured and procure the business on behalf of their principal. Insurance Brokers represent his client, someone in need of insurance, to one or more insurance houses and shops around for the bet insurance policy amongst many companies. Insurance surveyors/Claims Adjusters are those who evaluate the damage caused to property or people when an insurance-related accident occurs.

(22) Insurance Regulations are considered different from the Regulations in other businesses for various reasons:

(a) The product is bought and premium paid is for the promise of indemnification in the event of a loss.

(b) The insurer needs to act as per his promise only if the fortuitous event happens, which may arise only for a small number of policies.

(c) Regulations need to prevent fraudulent fly by night operators and ensure that the companies are there with sufficient funds to pay the claims when a loss occurs.

In contrast to the *laissez faire* philosophy in other areas of business, policy-holders protection has been the matter of regulatory concert.

(23) In insurance, the premium paid to the insurer is in return for a promise of indemnification in the event of the loss. The uniqueness of insurance necessities its regulations to be covered under the following aspects:

(24) *Watch on Funds:* The insurer thus has large amounts of public funds under his control and a much larger amount of promises to keep.

(25) *Ensuring Long-term Financial Solvency:* The insurer has to meet a financial obligation in the event of a loss that might happen at various degrees of probability. Financial solvency of the insurer is the foundation of the insurance mechanism and historical the primary objective of regulation.

(26) *Standardizing Insurance Products:* Customers of tangible goods and services can easily evaluate the products and promises made. The evaluating of an insurer's promises to perform certain obligations under certain specified future situation is not easy for customers of insurance.

(27) *Preventing Fraud and Speculation by Insurers:* The innovations in the economy have simultaneously created a class of hackers and tricksters. To avoid falling into the trap laid by 'fly by night operators', regulations and high pitch caution and watch have been prescribed by the Regulating Authority. As a large amount of public money gets pooled up in a few hands for long periods, there is a possibility of insurers mismanaging public funds through imprudent speculative investments, making risky money management decisions or being complacent, unless the market is well regulated.

(28) *Creating a Level-Playing Ground for all Players in Insurance:* Intensive unregulated competition in marketing insurance products can produce inadequate rates and lead to denial of claims. Abortive policy language is

also used, which is against public interest. So, the Regulator has to create a level playing field for all insurers.

(29) Regulators have to regulate reinsurance too. Insurers need to enter into different types of reinsurance contracts as part of their business. The regulator has to check whether foreign exchange is unduly drained off through reckless reinsurance programmes. Reinsurance should be for maximizing the country's capacity to retain its insurance business within and ensuring that local companies do not carry too much of risk, disproportionate to their capacity. Many Regulators insist that a percentage of the sum insured and written within the country shall be ceded to national reinsure(s) registered in the country.

Regulations should ensure that the insurers secure the best possible reinsurance protection and get competitive rates for placing their reinsurance business. They should prevent unhealthy practices such as ceding hundred per cent of their business to reinsures (i.e. with zero retention limit), or acting as 'fronting' companies of reinsures. Such activities are not regarded healthy for the market.

3

Foundation of Insurance (Nursery of Various Concepts)

INTRODUCTION

Insurance has been evolved by wise men, based on their life experiences, as the mantra to broaden the canvass of a particular risk over a number of persons who are exposed to it and who agree to insure themselves against it. Conceptualization requires imagination, creativity and quest to explore and devise new methods, ways and systems, and procedures. Salute to those who did this marvel of the schematic framework to add one more class of institution in society and that too so utterly fundamental !

Insurance helps to manage risks of various types. Risk is defined as uncertainty of a financial loss. The main functions of insurance include providing certainty, protection, risk sharing, and prevention of loss, and capital formation.

As has been discussed in the previous chapters, the term 'insurance' has been defined as the technique in which a sum of money as premium is paid in consideration for the insurer's undertaking to incur the risk of paying a large sum upon happening of a particular uncertainty.

Insurance is a contract whereby:

(a) Certain sum, called premium, is charged as consideration,
(b) Against the payment of the said premium, a large sum is guaranteed to be paid by the insurer,
(c) The payment will be made in the shape of a certain/definite sum, i.e. the loss incurred or the policy amount, whichever is less, and
(d) The payment is made only upon the happening of the contingency.

Therefore, insurance may be defined as a contract in which one party (insurer) agrees to pay to the other party (insured or beneficiary under the policy), a certain sum upon a particular unforeseen event (risk) taking place against which insurance was sought.

Every subject or discipline has certain generally accepted and systematically laid down standards or principles to achieve the underlying objectives. Insurance is also not an exception to this general rule. There is a body of doctrines commonly associated with the theory and procedures of insurance, guiding all stakeholders about the explanation and application of current policies and for making the best choice among the available alternatives.

These principles may be defined as the rules of action or code of conduct that are universally accepted by the different stakeholders involved in the business of insurance.

These are given in the figure on the next page for better and quick understanding due to visual effect:

ESSENTIALS OF INSURANCE CONTRACT

(i) Nature of Insurance Contract

All agreements are contracts if they are made by the free consent of parties, competent to contract; for a lawful consideration, for a lawful object and are not expressly declared to be void. As we know, an agreement enforceable by law is called a contract. Like all general contracts, a contract of insurance is also required to fulfil all basic requirements as prescribed under section 10 of the Indian Contract Act, 1872. These requirements are given below:

(1) Offer and Acceptance

It is the first requirement in the formation of a valid contract. The offer in insurance is intimation of the proposer's intention to purchase an insurance policy. When the insurer is ready to undertake the stated risk, it is called acceptance. In insurance, 'offer' is known as 'proposal'. It generally comes from the insured. If the insurer accepts the proposal, it is transformed into an agreement.

Therefore, when one party (potential policy holder) makes a proposal to another party (insurance company) and the latter accept it, the proposal is said to be accepted. The moment the notice of acceptance is communicated, it would be a valid acceptance and valid contract is born instantaneously.

The procedure goes like this: potential policyholder who wants to get his risk insured is required to fill a prescribed proposal form in an insurance contract. The insurance company studies the offer made in the proposal form. It may accept it. To complete offer and acceptance as conditions precedent for creating valid contract, the notice of acceptance must be communicated to the insured along with the information regarding the premium payable and first premium receipt is issued.

The basic principles of Contract Act apply in this case. Both the parties to the Contract—Insurer and the Insured/Policyholder—are supposed to be competent to contract and, at the time they enter into the contract, they should act of free volition and should be physically and mentally fit to understand the implications of contract. (Figure 3.1)

Figure 3.1: Principles of Insurance

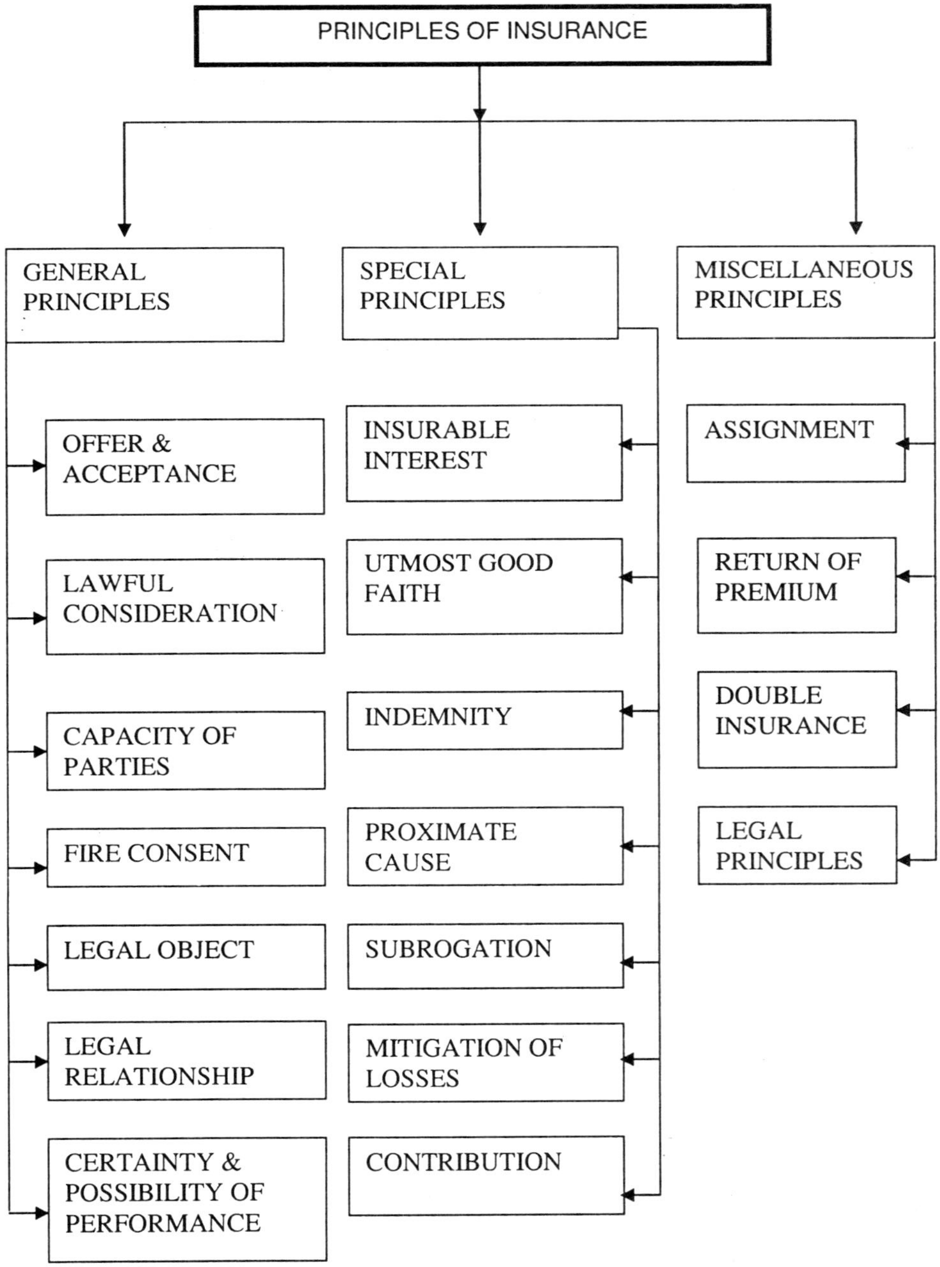

(2) Intention to Create Legal Relations

The second basic principle of valid insurance contract is that both the parties must have common intention and act to create the legal relationship between them. It needs to be reiterated that the intention of both the parties is to create the legal relationship between themselves. Under the insurance contract, an insured expresses his intention while making a valid offer and the insurer expresses his intention on the acceptance of that offer which will bind both the parties in accordance with the terms and conditions of the insurance policy.

(3) Parties Competent to make Contract

Both the parties to insurance contract should be competent/capable of entering into contract. Section II of Indian Contract Act, 1872, lays down that every person is competent to contract:

(a) Who is of the age of majority according to the law governing majority (under Indian Majority Act);
(b) Who is of sound mind (can understand the full implications of the terms and conditions of contract); and
(c) Who is not disqualified from entering into contract by any law to which he is subject (for example, undischarged insolvent, etc.).

A valid contract requires that both the parties should understand the legal implications of each other's conduct as obligations (rights and duties/obligations) under the contract. A minor is not competent to contract. A person is said to be of sound mind, who can understand the contract at the time of making it. An alien enemy, an insolvent and criminal cannot enter into contract. Contract made by incompetent party/parties will be void. Therefore, minor persons, persons of unsound mind and those with criminal background cannot take an insurance policy because they cannot enter into valid contract.

(4) Free Consent

It means when both the parties have agreed to a contract on the terms and conditions of the agreement in the same sense and spirit. They are said to have a free consent only when this happens. Under Section 14 of Indian Contract Act, 1872, the consent is to be free when it is not caused by: coercion; undue influence; fraud; misrepresentation; and mistake.

Contract without free consent is voidable at the option of the party whose consent is not free except when there is fraud. In case of fraud, the contract is void.

(5) Lawful Consideration

It means when a party to an agreement promises to do something, he/she must get something in return. This is called 'consideration' in law. In insurance contract, the payment of premium is the consideration on the part of the insured. The contract of insurance is the contract of indemnity under which an insurance company, in consideration of premium, undertakes to compensate the loss of the stated insured against a specified risk, e.g. fire, marine hazard, accident or death. The consideration for which the insurance company undertakes to compensate the risk of insured is called the 'premium'. Premium may be paid either in lump sum or in periodical instalments spread over the specified period of policy. The insurance contract cannot be initiated without the payment of premium.

(6) Lawful Object

There is another important basic principle of insurance contract and that is the legality (or lawfulness) of objects. The object of the insurance contract should be lawful. It is lawful when:

It is not forbidden by law, or
It is not immoral, or
It is not opposed to public policy, or
It is not against the provisions of any law

An unlawful object of any contract shall make it unenforceable at law. If the object of insurance, like the consideration, is found to be unlawful, the policy is void.

(7) Certainty and Possibility of Performance

Also important is the factor and that is the parties to a contract must agree on the terms of their mutually arrived agreement. They have to make their intention clear in their contract. The terms of contract must be definite or certain and capable of performance. If the agreement does not make it possible to ascertain its meaning and is impossible to perform, it cannot be enforced.

(ii) Fundamentals of Insurance Contracts

Insurance contracts, to whichever category they may belong, they are based on the following fundamental principles:

(1) Utmost Good Faith

The contracts of insurance are, therefore, included in the category of the contracts uberima fiddie, i.e. those contracts which require absolute and utmost good faith on the part of the parties concerned. In this respect, such contracts are different from the ordinary business contracts; the latter are based on the rule of Caveat Emptor (let the buyer beware). For instance, in an ordinary sale of goods, the buyer is expected to take reasonable care to satisfy himself as to the genuineness and quality of goods intended to be purchased. If the goods turn out to be otherwise, the buyer will have no remedy against the seller and will have to bear the loss.

This principle compels both the parties to the contract to make full disclosure of all martial facts. The material facts mean those facts which may affect the decision of either party whether to enter or not to enter into the contract. Both the parties should have the same state of mind when entering into contract, only then the correct risk, rights and obligations can be assessed. It also means that there should not be any concealment, misrepresentation, half-disclosure or fraud regarding the subject-matter to be insured. Otherwise, the contract would be null and void. Under the contract of insurance, greater degree of good faith is expected from the proposer.

Therefore, the insured must disclose the following facts in a life insurance contract:

Name, address and his occupation; date of birth, age, height, weight, etc., facts about his life and habits; family history; information about health; quantum and nature of his income; and a certification by the proposer that he has answered all questions truly and correctly and agrees that the proposal and declaration shall be the basis of contract.

The breach of obligation of disclosing material facts may arise as under:

Non-disclosure of material facts: intentional non-disclosure of facts; non-disclosure of material facts by negligence or through oversight; and misrepresentation of material facts with fraudulent purposes/intention.

In case of marine insurance, the offerer-maker is required to disclose the following information about the subject-matter of insurance:

Nature of goods; method of packing; particulars of vessel carrying the goods; the port of shipment and destination along the route of journey; insurance cover required and condition of insurance; sum to be insured; and past claims information and experience.

Section 20 of the Marine Insurance Act prescribes that in the following cases, the insured is not required to disclose the information:

Facts already known to insurer; facts which the insurer is expected to know in the normal course of his business; facts which may tend to reduce the risk; and facts covered under the warranty.

It generally happens, and that begins a controversy and promotes litigation, that the insurance company finds it a better way to cancel the contract or dismiss the claim on account of non-disclosure of material facts and as a consequent breach of utmost good faith. Similarly, the insured may also avoid contract, in case the insurance company does not conduct in good faith in disclosing the scope of insurance.

In the case of fire insurance also, this principle is applicable. But this duty lies more on the offer-maker, who is in possession of all material facts relating to the subject-matter to be insured. The insurer is also required to disclose important facts of policy to the prospective offerer also. The following material facts are required to be disclosed in contract of fire insurance:

Location of property; details of construction and description of property; particulars of occupier, i.e. whether used for office, residence, shop, godown, manufacturing unit or service undertaking, etc.; nature of goods or material; and particulars of previous loss, if any, suffered.

(2) Insurable Interest

No person could enter into a valid contract of insurance unless he had insurable interest in the object to be insured. If it were not so, and if everyone were at liberty to take out an insurance policy on any object or life in the world, irrespective of his insurable interest, the contracts of insurance would have been reduced to mere gambling. In such conditions, insurance contract would be reduced to wagering contracts, which are not valid and cannot be enforced in a court of law as wagering is unlawful activity.

It is important to understand insurable interest. It is understood as an interest in the preservation of a thing, or continuation of a life, recognized by law. Whoever has such interest in an object or a life may insure that object or life. Truly speaking, insurable interest is in the nature of pecuniary or financial interest in an object or a life. It follows that a person can have an insurable interest only when he would stand to benefit financially by the continuation of object or life insured. In other words, he would be put to a financial loss by the happening of the event against which an object or the life of the person has been insured. Moreover, insurable interest is not a mere sentimental interest in the object insured. It is a pecuniary interest and it follows that the loss caused by the risk insured against must be capable of measurement in term of money. It is important to know the views expressed by Prof. Mehra, "If the happening of the event insured cannot cost the insured in terms of money, then there is no insurable interest".

Essentials of Insurable Interest: The essentials of a valid insurable interest are as under:

> There must be a specific subject matter to be insured; the insured should have the monetary benefit in the subject matter; the insured should have legal relationship with the subject matter and that relationship must be recognized by law; the insured must be the owner or possessor of the legal right or interest in the subject matter; the insured should be economically benefited by the existence of the subject mater; and the insurance-maker should suffer an economic loss on its non-existence of the thing/subject-matter or at the death of the insured person.

Insurable interest in a life insurance should exist when a policy is purchased. In a life insurance policy, the insurable interest is as follows:

> A child has an insurable interest in the life of his father; a person has unlimited interest in his own life; a husband has an insurable interest in the life of his wife; a wife has an insurable interest in the life of her husband; a creditor has an insurable interest, to the extent of his debt, in the life of his debtor; a partner in a business has an insurable interest in the life or lives of his co-partner or co-partners; a company has an insurable interest in the life of a senior officer whose death may affect the profit of a business; and a servant has an insurable interest in the life of his employer.

Insurable interest in case of fire insurance must exist when insurance is effected as well as when the loss occurs. In fire insurance, however, insurable interest is as under:

> The owner of the property has in his property; every partner has an equitable interest in the properties of the firm; and an agent has an insurable interest in the property of his principal.

In marine insurance, insurable interest must exist only when the loss occurs. In Marine Insurance, the following persons have insurable interest:

> The owner of a ship has an insurable interest in the ship; the cargo owner has in its cargo; the master and the crew of the ship have it in respect of their wages; a creditor who has advanced money on the security of cargo or ship, up to his claim; a ship owner in the freight to be received on the completion of journey; a mortgagor has an insurable interest to the full value of the property; a mortgagee has it to the extent of the sum due to him; and a trustee holds property in trust up to the extent of value of such property.

(3) Indemnity

All contracts of insurance, except for life insurance, are contracts of indemnity. The basic principle of insurance is to transfer the loss of a person to the insurance company which can easily be spread over a large number of policyholders. It is, therefore, necessary that a person will get exactly the same amount as he has lost due to the loss of his goods or damage to the property. The insured cannot be permitted to make profit out of his loss. If insurance company were to agree to compensate a higher sum than the actual loss, there would be a constant temptation on the part of the insured to destroy his goods or property intentionally and thus to reap profit out of insurance. If it is so, it will be against the basic principle and also an anti-social act. For example, if the goods are insured for Rs. 10,000 and the insured suffers a loss of Rs. 5000, he will be compensated for Rs. 5000 only. But if the insured has taken a policy for a smaller value than the actual loss, the insurance company is bound to pay only the amount of policy and not the actual loss (assuming that average clause is not applicable). This is so because by insuring his goods for a lesser value, the insured has expressed his intention of transferring only a part of his actual loss to the insurance company. The balance of loss will justifiably be met by the insured himself. Thus, for a policy of Rs. 4000 instead of Rs. 10,000 and the actual loss being Rs. 6000, insurance company will pay only Rs. 4000 and no more.

Merits of Principle of Indemnity: There are merits in the principle of indemnity which are as follows:

(1) *Avoidance of Under or over-Insurance:* If this principle were not there, there would be tendency on the part of the insured to get things over-valued and then intentionally cause a loss and gain profit through enforcing insurance claim. Since in insurance only the actual loss is compensated, the insured would be discouraged to under or over value the policy's amount.

(2) *To avoid anti-social activity:* This principle avoids anti social act on the part of the insured. If the insured is allowed to make profit (which is against the principle of indemnity), there would be a constant temptation to destroy the property after it is insured. Therefore, the whole society will be doing only anti-social act to get easy money. But in insurance, only the cash value of loss of the insured is compensated even if it might have been insured for a greater amount.

(3) *To maintain premium at low level:* This principle helps the insurance company to maintain premium at low level because very few claims will be made and those will be genuine (within the actual value). If this principle is not made applicable, large amount of compensation will be required to be paid for a small loss. This will increase the cost of insurance and the companies would be forced to raise the premium. This will defeat the purpose of insurance.

Main Features of Indemnity: The following are the main features of the principle of indemnity:

(1) All contracts of insurance are contracts of indemnity except life insurance.

(2) There is an indirect relationship between the principle of indemnity and insurable interest because the insured is required to prove the amount of

his actual loss and his interest therein in order to get compensation.

(3) The amount of compensation cannot exceed the amount of actual loss or the value of policy, whichever is less.

(4) After the compensation of loss, the insured cannot hold the ownership right on the things insured, i.e. the ownership right will shift to the insurance company.

(5) Valued policies are not covered under the principle of indemnity.

Conditions for Indemnity: The following conditions are required to be satisfied in full for the application of the principle of indemnity:

Insured has to prove that he has suffered a loss on the subject matter insured and it is the actual monetary loss; the compensation cannot exceed the amount insured; insurer has a right to get back the extra amount, if any, paid to the insured; the insurer has a right to get back all amount received by the insured from the third party if the loss is fully indemnified by the insurer; and the principle of indemnity is not applicable in case of life insurance as the actual loss on death cannot be calculated.

Liability of Insurer to Pay Compensation: According to the application of the principle of indemnity, the insured can get only the actual loss of goods or property destroyed, or the insured amount, whichever is less. The loss payable is calculated after considering the following factors:

(a) *Sum insured or the value of policy:* Every insurance policy is issued for a specific sum, called sum insured, which is the maximum limit or liability of the insurer in respect of goods insured. But the actual amount payable is calculated with reference to his actual loss or the sum insured, whichever is less.

(b) *Excess and Franchise Clause:* It is a practice that certain insurance polices are issued subject to excess or franchise clause. This clause says that under certain conditions a part of the loss shall be borne by the insured himself. The liability of insurer is limited by the imposition of excess or franchise clause. In case of imposition of this clause, if the loss does not exceed the limit, it is not paid at all and if it exceeds the limit, only excess is paid under 'Excess clause' and total loss is indemnified under the franchise clause.

(c) *Pro-Rata Average:* Sometimes, the policy contains an average clause. This condition is incorporated with two objectives, i.e. to penalize the insured for taking a policy for a lesser sum than the actual value of property and secondly, to limit the liability of insurer.

According to the provision contained in this clause, the compensation payable by the insurer is proportionately reduced in case of under-insurance of goods or property. For example, a person may insure his property for Rs. 75,000. While the actual loss is assessed at Rs. 40,000 and the market value of the property at the time of loss is Rs. 1,00,000, the claim will be settled at Rs. 40,000 × 75,000/1,00,000 = Rs. 30,000. Obviously, in this case, the insured is penalized for Rs. 10,000 for under-insurance of his property. Formula is as under:

$$\text{Liability of Insurer} = \text{Actual Loss} \times \frac{\text{Insurance Policy taken}}{\text{Market value of property at the time of loss}}$$

(d) *Salvage:* In the event of loss of insured property, it may be partially destroyed, not completely. Anything left after the occurrence of loss is known as 'Salvage'. The salvage or scrap left of the damaged or destroyed goods or property is to be reduced from the amount of indemnity payable to the insured.

(e) *Subrogation:* The doctrine of subrogation is an extension and corollary of the principle of indemnity. According to the principle of indemnity, the insurer steps into the shoes of the insured and becomes entitled to all the rights of the insured regarding the subject matter of insurance after the claim of the insured has been fully and finally settled. In some cases, there may a possibility of his getting something in addition to what he has received from the insurer. If the goods are not fully destroyed, the insured may try to obtain some amount of scrap in addition to what to the money received by him in the settlement of his claim. This will be against the principle of indemnity because the insured will get more than what he lost. Therefore, whatever is left of the damaged or destroyed goods or property will automatically pass on to the insurance company after the claim of the insured has been settled.

(f) *Contribution:* Sometimes, the insured may get his goods or property insured with more than one insurer. This is referred to as 'Double Insurance'. In the event of loss, the insured will be indemnified only against actual loss incurred against the risk insured. In such cases, the companies concerned will follow the principle of contribution for the payment of compensation. According to this principle, each insurance company will contribute that proportion of the loss which the policy insured by it bears to the total amount for which insurance has been effected with all the insurance companies. But in case where the insured chooses to get the amount of loss from one particular company or two of them, the paying company or companies can later on adjust loss paid with other insurer by receiving their contribution according to the proportion of their insured amount.

Methods of Indemnifying: There are four alternative methods to indemnify an insured in the event of loss, damage or destruction of subject matter insured. These are as follows:

Cash Payment: Cash payment of the amount of claim of insurance is the easiest and a very common method of indemnification. After making proper enquiries of loss, the insurer accepts the claim by making cash payment through cheque to the insured.

Repairs: In some cases, where the subject matter of insurance is partially damaged and is capable of being repaired, the insurer, instead of making cash payment, prefers to settle claim of the loss or damage by means of getting the damaged subject matter, repaired. The repair is authorized to the insured and the insured has to submit bill of repairs along with a note of satisfaction and then the repair related bill is paid by the insurer.

Replacement: In case the subject of the insurance policy is damaged, lost or destroyed to such an extent that it is not possible and feasible to get it repaired, the insurance company may arrange the replacement of the property. Generally, this practice is followed in case of theft of property.

Reinstatement: Reinstatement is a method rarely used. In this case, the property damaged is reinstalled in its original position.

(4) Subrogation

This principle is also known as 'Doctrine of Rights Substitution'. It is an extension of the principle of indemnity. Subrogation is the transfer of rights and remedies of the insured in the subject matter (property) to the insurer after indemnification.

In other words, the insurer steps into the shoes of the insured and becomes entitled to all rights of action against the third party to cover the loss from the responsible person regarding the subject matter of insurance after the claim of the insured has been fully settled and paid.

The principle of subrogation refers to the right of the insurer to stand in the place of the insured after the settlement of a claim. The insurer can recover the loss from the third party. There always exists a possibility of getting something in addition to the claim received from the insurer by the insured, e.g. value of scrap, damages from the person responsible for the loss and several other alternatives.

Definition of Subrogation: According to Federation of Insurance Institutes (FII), "Subrogation is the transfer of rights and remedies of the insured to the insurer who has indemnified the insured in respect of the loss".

According to Dinsdale, "Subrogation may be defined as the insurer's right to receive the benefit of all the rights of the insured against third parties which, if satisfied, will extinguish or diminish the ultimate loss sustained".

Essentials of Subrogation

(i) *Extension of Principle of Indemnity:* It is the extension and corollary of the principle of indemnity. According to principle of indemnity, only the actual loss is compensated to the insured. If the goods or property are partially damaged or destroyed, the insurer can recover some amount after the claim is fully and finally settled with the insured. The loss to property may be caused by an act of a third party. Accordingly, the insured is required to subrogate all his rights in favour of the insurer to reduce his paid compensation.

(ii) *Subrogation is the substitution:* All rights and remedies available to the insured are transferred to the insurer after the settlement of claim. Insurance company is substituted in place of insured for all matters concerning the loss.

(iii) *Subrogation is only up to the amount of payment:* The insurer is substituted only up to the amount of compensation paid to the insured. If the insured has been compensated by the third party after he has been indemnified by his insurer, he (insured) is liable to compensate the insurer for the amount received by him from the third party.

(iv) *Subrogation may be applied before payment:* If the insured is compensated to some extent by the third party before being fully indemnified by the insurer, then the insurer can pay only the balance amount of the loss.

(v) *Personal Insurance:* The principle of subrogation is not applicable in case of personal insurance.

Need for Subrogation: The principle of subrogation has been introduced with the aim to protect the interest of insurers. In case of loss without it, the insured may be in a position to collect more money than his actual loss by selling the salvage. According to this principle, since the insured is required to subrogate all his rights in favour of the insurer after the loss is settled, cannot make profit out of insurance policy. Moreover, the insurer has a right to claim loss if it is caused by the act of third party.

Features of Subrogation: Subrogation has the following features:

(a) It is a corollary to and outcome of the principle of indemnity and is applicable in all contracts of indemnity.
(b) It is applicable only after the payment of loss by the insurer.
(c) It may also arise even before indemnification of loss except in case of marine insurance policies.
(d) The insured is required to provide all help to insurer while enforcing the claim against the defaulters.
(e) The insurer has a right to sue the third party in the name of the insured. But all expenses of litigation are to be borne by the insurer.
(f) The insured will hold the amount of compensation received from the third party in trust for the insurer if he has already been compensated by the insurer.
(g) The right of subrogation arises from the acts of torts, contract, salvage, etc.
(h) The principle of subrogation is automatically applied even without any express condition in the contract in this regard.
(i) Under this principle, the insurer cannot recover from the defaulter party anything more than the amount of compensation paid to the insured. The right of recovery is limited to the amount of claim paid to the insured.

How does Right of Subrogation Arise?: Subrogation rights arise in the following ways:

Tort: Where the insured has sustained some damage, lost right or incurred liability due to atrocious acts of some other person and the insurer has indemnified the loss, the insured is entitled to take action to recover the loss from the wrong doer.

Contract: Subrogation relates to rights, which arise out of certain contracts. This may arise where there is a custom of the trade to which the contract applies. Subrogation right may arise from contract where a person has contractual right to compensation regardless of fault.

Subject matter of Insurance: Sometimes, a situation may arise, whereas an insured has been indemnified and the subject matter treated as lost. Once the claim has been compensated, the insured cannot claim the salvage or scarp.

(5) Causa Proxima (immediate and the nearest cause)

The principle of proximate cause is also called 'causa proxima'. The term causa proxima is a Latin term which means, the nearest cause or proximate cause or immediate cause. Causa proxima is the real cause of loss and not the distant cause. It is helpful in deciding the actual cause of loss when a number of causes have contributed to the occurrence of loss. The maxim used in this regard is 'Sed Causa proxima non-remote spectator' which means that 'see the nearest or direct cause and not the remote or distant cause'. The real, nearest and direct cause of loss must be seen while making payment of the loss. If the real cause of loss is insured, the insurer is liable to compensate the loss, otherwise the insurer may not be responsible for loss.

In other words, while deciding the liability of the insurer, the direct, nearest or proximate cause and not the remote or indirect cause of the loss is to be taken into account.

Meaning and Definition of the Doctrine of Causa Proxima: The doctrine of causa proxima is in fact based on the law of cause and effect which means that having proved the cause and effect thereof, there remains no need to proceed further.

In case of *Pawsey* Vs. *South Union and National Insurance Co.*, it was observed that

> "Proximate cause means the active and efficient cause that sets in motion a train of events which bring about result, without the intervention of any force started and working actively from new and independent source".

Thus, the cause must be 'immediate cause' to be 'proximate'. The expression 'immediate' should be understood in terms of effectiveness or efficiency. In other words, proximate cause is the cause, which is effectual in producing that result.

The proximate cause means that direct, the most dominant and most effective cause of which the loss is the natural consequence. It is the cause, which is most closely and directly connected with the loss, not necessarily in time but in efficiency and effectiveness.

Practical Aspects of Doctrine of Causa Proxima: There is no problem in deciding the question of liability of the insurer if the loss is the outcome of only one event. But the loss may be the result of two or more events or causes. It becomes necessary to locate the effective and most powerful cause of loss. It is not easy to decide the proximate cause when it is caused by a large number of events.

Events or causes for the purpose of determining the practical use of doctrine of causa proxima may be divided into three categories:

(1) *Operation of a single Cause:* Where there is a single event which causes the loss, it will be a clear case of proximate cause and the insurer will be held liable for the event if it is insured under the policy, e.g. if a person dies in road accident, the accident will be the proximate cause under the personal accident policy.

(2) *Concurrent Causes:* In case of concurrent causes, i.e. causes occurring simultaneously, and the policy has not excluded perils, there arises liability of insurer if one of the causes is 'insured peril' and other causes may be

ignored. The concurrent causes may be separable and inseparable causes. Separable causes are those causes which can be separated from each other. The loss caused by a particular separable cause, if insured against peril, will be compensated by the insurer. In case the circumstances are such that causes are inseparable, then the insurer is not liable at all when there exists any expected event.

(3) *Successive Causes:* Where there is a chain of events causing a loss to the subject mater insured, the liability of insurer would arise if the original cause event is an 'insured peril'.

(6) Mitigation of Loss

Mitigation of loss means to minimize or to decrease the severity of the loss. Under this doctrine, it is prescribed that whenever the event insured against occurs, it will be the duty of the insured to take all such steps to minimize the loss as he would have taken when the subject matter was not insured. The logic behind the principle of mitigation of loss is that the insured should not become careless and passive at the time of loss simply because his property had been insured. He must act like any uninsured prudent person.

Accordingly to this principle, the insured must act reasonably to make the loss less severe and try to make each and every effort and arrangement to minimize the loss in the event of loss occurring.

(7) Contribution

Sometime, the same subject matter of insurance could be covered by different policies. It is possible that these policies are taken in different contexts under different portfolios or even multiple policies for extra protection. Here, as we saw in the case of subrogation, there is a possibility that the insured might get compensated more than once from different sources for the same loss, thereby making a profit. The principle of contribution is relevant in this context.

In the event of multiple policies covering the same subject matter of insurance, the principle of contribution provides for an equitable sharing of any loss between all the insurers according to their respective insurances. (Denis Riley, 1967). When a loss is insured under more than one insurance policy, for example, a travel policy and a household policy, in the event of a claim the two insurers share the cost. The principle of contribution like that of subrogation seeks to prevent the insured from getting compensations from different sources for the same loss, thereby violating the principles of indemnity.

Contribution is the right of an insurer who has paid claim under a policy, to call upon others insurer for the same loss, to contribute. This principle is applicable to all contracts of indemnity except the life insurance.

Definition of Contribution: According to the Federation of Insurance Institutes, Mumbai:

> "Principle of contribution refers to the right of an insurer who has paid for a loss under a policy to cover a proportionate amount from other insurers who are liable for the loss".

Therefore, contribution is the right of an insurer, to call upon other insurers liable for the same loss to contribute the payment to the one who has paid the loss under a policy. This doctrine ensures an equitable distribution of losses between different insurers.

Need of Principle of Contribution: Sometimes, a person may get his goods insured with more than one insures. This is known as double insurance. In the event of loss if he got his loss indemnified from all insures, he will receive more compensation than his actual loss. It is against the principle of indemnity. In case of loss, he may choose to get his loss compensated by one or more insurers taken together. In such a case when an insured chooses to collect his loss from one or two of them, the paying company or companies can later claim proportionate amount from other insurers.

Pre-Requisites of the Principle of Contribution: The principle of contribution is not applicable in all cases of 'double insurance'. The following are the pre-requisites for the application of principle of contribution:

(a) The subject matter or property of insurance must be common to all insurers. In simple words, it means that the goods or properties to be insured must be the same in case of all policies issued.
(b) The risk event which causes the loss must be common to all policies in order to attract the principle of contribution.
(c) The policies must be legally enforceable which means that the policies must be valid. These or none of these must not be invalid, void, null or defective at the time of loss.
(d) The policies must be in force at the time of loss. The principle of contribution is applicable only to those policies which shall be in force at the time of occurrence of loss.
(e) The insurable interest must be the same under all policies. All policies must be effected in favour of an insured.

(8) Miscellaneous

There are also certain miscellaneous principles of insurance beside the general and specific principles. These are as under:

(i) Principle of Assignment: Principle of assignment is also known as transfer of interest. It is necessary to distinguish between assignment of—the subject matter of property of insurance; the policy and the policy money when payable.

In case of marine and life insurance policies, assignments can be made freely without the prior consent of the insurer. But in case of fire insurance and accident insurance policies, assignment without advance consent of insurer is not valid.

The life insurance policy can be assigned freely for a legal consideration or even without consideration in case of love and affection.

Assignment refers to transfer of interest of policy to third party by the insured. The assignment shall be complete and effective only on the execution of such endorsement either on the policy itself or on a separate deed. Notice for this purpose must be given to the insurer who will acknowledge the assignment. Once the assignment is complete, it cannot be revoked by the assignor. The life policies are the only polices, which can be assigned whether the assignee has an insurable interest or not. A marine cargo policy is freely assignable unless it contains conditions expressly prohibiting assignment. It may be assigned either before or after loss. It may be assigned through endorsement or in any other customary manner.

Assignment of fire insurance cannot be done without prior consent of insurer. Change in insurable interest in fire insurance policies is not valid unless the consent of the insurer has been obtained.

(ii) Principle of Return of Premium: The amount of premium once paid cannot ordinarily be refunded. However, in the following cases the premium paid is returnable.

By agreement in the policy: The insured may pay full premium while effecting the insurance but it may be agreed in policy to return it wholly or partly on the happening of certain events.

For reasons of Equity: Equity implies a condition that the insured shall not receive the price of running a risk he bears. So, the contract does not come into effete in this case or it is held to be void. It can be established by the following points.

Non-attachment of Risk: Where the subject matter insured or part thereof, has never been imperiled, e.g. such policy is term insurance with returnable premium. Again, the premium is returned to the policy-holder if death does not occur during the period of insurance.

Undeclared Balance of an open Policy: Policy may be cancelled and premium may be returned for short interest allowed provided there was no further interest in the policy.

Payment of Premium is Apportional: The apportioned part of the consideration is refundable when a part of policy interest is not involved. For example, insurance may be taken for a voyage in stages, each stage being rated separately. In such a case if some stages are not completed, the premium, relating to the journey not completed, is returnable.

Where the assured has no insurable interest throughout the currency of risk, the premium is returnable provided the policy was not attached by way of wagering.

Unreasonable delay in commencing the voyage may also entitle the insurer to cancel the insurance by returning the premium.

(iii) Principle of over-insurance by Double Insurance: If there is over insurance by way of double insurance, a propitiate part of several premiums is returnable provided that if the polices are taken at different times and any earlier policy has at any time borne the whole risk or if a claim has been paid, premium on the first policy cannot be returned. When double insurance is effected knowingly by the insured, no premium is returnable.

(iv) Legal Principles: Life insurance is a contract and, therefore, the provisions of the Contract Act, 1872 are applicable. The provisions of other Acts like Transfer of Property Act, Estate Duty Act, Indian Stamp Act, Law of Limitation, etc., Succession Act, etc. are also applicable to life insurance.

New for Old Part(s) Principle

When a part of a machine or a vehicle is replaced following an accident, the insurer pays for the cost of a new part to see that the machine is reinstated to its working condition. Here, indemnity is seen as the process of putting the machinery back to working condition and not like replacement of the old part with another old part. In the bargain, the insured gets a new part instead of the old part and the insurer would be meeting the cost of new spare parts.

It is a term used to describe a basis of cover, usually within property insurance. Whereby the insurer agrees to pay the full replacement cost of the damaged insured item and not what the actual item is valued at the time of the loss. This principle is used in areas such as marine hull, machinery parts, vehicle parts and the like.

In other words, it denotes replacing old damaged parts or equipment with new ones rather than repairing them. In an insurance cover for property or equipment, an item if destroyed is replaced by the equivalent new item without deduction for age or wear and tear of the old item and regardless of price inflation. Items lost or damaged beyond repair will be at the present purchase price. The advantage is that the insured will not be left out of pocket when replacing items. However, new for old does not apply to items like clothing, household linen and pedal-cycles where wear and tear needs to be taken into consideration. New for old or replacement cost option is usually offered at the proposal stage of arranging insurance and will carry a higher premium charge than a strict indemnity only policy, which will take into account a deduction for wear and tear.

Reinstatement

Reinstatement is a claim settled on option agreed between the insured and the insurer, stating that the insurer would make good the damaged property of the insured, rather than pay a monetary amount. Reinstatement is the cost of making good the insured damaged property. Accordingly, the reinstatement clause or memorandum is usually used within a property policy that states the duty of the insurer if they decide to reinstate the property in the event of an insured loss. For this benefit, the insurer would usually charge a policyholder an additional premium.

However, reinstatement of the loss by the insurer is not followed strictly due to various practical issues. Reinstatement would be a costly exercise for the insurer. Again, if he were not able to reinstate to the satisfaction of the insured, his work would have to be abandoned. The insured may not practically prefer reinstatement, as he would like to have better buildings or newer technology or higher capacity equipment to replace the loss. In practical terms, the insured would prefer receiving the full cost of reinstatement in lieu of actual reinstatement. This cost would comprise of (i) the indemnity *per se*, (ii) wear and tear, depreciation, and (iii) cost of inflation between date of loss and probable time of reinstatement: this clause helps in bringing the insured closer to the state prior to the loss, instead of getting a lump-sum in the event of the loss suffered by the insured. However, there is a possibility of an insured getting away with a lower sum insured (and lower premium) utilizing this clause. Hence, the condition of average or adjusting the claim out of the sum, payable to the insured (chosen by the insured) is applied. Reinstatement at 85 per cent average is applied only to a claim settlement, if the building's sum insured is less than 85 per cent of the reinstatement value.

Apart from the above reinstatement that is applied in the case of a loss, there is a concept of reinstatement of premium. Under property insurance, reinstatement premium is the amount of premium payable by the policyholder to restore the sum insured to its original level, following an insured loss.

Agreed Value

Agreed value policies or valued policies are considered a practical way out in many cases where assessing the value of a loss post the event can pose problems. There could be different reasons for such situations and in the context of different types of policies. Moral and morale hazards may be involved in areas such as health insurance. In case of marine cargo, there could be difficulty in finding out the value at the location of the loss. In such cases, the value would be the invoice price plus some other objective measure such as freight, which seldom violate the principle of indemnity. In fire and engineering project insurance, the value of stock may have changed due to some processes involved, or by market conditions, inflation or currency fluctuations. In the case of rarities and personal possessions such as paintings, fitted items or prizes, sentimental reasons would make objective evaluation unacceptable. Values of such items can be extremely difficult to assess post loss. In areas like personal accident, measuring personal losses post event may be painful.

As situations of over insurance and total losses can cause overpayments, the reasonableness of fixing the agreed value becomes important. The agreed value concept has pitfalls as well. If the value reduces between the date of agreeing and the date of loss causing an over indemnification, the valuation in case of partial losses can be difficult. In some cases, partial losses may have to be treated on a different basis. In total losses, the value of salvage may vary widely between the insured and an objective assessor.

Material Fact

Any information that could affect the underwriter's assessment of the risk is regarded as a material fact. The underwriter's assessment can include fixing the insurance premium, framing the condition that would operate in the event of a claim, or even the decision to accept the risk itself. The Marine Insurance Act, 1906 defines the concept as follows:

> "Every circumstance is material which would influence the judgment of a prudent insurer in fixing the premium or determining whether he will take the risk".

Failure by the policyholder or proposer to inform insurers of all relevant material fats that affect the insured risk is referred to as non-disclosure. Non-disclosure of material facts could normally result in a reduced indemnity depending on the level of non-disclosure. However, if the material facts that were not disclosed are found to be very crucial or if there is any serious misrepresentation of facts, insurers are entitled to treat it as a serious matter and refuse to deal with any claims or void the policy from the start of cover.

Reciprocal Duty

Reciprocity is another guiding principle in insurance. Fundamental principles that are binding on one party call for reciprocal behaviour from the other party as well, whether stated or otherwise. While the insured is expected to disclose all material facts, the insurer should also disclose to him benefits under the policy that he (insured) normally may not know about. For instance, an insured has to inform the insurer that the old wiring in a block of the factory has caused short circuits in the recent past and due to insufficient budget allocation, rewiring has not been done yet. Reciprocally, the insurer should inform the insured that the automatic fire protection system he has installed in the block would entitle him to a discount, or that as a fire safe door had been fixed in the block, the loading for improper electrical installations would be applicable only to that block and not to other communicating blocks.

Condition of Average

The principle of average requires the amount of a claim payment to be reduced proportionately if a policyholder has not insured his property for its full value, or full replacement cost. The insurer has to meet the losses of a few employees from the money pooled from many. If an insured opts for a lesser sum insured and consequently pays a less than adequate amount as premium, it is only logical that the loss also gets reduced proportionally. An insured who contributes less to the common pool is allowed to reap only lesser benefits from the pool. If a policy is subject to average and if the sum insured at the time of a loss is less than the actual value of the property insured, the amount of claim under the policy will also be reduced in proportion to the under-insurance. In mathematical terms:

$$\text{Allowable Claim} = \frac{\text{Loss} \times \text{Sum Insured}}{\text{Value at Risk}}$$

The concept of average is applied by dividing the sum insured by the actual value at risk and applying the same proportion on the loss by multiplying the amount of loss by the result, making the loss proportionate to the sum insured. The remaining part of the sum insured is treated as actually covered by the insured himself who has retained the premium with him. Hence, he has to pay to himself the proportionate amount of the loss as well.

General Average

Concepts of general and particular averages are not to be confused with the condition of average stated above.

General average is a contribution made by all parties involved (usually) in a sea adventure, towards a loss occasioned by the sacrifice of the property of some of the parties in the common interest/for the benefit of all. In order to save a ship in peril of sinking during a storm, some of the cargo may have to be thrown overboard. In the exigencies of hazards faced at sea, crewmembers often have precious little time to determine precisely whose cargo they are jettisoning. Thus, to avoid quartering that could waste valuable tie, there arose the equitable practice whereby all the merchants whose cargo was on board would be called on to contribute a portion, based upon a share or percentage, to the merchant or merchants whose goods had been tossed overboard to avert imminent peril. The ship owner and the owners of the saved cargo obviously benefit at the expense of the owners of the jettisoned cargo. It is called general average, because the loss is applicable in general to the ship, the cargo and the freight at risk saved by the sacrifice. This was unfair demand and the principle of general average evolved so that all parties would contribute in such a situation.

It is believed that the inhabitants of Rhodes invented the concept of the general average. Merchants whose goods were being shipped together would pay a proportionally divided premium that would be used to reimburse any merchant whose goods were jettisoned during storm or sinkage. While general average traces its origins in ancient maritime law, it still remains a part of the admiralty law of most countries. The first condition of general average was the York Antwerp Rules of 1890. American companies accepted it in 1949. General average requires three elements as stated by Justice Grier in *Barnard* v. *Adams.*

(1) "*A common danger:* A danger in which vessel, cargo and crew all participate, a danger imminent and apparently "inevitable, except by voluntarily incurring the loss of a portion of the whole to save the remainder".

(2) "There must be a voluntary jettison, jactus, or casting away, of some portion of the joint corner for the purpose of avoiding this imminent peril, periculi imminent is evitandi causa, or in other words, a transfer of the peril from the whole to a particular portion of the whole".

(3) "This attempt to avoid the imminent common peril must be successful".

In simple words, the law of general average is a legal principle of maritime law, according to which all parties in a sea venture proportionally share any loss resulting from a voluntary sacrifice of a part of the ship or cargo to save the whole in an emergency. Thus, if one ships cargo on a vessel that is involved in a loss, he may face a claim against him even though his goods are not damaged. This aspect is questioned by some insured as unfair. However, actually it is not unfair because all the insured are part of the same marine venture, went through the same situations, and anyone could have suffered the loss.

Particular Average

Particular average is the damage or partial loss happening to the ship or cargo or freight, in consequence of some fortuitous or unavoidable accident, and it is borne by the individual owners of the articles damaged or by their insurers. The term is usually used in marine insurance. In contrast to general average, particular average does not deal with damage voluntarily incurred in case of a cargo consignment; the measure of indemnity varies depending on whether there was a total loss to some of the cartons sent, or whether damage was sustained by some part of the consignment. The value is derived as an average of the CIF invoice value (comprising cost, insurance and freight) for the entire consignment. As particular average means a partial loss insurance cover, policies issued on total loss cover are said to be on free of particular average (FPA) which means excluding partial losses (or total loss only). FPA is a set of marine insurance conditions providing a very narrow cover. Another term relating to average that is used in marine insurance are petty averages that are sundry small charges, which occur regularly, and are necessarily defrayed by the master in the usual course of a voyage. These include port charges, common pilotage, and the like, which could be borne partly by the ship and/or partly by the cargo.

Sue and Labour/Particular Charges

Sue and labour/particular charges are charges incurred by or on behalf of the insured for the safety and preservation of the subject matter insured. These are different from general average, particular average and salvage charges. In practice, particular average is treated synonymously with sue and labour.

The principles stem from the theory that the insured should at all times, act as if he/she were uninsured. That is, he should take all reasonable care that he would have taken had the subject matter been uninsured. The sue and labour clause requires the shipowner to make every attempt to reduce or save the exposed interest from loss. Under the terms of the values, the insurer pays for any necessary costs incurred in carrying out the retirements of the 'sue and labour' clause. Thus, if a ship is stranded, under the 'sue and labour' clause, the hull owner would be required to hire salvers and get it towed to the nearest port. In case of fragile cargo such as bottles of jam, this logic applies in taking due care of the consignment, say, with adequate packing and proper labelling. If a heavy machine tilts and damages the cartons containing the jam bottles, the cartons may have to be shifted to a safer place on the ship. Also, the damaged cartons may have to be opened and broken bottles removed so that the leaking contents do not rot and damage the remaining jam bottles by spoiling the labels or by attracting ants and insects. Such ensuring costs reasonably and incurred short of destination. In averting or minimizing the loss are termed sue and labour charges and are payable by the insure if these cost are incurred after the goods reach their destination, such as some additional costs are incurred for cleaning up the remaining bottles and re-labelling them to make them saleable, these are treated as particular charges. Sue and labour follows a loss or damage making incident, whereas particular average can be incurred to avoid or avert the threat of an imminent loss. Differences like these are treated as academic by many authors, and in actual practice both the terms are treated almost synonymously.

Excess and Deductibles

In an insurance policy, the deductible or excess is the portion of any claim that is not covered by the insurance provider. That is, only the amount that is in excess of the deductible is recoverable. It is normally quoted as a fixed amount and is a part of most policies covering losses to the policyholder. The deductibles must be met by the insured, or in other words, paid by the insured before the benefits of the policy can apply. An excess can apply is two ways: either as a voluntary excess at the instance of the insured to obtain a discount on the premium, or as a compulsory excess imposed by the insurer for underwriting reason such as avoiding larger numbers of small claims and their associated administration costs. Often, the second case is specifically referred to as a deductible.

Either way, the excess or deductible is the amount of a claim that is the responsibility of the insured or where he is his own insurer. In simple terms, it is the amount of the claim that you have to pay out of your own pocket. In a typical automobile insurance policy, a deductible will apply to claims arising from damage to or loss of the vehicle, caused by accidents for which the holder is responsible, or by theft. If a person has an insurance policy for his car with Rs. 5000 as deductible for damages, in the event of an accident costing Rs. 8000 worth of damage to the car, the insurance company would pay not Rs. 8000 but Rs. 3000 only. The insured is responsible for the first Rs. 5000 worth of damage (the deductible). Most health insurance policies and some travel insurance policies have deductibles as well. Generally, for a higher deductible, the premium is lower and *vice versa*. Some medical insurance policies have a deductible that does not cover the cost of routine outpatient visits (e.g. to a doctor's clinic). The concept can operate on per event (per condition) basis or a per year basis, explained below:

Per Event Basis: This most common form of deductible is applied on a per event basis. The deductible amount is agreed upon between the insurance company and the policyholder on each occasion that a claim arises for each medical condition that requires treatment, the insured will be required to pay a percentage over fixed sum of the treatment costs. For example, a deductible of Rs. 1000 is applied for the treatment of an illness. If the total bill comes to Rs. 5000, then the insurance company reimburses Rs. 4000. If the total bill from three occasions of treatment comes to Rs. 15,000 in a year, the insurance company reimburses Rs. 12,000 (Rs. 15,000 less Rs. 3000) as deductibles for three occasions @ Rs. 1000 per occasion).

Per Year Basis: In a per year form of deductible, an annual limit for deduction applies instead of a per event basis. The insurance company and the policyholder agree upon an annual limit of deductible and not a claim by claim deductible. Once the claims have reached this limit, the insurance company reimburses all further expenses in full. The insured will be required to pay for their treatment up to the agreed annual limit and the insurance company will be responsible for all further costs. In the above case, if Rs. 1000 is agreed as the deductible, the insured will be required to bear the first Rs.1000 for the treatment he receives in the year. If the total bill comes to Rs. 5000 for the first occasion of treatment, the insurance company reimburses Rs. 4000. If there are two more occasions of treatment of Rs. 5000 each in the same year, the insurance company does not make any further deductions and the full claim is reimbursed on these subsequent two occasions.

Co-insurance or Co-pay

This is a form of excess used in some markets, where the insurance company requires the policyholder to pay a certain amount, most often expressed as percentage of the total cost. Co-insurance usually applies for dental, maternity treatments and outpatient treatment where the client will bear a percentage of the total expenses. For example, if an insurance company requires 20 per cent co-insurance and the total bill comes to Rs. 1000 the policyholder will bear Rs. 200 and then the insurance company will pay the remaining Rs. 800.

Franchise

This concept is similar to excess and deductibles in that the insurer makes no settlement if the total claim is below the franchise figure. In case of excess, deduction is made when a loss crosses an agreed figure. Franchise is different from excess in that no deduction is made once the loss crosses the agreed figure. This figure, however, applies as a threshold level for a claim to be considered. If the claim is more than the franchise figure, the claim is paid in full. In the above example, if the franchise figure is Rs. 1000, no claim under Rs. 1000 is payable, just as in the case of excess. However, if a loss exceeds Rs. 1000, the entire amount is paid without any deduction. Franchisees are becoming less and less common in modern insurance practice though machinery breakdown covers sometimes use time franchise.

First Loss

First loss denotes a policy where the sum insured is accepted to be less than the value of the property but the insurer undertakes to pay claims up to the sum insured, without application of average. It is a contract written on such an amount as to cover only an insured's expected loss during the policy period with no other insurance in existence. It is a type of partial insurance (which covers less than the full value of goods or property at risk) where both the insured and the insurer acknowledge that the 'subject to average (se average) rule' does not apply. 'First Loss Policies' cover only the estimated largest possible loss and are often used in theft insurance, covering high value goods that would be physically impossible to steal in a single burglary, that is where the possibility of total loss is extremely remote (such as in case of a large store).

In other words, it is an accepted form of partial insurance where the insured decides he would not suffer a total loss and selects a maximum insured sum for any loss that is probable. The sum insured is often decided by calculating the maximum probable loss (MPL) or probable maximum loss (PML). The PML of a particular risk is the estimate of the maximum loss that would occur as a result of damage caused by the most destructive peril to be insured, in regard to the location, construction, occupation and protection of the risk. PML is usually expressed as a percentage of the sum insured. It is important that first loss sums insured are used only on first loss policies where average does not apply. In the usual insurances if the sum insured does not represent the full value, the insured will not get a full settlement of any loss. In some markets, first loss is used to refer to a policy whose limits are reduced (and not reinstated) by loss payments. There are also contexts where the term first loss is used to denote a policy that covers only a single loss during the policy period or that provides coverage of multiple locations for only the first loss at each location during the policy period.

Performance Ratios

Insurance companies have to constantly assess and reassess the effectiveness of their various strategies and readjust them based on their findings. The assessments have to be objective, scientific and based on quantifiable parameters so that they are reliable. Performance is assessed essentially from three angles, the company's exposure, the company's actions, and its results.

(1) Exposure Ratios

These ratios essentially assess where the company is placed in the insurance market and in comparison to the other companies. In other words, it indicates the relative position of the insurer in the environment in which it operates.

Market Share

It indicates the insurer's share in the total pie (market). That is considering the total market as 100, how much of it the company has been able to capture for itself. This is often expressed as line graph or in table or in pie chart.

$$\text{Market Share} = \frac{\text{GDP of the particular company}}{\text{Total GDP of the market}} \times 100$$

The pie chart enables an insurance company to visualize its standing in terms of the share of the market that it controls.

Relative Market Share is another term used for comparison purposes. The comparison can be with the share of the biggest player or with an average share.

Relative Market Share (against biggest share)

$$\text{RMS} = \frac{\text{GDP of the particular company}}{\text{Highest individual GDP in the market}} \times 100$$

In the line graph given in figure, the market share of the company with the largest market share (the highest market share) is taken to be 100 per cent. The company that wants to compare itself with the largest company works out its share as compared to that of the largest company's share.

Similarly, an average company is taken as 100 for comparison to find out where the company comparing its share stands as compared to the Average Company:

$$\text{Average GDP Share} = \frac{\text{Total GDP of the market}}{\text{Number of Players}}$$

$$\begin{array}{l}\text{Relative Market Share}\\ \text{(Against average shares)}\end{array} = \frac{\text{GDP of the particular company}}{\text{Average GDP share}} \times 100$$

Persistence Ratio is considered a yard-stick to evaluate the market performance of the company *vis-à-vis* a past period. The most common comparison is between the premium collection of the current month and the premium collection of the corresponding month of the previous year, i.e. premium amount of January 2008 vs. premium amount of January 2007. Comparison is also made between the current month's premium incomes as a percentage of the total Gross Direct Premium (GDP) vs. the corresponding month's premium of the previous year as a percentage of that year's total GDP. For example, only 5 per cent of this year's GDP came from this January premium, whereas 15 per cent of last year's GDP had come from the business done in last January.

Premium Persistence Ratio refers to the tendency of the policyholders to renew the insurance with the same company. It is taken as an indication of the trust the market reposes in the company. It represents a level of satisfaction of policyholders towards their policies. This indicator is often used as an important reference when evaluating the potential growth of business. As most general insurance policies are one-year policies, substantial thrust is given on the ability of the company to retain existing customers. Customers often seek best rates and services at the point of renewal. Hence, retaining customers is taken as a barometer for the company's ability to keep its rates reasonable, give good service and maintain a healthy level of credibility in the market. It is often indicated as the amount of the premium coming from renewed business *vs.* the premium expectation as per the company's renewal register.

Premium Persistence Ratio (PPR) works as under:

$$\text{PPR} = \frac{\text{Premium in respect of renewed business}}{\text{Premium expected as per renewal register}} \times 100$$

Insurers take pride in stating that they have a premium/policy persistence ratio of 95 per cent, indicating a high level of satisfaction among its customers.

In some markets, the terms Policy Persistence Ratio/Policy Retention Ratio are used to make similar comparisons between the number of policies issued in a given period and those issued in a previous period (same season).

The gap between the policy retention ratio and the ideal ratio of 100 per cent is referred to as the Policy Lapse Ratio. That is, if 98 per cent of the policies due for renewal have been renewed, it indicates a policy retention ratio of 98 per cent and a policy lapse ratio of 2 per cent.

Policy Lapse Ratio (PLR)

$$\text{PLR} = \frac{\text{Number of Policies not renewed as per renewal register}}{\text{Number of Policies expected to be renewed as per renewal register}} \times 100$$

Reinsurance Retention Ratio (net premiums/gross premiums) is different from the policy retention ratio mentioned above. This retention ratio indicates a company's dependence on reinsurers and the potential scope of reinsurance cover purchased. This is done by comparing the amount of premium paid for reinsurance protection *vis-à-vis* the gross amount received by the company.

$$\text{Re-insurance Retention Ratio} = \frac{\text{Net Premium Written}}{\text{Gross Premium Written}} \times 100$$

It is a rough measure of how much of the risk is being carried by an insurer rather than being passed on to reinsurers.

Loss Retention Ratio (LRR) is calculated by dividing net claims incurred by gross claims incurred. If this ratio is materially lower than the premium retention ratio, for consecutive years, it indicates a potential excessive reliance upon reinsurer's support for generating underwriting profits. Heavy dependence on re-insurance support for meeting claims for continuous period can impact an insurer's reputation among reinsures.

$$\text{Loss Retention Ratio} = \frac{\text{Net claim Incurred}}{\text{Gross claims incurred}} \times 100$$

(2) Action Performance Ratios

These ratios relate to the various activities carried out by the insurers as part of their business actions or activities. These are often direct indicators of the company's efficiency and customer satisfaction. Ratios relating to the expeditious settling of claims, claim amount carried forward from previous years, the company's preparedness for settling claims by maintaining solvency margins, keeping sufficient liquid reserves, etc. are often considered indicators of the company's efficiency. An insurer's underwriting performance is measured by a set of ratios. Some such ratios are discussed below.

Claims Ratio is one of the most commonly used ratios. Claims ratio is often used synonymously with loss ratio. It is the percentage of the premium paid towards settlement of claims. In other words, the total losses of the company are diyided by the premium collected during the same period; it is expressed as a percentage. This is worked out as under:

$$\text{Claims Ratio} = \frac{\text{Claims}}{\text{Gross Premium}} \times 100$$

A loss ratio of 60% indicates that out of Rs. 10,000 premium collected, Rs. 6000 has been paid towards claims in the particular period. This ratio does not reflect the costs or expenses that are necessarily incurred by the insurers, and refers purely only to the premium and claim, this is more appropriately called as burning cost or pure risk cost.

Incurred Claims Ratio is an accounting mechanism of apportioning the claims ratio to a particular year as closely as possible. As the insurer continues with the process of settling claims all through the year and claims constantly spill over to one or more future years, it becomes difficult to apportion claims to a particular period and calculate such ratios. Incurred claims ratio is an accounting mechanism of appropriating claims to a year. The amount of claims paid in a year and the amount of claims outstanding at the end of the year are added, from which the amount of claims outstanding at the beginning of the year is deducted. This figure is called incurred claims.

Incurred Claims = claims paid during the year + Claims outstanding at the end of the year – Claims outstanding at the beginning of the year

Gross Premium is the total amount of premium that comes in from the policies issued. Net written premium or net premium prefers to gross premium less premium on re-insurance ceded to re-insurers plus premium on re-insurance accepted.

Net Premium = Gross Premium + Premium on reinsurance accepted – Premium on reinsurance ceded.

When amount of incurred claims is divided by the net written premium, we get the incurred claims ratio that gives a closer picture of the insurer's performance.

$$\text{Incurred Claims Ratio} = \frac{\text{Incurred Claims}}{\text{Net Premium}} \times 100$$

This exercise primarily tries to allocate claims to a particular year to ensure that the claims are more or less matched to the premiums received during the period. In other words, there is no mis-match between assets and liabilities (or tolerable mis-match).

Claims Coverage Ratio is a relative term that seeks to compare the company's claim experience *vis-à-vis* the industry's claim experience in a particular portfolio or a given market segment. This analysis would give insight into having a disproportionate share of claims *vis-à-vis* the market share, if such be the case. For instance, a company can find that it has only 10 per cent share of the industry's own damage insurance in respect of goods carrying vehicles, whereas it is paying 20 per cent of the claims paid by the industry on the particular segment.

Claims Duration Ratio helps in finding out the company's internal effectiveness in settling claims. Claims due to certain occupations and use of certain products take a long time to get noticed. In some cases, the courts take long periods of time, for instance 10-15 years, for settling liability claims (when there is litigation). The types of claims that get settled fast are called short tailed claims and those that take a longer settlement time are referred to as long tailed claims. While making provisions and allocating reserves, actuaries deal with these claims differently based on their devolvement period and duration ratios.

Complaints Ratio of a company is another core indicator. This figure indicates how a company's track record for satisfied customers stacks up against the competition. The common practice is that a ratio less than 0.3 indicates good performance *vis-à-vis* the median for a particular insurance market (marked by a score of "1"). A number higher than 1 suggests a relatively large number of complaints per customer served. Another thumb rule is to count the number of established complaints for every 1,00,000 customers served.

Capital Risks Ratio or Solvency Ratio tries to assess whether an insurer is solvent. In other words, if an insurer has adequate assets (over its liabilities) that can be utilized to pay the claims that can arise, it is solvent. It should have adequate technical reserves to meet the obligations entered into, and adequate capital as security. In simple terms, solvency margin can be defined as the surplus of assets over liabilities. A company's ability to pay claims denotes its solvency. Regulators expect that a certain minimum level of solvency margin is maintained so that the fluctuations in the overall results of a year are sufficiently cushioned without directly affecting the company. Solvency ratio from the Indian regulatory perspective is dealt with as a separate topic a little afterwards.

(3) Result Performance Ratios

These ratios indicate the end-product or the final result of all the performance parameters of the insurers. This includes concepts such as management expenses ratio and combined ratio. However, before dealing with them directly, we have to be clear about a few more terms.

Net Claims Paid is worked out by adding the claims paid on the re-insurances accepted and reducing the claims received on reinsurance ceded, to the gross claims paid. (Gross Claims paid refers to the total claims paid, including all claim-related expense and interest). When net claim paid is adjusted to the current accounting year, by reducing the effect of the previous year's accumulated claims, we get Net Incurred Claims.

Net Incurred Claims = Net claim paid + Amount of claims outstanding at the end of the year – Amount of claims outstanding at the beginning of the year

Net Earned Premium: In respect of almost all policies, (other than those effective from April 1 of the year), some part of the premium received and accounted in an particular year would relate to the same accounting year while the remaining part would relate to the un-expired part of the policy falling in the next accounting year. Claims on the un-expired part of these policies would fall in the next year whereas the premium would not. Insurers use the term Earned Premium to refer to the proportion of the premium pertaining to the policy period in which it was received. The part of the premium proportionate to the un-expired period which would fall in the next accounting year is called Unearned Premium (or premium received in advance). The net premium received in a year is apportioned on a 1/365 days basis to take care of the risks that the company is exposed to within the same year, i.e. excluding the premium on the un-expired part of the policies that would spill over to the next accounting year. This share is called net earned premium. On a thumb rule basis, instead of the 1/365 day basis, insurers usually apportion 50 per cent of the previous year's net written premium and the current year's net written premium to work out the current year's net earned premium. (There is a view that as the company continues in business for many years and premiums keep coming every year, the simple written premium and incurred claims are good enough indictors for all practical purposes, as the premium and claims experience tend to even out over long periods, even without such apportionments. However, such simplistic stands do not find favour with actuaries who find that these indicators do not support the kind of precise calculations required in the modern day's competitive environment).

NIC-NEP Ratio tries to give a more accurate ratio than the ones seen above. However, one needs to understand the following concepts to appreciate this ratio. Net incurred claims (NIC) divided by net earned premium (NEP) is referred to as Loss ratio or NIC-NEP ratio in common parlance. It may be observed that both the denominator and numerator in this calculation are business figures duly appropriated to a specific year. (It may be noted that loss adjustment expenses are considered part of incurred losses for such calculations).

$$\text{NIC-NEP Ratio} = \frac{\text{Net Incurred Claims}}{\text{Net Earned Premium}} \times 100$$

Insurers have to take care of various overheads other than settlement of claims. They incur business promotion expenses, agency commissions, administrative expenses, establishment costs, etc. The main variable costs having a direct bearing the insurer's performance are management expenses and agency commissions. The sum total of all such expenses incurred in a year is compared with the net written premium of a given year to assess the insurer's performance. Expense ratio is a commonly accepted term indicating the sum total of management expenses plus commissions, divided by net written premium. Here, it may be borne in mind that as the expenses relate to the payments made in the current year only, the net written premium, i.e. the premium received in the current year is taken into consideration. Both the denominator and numerator are, therefore, actual figures relating to the inflow/outflow in the particular year.

$$\text{Management Expenses Ratio} = \frac{\text{Management Expense}}{\text{Net Written Premium}} \times 100$$

In some markets, expenses ratio refers specifically to management expenses divided by net written premium, while commission ratio is calculated separately as commissions divided by net written premium.

Combined Ratio is obtained when

NIC-NEP ratio + Expense Ratio

The combined ratio is a reflection of the company's overall underwriting profits ability. A combined ratio of less than 100 per cent indicates profitability, while anything over 100 indicates a loss. These ratios are used to assess an insurance company's performance. Over and above these performance indicators, insurers make reserves/provisions for catastrophic losses as well. The insurer has to provide for his company's profit as well. The insurer's profit in the simplest terms can be stated in the form of the following equation:

Profit = Earned premium + Investment Income – Incurred Loss – Underwriting Expenses – Provisions

Solvency Margin

Solvency margin is important for an insurance company. It explains as having sufficient assets in terms of capital, surplus and reserves, and being able to satisfy financial requirements to be eligible to transact insurance business and meet liabilities. Certain mathematical comparisons of different components of an entity's financial statement have been prescribed to determine its solvency. Solvency ratios are calculated in India by a three-step method as prescribed by the regulator (IRDA) in the IRDA (Assets, Liabilities and Solvency Margin of Insurers) Regulations, 2000.

The first step that is prescribed for the calculation of the Required Solvency Margin (RSM) is based on (a) net premiums, termed RSM-1, and (b) net incurred claims, termed RSM-2. RSM on net premiums (i.e. RSM-1) is determined as 20 per cent of the amount, which is the higher of (i) the gross premiums multiplied by a set of factors prescribed for the purpose, and (ii) the net premium. In other words, the RSM on net incurred claims (i.e. RSM-2) is determined as 20 per cent of the amount, which is the higher of (i) the gross net incurred claims multiplied by a set of prescribed factors, and (ii) the net incurred claims. The Required Solvency Margin (RSM) for the company is higher of the two. The second step is to calculate the Available Solvency Margin (ASM), which is the net assets in the policyholder's funds plus the net assets in the shareholders funds. The third step is to calculate the solvency ratio, which is the total ASM divided by the total RSM.

Stated in simple terms, solvency margin denotes the surplus of assets over liabilities. A company's ability to pay claims denotes its solvency. As already stated, it should have adequate technical reserves to meet the obligations entered into, and adequate capital as security. Regulators expect that a certain minimum level of solvency margin is always maintained so that the fluctuations in the overall results of a year are sufficiently cushioned without directly affecting the company.

INTERNATIONAL ASSOCIATION OF INSURANCE SUPERVISORS (IAIS)—IAIS CORE PRINCIPLES

Like other professional associations, the International Association of Insurance Supervisors (IAIS) sets standards that are fundamental to developing effective insurance regulation and supervisory practices. IAIS has prescribed a set of legally accepted standards called Insurance Core Principles that are fundamental in developing effective regulation and supervisory practices for the insurance sector. IAIS principles, standards and guidance papers provide the basis for evaluating insurance legislation, supervisory systems and procedures. The IRDA in India has successfully taken care of most of the 28 core principles (which are in seven clusters). However, in its adherence to standards, India needs to focus on certain perceived gaps that are based on internationalization of the Core Principles (Core Principles by Dr. K.C. Mishra). For a core principle to be regarded as being "observed", the essential criteria must be met without any significant shortcomings. We may refer to the Basel Committee on Banking Supervision (BCBS) which has formulated the Core Principles of Banking Supervision, which ensure best supervisory practices in the area of banking supervision.

Insurance Core Principles and Methodology

(International Association of Insurance Supervisors (IAIS), October 2003)

ICP-1: Conditions for Effective Insurance Supervision

Insurance supervision relies upon:

- A policy on institutional and legal framework for financial sector supervisions.
- A well developed and effective financial market infrastructure.
- Efficient financial markets.

ICP-2: Supervisory Objectives

The principal objectives of insurance supervision are clearly defined.

ICP-3: Supervisory Authority

The supervisory authority:

- It has adequate powers, legal protection and financial resources to exercise its functions and powers.
- It is operationally independent but accountable in the exercise of its functions and powers.
- Hires, trains and maintains sufficient staff with high professional standards.
- Treats confidential information appropriately.

ICP-4: Supervisory Process

The supervisory authority conducts its functions in a transparent and accountable manner.

ICP-5: Supervisory Cooperation and Information Sharing

The supervisory authority cooperates with other agencies and shares information with other relevant supervisors subject to confidentiality requirements.

ICP-6: Licensing

An insurer must be licensed before it can operate within a jurisdiction. The requirements for licensing are clear, objective and public.

ICP-7: Suitability of Persons

The significant owners, board members, senior management, auditors and actuaries of an insurer are fit and proper to fulfil their roles. This requires that they possess the appropriate integrity, competency, experience and qualifications.

ICP-8: Change in Control and Portfolio Transfers

The supervisory authority approves or rejects proposals to acquire significant ownership or any other interest in an insurer that results in that person, directly or indirectly, alone or with an associate, exercising control over the insurers.

The supervisory authority approves the portfolio transfer or merger of insurance business.

ICP-9: Corporate Governance

The corporate governance framework recognizes and protects rights of all interested parties. The supervisory authority requires compliance with all applicable corporate governance standards.

ICP-10: Internal Control

The supervisory authority requires insurers to have in place internal controls that are adequate for the nature and scale of the business. The oversight and reporting systems allow the board and management to monitor and control the operations.

ICP-11: Market Analysis

Making use of all available sources, the supervisory authority monitors and analyses all factors that may have an impact on insurers and insurance markets. It draws conclusions and takes action as appropriate.

ICP-12: Reporting to Supervisors and Off-site Monitoring

The supervisory authority receives necessary information to contact effective off-site monitoring and to evaluate the condition of each insurer as well as the insurance market.

ICP-13: On-Site Inspection

The supervisory authority carries out on-site inspections to examine the business of an insurer and its compliance with legislation and supervisory requirements.

ICP-14: Preventive and Corrective Measures

The supervisory authority takes preventive and corrective measures that are timely, suitable and necessary to achieve the objectives of insurance supervision.

ICP-15: Enforcement or Sanctions

The supervisory authority enforces corrective action and, where needed, imposes sanctions based on clear and objective criteria that are publicly disclosed.

ICP-16: Winding-up and Exit from the Market

The legal and regulatory framework defines a range of options for the orderly exit of insurers from the marketplace. It defines insolvency and establishes the criteria and procedure for dealing with insolvency. In the event of winding-up proceedings, the legal framework gives priority to the protection of policyholders.

ICP-17: Group-wide Supervision

The supervisory authority supervises its insurers on a solo and a group-wide basis.

ICP-18: Risk Assessment and Management

The supervisory authority requires insures to recognize the range of risks that they faced and to assess and manage them effectively.

ICP-19: Insurance Activity

Since insurance is a risk taking activity, the supervisory authority requires insurers to evaluate and manage the risks that they underwrite, in particular, through re-insurance, and to have the tools to establish an adequate level of premiums.

ICP-20: Liabilities

The supervisory authority requires insurers to comply with standards for establishing adequate technical provisions and other liabilities, and making allowance for re-insurance receivables. The supervisory authority has both the authority and the ability to assess the adequacy of the technical provisions and to require that these provisions be increased, if necessary.

ICP-21: Investments

The supervisory authority requires insurers to comply with standards on investment activates. These standards include requirements on investment policy, assets-mix, valuation, diversification, asset-liability matching, and risk management.

ICP-22: Derivatives and Similar Commitments

The supervisory authority requires insurers to comply with standards on the use of derivatives and similar commitments. These standards address restrictions in their use and disclosure requirements, as well as internal controls and monitoring of the related positions.

ICP-23: Capital Adequacy and Solvency

The supervisory authority requires insurers to comply with the prescribed solvency regime. This regime includes capital adequacy requirements and requires suitable forms of capital that enable the insurers to absorb significant unforeseen losses.

ICP-24: Intermediaries

The supervisory authority sets requirements, directly or through the supervision of insurers, for the conduct of intermediaries.

ICP-25: Consumer Protection

The supervisory authority sets minimum requirements for insurers and intermediaries in dealing with consumers in its jurisdiction, including foreign insurers selling products on a cross-border basis. The requirements include provision of timely, complete and relevant information to consumers both before a contract is entered into to the point at which all obligations under a contract have been satisfied.

ICP-26: Information, Disclosure and Transparency Towards the Market

The supervisory authority requires insurers to disclose relevant information on a timely basis in order to give stakeholders a clear view of their business activities and financial position and to facilitate the understanding of the risk to which they are exposed.

ICP-27: Fraud

The supervisory authority requires that insurers and intermediaries take the necessary measure to prevent, detect and remedy insurance fraud.

ICP-28: Anti-Money Laundering, Combating the Financing of Terrorism (AML/CFT)

The supervisory authority requires insurers and intermediaries, at a minimum those insurers and intermediaries offering life insurance products or other investment-related insurance, to take effective measures to deter, detect and report money-laundering and the financing of terrorism consistent with the Recommendations of the Financial Action Task Force on Money Laundering (FATF).

SUMMARY

The foregoing description has provided the reader/student with a detailed understanding of the fundamental principles of insurance. It would have been realized that insurance as a branch of learning uses its own set of terms and principles. The terms used are numerous and it may not be possible to cover them here. Suffice it to say that this account has familiarized readers with a good number of principles and terms used in the insurance market so that a reasonably good understanding of all the important aspects of insurance is obtained. Effort has been made to give a brief idea of the core principles developed by the International Association of Insurance Supervisors (IAIS).

(1) Although trust or good faith is cardinal to all financial transactions yet the position in insurance emphasizes greatly the importance of trust. As the underwriter knows nothing of the risk and the proposer knows everything about it, it is the duty of the proposer to make a full disclosure of all the material circumstances and facts to the underwriter without being asked. That is expressed by saying that it is a contract of utmost good faith.

(2) When a ship is proposed for insurance, if the proposer does not state the factual negative details such as the ship's machinery being worn out, or that repairs are needed to make it seaworthy, or that it is carrying hazardous goods that it is not designed to carry, the insurer will not be reasonably expected to know of these. If the insurer had come to know of these details, he might have insured it only with some additional conditions or with an additional premium or he might not have insured the ship at all. In such cases, the withholding of these vital details from the insurer is a breach of the principle of utmost good faith.

(3) Insurance does not allow anyone to insure or get an insurance claim on any risk. It is important that the insured has a real interest on the subject offered for insurance. This is termed 'insurable interest' and is a prime requirement for an insurance contract to be valid.

(4) The requirement of 'insurable interest' is to ensure that the insured does not insure the risk with an intention of speculation, i.e. to make a profit out of the loss.

(5) The importance of 'insurable interest' can be made clearer by the following example. If a person insures his neighbourer's car, he is not at any financial loss if some damage happens to that car. Primarily, he has no financial interest in the car and his contract can only be a bet or wager on someone else's property. Further, as any damage happening to the car is to his advantage (with no loss to him). It is possible that he causes to become instrumental in causing damage to the car. The requirement of insurable interest is to ensure that the insured does not indulge in wagering or making a profit out of the loss.

(6) The principle of indemnity goes hand in hand with insurable interest and implies that the insured will be compensated only to the extent of the financial loss he has suffered or only up to the value previously agreed as the cost of the loss. The principle ensures that an insured should get a full

indemnity and that he should get no more, i.e. he does not make a profit from the transaction.

(7) In the cases of health and personal accident insurance where the principle of indemnity does not strictly apply, the insurer promises to pay a predetermined amount to the insured on account of a disability due to an accident and/or to reimburse his medical expenditure. Although indemnity can not be possible for physical suffering yet the unfortunate or their families are moved closer to their former economic position.

(8) Subrogation is a provision by which the insurer is placed in the position of the assured to ensure that the assured is prevented from recovering more than the indemnity from any source. By this principle, on payment of the loss, the insurer is entitled to be placed in the position of the insured and success to all his rights and remedies against third parties in respect of the subject matter of insurance.

(9) In a road accident, if an insured vehicle gets totally damaged beyond repair, the insurer would pay the full sum insured of the vehicle to the insured. However, if the accident was caused entirely due to the fault of another vehicle, the insured has the legal right to claim compensation from the owner of the vehicle that caused the accident. The debris of the damaged vehicle can also be sold as scrap for some amount of money. Such as situation can give opportunity to the insured to recover more money than his loss. By the principle of subrogation, on payment of the loss, the insurer takes over the right of the insured to sue and to recover from any third party in respect of the loss that occurred

(10) Proximate cause is explained as the active, efficient cause that sets in motion a chain of incidents which brings consequences without the intervention of any force and working actively from a new and independent source. It indicates the proximity or closeness of a loss to its cause or *vice-versa*. It refers to the most dominant and most effective cause from which the loss emanated.

(11) A vessel was insured for marine perils but not against war like operations. The vessel was torpedoed and had to berth at a neighboring harbour. When the tide fell, she grounded in the shallow waters and later became a total wreck. The assured claimed for a loss of perils of the sea. As the proximate cause of the loss was the torpedoing, which was not covered under the policy, the claim was not paid.

(12) When a part of a machine or a vehicle is replaced following an accident, the insurer pays for the cost of a new part to see that the machine is re-instated to its working condition. Here, indemnity is seen as the process of putting the machine back to its working condition and not for a like replacement of the old part with another old part. In the bargain, the insured gets a new part instead of the old part and the insurer would be meeting the cost of new spare parts.

(13) 'New for old' is a term used to describe a basis of cover, usually within property insurance, whereby the insurer agrees to pay the full replacement cost of the damaged insured item and not what the actual item is valued at

the time of the loss. This principle is used in area such as marine hull, machinery parts, vehicle parts, and the like.

(14) Sometimes, the same subject-matter of insurance could be covered by different policies. Here, there is a possibility that the insured might get compensated more than once from different sources for the same loss, thereby making a profit. In the event of multiple policies covering the same subject-matter of insurance, the principle of contribution provides for an equitable sharing of any loss between all the insurers according to their respective insurance amount.

(15) Re-instatement is a claim settlement option agreed between the insured and the insurer, stating that the insurer would make good the insured damaged property, rather than pay a monetary amount. For this benefit, the insurer would usually charge the policyholder an additional premium.

(16) Re-instatement of the loss by the insurer is not strictly followed due to various practical issues. Re-instatement would be costly for the insurer. Again, if he were not able to re-instate to the satisfaction of the insured, his work would have to be abandoned. The insured may not practically prefer reinstatement, as he would like to have better buildings or newer technology or higher capacity equipment to replace the loss. In practical terms, the insured would prefer receiving the full cost of re-instatement in lieu of actual re-instatement. This cost would comprise: (i) the indemnity *per se*, (ii) wear and tear and depreciation, and (iii) cost of inflation between date of loss and probate time of re-instatement.

(17) In some contexts, there can be practical difficulties in finding out the value of the loss due to change of value of stock due to processing, market conditions, location of the goods (especially in cargo insurances), inflation or currency fluctuations. In the case of rare objects and personal possessions, objective evaluation values can be extremely difficult to assess post-loss. In areas such as personal accident, measuring personal losses post-event may be offending and painful. Agreed value policies or valued policies are considered a practical way out in many cases where assessing the value of a loss post the event can create difficulties.

(18) Any information that could affect the underwriters' assessment of the risk is regarded a material fact. The underwriter's assessment can include fixing the insurance premium, framing the conditions of acceptance. Framing the conditions that would operate in the event of a claim or the decision to accept the risk itself.

(19) Reciprocity means that principles that are binding on one party call for reciprocal behaviour from the other party also whether stated or otherwise. While the insured is expected to disclose all material fats, the insurer should also disclose the benefits under the policy that the insured normally may not know.

(20) The principle of 'average' requires the amount of a claim payment to be reduced proportionately if a policyholder has not insured the property for its full value. If an insured opts for a lesser sum insured and consequently pays a less than adequate amount as premium, the loss also gets reduced

proportionately. The concept of average is applied by dividing the sum insured by the actual value multiplied by the loss incurred. If the sum insured is only 50 per cent of the value, the loss will also be reduced to 50 per cent.

(21) General average is a contribution made by all parties involved (usually) in a sea adventure towards a loss occasioned by the sacrifice of the property of some of the parties in the common interest/for the benefit of all.

(22) The law of general average is a legal principle of maritime law according to which all parties in a sea venture proportionally share any loss resulting from a voluntary sacrifice of part of the ship or cargo to save the whole in an emergency. Thus, if an insured ships' cargo on a vessel that is involved in sea hazard/unworthy sea and meets with a loss, he may face a claim from the insurer against him even though he was lucky that his goods were not damaged. This aspect is criticized by some insured as unfair. However, actually it is not unfair because all the insured were also part of the same venture went through the same situation and all could have suffered the loss.

(23) Particular average means a partial loss. Insurance cover is taken and policies issued on total loss cover only are said to be free of particular average, which means excusing partial losses. 'Sue and Labour' denotes charges incurred by or on behalf of the insured for the safety and preservation of the subject-matter insured.

(24) In an insurance policy, the deductible or excess is the portion of any claim that is not covered by the insurance provider. That is only the amount that is in excess of the deductible is recoverable from the insurer.

(25) This most common form of deductible is applied on a per event basis. The deductible amount is agreed upon between he insurance company and the policyholder on each occasion that a claim arises.

(26) In a per year form of deductible, an annual limit is applied instead of per event basis. The insurance company and the policyholder agree upon an annual limit of deductible and not go by claim deductible.

(27) This concept is similar to the excess/deductible, in that the insurer makes no settlement if the total claim is below the franchise figure. In the case of excess, a deduction is made when a loss crosses an agreed figure. The difference is that in franchise, no deduction in made once the loss crosses the agreed figure. It rather applies as a threshold level for a claim to be considered.

(28) Usually the sum insured is the limit of indemnity and in case of under-insurance, the condition of average applies. The Probable Maximum Loss (PML) of a particular risk is the estimate of the maximum loss that would occur as a result of damage caused by the most destructive peril to be insured with regard to the location, construction, occupation and protection of the risk. PML is usually expressed as a percentage of the sum insured. Where the sum insured is decided based on the PML, as in the case of First Loss Policies, the sum insured is accepted to be less than the value of the property, but the insurer undertakes to pay claim up to the sum insured, without application of average.

(29) The simplest form of loss ratio or claims ratio is the total loss divided by net premium. It is expressed as a percentage. As this ratio does not reflect all the costs or expenses that are necessarily incurred by the insurers, this is more appropriately called as the burning cost or pure risk cost.

(30) Incurred claims ratio is an accounting mechanism of appropriating claims to a year. The amount of claims paid in a year and the amount of claims outstanding at the end of the year are added, from which the amount of claims outstanding at the beginning of the year is deducted. This figure is called the incurred claims which are divided by the net premium to get the incurred claims ratio.

(31) The loss ratio (incurred losses and loss adjustment expenses divided by net earned premium) is added to the expense ratio (underwriting expenses plus commissions divided by net premium written) to determine the company's combined ratio. Thus, combined ratio = loss ratio + expense ratio.

4

Concept of Risk as Basis of Insurance

Organizations face a very wide range of risks that can impact the outcome of their operations. The desired overall aim may be stated as a mission or a set of corporate objectives. The events that can impact an organization may inhibit what it is seeking to achieve (hazard risks), enhance that aim (opportunity risks), or create uncertainty about the outcomes (control risks).

Risk management needs to offer an integrated approach to the evaluation, control and monitoring of these three types of risk. This book examines the key components of risk management and how it can be applied. Risk management also has an important part to play in the success of not for profit organizations such as charities and (for example) clubs and other membership bodies.

The risk management process is well established, although it is presented in a number of different ways and often uses differing terminologies. The different terminologies that are used by different risk management practitioners and in different business sectors are explored in this book. In addition to a description of the established risk management standards, a simplified description of risk management that sets out the key stages in the risk management process is also presented to help in understanding.

The risk management process cannot take place in isolation. It needs to be supported by a framework within the organization. Once again, the risk management framework is presented and described in different ways in the range of standards, guides and other publications that are available. In all cases, the key components of a successful risk management framework are the communications and reporting structure (architecture), the overall risk management strategy that is set by the organization (strategy) and the set of guidelines and procedures (protocols) that have been established. The importance of the risk architecture, strategy and protocols (RASP) is discussed in detail in this book.

The combination of risk management processes, together with a description of the framework in place for supporting the process, constitutes a risk management standard. There are several risk management standards in existence, including the IRM Standard and the recently published British Standard BS 31100. There is also the American COSO ERM framework. The latest addition to the available risk management standards is the international standards, ISO 21000, published in 2009. The well-established and respected Australian Standard AS 4360 (2004) was withdrawn in 2009 in favour of ISO 31000. As far as 4360 is concerned, it was first published in 1995. The ISO 31000 includes many of the features and offers a similar approach to that previously described in AS 4360.

TERMINOLOGY OF RISK

Most risk management publications refer to the benefits of having a common language of risk within the organization. Many organizations manage to achieve this common language and common understanding of risk management processes and protocols at least internally. However, it is usually the case that within a business sector, and sometimes even within individual organization, the development of a common language or risk can be very challenging.

Appendix A sets out the basic terms and definitions used in risk management. It also provides cross-reference between the different terms in use to describe the same concept. Where appropriate and necessary, a table setting out a range of definitions for the same concept is included within the relevant chapter of the book and these tables are cross-referenced in Appendix A.

BENEFITS OF MANAGING RISK

There are a range of benefits (like a bouquet) arising from the successful implementation of risk management. These benefits are summarized in this book as compliance, assurance, decisions and efficiency/effectiveness/efficacy (CADE3). Compliance refers to risk management activities designed to ensure that an organization complies with legal and regulatory obligations.

The board of an organization will require assurance that significant risks have been identified and appropriate controls put in place. In order to ensure that correct business decisions are taken, the organization should undertake risk management activities that provide additional structured information to assist with business decision-making.

Finally, a key benefit from risk management is to enhance the efficiency of operations within the organization. Risk management should provide more than assistance with the efficiency of operations. It should undertake risk management activities that provide additional structured information to assists with business decision-making. It should also help ensure that business processes (including process enhancements by way of projects and other change initiatives) are effective and that the selected strategy is efficacious, in that it incapable of delivering exactly what is required.

Risk management inputs are required in relation to strategic decision-making, but also in relation to the effective delivery of projects and programmes of work, as well as in relation to the routine operations to the organization. The benefits of risk management can also be identified in relation to these three time scales of activities within the organization. The outputs from risk management activities can benefit organizations in three timescales and ensure that the organization achieves:

- Efficacious strategy;
- Effective process and projects; and
- Efficient operations.

To achieve a successful risk management contribution, the intended benefits of many risk management initiatives have to be identified.

It goes without saying that good risk management must have a clear set of desired outcomes/benefits, appropriate attention should be paid to each stage of risk management process, as well as to details of the design, implementation and monitoring of the framework that supports these risk management activities.

FEATURES OF MANAGING RISK

Failure to adequately mange the risks faced by an organization can be caused by inadequate risk recognition, insufficient analysis of significant risks and failure to identify suitable risk response activities. Failure to set a risk management strategy and to communicate that strategy and the associated responsibilities may result in inadequate management of risks. It is also possible that the risk management procedures or protocols may be flawed, such that these protocols may actually be incapable of delivering the required outcomes.

The consequences of failure to adequately manage risk can be disastrous and result in inefficient operations, projects that are not completed on time and strategies that are not delivered, or were incorrect in the first place. In order to be successful, the risk management initiative should be proportionate, aligned, comprehensive, embedded and dynamic (PACED).

By proportionate, it means that the effort put into risk management should be appropriate to the level of risk that the organization faces. Risk management activities should be aligned with other activities within the organization, and those activities will also need to be comprehensive, so that any risk management initiative covers all the aspects of the organization and all the risk that it faces. The means of embedding risk management activities within the organization are discussed in this book. Finally, risk management activities should be dynamic (not static) and responsive to the changing business environment faced by the organization, either because of competition or due to development of science and technology and/or as a result of socio-political/economic forces at play.

FUTURE OF MANAGING RISK

Due to the global financial crisis, economists, policy-makers and socio-political thinkers have come out with many critical/radical solutions; the global crisis has unfolded many truths relating to myriads of risks in business and service organisations. There is an increasing tendency for news reports to indicate that risk is bad and risk management has failed. In reality, neither of these two statements is correct. Organizations have to address the risks that they face because many of them have to undertake high risk activities, either because these activities cannot be avoided, or because the activities are undertaken in order to produce a positive outcome for the organization and its stakeholders.

It is the other way round: the global financial crisis does not demonstrate the failure of risk management, but rather the failure of the management of organizations to successfully address the risk that they faced. Achieving benefits from risk management requires carefully planned implementation of the risk management process in the organization, as well as the design and successful embedding of a suitable and sufficient risk management framework.

GLOBAL FINANCIAL CRISIS

The extract penned below offers a summary of the actions that would help to avoid recurrence or repeat of the global financial crisis. Many organizations lack a common risk management framework across the enterprise; there is sense of utter neglect or low priority to risk management. This has many elements, each of which is required to help avoid similar disasters in the future:

- First, there should be common processes, terminology and practices for managing risk of all kinds;
- Second, it is essential that risk tolerance be fully understood, communicated and monitored across the enterprise;
- Third, risk management practices should be incorporated into all key business processes and decisions; and
- Fourth, management should make most objective and data-based risk-related decisions using dedicated high quality risk information.

APPROACHES TO DEFINING RISK: DEFINITIONS OF RISK

The Oxford English Dictionary contains definition of risk that is as follows: 'a chance or possibility of danger, loss, injury or other adverse consequences' and the definition of stake at risk is 'exposed to danger'. In this context, risk is used to signify negative consequences. However, taking a risk can also result in a positive outcome. A third possibility is that risk is related to uncertainty of outcome.

Take the example of owning a motorcar. For most people, owning a motorcar is an opportunity to become more mobile and gain the related benefits. However, there are uncertainties in owning a motorcar that are related to maintenance and repair costs. Finally, motor cars can be involved in accidents; so, in all fairness, there are obvious negative outcomes that can occur.

Definitions of risk can be found from many sources and some key definitions are set out in Table 4.1. An alternative definition is also provided to illustrate the broad nature of risk that can affect organizations. The Institute of Risk Management (IRM) defines risk as "the combination of the probability of an event and its consequences". Consequences can range from positive to negative. This is a widely applicable and practical definition that can be easily applied.

The international guide to risk related definitions is ISO Guide 73 and it defines risk as "effect of uncertainty on objectives". This definition appears to assume a certain level of knowledge about risk management and it is not easy to apply to everyday life. The meaning and application of this definition would become clearer as the reader progressed through this book.

We find that Guide 73 also notes that an effect may be positive, negative, or a deviation from the expected. These three types of events can be related to risks as opportunity, hazard or uncertainty, and this relates to the example of motorcar ownership outlined above. The Guide 73 notes that risk is often described by an event, a change in circumstances, a consequence, or a combination of these and how they may affect the achievement of objectives.

Table 4.1: Various Definitions of Risk

Organization	*Definition of Risk*
ISO Guide 73 ISO 31000	Effect of uncertainty on objectives. Note that an effect may be positive, negative, or a deviation from the expected. Also, risk is often described by an event, a change in circumstances or a consequence.
Institute of Risk Management (IRM)	Risk is the combination of the probability of an event and its consequence. Consequences can range from positive to negative.
"Orange Book" from HM Treasury	Uncertainty of outcome, within a range of exposure, arising from a combination of the impact and the probability of potential events.
Institute of Internal Auditors	The uncertainty of an event occurring that could have an impact on the achievement of the objectives. Risk is measures in terms of consequences and likelihood.
Alternative Definition by Paul Hopkin	Event with the ability to impact (inhibit, enhance or cause doubt about) the mission, strategy, projects, routine operations, objectives, core processes, key dependencies and/or the delivery of stakeholder expectation.

The Institute of Internal Auditors (IIA) defines risk as "the uncertainty of an event occurring that could have an impact on the achievement of objectives". The IIA adds that risk in measured in terms of consequences and likelihood of occurrence. Different disciplines define the term 'risk' in very different ways. The definition used by health and safety professionals is that risk is a combination of likelihood and magnitude, but this may not be sufficient for more general risk management purposes.

Risk in an organizational context is usually defined as "anything that can impact the fulfilment of corporate objectives". Risk is best defined by concentrating on risk as event, as in the definition of risk provided in ISO 31000 and the definition provided by the Institute of Internal Auditors, as set out in Table 4.1.

On the basis of 'types of Risks' as in the Guide 73 definition, risks are divided into three categories:

- Hazard (or pure) risks;
- Control (or uncertainty) risks;
- Opportunity (or speculative) risks.

There is no 'right' or 'wrong' sub-division of risks; readers will encounter other sub-divisions in other texts and these may be equally appropriate.

There are certain risk events that can only result in negative outcomes. These risks are hazard risks or pure risks, and these may be thought of as operational or insurable risks. In general, organizations will have a tolerance of hazard risks and, as of necessity; risks need to be managed within the levels of tolerance of the organization. A good example of a hazard risks faced by many organizations is that of theft.

Often, there are certain risks that give rise to uncertainty about the outcome of a situation. These can be described as control risks and are frequently associated with project management. The management of control risks will often be undertaken in order to ensure that he outcome from the business activities falls within the desired range.

In the interest of business, at the same time, organizations deliberately take risks, especially market place or commercial risks, in order to achieve a positive return. These can be considered as opportunity or speculative risks, and an organization will have a specific appetite for investment in such risks.

It is observed that there are risks/dangers associated with taking an opportunity, but there are also risks associated with not taking the opportunity. Opportunity risks may not be visible or physically apparent, and they are often financial in nature. Although opportunity risks are taken with the intention of having a positive outcome, this is not guaranteed. Opportunity risk for small businesses include moving a business to a new location, acquiring new property, expanding a business and diversifying into new products.

COMPUTER VIRUSES: AN EXAMPLE

In order to understand the distinction between hazard, control and opportunity risks, the example of the use of computers is useful. Virus infection is an operational or hazard risk and there will be no benefit to an organization suffering a virus attack on its software programs. When an organization installs or upgrades a software package, control risks will be associated with the upgrade project.

The selection of new software is also an opportunity risk, where the intention is to achieve better results by installing the new software, but it is possible that the new software will fail to deliver all of the functionality that was intended and the opportunity benefits will not be delivered. In fact, the failure of the functionality of the new software system may substantially undermine the operations of the organization.

RISK AT THE LEVEL OF INTERNET

Identifying the inherent level of the risk enables the importance of the control; measures in place to be identified. The Institute of Internal Auditors (IIA) has the view that the assessment of all risks should commence with the identification of the inherent level of the risk. The guidance from the IIA states that in the risk assessment, we look at the inherent risk before considering any controls. The new international risk management standard, ISO 31000, recommends that risks are assessed at both inherent and current levels.

Often, a risk matrix will be used to show the inherent level of the risk in term of likelihood and magnitude. The reduced or current level of the risk can then be identified, after the control or controls have been put in place. The effort that is required to reduce the risk from its inherent level to its current level can be clearly indicated on the risk matrix.

Figure 4.1: Likelihood of Risk and its Magnitude

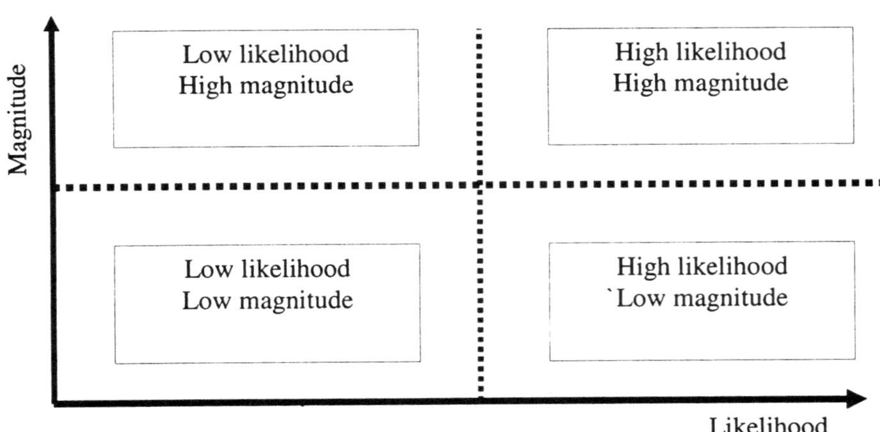

Terminology varies and the inherent level of risk is sometimes referred to as the absolute risk or gross risk as the residual level or the managed level of risk. The example in the box above provides an example of how inherently high risk active are reduced to a lower level of risk by the application of sensible and practical risk response options.

CROSSING THE ROAD: INHERENT RISK

Crossing a busy road would be inherently dangerous if there were no controls in place and many more accidents would occur. When a risk is inherently dangerous, greater attention is paid to the control measures in place, because the perception of risk is much higher. Pedestrians do not cross the road without looking and drives are always aware that pedestrians may step into the road. Often, other traffic-lane control measures are necessary to reduce the speed of the motorists or increase the risk awareness of both motorists and pedestrians.

LIKELIHOOD OF RISK AND ITS MAGNITUDE

Risk likelihood and magnitude are best demonstrated using a risk map, sometimes referred to as a risk matrix. Risk maps can be produced in many formats. Whatever format is used for a risk map, it is a very valuable tool for the risk management practitioner. The basic style for a risk map, it is a very valuable tool for the risk management practitioner. The basic style of risk map plots the likelihood of an event against the magnitude or impact should the event materialize.

The vertical axis is used to indicate magnitude in Figure 4.1. The word magnitude is used rather than severity, so that the same style of risk map can be used to illustrate hazard, control and opportunity risks. Severity implies that he event is undesirable and is, therefore, related to hazard risks.

As a practical example of risk management in action at strategic level, consider the uncertainties embedded in the merger involving Delta Airlines and Northwest Airlines. This illustrates that organizations take strategic decision that involve high levels of risk and uncertainty. There will be considerable uncertainties relating to whether all of the benefits outlined below can be delivered in practice.

Uncertainty in Strategic Decisions

An agreement has been reached and, barring any roadblocks from antitrust authorities, Delta Airlines and Northwest Airlines are merging and will operate under the Delta Airlines name. Delta Airlines released information outlining the basic elements of the deal and the ramifications it foresees for the new airline and its passengers.

List of Benefits Delta Airlines Sees by Merging

- Combining Delta and Northwest will create a global US carrier that can compete with foreign airlines that continue to increase service to the United States.
- Customers and communities will benefit from access to a global route system and a more finically stable airline.
- More destinations will result in more schedule options and more opportunities to earn and redeem frequent flyer miles.
- Delta customs will benefit from Northwest's routes to Asian markets and Northwest's customer will benefit from Delta's routers to other markets.
- Delta and Northwest complementary common membership in the sky Team alliance will ease the integration risk that has complicated some airline mergers.

5

Market Concept: Insurance Market

This topic has assumed great significance in view of the internationalization of economy and open competition. Banking and insurance sectors are the fastest emerging sectors of economy in India. This subject gives awareness about the general insurance market as it exists now. We have discussed the evolution of the market till the point of enactment of the General Insurance Nationalization Act in 1973. In this chapter, we deal with the appointment of the Committee on Reforms in Insurance Sector, which signaled a new era of liberalization and is generally regarded as the advent of the present-day insurance market in India. A set of figures that indicate the nation's progress from both the economic and insurance angles are eye-openers and encouraging.

A brief mention about the current trends in the insurance market was made before. Having acquired a basic understanding of the principles and terms of insurance, the reader should be able to understand and appreciate the present-day market trends discussed hereinafter.

This chapter will, therefore, familiarize the readers with the legal and economic environment, as well as the systems prevailing in the market.

RECENT CHANGES IN THE INSURANCE MARKET CONCEPT

The history and evolution of the Indian general insurance market have already been discussed in detail. It is generally regarded that the market evolved into a fairly modern form by the middle of the 1930s. During this period, the Indian market came out of its adolescence and started addressing problems similar to those faced by more mature markets. We have seen that the combined efforts of the market and the government led to the enactment of the Insurance Act, 1938.

In the early 1990s, the need for further changes in the insurance market was voiced by various segments in both the national and international markets. The consequent changes and the succession of events that have formed the market the way it is today are discussed here. The insurance companies were widely criticized for inefficiencies arising out of overstaffing, governmental interference in management, lack of freedom in decision-making, waning company loyalty, as well as deficiencies in the system, which could neither provide enough motivation for meritorious employees nor effectively penalize employees for non-performance or lethargy. Professionalism in the industry started declining, and the industry's growth rate got largely limited to the rates of inflation and the returns the companies could earn by investing their surplus funds. With market penetration becoming static, the insurers were criticized as indifferent to the country's needs and the Government was criticized for being over-protective of the nationalized industry by not allowing competition from private players which could improve matters.

REFORMS IN INSURANCE

Malhotra Committee Report on Insurance Reforms, 1994

The Central Government responded to the situation by setting up a high power Committee on Reforms in Insurance Sector on April 7, 1993 headed by R.N. Malhotra, former Governor, Reserve Bank of India, "to examine the reforms required in the insurance sector". This Committee is popularly referred to as the Malhotra Committee. The committee interacted with the insurance companies, their staff unions, various chambers of commerce, trade bodies and a cross section of the country's public, and made a detailed analysis of the present Indian insurance industry. It also visualized the shape of things to come in the future and put forward its recommendations for the insurance industry on January 7, 1994.

The Malhotra Committee's report recommended that both life and non-life insurance sectors should be gradually opened for private participation and recommended entry to foreign companies through joint ventures established in India with Indian partners. The Committee prescribed a minimum paid up capital for new insurers as not less than Rs. 100 crore, which would be backed by well-defined solvency standards. The Committee recommended that the regulatory apparatus should be activated even in the present set-up of nationalized insurance sector and, among other things, recommended the establishment of a strong and effective Insurance Regulatory Authority (IRA) in the form of a statutory autonomous board on the lines of Securities and Exchange Board of India (SEBI). By way of detail, the Committee recommended retention of all major tariffs for some period of time, and progressive liberalization therein. The recommendations of the Committee were discussed across the country at different forums, including the managements of the Life Insurance Corporation, the General Insurance Corporation, the subsidiary companies of the latter, trade unions, Chambers of Commerce and various consumer interest groups. The Consultative Committee of the Parliament and the Ministry of Finance also held discussions on the Report of the Committee on Reforms in Insurance Sector with the various stakeholders in the markets. After prolonged deliberations, the government accepted the Committee's recommendation to set-up an autonomous interim Insurance Regulatory Authority (IRA).

The (Interim) Insurance Regulatory Authority, 1996

In his 1995 Budget Speech, the Finance Minister announced the government's views on the subject as follows:

"As a first step, I propose to establish an independent regulatory authority for the insurance industry. Necessary legislation will be introduced shortly".

An interim Insurance Regulatory Authority (IRA) was formed accordingly on January 23, 1996 by a Government resolution, pending the enactment of comprehensive legislation, which would take time. The IRA came into existence with Mr. N. Rangachari as its full time Chairman, two part time members and a skeletal secretariat. The IRA, through seminars, discussions and press releases, made an attempt to create awareness about modern trends in insurance among various segments of the insured and potential insured. However, it did not have sufficient legislative powers to bring about any significant change in the insurance industry. Although the government had vested the powers of the Controller of Insurance with the Chairman of the IRA yet no serious change could be made in the working of the government-owned public sector insurers.

The then Finance Minister, in his Budget Speech of July, 1996, announced that in keeping with the trend of liberalization, the non-statutory insurance regulatory authority would be made statutory and suitably empowered so that it would have sufficient teeth to play an effective regulatory role. In the statement of objects and reasons, necessitating the vesting of the insurance regulatory authority with powers to direct, advise, caution, prohibit, investigate, inspect, prosecute, search, seize, fine, amalgamate, register and regulate insurance companies, it was also conceded that the government was seized of the fact that after the nationalization of the life insurance industry in 1956 and the General insurance industry in 1972, the role of the Controller of Insurance had gradually diminished in its significance.

The Insurance Regulatory Authority Bill was submitted to the Parliament in December, 1996 but had to be withdrawn to incorporate certain changes suggested by the Members of Parliament. With certain amendments, the next government resubmitted the Bill to the Parliament in 1997 when it was shelved once again due to opposition from some quarters. In 1997, the Bill was presented a third time by the new government. The House felt that the Bill needed to be studied by Multi-party Parliamentary Committee under Mr. Murli Deora, then M.P. This Committee made fresh changes to the bill and the same was subsequently cleared by the Council of Ministers. The revised bill termed as the Insurance Regulatory and Development Authority Bill was accordingly submitted to the Parliament for its consideration.

The Insurance Regulatory and Development Authority (IRDA) Act, 1999

The Insurance Regulatory and Development Authority Bill was approved by the Lok Sabha on December 1, 1999 and after approval of the Rajya Sabha, it was enacted as the Insurance Regulatory and Development Authority (IRDA) Act, 1999. The IRDA Act, 1999 was notified in the Gazette on April 19, 2000. As per the First Schedule to the IRDA Act, 1999, certain amendments were made to the Insurance Act, 1938, the Life Insurance Corporation Act, 1956 and the General Insurance Business Nationalization Act, 1972 to pave the way for liberalization of the insurance sector.

As per the Preamble of the IRDA Act

"An Act to provide for the establishment of an authority to protect the interest of holders of insurance policies, to regulate, promote and ensure orderly growth of the insurance industry and for matters connected therewith or incidental thereto...."

In terms of the IRDA Act and amendments to the Insurance Act, the office of the Controller of Insurance had become redundant under normal circumstances. However, the Central Government has certain powers to appoint a person to be the Controller of Insurance in certain specific situations.

The authority is body corporate having perpetual succession and common seal. It consists of a Chairperson and other members not exceeding nine in number, of whom not more than five would serve full time and not more than four would serve part time, to be appointed by the Central Government from amongst persons of ability, integrity and standing who have knowledge or experience of life insurance, general insurance, actuarial science, finance, economics, law, accountancy, administration or any other discipline which in the opinion of the Central Government shall be useful to the Authority. As per the Act, the Chairperson would hold office for a term of 5 years, or until the age of 65 years. The whole-time members would hold office for a term of 5 years, or until the age of 62. A part-time member would hold office for a term not exceeding 5 years.

The duties of IRDA have been spelt out in the Act as to regulate, promote and ensure orderly growth of the insurance business and re-insurance business. The powers and functions of IRDA have been listed out as follows:

(1) Issue to the applicant a certificate of registration as well as to renew, modify, withdraw, suspend or cancel such registration.
(2) Protection of the interest of the policy-holders in matters concerning assigning of policy, nomination by policyholders, insurable interest, settlement of insurance claims, surrender value of policy and other terms and conditions of contracts of insurance.
(3) Specifying the requisite qualifications, code of conduct and practical training for intermediary or insurance intermediaries and agents.
(4) Specifying the code of conduct for surveyors and the loss assessors.
(5) Promoting efficiency requisite in the conduct of insurance business.
(6) Promoting and regulating professional organization connected with the insurance and re-insurance business.
(7) Levying fees and other charges for carrying out the purposes of the IRDA Act.
(8) Calling for information from, undertaking inspection and conducting enquiries and investigations including audit of the insurers, insurance intermediaries and other organizations connected with the insurance business.
(9) Control and regulation of the rates, advantages, terms and conditions that may be offered by insurers in respect of general insurance business not so controlled and regulated by TAC under Section 64U of the Insurance Act, 1938.
(10) Specifying the form and manner in which books of accounts will be maintained and statements of accounts will be rendered by insurers and insurance intermediaries.

(11) Regulating investment of funds by insurance companies.
(12) Regulating maintenance of margins of solvency.
(13) Adjudication of disputes between insurers and intermediary or insurance intermediaries.
(14) Supervising the functioning of the Tariff Advisory Committee.
(15) Specifying the percentage of premium income of the insurer to finance schemes for promoting and regulating professional organizations referred to in clause (f).
(16) Specifying the percentage of life insurance business to be undertaken by the insurers in the rural as well as/or social sector.
(17) Exercising such other powers as may be prescribed.

The IRDA Act, *inter-alia*, allows the issue of necessary regulations consistent with the Act and to carry out the purposes of the Act, the IRDA is empowered to constitute an Insurance Advisory Committee to advise it while framing any regulations.

As a sequel to these changes, the General Insurance Business (Nationalization) Amendment Act, 2002 was passed and the General Insurance Corporation ceased to be the holding company of the four public sector insurance companies. The four public sector insurers were given functional autonomy in order to equip them better to face the challenges of liberalization. General Insurance Corporation of India became the national reinsurer and ceased to do direct insurance business. Consequently, Crop insurance, which was one of the major direct lines handled by GIC, got transferred to the newly formed Agricultural Insurance Corporation of India.

REGULATIONS FRAMED BY IRDA

In exercise of its powers under Section 26 of the IRDA Act, IRDA is authorized to make rules and regulations consistent with and to carry out the purposes of the Act in consultation with its Insurance Advisory Committee. The regulations would be notified by IRDA and submitted to the Parliament for its approval.

The IRDA has issued various regulations covering areas such as 'regulation of companies', protection of policyholders, obligations of insurers to rural and social sectors, appointment of actuaries, licensing of insurance agents, maintenance of solvency margins, preparation of financial statements, investment of funds, licensing of brokers, micro-insurance, etc.

Regulations came over various areas, some examples are: fixing financial requirements for licensing companies and intermediaries, specifying professional and academic standards for key-personnel in the insurance sector, setting codes of conduct for intermediaries such as surveyors, brokers and third party administrators, fixing common methodology for working out solvency margins prescribed for insurers, and prescribing uniform formats for submitting financial returns.

Some of the regulations specify standards for the functioning of the insurance regulatory bodies, IRDA itself and the Tariff Advisory Committee (TAC), covering matters such as holding meetings, fixing salaries, and service terms and conditions of the IRDA members and personnel.

COMPREHENSIVE REVIEW OF THE INSURANCE LAW

The Government of India (GOI) initiated a comprehensive review of the insurance regulatory framework through the Law Commission in 2004. This initiative was in response to the market's pleas for review of the laws. The laws relating to the insurance market, as we have seen, are spread beyond the insurance Act and its amendments, over various acts, regulations, circulars and court judgments. The review process involved removing incongruities and inconsistencies in the present framework and putting in place an integrated set of rules for the country. The Law Commission had a series of discussions with different stake-holders and put up a notice on their website inviting views of the public. After deliberations, it submitted its report to the GOI on June 1, 2004, and suggested that a detailed examination by experts was needed in the following specialized domains of the Insurance Act: (1) Provisions relating to investments, (2) Shareholders' Funds and Policyholders' Funds, (3) Sufficiency of Assets, (4) Insurance Surveyors, and (5) Tariff Advisory Committee. In accordance, the IRDA constituted a Committee of 11 experts chaired by Mr. K.P. Narasimham, which submitted its Report for the government's consideration. Once the views of the Committee are integrated with the Law Commission's recommendations and the necessary enactments made, the country can hope to be free from the present maze of regulations and have a simplified and efficient regulatory framework for the insurance sector.

BUSINESS INDICATORS

All through the centuries, the insurance industry has grown alongside the growth of the economy. Economists the world over consider insurance penetration a yardstick of economic development. Over the last decade, India has made significant strides in both economic and insurance reforms. The reform process is still going on, as seen in various monitoring/assessing barometers of the economy.

A BRIEF OF THE ECONOMY FOR INSURANCE SOLICITATION

A student of insurance should have an overview of the external environment, in which the insurers are functioning at present and are expected to function in the future. The trends culled out from contemporary literature give a rough indication of the extent to which the insurers need to prepare themselves to face the challenges.

Economic liberalization has caused cascading effects on various aspects of the Indian economy. The country's transformation from a conventional agricultural economy to an industrialized economy has raised an array of new challenges to the nation's infrastructure, especially in the services sector. India has crossed new milestones in diverse areas such as exploration of oils in the high seas, launching of artificial satellites, creation of state of the art power plants and refineries, acquiring of business processes from different countries, and higher inflow of foreign direct investment to invigorate the backward economy. All these have created a bigger market for the support systems, including insurance.

Growth potential in insurance sector is a well-researched phenomenon anywhere in the world. It depends on several macro-economic parameters. Collectively exhaustive but not mutually exclusive parameters of insurance growth are gross domestic product (GDP) level and growth rate, agricultural production and productivity, energy generation and incremental consumption, infrastructure level and strategy of further implementation, corporate sector and industry, inflation targeting and containment, capital market volume and returns, money and banking, growth rate projections of economy and business confidence level to determine the spirit of times.

Changes in consumer demographics largely determine reorientation of insurance business. The insurance sector has to strive to translate demographic relatives into opportunities for growth. The country's progress in terms of financial knowledge, rapid technological innovation, communication and internet technologies, emerging/evolving business environment, globalization, liberalization, trend to conglomerate, more distribution channels, and increasing education are drivers of change that the insurance sector can tap for its growth.

As per the Swiss Investment Bank 'Credit Suisse', India's Gross Domestic Product (GDP), at around Rs. 41,00,000 crore, has crossed the trillion dollar mark for the first time in history in April 2007 when the rupee appreciated to below 41 level against the US dollar. India has thus joined the elite club of 12 countries with a trillion dollar economy. The annual growth rate of 2007 is over 9 per cent and over a period of time hovering around 8 to 9 per cent.

During the first three quarters of 2006-07, the six core infrastructure industries, viz. crude petroleum, petroleum refineries, electricity, finished steel, cement and coal grew approximately at 8.3 per cent as compared to 5.5 per cent in the previous year. The index of industrial production showed a rise of 10.6 per cent as against the 8.3 per cent of the previous fiscal. The three categories of industry—manufacturing, mining and electricity sectors—also fuelled the growth of the economy.

The automobile industry registered a total production of 8.2 million vehicles in the same period with a growth percentage of 15.91 per cent. The number of passenger cars grew by 20.76% two-wheelers grew by 13.45 per cent, three-wheelers grew by 17.94 per cent and commercial vehicles grew by 37.5 per cent. Automobile exports registered a growth of 28.74 per cent over the previous year. Till December 2006, India had total of nearly 190 million phones.

The responsibility of providing insurance coverage to have these landmark achievements of the nation's progress rests with Indian insurance companies which have to assess and accept the risks for insurance and reinsure the portion of the risk that is beyond their retention capacity, in the international market.

Growth in various sectors calls for corresponding regulatory changes as well. In acknowledgement of the scope of regulatory overlap and realizing the increasing need for regulatory convergence, a high level co-ordination committee on capital and financial markets, comprising the heads of the regulatory institutions, meet periodically to ensure a certain degree of effectiveness of supervision, consistency in regulation and harmonization of supervisory practices between the banking, securities and insurance supervisors.

A Brief of the Insurance Market

Experts in the industry have forecasted that challenges will emerge in four distinct areas of the insurance industry in the next generation. Challenges can be reasonably expected from the following areas:

(1) New potential hazards resulting from rapid innovation and scientific advancement and the resultant demands on risk management,
(2) New vulnerabilities caused by massive levels of interconnectivity and independency, especially in strategic partnership, electronic networks and supply chains,
(3) New forms of untested insurance such as tsunami, terrorism or even genetic risks including avian flu, SARS and AIDS,
(4) New need of international coverage in many of these areas where risk could be fall out of trans-border occurrences such as terrorist strikes, natural catastrophes, hacking or epidemics, and
(5) New liability issues that can arise from areas such as data confidentially, errors, negligence or breaching of deadlines, relating to the business processes outsourcing (BPO) industry that is booming in India.

While the insurance market is growing, the growth has also expanded the scope of training and research in insurance, increased competition in the native market, shrunk margins, necessities of new insurance products; these have increased the pressure on insurers' efficiency and performance, blurred boundaries between financial instruments, and institutions, caused international integration/internationalization of financial markets. The emerging situation has increased the need for cross-border financial services, attracted investors from domestic markets to foreign markets and *vice versa*.

TRENDS/CHALLENGES OF THE INSURANCE MARKET

The Indian general insurance market has mostly been a tariff market for many years. A tariff market is one in which insurance products are standardized along with all related rates, terms and conditions. In the Indian market, the Tariff Advisory Committee is statutory body designated under the Insurance Act to design and regulate the products and their rates. The rates fixed by the Tariff Advisory Committee are mandatory for all insurers; these are the lowest rates. This mechanism of fixing lowest rates is to ensure that insurance companies have sufficient funds at their disposal to settle claims when they arise. In the Indian market, major portfolios such as fire insurance, marine insurance, marine hull, motor insurance, engineering insurance and workmen's compensation have been all through the tariff system. Areas such as crop insurance, cattle insurance and health insurance have been all through the non-tariff system and are controlled by the inter-company arrangements called market agreement. Some portfolios such as personal accident insurance, marine cargo, and insurances of tea, coffee, rubber and cardamom were governed by tariffs for some time but de-tariffed in the 1980s and 90s.

In essence, the philosophy was that core areas were tariff controlled. Areas where frequent product innovation was called for (e.g. crop and cattle insurance) or where rates had to be entirely re-insurance driven (e.g. aviation and satellite insurance) or where the fortunes of the portfolios did not count much in terms of premium and claims (e.g. pedal cycle insurance, bee-hive or poultry insurance) were left out of the scope of tariffs.

Experts in the field point out that the demise of the tariff in any insurance market is at best an unsetting time and at worst a disastrous path leading to significant losses to major companies. When the UK motor tariff was withdrawn in the late 1960s, the position was compounded by the lack of any reliable data or statistically robust methodologies.

De-tariffing has made the insurers' job more challenging as they have to design more and more products and price them correctly. The provider-scene has changed, more professionalism has come in, the distribution network is getting overhauled, and brokers have come into the market and are expected to add value to services.

Changes have brought with them new challenges for the insurers, the insured and the regulator.

The Organization for Economic Co-operation and Development (OECD), an international body that promotes policies for efficient functioning of markets and encourages convergence of policies, laws and regulations covering financial markets and enterprises, issued twenty guidelines on insurance. The magnitude of the challenges a regulator expects to meet can be visualized from the first of these guidelines, which reads as follows:

> "Adequate prudential and regulatory provision should be enforced in order to ensure the soundness of the insurance markets, the protection of the consumers and the stability of the economy as a whole. Over-regulation should be avoided. The insurance regulatory framework should be adapted to the characteristics of individual countries and encourage the stability, whilst maintaining the necessary flexibility to meet development in the market".

PRODUCTS OFFERED/TO BE OFFERED IN INSURANCE

The Indian market has moved over to a tariff-free regime from January I, 2007, though in phased manner. The de-tariffing process has not been effected in the complete sense as only the rates are unfrozen while the products continue to be frozen, i.e. the cover, terms and conditions still continue to be as per the tariffs. Pricing of insurance products in both tariff and tariff-free regimes ideally has to be based on certain actuarial and statistical techniques. Most of this scientific decision-making has to rely heavily on statistical data. For improving the quality of decisions and to provide the industry with correct technical rates and burning costs in a non-tariff regime, the industry needs a national database to bank upon.

Different markets do standardization of products using different methods. Self-explanatory terms of standardization such as 'prior approval', 'modified price approval', 'flex rating', 'file and use', 'use and file', 'no file/record maintenance', 'state prescribed', etc. are internationally used to denote the degree of control exercised by the regulator on insurance products. The Indian tariff products fall under the 'state prescribed' category while the non-tariff products can possibly be categorized as 'no file/record maintenance' type. Some countries have scientific systems such as 'Risk Factor Based Rating Systems' (RFBRS) and 'Risk Based Pricing Models' (RBPM) for pricing their products.

Insurance Information Institute (an international academic body) states that under the 'file and use' mechanism, an insurer has to file a proposed product with the regulator along with all details, terms, conditions and justification for rates. The filing becomes effective immediately or from a future date specified by the filer. The regulator may disapprove a filing at any time if it is not in compliance with the law, after holding a hearing to establish non-compliance. Systems of justification of rates and/ or terms are also not uniform and some products need prior re-filing. However, actual implementation of the system varies from product to product and country to country.

The Indian variant of 'file and use' system has a specified waiting period days in the case of 'prior approval' category of products, where the products are deemed approved automatically if the regulator does not take any specific action during the waiting period. Usually, rate revisions under 'file and use' are based solely on a change in loss experience, while in terms of modified period approval, rate revision is based on a change in expense relationships and rate classifications. Although guidelines on 'file and use' norms have been set by IRDA in India, the system is still is its nascent stage and yet to crystallize as a full-fledged regulation. The philosophy is that the players will be able to set their own rates and justify them. Also, each company will have to explain whether the rating of the risk is adequate, based on data, and justifiable. When there is no one official fixing rate, there is an increased need for self-regulation and better governance. Probably, the IRDA selected this hybrid 'file and use' system for the Indian market to provide a stable alternate system before removal of tariffs. The hybrid is expected to prevent volatility in the market, promote scientific rating, and usher in a culture of self-regulation with responsibility.

The 'file and use' system makes it mandatory that the wordings of every product sold in the market are legally vetted, the rates actuarially vetted and the product as such certified to be in line with the company's underwriting policy by the Chief Officer or a nominated Compliance Officer.

INSURANCE PROVIDERS AND INTERMEDIARIES

The providers of general insurance (the insurers) in the Indian market are four public sector companies, eight private sector companies, two health insurance companies, one agricultural insurance company, five state government departments, two specialized companies (each on credit guarantee and deposit insurance), and health benefits association.

The State Government Insurance Departments insure properties owned by the respective states or where these states have substantial financial interests. The Calcutta Hospital and Nursing Home Benefits Association Limited provides certain health benefits to its members. Export Credit and Guarantee Corporation Limited (ECGC) is the fifth largest credit insurer in the world and provides a set of specialized services for the export industry. The Deposit Insurance Guarantee Corporation (DIGC) gives covers to all bank deposit-holders up to a maximum of Rs. 1,00,000 (Rupees one lakh) for principal and interest amount held by him, in case the bank gets liquidated or its licence gets cancelled. The Credit Guarantee Corporation provides guarantees credit to the priority sectors under schematic lending made by the banks (on project basis) approved by appropriate authorities up to a specified percentage of limits or outstanding balances, whichever is lower. A few international insurers have opened liaison offices in India and are waiting with their Indian joint venture partners for the necessary regulatory compliances.

The General Insurance Corporation of India (GIC) is the sole re-insurer in the market and is sometimes referred to as the national re-insurer. There are a few international re-insurers who have also opened representative offices in India for facilitating placement of outward/inward reinsurance business.

The General Insurance Council of India (GICI) and the Life Insurance Council of India (LICI) are now statutory bodies under the Insurance Act that have recently been revived under the auspices of IRDA. These are intended to function as self-regulatory organizations and reduce the gaps between the insurers, the insured, trade bodies, regulators and the government. The Insurance Association of India (IAI) is another statutory body under the Act, which is yet to be formed.

IRDA has granted licenses to 382 insurance brokers till September 30, 2008. They have set-up offices in different parts of the country. There are a few reinsurance brokers as well in the country which interact between the insurers and the reinsurance providers to facilitate placement of risks.

The bancassurance model allows banks to work with the insurers either on a corporate agent model or for referral services. Experts in the field state that regulatory changes have made bancassurance possible and feasible, and found a large untapped growth potential in banks and insurers working together.

Micro insurance groups are also growing as key players in increasing the country's insurance penetration by interacting with rural and sub-urban population. IRDA has brought about regulations to develop and regulate this sector also.

Surveyors are another group of professionals who have got more organized under the initiatives of IRDA. The Indian Institute of Insurance (III), loss surveyors and assessors have been formed to increase professionalism in the field.

The role of independent insurance arbitrators is getting recognized more than ever by the market, as there is an increased interest in 'out of court' settlement of claims and is thus an 'alternative dispute resolution' (ADR) mechanism to court cases.

PRICING AND INFORMATION TECHNOLOGY

For scientific rating to be possible, the market would need a substantial amount of transactional data of reasonable quality and accuracy. Both historical and contemporary data require to be analyzed for making business decisions, product innovations, pricing and effective claims management. Statistical databases for various classes of business, detailing various segments based on nature of risk, type of insurance cover, and probable risk exposure would be needed for proper product pricing. IRDA has taken the initiative for creating a centralized national data repository with the Tariff Advisory Committee (TAC) to cater to the multifarious needs of the industry.

Although the TAC was all along having the powers under Section 64 UE of the Insurance Act to collect this data from the insures yet the power had seldom been effectively exercised. From 2000-01, IRDA and TAC renewed their efforts of colleting data on tariff area of business from both public and private sector players and started a system of charging penalties for non-compliance in submission of the requisitioned data. However, success was limited as the public sector insurers were not able to consolidate the data of their operating offices at their Regional Office or Head Office level.

The new version of software installed by the pubic sector insurers in late 2004 and 2005 gave the PSU insurers the technical capability to consolidate data at their Head Office levels. As a result of this technological breakthrough and the relentless pressure built up by IRDA on the insurers, the insurers have taken up data collection and compilation more seriously. Motor data collation is perceived difficult in terms of numbers and spread, and the insurers require putting in a lot of efforts in culling out and submitting the data, notwithstanding the manifold errors and inconsistencies. Health insurance data available with third Party Administrators and submission thereof is relatively easy to collect. The TAC has been able to collect data in respect of motor and health insurance from 2003-04 onwards and has published certain basic information tables at its website http://www.tac.org.in. The TAC has designed elaborate data format and data dictionaries for fifteen lines of business to streamline the process of data compilation.

In the tariff-free scenario, the TAC is expected to publish technical rates or burning costs, provide the insurers with information on segment-wise claims experience, and analyze data on frequency and severity aspects at a national level. The end objective is that the domestic insurers would develop in-house information technology skills and actuarial systems for more effective pricing and underwriting.

Advanced markets use scientific methods for insurance pricing. Three popular types of pricing are: (i) individual rating, (ii) class or manual rating, and (iii) modification rating, usually referred to as merit rating. Modification rating methods include schedule rating, experience rating, retrospective rating and premium discount plans. These rating methods are dependent on the terms cover and past loss experience of the insurance segment, duly considered. The accuracy of the calculation that goes into rating depends heavily on situational data of the frequency and severity of past losses. The data should be of sizeable quantity, of reasonable quality, creditability and relevance. For large property risks, the Probable Maximum Loss (PML) of the risk is also estimated. The PML of a particular risk is the worst possible scenario that an insurer can estimate in terms of the maximum loss that would occur as a result of damage caused by the most destructive peril to be insured. PML is usually expressed as a percentage of the sum insured.

For the purpose of making reserves or estimating its anticipated liabilities accurately and creating reserves for settling them, the insurer has to go for an actuarial process which, to a large extent, is based on the data.

Although individual insurers have their own data yet they may mot have a comprehensive picture of the entire market. They may not have any legal and ethical means to know how the industry is performing in general and how a particular branch or segment of insurance is behaving. For instance, no single insurer will be able to accurately assess how much money the industry is losing by way of interest on motor liability claims or what the annual payout in maternity claims is or even what the total impact of the Mumbai floods on the insurance industry was. Answer to these and many more questions on the total market or on particular market segment can be derived only from a centralized national data repository.

Beyond the realms of product pricing and reserving, the data repository can be used for many purposes such as claims managements, risk management, fraud detection and finding areas in the market where new products would be required.

For instance, if there is a large gap between amounts of claims paid for eye surgeries, the insurers can probably devise a product for the purpose with higher limits. In the life insurance segment, the insurers share data on declined lives, a term used to denote proposals that are uninsurable due to various reasons such as bad health, financial insolvency, moral turpitude, bad habits, or hazardous hobbies or occupations. General insurers are planning to share their data of stolen vehicles so that a vehicle once reported as stolen and paid for as a total loss, doesn't get insured with another insurer. The changed market is expected to usher in more of such co-operative endeavors.

Although a data warehouse is generally regarded a good idea yet one may observe that in the developed nations like the US and the UK, the insurers have been dissuaded from compiling similar data banks owing to issues regarding the insurer's proprietary rights. The insurers are guarded on issues of confidentiality whether company-specific information will get into the hands of competitors, whether their standard of service would get exposed, whether insured entity's rights to confidentiality of personal data get compromised, whether the data will expose the insurers' errors to regulatory scrutiny, etc.

DEVELOPMENTS IN INSURANCE-RELATED BUSINESS

The changes in the country's business environment have introduced a variety of new activities in the insurance market and those have added to its complexity.

For instance, with the tariffs becoming non-existent, products and prices have become more competitive for the insurers' survival. Further, the insurers have to look more closely at their costs. The company's manpower requirements need to be optimized to cut expenses. Claim-costs have to be reduced by way of correct assessment of losses, reduction of litigation, structured scales of compensations, effective methods of preserving subrogation rights, getting better value for salvage, etc. Speedy claim-settlements having effective distribution system, better information technology systems, better financial planning and control systems, and effective investment policies—all these areas are expected to get a closer look in the near future. These expectations can be summarized as having a more professional approach in the market. This leads to the creation of a better genre of professionals by way of qualitative changes in recruitment and training.

The regulator will require more alertness in its watchdog role as cut-throat competition in the market can bring in disruptive trade practices, abortive policy wordings, truncated claim settlements as well as expose the industry to unfamiliar civil and criminal offences. The regulator may have to locate early warning symptoms in the market and monitor aberrations to their source.

The modern insurance market calls for better interaction with many external agencies as there are many common areas of interest. Central Building Research Institute (CBRI) sets standards/designs for the construction of buildings. The insurers should understand the import of these guidelines for the buildings that they are insuring. The National Fire Protection Association (FPA) sets standards for fire protection, which are again important for the insurers in granting discounts for risks with better protection. There is scope for interaction with the Road Transport Authorities and the Traffic Police for tracking uninsured vehicles. Similarly, interaction with Automobile Manufacturers' Associations and Automobile Owners' Associations can help in understanding the motor insurance industry better.

The international market will have to be watched with care. For instance, the Sarbanes Oxley Act (2002) of the USA made it mandatory for the senior management and business process owners to establish and maintain adequate internal control structures for their business ventures. In India, the Securities and Exchange Board of India (SEBI) came up with a corresponding regulation 49 in India. Experts predict a spurt in the demand for directors and officers (D&O) policies in the Indian market shortly.

Two modern innovative technologies that are making global rounds, viz. Parametric Insurance and trans-human insurance are yet to enter the Indian general insurance market. Parametric insurance is a type of insurance that does not indemnify the pure loss, but agrees in advance to make a payment upon the occurrence of a triggering event. The triggering event is often a catastrophic natural event that may ordinarily precipitate a loss or a series of losses. The attraction of parametric insurance that supplements traditional insurance recoveries lies in its commitment to pay for collateral damages that are not covered. The pay-out is a percentage of the recovery from a traditional insurance policy, the proceeds of which can be used as the policyholder sees fit. Both the Indian regulators and the general insurance companies have to realize the importance of such new technologies coming up in the international market.

Insurance industry in India is lagging behind its counterparts in the developed countries in fields such as risk management, loss prevention technique, non-life actuarial studies and arbitration.

Apart from the National Insurance Academy (NIA) situated at Pune, which provides short-term 'on the job' training in almost any insurance related areas, there is no professional institution in India that specialists in risk management, teaches risk improvement techniques and promotes loss prevention as a science. NIA which is running an AICTE approved MBA programme with insurance as an area of specialization, has developed its own academic talent pool supported by industry experts who constitute its guest faculty. NIA has practically become the only specialized academic forum for holistic solutions for the insurance industry's academic needs. The academy has contributed to information technology and actuarial education apart from the traditional risk management and insurance areas.

In the 1980s and the 1990s, the Loss Prevention Association of India (LPAI), an organisation totally owned by the public sector companies, had made some attempts in creating public awareness on the subject. The Indian Institute of Risk Management (IIRM) floated by a few corporate houses in the 1980s could not make any significant achievement in the field. The IIRM, Hyderabad is yet to make its mark in insurance academics. The Institute of Actuaries of India (IAI) conducts actuarial courses for the industry leading to Associateship and Fellowship qualification. The Indian Insurance institute of India, one of the oldest institutions in the country for insurance academics, awards the licentiate associate and fellowship qualification in insurance. The Institute is headquartered in Mumbai and has local institutes in many states. The College of Insurance, Mumbai, a wing of the Insurance Institute of India concentrates mainly on conventional areas of insurance training designed for junior staff and officers.

The process of liberalization in the insurance sector has created a substantial requirement of training for brokers and agents. A few private institutes have been established to cater to this need.

Scope of Insurance

People in India are not risk conscious; insurance, in 90% cases, is taken out of compulsion. Users of credit have to get assets created out of credit proceeds insured as it is one of the covenants while granting credit for purchase of assets. Individuals in urban areas only get their lives insured. There is, therefore, vast scope for insurance coverage in India. Privatisation and permitting foreign companies to do insurance business here will definitely create awareness about insurance among the masses. Under 'Poverty Alleviation Programmes', the governments are engaged in extending insurance—both personal (life insurance of the bread-earner) and assets-insurance. Otherwise, too, the government grants relief out of the state exchequer. Truth is that risks of life and to property have to be insured to provide succour to the affected.

SUMMARY

After going through this chapter, the readers should be able to understand how the insurance market has developed into what it is today. Also, they should be able to recognize the importance of the insurance sector in the country's economy. This chapter would have also enabled them to appreciate the modern day developments in insurance market and familiarized them with the different constituents of the insurance market.

(1) The Malhotra Committee report recommended private participation and entry to foreign companies through joint ventures with Indian partners in both life and non-life insurance sectors. It prescribed a minimum paid-up capital for new insurers as not less than Rs. 100 crore. It recommended the establishment of a strong and effective Insurance Regulatory Authority (IRA). It recommended retention of all major tariffs, for some period of time, and progressive liberalization.

(2) The recommendations of Malhotra Committee were discussed across the country at different forums including the managements of the Life Insurance Corporation, the commerce world, industrialists and various consumer interest-groups. The Consultative Committee of the Parliament and the Ministry of Finance also held discussions on the report of the Committee on reforms in insurance sector with various stake-holders in the market. After prolonged deliberations, the Government accepted the Committee's recommendation to set-up an autonomous interim insurance regulatory authority (IRA).

(3) Mr. N. Rangachari was appointed the Chairman of the interim IRA.

(4) As per the preamble, the IRDA act was created to provide for the establishment of an authority to protect the interest of holders of insurance policies, to regulate, promote and ensure orderly growth of the insurance industry, and for matters connected therewith.

(5) As per the Act, some of IRDA's functions are:

(a) Issuing certificate of registration to the insurance companies.
(b) Protection of the interests of the policy-holders.
(c) Specifying qualifications and code of conduct for insurance intermediaries and agents.
(d) Specifying the code of conduct for surveyors and the loss assessors, and
(e) Promoting and regulating professional organizations connected with the insurance and re-insurance business.

(6) The Authority is a body corporate having perpetual succession and common seal. It consists of a Chairperson and other members, not exceeding nine in number, of whom not more than five would serve full-time and no more than four would serve part-time, to be appointed by the Central Government from amongst persons of ability, integrity and standing who have knowledge or experience of life insurance, general insurance, actuarial science, finance, economics, law, accountancy, administration or any other discipline which, in the opinion of the Central Government, shall be useful to the Authority. As per the Act, the Chairperson would hold office for a term of five years or until the age of 65 years. The whole-time members would hold office for a term of five years or until the age of 62 years. A part-time member would hold office for a term not exceeding five years.

(7) IRDA has issued various regulations covering areas such as registration of companies, protection of policyholders, obligations of insurers to rural and social sectors, etc.

(8) The laws relating to the insurance market are spread beyond the Insurance Act and its amendments, over various Acts, Regulations, Circulars and Court judgments. As such, in response to the market request for review, the Government initiative involves removing incongruities and inconsistencies in the present framework and putting in place an integrated set of rules for the country.

(9) The Law Commission of the Government of India initiated the review process.

(10) The Law Commission's Report suggested that the following five specialized domain areas of the Insurance Act be deliberated upon by experts:
(a) Provisions relating to investments,
(b) Shareholders' funds and Policyholders' funds,
(c) Sufficiency of Assets,
(d) Insurance Surveyors, and
(e) Tariff Advisory Committee (TAC).

(11) Some of the indicators of growth are:
(a) Gross Domestic Product (GDP),
(b) Performance of core intrastate industries such as crude petrol., petroleum refining, electricity, finished steel, cement and coal,
(c) Index of industrial production, and
(d) Performance of industry, manufacturing, mining, electricity and tele-communication sectors.

(12) The responsibility of providing insurance coverage for the nation's assets, trade and people is entrusted to the insurance companies which have to assess

and accept the risks for insurers and reinsurers which apportion the risk that is beyond their retention capacity, in the international market. Rapid growth in these sectors demands corresponding growth in the insurance sector as well.

(13) GDP denotes Gross Domestic Product for the economy and Gross Direct Premium for the insurance market, currently Rs. 24,993 crores.

(14) Health, motor owner damage, motor third party damage and personal accident are some areas that are poised for growth.

(15) The National Insurance Company Ltd., The New India Assurance Company Ltd., The Oriental Insurance Company Ltd., The United India Insurance Company Ltd., The Reliance General Insurance Company Ltd., the IFFCO Tokyo General Insurance Company Ltd., The Tata AIG General Insurance Company Ltd. and the ICICI Lombard General Insurance Ltd. are a few of the companies operating in the Indian market.

(16) Regulators internationally use controls such as Prior Approval, Modified Prior Approval, Flex Rating, File and Use, Use and File, No File/Record Maintenance, State Prescribed, etc. to control insurance products.

(17) India uses a variant of 'File and Use' system with a specified waiting period as in the case of 'Prior Approval' category of products, where the products are deemed approved automatically if the regulator does not take any specific action during the waiting period. Usually, rate revisions under 'File and Use' are based solely on a change in loss experience, while in 'Modified Prior Approval' terms, the rate·revision is based on a change in expense relationship and rate classification. Although guidelines on 'File and Use' norms have been set by the IRDA in India yet the system is still in an early stage and yet to develop as full-fledged regulations. The philosophy is that the players will be able to set their own rates and justify them.

(18) For scientific rating to be possibility, the market would need a substantial amount of transitional data of reasonable quality and accuracy. Both historical and contemporary data requires to be analyzed for making business decisions, product innovations, pricing, and effective claims management. Statistical databases for various classes of business detailing various segments based on nature of risk, type of insurance cover, and probable risk exposure would be needed for proper product pricing. This would be possible only with a robust IT back-bone and a centralized national data repository.

(19) Beyond the realms of product pricing and reserving, information technology and a data repository can be used for many purposes, such as claims management, risk management, fraud detection and for finding areas in the market where new products would be required. For instance, if there is a large gap between amounts claimed and paid for eye surgeries, the insurers can probably devise a product for the purpose with higher limits.

(20) In developed nations like the US and the UK, the insurers have been dissuaded from compiling similar data-banks owing to issues regarding the insurers' propriety rights. The insurers are guarded on issues of confidentiality whether company specific information will get into the hands of competitors, whether their standards of service would get exposed, whether the insured's

right to confidentiality of personal data get compromised, whether the data will expose the insurers' errors to regulatory scrutiny, etc.

(21) Two modern innovations in insurance are 'Parametric Insurance' and "Trans-insurance' that are yet to enter the Indian general insurance market. Parametric insurance is a type of insurance that does not indemnify the pure loss, but agrees in advance to make a payment upon the occurrence of a triggering event. The triggering event is often a catastrophic natural event, which may ordinarily precipitate a loss or a series of losses. The attraction of parametric insurance for the insurers is the expected reduction in transition costs involved in loss assessment for payment of claims. Trans-human insurance is yet new form of insurance that supplements traditional insurance recoveries to pay for collateral damages that are not covered. The pay-out is a percentage of the recovery from a traditional insurance policy, the proceeds of which can be used as the policyholder sees fit.

(22) The Sarbanes Oxley Act (2002) of the USA made it mandatory for the senior management and business process owners to establish and maintain adequate internal control structures for their business ventures. In India, the Securities and Exchange Board of India (SEBI) came up with a corresponding Regulation 49. As consequence thereof. The experts predict a spurt in the demand for Directors and Officers (D&O) policies in the Indian market any time.

(23) National Insurance Academy (NIA), situated at Pune provides short-term 'on the job' training in almost any insurance related area; teaches risk management, risk improvement techniques and loss prevention. NIA is running an AICTE approved MBA programme with insurance as an area of specialization. The IIRM, Hyderabad, Institute of Actuaries of India, the Insurance Institute of India, which award, respectively, the Licentiate, Associate and Fellowship qualifications in Insurance, and a few Institutes established to train agents, approved by IRDA, are the main providers of insurance education in India.

Acts Relevant to the General Insurance Market

Apart from the Insurance Act, 1938 and the Insurance Rules made thereunder, the Insurance Regulatory and the Development Act, 1999, Regulations framed under the IRDA, Act, and the General Insurance Business (Nationalization) Amendment Act, 2002 that directly focus on the conduct of insurance business, there are many miscellaneous pieces of legislation, which historically have influenced court judgments on non-life insurance, some of which are listed below:

(1) The Indian Fatal Accidents Act, 1865 deals with accidents and liability to various parties.

(2) The Carriers Act, 1865 with amendments of 1993 defines the rights and liabilities of common carriers engaged in the business of transporting on hire, property from place to place by land or inland navigation.

(3) The Insurance (marine and fire) Assignment Act, 1886 deals with assignment of insurance policies.

(4) The Indian Contract Act, 1872 sets the rules on validity and enforceability of insurance contracts.

(5) The Transfer of Property Act, 1882 and its amendment Act, 1944 set rules on assignment of Insurance policies.

(6) The Marine Insurance Act, 1906 defines concepts of insurance such as description of subject-matter and extent of interest.

(7) The Indian Ports Act, 1908 and the Major Port Trusts Act, 1963 spell out the laws relating to port charges, safety in shipping, safety in Indian ports, etc. The Act contains several provisions for conservation of ports and prescribes penalties for infringements.

(8) The Marine Insurance (Gambling Policies) Act, 1909 differentiates between bona-fide insurance contracts and wager arrangements.

(9) The Indian Companies Act, 1913 contains the rules relating to formation of companies.

(10) The Workmen's Compensation Act, 1923 speaks about employers' liability, compensation to workmen and insurance protection.

(11) The Carriage of Goods by Sea Act, 1925 covers carriage of goods by sea between any port in India and any other port in India or abroad, establishes the responsibility, liabilities, rights and immunities attaching to carriers, and is largely aligned to the recommendations of the international conferences on maritime Law.

(12) The Law of Property Act, 1925 speaks about exercising subrogation rights over contract breakers/tort flab. The Indian Sales of Goods Act, 1930 specifies details on transfer of ownership, contracts of sale, etc.

(13) The Law Reforms (Miscellaneous Provision) Act, 1934 sets the rules on rights of legal heirs of accident victims.

(14) The Motor Vehicles Act, 1939 (amending Indian Companies Act, 1862) deals with formation and ownership of companies.

(15) The Companies Act, 1956 (amending Indian Companies Act, 1882) deals with formation and ownership of companies.

(16) The Merchant Shipping Act, 1958 and its amendments from time to time keep Indian shipping (and related insurance) in line with international conventions in matters such as liabilities of ships and ship-owners, collisions, limitation of liability for maritime claims, and make insurance mandatory for certain types of ships.

(17) The Emergency Risks (Goods) Insurance Act, 1962 which was framed in the wake of the Chinese aggression, provides for compulsory insurance against emergent risks to person carrying on business in India as a seller or suppliers of goods, if the insurable value of such goods lying in the same residency town or district exceeds Rs. 30,000. The Act was intended to provide indemnity against loss or damage due to enemy action.

(18) The Emergency Risks (Factories) Insurance Act, 1962, which was also framed in the wake of the Chinese aggression, provides for compulsory insurance against emergency risks of all factories falling within the purview of the Factories Act, 1948. For standing tea crops, inland vessels, plant, machinery and equipment of mines and oil companies, distribution system of fast

supply undertakings, and the whole of the generation, distribution and transmission systems of hydroelectric and electric systems, this Act, like its twin, was intended for providing indemnity against or damage due to enemy action.

(19) The Marine Insurance, Act, 1963, based substantially on the similar English Act of 1906, governs transactions of marine insurance in India. It defines marine insurance and includes perils incidental to local or inland transit also within its scope. The Act defines many insurance concepts such as insurable interest, insurable value, and disclosure by the assured, valued policy, unvalued policy, flatting policy, double insurance, warranties and assignment of policy, actual total loss, constructive total loss, general average loss, general average contributions, salvage charges, liability to third parties, etc., and prohibits wagering contracts.

(20) The Carriage by Air Act, 1972, applies to international carriage of goods and passengers. It fixes the liability of the carrier for injury or death of passengers and loss of or damage to goods.

(21) The Consumer Protection Act, 1986 deals with consumer rights, product supplers' liability and the insured persons' rights as consumers.

(22) The Railways Act, 1989 holds railway administration responsible for the loss, destruction, damage, deterioration or non-delivery in transit, to the consignee.

(23) The Multi-modal Transportation of Goods Act, 1993 regulates the business of multi-modal transportation of goods from any place in India to a place outside India on the basis of a multi-modal transport contract. As per the Act, a multi-modal transport operator is liable for loss of or damage to the consignment.

(24) The Environment Protection Act, 1986 makes entrepreneurs duty bound to protect the environment and responsible for liabilities attaching in case of degradation of the environment due to negligence and/or hazardous activities.

(25) The Arbitration and Conciliation Act, 1996 (in amendment of the Indian arbitration Act, 1940) specifies the arbitration provisions in insurance contracts.

(26) The redressal of Public Grievance Act and Rules, 1998 requires general and life insurance companies to resolve complaints relating to the settlement of claim in a cost-effective, efficient and impartial manner through grievance redressal machinery. The Act is the basis of the Ombudsman system.

(27) The Right to Information Act, 2005 requires public authorities to maintain the records, duly catalogued, and make information on matters that affect the public accessible to the affected persons.

6

Concept of Underwriting and Rating of Insurance

INTRODUCTION

This unit introduced you the concept of underwriting in the general insurance context. The common practices followed in underwriting have been elaborated. Rating practices as followed in the general insurance market are discussed in this unit. The unit gives you a broad idea of risk management practices as well.

UNDERWRITING CONCEPT

Insurance underwriting, for the common man, is the process of issuing insurance policies. The formalist theory of contract stipulates that every contract must have six elements, offer, acceptance, consideration, meeting of the minds, capacity and legality. When we look at insurance as a contract, the offer part is done by the insured through the proposal form. The insurer has to carry out the four of the other five parts and inform the proposer the consideration or amount of premium payable by him.

Underwriting involves evaluating the risk, measuring the risk exposure, determining the premium that needs to be charged to insure that risk, and taking the decision to accept or reject a risk. Insurance underwriters decide how much coverage the client can be given, how much they should pay for it, or whether to even accept the risk and insure them. The function of the underwriter is to acquire or to "write" business that will make money for the insurance company, and to protect the company's book of business from risks that they feel will make a loss. Underwriting involves checking whether there is a meeting of minds between the insured and the insurer. If the underwriter is satisfied on these aspects, using the accepted practice of the company, he finds out the cost at which the risk can be accepted and conveys the same to the insured, which indicates that the insurer is willing to accept the risk at the quoted price. Once the consideration is paid by the proposer and accepted by the insure, the contract comes into force.

Before conveying his acceptance or before the finer details of the contract are finalized, the insurer has to go through various steps. He has to evaluate the risk offered and its exposure. He has to decide how much cover can be given to the risk offered how much they should receive for accepting it, or whether to even accept the risk for insurance. Any factor that causes a grater likelihood of loss should theoretically be charged a higher rate. This basic principle of insurance must be followed if insurance companies are to remain solvent. Every insurance company sets its own set of underrating guidelines to help the underwriting determine whether or not the company should accept the risk. Over a period of time, markets evolve a set of guidelines that become standard for all the players in the market. However, each company will have its internal set as well.

ACCEPTANCE OF NEW BUSINESS

The insurers usually prescribe an elaborate state of conditions while accepting new businesses. This is to ensure that the company's finances are not put to risk by aggressive marketing without proper quality checks. If the particular risk offered for insurance has a greater chance of making a loss than other similarly placed risks, it can be called bad business, if, in the case of the particular business, there are reasons to expect that practically the loss will not be an uncertainty but a certainty or almost a certainty, the insurance has to be understood as bad business. In other words, the element of uncertainly that is normally expected in insurance contract would not be the same in a bad risk and the insurer would have to pay for it. Due to competition, the insurers may have to knowingly accept bad business, but the decision to do so would be at the discretion of the underwriter. Such decisions are made by seniors in the company with sufficient safeguards to bring the business as close as possible with other similarly insured.

Internal Guidelines: The insurers have to decide up to what sum insured risks can be underwriter at a particular hierarchical level in the company. Further, the standards to be set for bringing the risk or the operation of the insured peril more or less to the level of other risks in the same category have also to be decided by the insurers. So, in respect of each type of insurance, the insurers have to decide upon the following:

(1) Irrespective of sum insured, at what level should a business be underwritten?
(2) Up to specified levels of sum insured, specify who all can underwriter?
(3) Which types of sum insured need approval of the controlling office?
(4) What underwriting safeguards should be specified for each type of risk at different levels of sum insured?
(5) What procedures should be followed to evaluate the risk?
(6) What internal procedures should be followed for collecting premium, after sales services, etc.?

The decision regarding acceptance would very depending on the type of insurance, as the exposure can be different in different types, hence, the guidelines would be in detail. The Alabama Insurance Association defines the underwriting guidelines as a rule, standards, guidelines, or practice, whether written, oral, or electronic, that is used by an insurance company (or its agent) to decide whether to accept or reject an application for insurance policy, or to determine what rate will apply once the application is accepted.

REJECTION

There are many occasions when risks offered for insurance are rejected if they are not found food enough to be accepted as per the insurers internal standards prescribed for accepting businesses. For example, military vehicles are not accepted for comprehensive insurance. People beyond a particular age and those who are seriously sick are not covered for life insurance or health insurance. In short, risks that the underwriter perceives as extra hazardous as per the company's standards are declined. For instance, as per the Alabama Insurance Association's Underwriting Guidelines, underwriters are allowed to accept buildings. Less than 25 years of age for fire insurance, whereas if the building is more than 25 years of age. Insurance can be given only if written documentation is provided, stating that the electrical wiring, heating system, plumbing and roof have been renovated within the previous 20 years.

Limits on Sum Insured: In a tariff market, fairly high limits of acceptance are allowed to lower offers in the case of standard policies. In some cases such as motor, agents are allowed to accept business and issue cover notes and certificates of insurance. In case of insurances such as all risks on jeweler, baggage, personal accident, special contingency, etc. that involve risk with higher sum insured. Many insurers prescribe approval of the controlling office. Private sector insurers in India practically have more centralized systems for acceptance.

Limits by Types of Insurance: Usually, certain classes of business, such as aviation, bankers' indemnity, bloodstock, jewelers block, public liability, product liability, professional indemnity and certain types of engineering insurances are accepted only at the controlling office level. In India, insurances for satellites, offshore drilling aviation, etc. are accepted only at the head office level, often after elaborate discussions with the reinsures.

Accommodations Risks: There are certain categories of risks categorized as bad risks, which are fit to be declined and are sometimes called declined risks., however, in many cases, due to market compulsions, the insures have to cover these risks. In such cases, the proposal form, risk inspection report, details of other business from the same client, loss experience, special situation justifying acceptance, etc. are submitted to the controlling office. Acceptance of such risks would be usually subject to restrictive conditions, special clauses, warranties and loadings on premium. Examples of risk of this type are marine transit risk of cement in bags, sugar on all risk basis, perishable goods on all risks basis, gold and currency above specified values, etc. fire risks of explosive factories, ammunition works, fire works factories, and celluloid factories, etc. also come under this category. Burglary policies for jewelers, workmen in explosives factories, fidelity guarantee of gold shop employees, etc. are some other examples. These bad risks once accepted are referred to as accommodation risks.

CONTROL BY INSPECTION

In some cases, the insurers insist on pre acceptance survey of the risk. Some acceptance would be subject to inspection. Post acceptance inspections are mostly to finalize the rates and impose restrictive wordings. Inspections are done by the insures own engineers or by outsourced inceptors. This topic will be elaborated later on when risk management is discussed. Business interruption policies are sometimes issued only if the insured's books of accounts are being regularly audited by reputed agencies.

Restrictive Wordings: Certain clauses and warranties are imposed depending on the special features of the risk. Examples of such wordings used in marine insurance are:

(1) Breakage excluded—for asbestos sheets and cement pipes.
(2) Denting/scratching excluded for refrigerators
(3) Denting/scratching excluded for motor vehicles.
(4) Bursting/tearing excluded for cargo in paper bags.
(5) Breakage excluded for transformers and second hand machinery.
(6) Breakage excluded for sheet glass and glassware.
(7) Leakage and contamination excluded oil in second hand drums.
(8) Buckling excluded for cattle prone to buckling of knees while standing in transit.
(9) Cutting clause, damaged end of pipes to be cut and balance used.

Conditions of Excess: Compulsory excess (or co-payment) is imposed for certain risks, such as own damage of old vehicles, health insurance, leakage from transformers in transit, pilferage in fast moving consumer goods, fires in spray painting units, theft losses in a shopping mall, etc. Comprehensive insurance of costly imported cars is often subject to an excess clauses.

Other Restriction: Motor vehicles of older age attract higher rats. Cargo sent by overage vessels, under tonnage vessels and tramp vessels attract higher rates as a disincentive for using substandard modes of transit. Certain parts of the factory carrying out hazardous operations may require to be serrated by brick walls or fire proof doors to make the rest of the factory safer.

Provisional Acceptance: Sometimes the insurers take the decision to accept the risk without having the necessary information about the risk to price it appropriately. In such cases, the insurers may have to wait for the risk to be inspected or wait for a confirmation of the rates with conditions from the controlling office. Sometimes, through the details of a high value risk would be known, matter such as the insurers' capacity to retain the risk, co-insurance terms, and reinsures quotations based on international rates and terms may not be clear for some time. In such cases, the insured may not be willing to wait for the procedural informalities. He may be under obligation to his financiers, or his consigner/buyers to show the proof of insurance. Sometime she has to prove the existence of the cover to certain government agencies. In cases such as motor third-party insurance and public liability insurance, the insured requires a certificate of insurance, which is also required to be issued along with the cover note. Also, there would be market pressures on the insurer from competitors who would like to snatch away the business. In such a case, inspection of the risk or confirmation of rates is done. Conditions from the controlling office are yet to be received; depending upon the fact that the risk is provisionally accepted by the underwriter. The insurance act and the respective tariffs allow for this contingency and provide for the insurance cover to be effected subject to collection of a provisional premium. Acceptance of risk conveyed by the insure is evidenced by issuance of the cover note. Cover notes are easily numbered and strictly account for by way of cover note registers.

Policies are Issued: Once the complete details are collected and all the integrities of the contract are finalized, the policy is issued as a composite document covering all information of the risk and the contract. Policies are also serially numbered and entered in a register for effective control. The policy numbers are included or updated in the cover note register and the premium register. The policy document is stamped in accordance with the Indian Stamp Act and delivered to the insured.

RENEWAL OF BUSINESS

Policy numbers and details are entered in an expiry register (renewal register) according to the scheduled date of renewal. This register helps the insurers to track the insured ahead of the expiry date of the policy and try to retain the business. With increased competition, the insures are increasingly keen on retaining their good businesses. This is advantageous to them in many ways. In some cases, the acquisition costs are saved or reduced on the renewals. The insurers is comfortable in dealing with an existing insured as the risk is a known one, the claims history is related available, and administrative costs on risk inspection, etc. are saves. Another reason for retaining the insured with him is to improve the brand loyalty factor. That is a an insurer can expect a satisfied regular customer to get his other insurance transferred to the company. He may also talk good about his insurance experience to other and eventually bring in more business. Though renewal is a fresh contract of insurance on fresh terms and issuance of a renewal notice may to be mandatory, most insured consider it a matter of courtesy and a good gesture.

In accident insurance, a fresh proposal from is not asked for at renewal. However, the terms are fresh depending on the current age of the vehicle, revised IDV, etc. in fidelity guarantee policies or personal accident policies, the individual limits may have to be revised or changes in employee cadres given effect to.

Bonus: The insurers offer an incentive on claims free insurance by granting a bonus on renewal. The bonuses are often linked to the number of claim-free years completed, as well as works as a disincentive for making minor claims. This helps the insurers in retaining good business in certain classes where frequent transfers of business are expected. Motor own damage and health insurance are such examples. Conversely, a malls or loading based on bad claims experience is applied when the insurance is offered for renewal. When it comes to portability of insurance policies or insurance shifting from one insures to another, different practices are followed in the market as regards to bonus, etc. A view is that the insured has earned it and has a right to keep the discount. Another view is that if the insurer, who has already enjoyed claims free years, is willing to give a bonus, it can be binding on another insurer, who will be getting only a reduced premium from day one. In tariff marks, generally such bonuses are honoured. Portability of malaises is generally not a matter for dispute as the insured would not shift the business to a new insurer unless he has a good reason for doing so.

RATING PRINCIPLES

Insurance rate refers to the consideration that is vital to the contract. The price of the insurance usually expressed as the cost of a unit of cover, e.g. Rs. 'x' per mile or in some cases as Rs. 'x' per cent. Until December 31, 2006, in the Indian market, rates were fixed for all major lines of business by the Tariff Advisory Committee (TAC), after which a tariff-free regime has come into place. The tariff-free regime follows a File and Use model where the individual insurers have to actuarially justify the rates charged by them. Post de-tariffing from January 1, 2007, the insurers are by and large allowed to charge their own rates except for motor third party policies where the IRDA has fixed a guideline rate. In other lines also, some minor restrictions exists. There are, however, only transient provisions to prevent a sudden plunge of the rates.

Correct pricing ensures stability in the insurance market, which in turn bolsters the confidence of the insuring public in the system of insurance. In short, in developing markets, policy-holders' interests are protected by standardization of products and administered prices. Insurance polices have to be priced correctly to ensure on the one hand that the insured do not end up paying more, and on the other hand to provide the insurers with sufficient funds to pay the claims to the insured, whenever the need arises.

In the Indian context, Section 64 UC(2) of the Insurance Act, 1938 prescribes that in "fixing, amending or modifying any rates, advantages, terms or conditions relating to any risk, the Advisory committee shall try to ensure that there is not unfair discrimination between risks of essentially the same hazards".

RATING CONCEPTS

An insurer's pricing objectives depend on the overall objectives of the insurers and the state of the insurance market. These pricing objectives may be expressed in three main ways:

(1) To achieve a specified rate of return on capital,
(2) To maximize profits, and
(3) To maintain or extend market share.

The basis principle followed in rating all businesses is that insurance companies should remain solvent to satisfy their obligations to the insured and the society. This would include ensuring the survival of the insurance company, achieving optimum strategic positioning, providing quality and value for the service, contributing to the society's well-being, and maximizing the returns on a given type of risk.

As per the guidelines issued by the Motor Accidents Authority (MAA), the regulatory body of the New South Wales State of Australia, for the preparation of rate filing reports.

"Premiums must be sufficient to pay all acquisition and policy administration costs, provide a sum of money to meet the best estimate of the cost of claims (including claims management expense), provide a profit margin representing an adequate return on capital invested and compensation for the risk, and provide for other matters a prudent insurer would make provision for".

Insurance pricing methods can be divided into three major categories:

(1) "Manual rate", which refers to a rate designed to apply on a generic basis to similar risks within the same market, filed with the department by an insurer or rate service organization, and made part of the rating manual used by an insurer or rate service organization.
(2) Experience rating, which refers to a rating systems whereby a manual rate for insurance is adjusted or modified, based on the past loss experience of the insured.
(3) "Modification rating", which refers to a rating procedure that provides a listing of various risk characteristics or conditions and a range of modification factors that may be applied for the characteristics or conditions of the manual rate of a particular insurance risk. The effect of the modification factor is to increase (debit) or decrease (credit) the manual rate (definitions are as per the Utah State Insurance Rules in the USA).

The terms of the insurance contract, the conditions under which losses are payable (the insurance cover), and the past experience of losses in the particular type of insurance are taken into reckoning. The rating hinges on the frequency and severity of past losses. The calculations that go into the rating depend on the accuracy of the statistical data. The data should be of a sizeable quantity, reasonable quality, credibility and relevance. For large property risks, the probable maximum loss (PML) of the risk is also estimated. The PML of a particular risk is the estimate of the maximum loss that would occur as a result of damage caused by the most destructive peril to be insured with regard to the location, constitution, occupation and protection of the risk. PML is usually expressed as a percentage of the sum insured (Hart, Buchanan & Howe).

PREMIUM OF POLICIES

Any factor that causes a greater likelihood of loss should theoretically be charged a higher rate. Thus, for rating purposes, the insurers try to see the insured risks as forming part of some class of risks that share similar characteristics. At the same time, for rating purposes, the insurers have to try to distinguish the specific risk from the class of risks to find out the degree of differential treatment the risk would attract depending on its individual characteristics. For instance, for a health insurance cover, the insurers charge older people a significantly higher premiums than they charge younger people for term life insurance. Old people are more likely to fall sick than younger people. That is, a particular old man proposing himself for health insurance would be seen as part of the common class of other old men and rated accordingly. But if the insurer finds that the old man enjoys excellent health, has healthy exercising habits, is a non-smoker and non-drinker, and that both his parents had lived into their nineties, the insurers would distinguish him as a specific risk, and would like to reduce his rates substantially from the common rates applicable to other old men.

In a motor insurance, information on the driver's experience and claim-free record are significant. The insurance company uses the information to assess the likelihood that a driver will have an accident, and adjusts premium accordingly. A driver who drives great distances at high speeds, for example, might be charged a different rate than a deriver who drives short distances at low speeds. The rate will be justifiable only if the insure is sure that a high-speed long distance river incurs greater risk to an insurance pool than the slow, around town drier. Therefore, in treating the insured differently, the insurers should be able to logically and actuarially justify their reason for doing so, so that the discrimination is not unjust or unlawful.

RATING CONCERNS

We have seen that the rate would depend on various factors, deciding the factors and ascribing appropriate weights to them is the insured's challenge. Depending on the type of insurance product (line of business), the insurance companies sometimes use automated rating packages by encoding the rating rules, thereby reeducating the amount of manual work in working out premiums.

In marine cargo insurance, the rate would depend on factors such as nature of cargo, scope of cover, packing, mode of conveyance, distance and past claims experience. An example of a Risk Based Pricing Model (RBPM) in Marine Cargo Insurance is given below:

Example

Factors and Weights—1

On a composite matrix, a range of weightage points can be ascribed to multiple rating factors based on the loss propensity of marine cargo consignment, as given below:

Sl. No.	*Factor*	*Weightage*
1.	Frequency/periodicity of dispatch	05%
2.	Mode of transit	10%
3.	Per bottom value	05%
4.	Nature of goods sent (perishable, hazardous, high value, unstable by design/weight)	20%
5.	Transshipment single or multiple	20%
6.	Duration of transit	05%
7.	Storage location single or multiple	05%
8.	Duration of storage	05%
9.	Consignment in bulk/containerized, packing type and material	05%
10.	Claims history of insured	05%
11.	Claims history of carriers	05%
12.	Geographical location(s) of transit	05%
13.	Season of shipment	03%
14.	Salvage value of consignment	02%
	Total	100%

The total rate to be charged for a marine cargo policy can be distributed over the 14 factors mentioned above, contributing to 100 per cent of the premium. Such mathematical rating models help companies in fixing rates in a balanced manner, i.e. the underwriter would be more objective in his decisions if there is a rating structure in place.

Factors and Weights—2

In the motor context, weightage points can be ascribed to multiple rating factors to rate a vehicle, as given below. It is possible that many more rating factors could be added or a few removed depending on the conditions of a particular market.

Sl. No.	*Factor*	*Weightage*
1.	Vehicle colour	10%
2.	Vehicle age	20%
3.	Vehicle engine capacity	20%
4.	Vehicle make	05%
5.	Anti-theft protection	05%
6.	Age of driver	05%
7.	Gender of driver	05%
8.	Profession of driver	05%
9.	Lifestyle of driver	05%
10.	Driving experience of driver	05%
11.	Accident history	05%
12.	Average distance commuted daily	05%
13.	Regular place of packing	03%
14.	Type of road mostly used	02%
	Total	100%

The total rate to be charged for a motor vehicle can be derived from the above weightage proportionate to their loss-making potential, which can be spread over the above 14 factors mentioned, contributing to 100 per cent of the premium. Such rating factors and weightage become the back bone of a Risk Factors Rating System (RFRS) or Risk Factors Based Rating System, which is used in countries like Japan.

RISK ASSESSMENT

We have seen that risks are evaluated before acceptance or immediately after acceptance for finalizing intricacies of the rates. Risk evaluation can involve an inspector's visit to check the site and seeing the physical features of the risk. This can include checking the construction of the building, its height, the processes done in it, its proximity to other risks, the geographical location for chances of flood or earthquake or cyclone prone areas, etc. The insurers may suggest risk improvements such as installation of fire proof doors, burglar alarms and smoke detectors, or offer incentives by way of discounts for improving the risk. The insurers do mathematical modeling based on risk perceptions. Methods of identifying hazards, objectively assessing them, and weighing their loss potential on mathematical scales in all, finding out the probability of an operating hazard is studied by risk managers, the perceived

Hazard Operability Model

Mitigation	*Severity*		*Improbable*	*Unlikely*	*Possible*	*Likely*	*Probable*
Prevention		likelihood	1	2	3	4	5
Light		-1	-1	-2	-6	-4	-5
Serious		-2	-2	-4	-9	-8	-10
Major		-3	-3	-6	-12	-12	-15
Catastrophic		-4	-4	-8	-16	-16	-20
Multi-catastrophic		-5	-5	-10	-20	-20	-25

Legand Hazard Operability Model

–25 to –20	Non-operatable	Evacuate area/zone/country
–16 to –10	Intolerable	Do not take this risk
–9 to –5	Undesirable	Evaluate risk thoroughly before insuring
–4 to –2	Acceptable	Proceed carefully planned risk improvement
–1	Negligible	Safe to proceed

frequencies and severities with which hazards can operate on a given risk are studied using certain models called hazards, can operate on a given using certain models called Hazards Identification Study (HAZID) and Hazard and Operability Studies (HAZOP), which enable the insures to evaluate risk potential accurately and scientifically. The basic HAZOP model given indicates how the mathematical weights work in risk evaluation.

As the likelihood increases, the loss becomes more of a certainty than fortuitous event. As the severity goes up, it becomes increasingly difficult for the insurers to absorb the losses. Risk management reduces the likelihood (or probability) of a loss and reduces the severity (or intensity) of a loss. Loss prevention and loss minimization activities are initiated at the instance of the insurers. They form agencies to educate target groups on reducing losses by various methods. Drivers of tanker carrying hazardous goods are trained on fire prevention, cargo handlers at ports are trained to handle cargo with care, pedestrians are taught road discipline, and the general public is advised on precautions to be taken while bursting crackers during festival season. The philosophy is that if any loss is averted or any risk prevented, the insurers gain; beyond this, of course, the preservation of the nation's wealth is everyone's responsibility.

CUSTOMER SERVICE/CUSTOMER DELIGHT

Customer service is an integral part of an insurer's business, just like in any other business enterprise. In insurance, the customer comes in for a long-term relationship and not an across the counter dealing. He looks forward to the insurer as a friend in need who will come to his help when he needs him the most. In a way, having parted with the premium, he would also feel weak and dependent on the insurer for fulfilment of his part of the promise. In this background, retaining the insured's trust and goodwil is very important. In general insurance, conventionally there are mainly two aspects of customer service. The first is the prompt completion of all formalities and issuance of the policy. The second is prompt settlement of claims. However, there are areas such as easy to read literature, customer-friendly forms, clarity on the contract trust, courteous behaviour from staff and intermediaries, updating of changes in address, hassle-free endorsement process, sending of information mailers, advertisements that endorse the trust aspects, receiving a timely renewal notice, etc. that keep the customer relations on a happy note.

The acid test of the insurance contract is when the claim occurs and that is where the insured expects wholesome customer service that the insurers can provide. This aspect will be discussed in other chapter.

SUMMARY

After going through this unit, you should develop a basic understanding of underwriting as a professional understands some of the common underwriting practices, and familiarize yourself with general insurance pricing practices. You should also be able to integrate your understanding of risk management in the context of general insurance.

(1) Underwriting involves evaluating the risk, measuring the risk exposure, determining the premium that needs to be charged to insurer that risk, and taking the decision to accepting or rejecting a risk.

(2) Ever insurance company sets its own set of underwriting guidelines to help the under writer determine where the or not the company should accept the risk.

(3) The insured internal guidelines are usually the following:
   (a) At which level should a business be underwritten?
   (b) Which types/what sum insured levels need approve of the controlling office?
   (c) What underwriting safeguards should be specified for each type of risk at different levels of sum insured?
   (d) What procedures should be followed to evaluate the risk?
   (e) What internal procedures should be followed for collecting premium, after sales services, etc.

(4) Risks offered for insurance are rejected if they are not found good enough to be accepted as per the insurers' internal standards prescribed for accepting businesses.

(5) Sometimes, due to market compulsions, the insurers cover certain bad risks, though fit to be declined. This would be usually subject to restrictive conditions, special clauses, warranties and loadings on premium. Once accepted, these risks are called accommodation risks.

(6) Examples of restrictive wordings are:
   (a) Breakage excluded for asbestos sheets and cement pipes.
   (b) Denting/scratching excluded for motor vehicles.
   (c) Bursting/tearing excluded for cargo in paper bags.
   (d) Breakage excluded for sheet glass and glassware.

(7) In certain cases, though an inception of the risk or a confirmation of rates/ conditions from the controlling office is pending, the risk is provisionally accepted by the underwriter.

(8) The insurers are keen on retaining their good businesses. This is advantageous to them as acquisition costs are saved or reduced on the renewals. The insurer is comfortable dealing with an existing insured as the risk is a known one and the claims history is already available. Renewals also improve the brand loyalty factor and most insured consider it a matter of courtesy and good gestures.

(9) The insurers offer an incentive on claims free insurances by granting a bonus on renewal. The bonuses are often linked to the number of claims free years completed, as well as works as disincentive for making minor claims. This helps the insurers in retaining good business in certain class where frequent transfers of business are expected.

(10) Insurance rates are usually expressed as the cost of a unit of cover, e.g. Rs. 'x' per mille, or in some cases as Rs. 'x' percent.

(11) Section 64 UC(2) of the Insurance Act, 1938 prescribes that in "fixing, amending or modifying any rates, advantages, terms or conditions relating to any risk, there should be no unfair discrimination between risk of essentially the same hazard".

(12) This basic principle followed in rating is that insurance companies should remain solvent to satisfy their obligations to the insured and the society.

This would include ensuring the survival of the insurance company, achieving optimum strategic positioning, providing quality and value for the service, contributing to the society's well-being, and maximizing the returns on the given type of risk.

(13) Manual rate refers to a rate designed to apply on a generic basis to similar risks within the same market or filed with the department by an insurer or rate service organization and made part of the rating manual used by an insurer or rate service organization.

(14) Experience rating refers to a rating system whereby a manual rate for insurance is adjusted or modified based on the past loss experience of the insured.

(15) Modification rating refers to a rating procedure that provides a listing of various risk characteristics or conditions and a range of modification factors that may be applied for the characteristics or conditions of the manual rate of a particular insurance risk. The effect of the modification factors is to increase (debit) or decrease (credit) the manual rate.

(16) By PML of a particular risk, the insurers come to estimate the maximum loss that would occur as a result of damage caused by the most destructive peril to be insured, with regard to the location, construction, occupation and protection of the risk.

(17) In contrast to other old men, if the insurer finds that particular old man enjoys excellent health, has healthy exercising habits, is a non-smoker and non-drinker, and that both his parents had lived into their nineties, the insurers would distinguish him as a specific risk and would like to reduce his rates substantially from the common rates applicable to other old men.

(18) Mode of transit, per bottom value, and duration of storage.

(19) Vehicle age, vehicle engine capacity, and vehicle make.

(20) A score of '1' indicates that the possibility of the loss-making event occurring improbable and if it happens, the loss would be light.

(21) A score of '-25' indicates that the possibility of the loss-making event occurring is probable and if it happens, the loss would be multi-catastrophic.

(22) The first score of '-5' indicates that the possibility of the loss-making event occurring is 'probable' and, if it happens, the loss would be 'light'. The other score of '-5' indicates that the possibility of the loss-making event occurring is 'improbable', and if it happens, the loss would be multi-catastrophic.

(23) The customer looks forward to the insurer as a friend in need who will come to his help when he needs him the most. He expects prompt completion of all formalities and issuance of the policy. He also expects prompt settlement of claims, courteous behaviour from staff, intermediaries, and timely information such as renewal notice.

7

Privatisation Concept for Efficient Customer Service in Insurance Sector

INTRODUCTION: PRIVATE ENTERPRISING AS A DEMOCRATIC TOOL FOR EFFICIENCY

It has been observed that the Public Sector Enterprises (PSEs) cannot perform their economic and business activities effectively and efficiently in any country as their focus is on general welfare. Without profit planning, wasteful expenditure can not be avoided and bureaucratic functioning has no place in private enterprises. It is no secret that the public enterprises are not discharging their full responsibilities even in a socialist country. The total nationalization of business industry will lead to serfdom or anarchism. The tenets of democracy demand full freedom in all matters with people's choice, not forced. But, it is stark reality that it is difficult for every enterprise to compete in the market. The government has to restructure society and economy in such a manner that the poor, the unemployed, can be profitably employed. Entrepreneurship has to be developed and all the educated persons have to set-up their ventures with the latest technology and under franchisee system or through ancilliarization in the industrial sector.

India has been planning for development using the Nehruvian-Mahalonovis economic model of mixed economy. Too much expectation from public enterprises will distort the economy and will ultimately lead towards wastage of precious and valuable scarce resources. Therefore, the government is going to recast the industrial policy considering the productivity and efficiency as criteria to continue particular units whether as public enterprises or private enterprises. It is a matter of satisfaction that the government has started taking pragmatic criteria for the development of enterprises. The restriction on the use of full capacity by private enterprises is being removed to increase the output and productivity of the economy.

Time has come when the public enterprises will have to compete with the private enterprises. If the public enterprises are losing in the efficiency and productivity criteria, they should be closed down. If the private enterprises have more efficiency and higher productivity, those should be encouraged to increase production and output of the economy. It is universally agreed that the government cannot perform all the functions with equal efficiency. It should have nothing to do with business or industry as far as the ownership is concerned. Ownership should pass on to the private hands as the private sector has entrepreneurship. The regulatory role, promotional role, entrepreneurial role and planning role have not been fully performed by any government with the level of efficiency of the private sector. The government should concentrate more on regulatory and planning roles at the macro-level. The entrepreneurial role should be confined only to those areas where the private entrepreneurs are hesitant and cannot discharge their functions satisfactorily at national level. Non-profitable business activities like defense, transport, education, communication and other such types of activities concerning general welfare and national security should only be undertaken by the Government.

According to W.A. Levis, the nationalization of industry is not essential to development planning. A government can do anything it wants to do by way of controlling industry without resorting to nationalization or ownership.

There should not be a state monopoly in the country in all fields. Competition is the backbone of an economy and it pushes up productivity. Therefore, competition should be encouraged to promote production and productivity in the economy. Competition may be between the public and private enterprises. The public enterprises should be preferred in some areas than private sector, and so, they should be permitted to continue to accelerate the growth of the economy. On the other hand, many public sector enterprises are wasting public money because of continuous losses or less than optimal production. Such enterprises should be handed over to the competent private entrepreneurs.

However, privatization may be done after analyzing the efficiency of the organizations and their role in the economy. Insurance industry along with other financial institutions has been constantly under pressure of privatization without going into the grass-root problems and their potential consequences. Many Committees and government agencies have been arguing in favour of privatization, denationalization and permitting foreign institutions to conduct insurance business in India.

PRIVATIZATION OF INSURANCE INDUSTRY IN INDIA—STEPS TAKEN BY GOVERNMENT TO PRIVATIZE INSURANCE SECTOR

In 1993, the Government of India had set-up a high powered committee under the Chairmanship of R.N. Malhotra, former Governor of Reserve Bank of India, to examine the structure of the insurance industry and to recommend changes to make it more efficient and competitive, keeping in view the structural changes taking place in other parts of the financial system of the country.

OBJECTIVES OF MALHOTRA COMMITTEE

The following were the purposes of the Malhotra Committee:

In terms of the objectives before the Malhotra Committee, it had surveyed, studied and analysed in its report the structure of insurance industry, to assess the strengths and weaknesses of insurance companies in terms of the objectives of creating an efficient and viable insurance industry, to have a wide coverage of insurance services, to have a variety of insurance products with a high quality services component, and to develop an effective instrument for mobilization of financial resources for development. The report also contained the arguments and made recommendations for changing the structure of insurance industry, for changing the general policy framework, etc. The Committee had the task of making suggestions regarding the following:

(a) To make specific suggestions regarding Life Insurance Corporation of India (LIC) and General Insurance Corporation of India (GIC) with a view to improve their functioning.
(b) To make recommendations on regulations and supervision of the insurance sector in India.
(c) To make recommendations on the role and functions of surveyors, intermediaries like agents, etc. in the insurance sector.
(d) To make recommendations on any other matter which is relevant for development of the insurance industry in India.

MALHOTRA COMMITTEE'S RECOMMENDATIONS

Let us be briefed about the recommendations of the Malhotra Committee. The Committee submitted its report in January 1994 recommending that private insurers be allowed to co-exist along with government companies like LIC and GIC. This recommendation had been supported by several factors, the most important being the need for wide insurance coverage in the economy. Major recommendations of Malhotra Committee are as follows:

(i) Raising the capital base of LIC and GIC up to Rs. 200 crores each, half to be retained by the government and rest sold to the public at large with suitable reservations for employees.
(ii) Private sector be granted permission to enter insurance industry with a minimum paid up capital of Rs. 100 crores.
(iii) Foreign insurance companies be allowed to enter by floating an Indian company preferably joint venture with Indian partners.
(iv) Steps to be taken to set-up a strong and effective insurance regulatory body in the form of statutory autonomous board on the lines of SEBI.
(v) Limited number of private companies to be allowed in the sector. But no firm be allowed to operate in both lines of insurance (Life and non-Life).
(vi) Tariff Advisory Committee (TAC) is to be delinked from GIC to function as a separate statutory body under necessary supervision by the Insurance Regulatory Authority.
(vii) All the insurance companies be treated on equal footing and governed by the provisions of the Insurance Act. No special dispensation is to be given to government companies.
(viii) Setting up of a strong and effective regulatory body with independent source for financing before allowing private companies into this sector.

(ix) The committee suggested that settlement of claims was to be done within a specific time frame (without delay).

(x) The committee has made several recommendations on product pricing, vigilance, systems and procedures, improving customer service and use of technology.

(xi) It also made a number of recommendations to change the existing structures of the LIC and GIC.

(xii) The committee insisted that insurance companies should pay special attention to the rural insurance business (rural coverage).

IMPACT OF PRIVATIZATION OF INSURANCE INDUSTRY

The opening up of insurance sector for competition offers ample opportunities to both existing as well as new players to penetrate into untapped areas, sectors and sub-sectors and unexploited segments of population as presently both insurance density and penetration are at low level. Both indices being at very low level in the country, even compared to the countries with the same level of economic development and per capita income, are indicative of the vast potential of the growth of this sector in future.

The impact of privatization can be studied under three heads:

(i) Opportunities; (ii) Challenges or Threats; and (iii) Strategies.

(i) Opportunities

The privatization of insurance industry will provide the following opportunities:

Untapped Market: New comers in insurance industry will get the advantage of untapped market. The untapped potential market for insurance products is quite large in spite of the efforts made by general insurance companies and LIC to extend their services throughout the country. But the choices available to the insuring public are inadequate in terms of services, products and prices. The Malhotra Committee estimated that in life insurance, 22% of the insurable population has been tapped so far. Premium per capita is only 2% in India. Premium percentage of GDP is 0.55% which is very less in comparison to the USA where premium per capita is equivalent of Rs. 1381 and premium as percentage of GDP is 4.80%. This huge gap from the global bench-mark is itself indicative of huge untapped potential.

Mandatory Insurance: In disaster prone areas, Government of India is going to make insurance mandatory. The interim report of the high powered committee set-up by the centre on disaster management has proposed mandatory insurance of life and property by people residing in a disaster prone area such as coastal belts, flood prone areas, site near nuclear, chemical and hazardous industries and thickly populated areas.

More Products Offered: A state monopoly has little incentive to offer a wide range of products. It can be seen by a lack of certain products from LIC's portfolio and lack of extensive categorization in several GIC products such as health insurance. More competition in this business will spur firms to offer several new products with more complex and extensive risk categorization.

Growth of Economy: With the allowing of holding of equity shares by foreign company either itself or through its subsidiary company or nominee, not exceeding 26% of paid-up capital of insurance company, various joint ventures between foreign investors and Indian partners will be operated resulting into supplementing domestic savings and economic progress of the nation.

Opportunity for Banks: Banks, with their wide area network with branches in all parts of the country, will have good opportunity to enter insurance business or industry. Banks will succeed in this sector because they have data of customers, trained staff, a good network

Better Customer Services: Privatization would result in better customer services and would help in improving the variety and price of insurance products. Competition will compel the players to bring new and innovative products, wider choice of prices and quality service to the policyholders (consumers).

(ii) Challenges

Whether the insurer is old or new, private or public, expansion and extension of market will present multitude challenges, as described hereunder:.

New Insurers: New insurance companies will have to invest a minimum capital of Rs. 100 crore. The normal gestation period is five years. Hence, the new insurers will have to lock up their capital for at least five years before earning any profits. Besides, they will face problems of shortage of trained manpower for the insurance industry. The setting up of various offices and distribution of network is a time-consuming process. Further, the new insurer-companies will have to compete with the established insurance companies like LIC and GIC, which have a corporate image and market presence for several years.

Expectations of the Consumers: Today, LIC has more than 60 products and GIC has more than 180 products to offer in the insurance market. But most of them are outdated, as they are not suitable to the needs of the present-day consumers. Hence, all the insurance companies will have to offer innovative products to the consumers. The consumers are particularly expecting good pension plans, health insurance, term insurance, and investment products like unit linked insurance from the life insurance companies. Similarly, the consumers expect innovative products from the general insurance for managing health care, property insurance, accident insurance and other products on an attractive terms and competitive premium. The consumers also expect reduction in the premium of the insurance products for another reason; that the mortality rate in India has come down three times in the last five years.

Premium on Customer Service: The days of giving fixed insurance products are over. Now the customers need insurance solutions that match their needs or wants. The large-scale of operations, public sector bureaucratic and cumbersome procedures hamper nationalized insurers. Therefore, potential private entrants expect to score in the areas of customer service, speed and flexibility. It may mean better products and wider choice for the customers. For extending better service, insurance companies will have to build call centres to provide call-free telephone-based sales and services. The call centres will provide product-related information, customers' accounts' information, queries and complaint handling. These call centres can be used for outbound sales and marketing companies.

Distribution Channel: In the privatized insurance market, there will be multiple distribution channels which will include agents, brokers, corporate intermediaries, bank branches, affinity groups and direct marketing through tele-sales and internet. There will be competition among the channels also. Intense competitions will grow among the old and new insurers in the liberalized insurance market.

There would be substantial shift in the distribution of insurance in India. Many of these changes are due to international trends. World-wide insurance products move from pure service produces to pure commodity products. Then they could be sold through the medical shops, groceries, novelty stores, etc. Once the products gain awareness and popularity, then they can move to remote channels such as telephone or direct mail.

Consumer Education: The existing level of consumes' education and awareness about insurance products is very low. Only 62% of the Indian population is educated and less than 10% are well educated. Even the educated are ignorant about the various products of insurance. Hence, it is necessary that all the insurance companies should undertake the executive plan and policy for education and awareness of consumers about insurance policies. The consumer organizations and media can also play very important role in education of the consumers. This will result in expansion and depth of the insurance market and will also enable the needy consumers to purchase appropriate policies. In fact, the private new comer-insurers have already started putting a lot more emphasis on advertising and using creative tactics to educate the consumers.

Consumer Grievance Redressal Mechanism: The insurance companies have to face an acute problem of the redressal of grievances of consumers for deficiency in products and services. The IRDA has already appointed ombudsman for looking into the grievances of the policyholders and its judgment will be binding on insurers. In the competitive market, awareness level of consumers will increase and it will help consumers to fight for their legal right in case of deficiency in services. Therefore, the number of legal cases filed by the consumers against the insurance companies is likely to increase substantially in future. This will be a challenge to the insurers.

New Product Innovations Needed: In India, only two products of LIC dominate with majority share out of 52 products. With more competition, good products will become an important differentiator among the various competing insurance products. A lot will depend on the kind of products that these outfits would launch. Initially, after launching simple products, the multinationals will shift to specialized products, e.g. Royal Sundaram Alliance will launch a mix of personal and commercial insurance policies. This will cover fire, marine, motor, personal accident and health insurance. HDFC Standard Life will launch two core life insurance products and then another dozen of the same type.

Positioning of Varied/Multiple Insurance Products in the Market: First and the biggest challenge before the insurance companies is to bring about a change in the mindset of people, especially in regard to the object of life insurance. Life insurance is seen more as a tax saving mechanism rather than safety net in case of death, in India, e.g. ICICI Prudential Life Insurance's Chief Marketing Officer, Saugata Gupta says that "Working on consumer attitude will be the greatest challenge". New types of products should be futuristic in outlook. To start with, low premium high cover policies should be introduced and better savings products may be introduced at a later stage.

Rural Area Exploitation the Best Bet: Life insurance business in India suffers from high premium and low returns. A normally competitive industry should be able to increase coverage, mobile large savings, and provide high returns. In terms of mobilizing savings in the form of insurance, India is ranked at 27th in the world. In developed countries like the U.K., the USA and South Africa, life insurance premium accounts for over 25% population only. Now with the entry of numerous private companies in rural areas, it is expected that rural sector will be tapped as well. IRDA has made it mandatory for life insurance companies to sell 5% of their aggregated polices in the rural areas during the first year of operation and that will progressively be increased to 15% by the fifth year. But with gestation period being long and investment required being large, new entrants will feel very difficult to achieve it.

Information Technology—the Highly Facilitating Factor: Information technology has become an integral part of the insurance industry worldwide from general accounting to customer service, re-insurance, underwriting and risk management. These have integrated application and are decision-oriented. In the Indian insurance industry, information technology is used as a reporting tool whereas overseas it is used more as a decision-making instrument. The policyholders would be able to check policy details, to identify schemes, make (or change) nominations, the type of loans available and the amount in their investment accounts on-line and through Internet connectivity. The insurers' advisors can also check accounts of their customers as well as their own accounts.

(iii) Strategies

The insurance players would be required to concentrate on the following main strategies to become more competitive and responsive to the needs of the societies:

Environmental Analysis: The companies should concentrate on environmental change, its direction, magnitude and its short-term and long-term impact, formulating strategies to meet the challenges of high competition, preparing contingency plans and then designing action plans for effective implementation of formulated strategies.

Restructuring Organization will Help: The traditional hierarchy system is very slow in making decisions due to several levels of management involved, its procedural inflexibility and slow communication process/system. A manager in the privatized scenario is required to be an organizational specialist, country specialist and global specialist.

Speed, Cost Effectiveness and Innovations Required: The private insurance companies will have to make substantial investments in customer relationship management technologies. They will be required to have wide area network (WAN), connecting branches spread across wide geographical locations and work out modalities for facilitating premium payment through the Internet. LIC is setting up an interactive response system in more cities so that a policyholder need not travel to the office of company for information. After all, the customer should have the choice of getting work done in the shortest possible time without having to visit the office of insurance companies.

Human Resources Development the Key to Business Development and Client Servicing: Human resource is important for any organization, more especially for organizations activities of which revolve around special human interactions. The new private insurance companies need people with the right set of knowledge, skills and aptitude for insurance alongwith right type of products and services. The persons who are involved in selling the product and those who are doing the back office work need to equip themselves with newer skills and insights into every aspect of functioning of the company. They have a daunting task of exploiting potential in the industry and at the same time bring down risk level to the company for providing insurance coverage. They have to retain the existing customers for which they need to have better understanding of products and services by creating healthy internal environment with group harmony. Existing companies will have to frame their human resource policies to retain the competent personnel and motivate staff continuously since new companies entering insurance business will be eyeing them by offering lucrative salaries.

Efficiency in Distribution to be Assured: It is very important factor and may prove bottleneck to the new players. Insurance companies are making the products available through the ready distribution channels of banks, non-banking finance companies and housing companies. One has to be careful doing this, since creating distribution with distances does not automatically mean controlling them. There will be more places from where customer can purchase insurance polices with the starting of corporate agencies besides the consultants and agents currently selling these policies. Due to this, a new concept of Bancassurance has emerged which is defined as a kind of service that the insurance companies use to offer their products though the distribution channels of banking industry. There is need to augment sources of revenues for survival. Bancassurance has promoted two big classes of financial institutions to combine their strengths and create a new means of marketing and servicing their products. Convergence of banking sector traditionally considered being more competitive and insurance sector having a vast untapped potential of growth has resulted into bancassurance.

Risk Management: Insurance companies will have to bring new approach and sophistication in market research techniques, future portfolio expansion like all intermediaries in financial markets do.

Efficient Marketing Strategies: Marketing strategies for insurance products in the emerging scenario could be understood in the following steps:

$$R \rightarrow STP \rightarrow MM \rightarrow I \rightarrow C$$

where

R = Market Research,
STP = Segmentation, Targeting, Positioning,

MM = Marketing Mix,
I = Implementation, and
C = Control.

The focus of emerging marketing strategies would centre on the prepositions like reduced costs, increased profitability, reduced time to market, improved customer intimacy, retained customers for life, establishing strong partnership. Formulation of a marketing strategy is more a process than an event. Environmental factors like macro-economic parameters, regulatory norms and theme, technology, infrastructure, legal set-up, competition by way of new entry, degree of globalization, etc. need to be scanned and considered in framing the likely scenarios. The competitive advantage of a company may stem from the many discrete activities in value chains. Each of these activities can contribute to a company's relative cost position or create a basis for differentiation.

Ethical Issues: The governance problems in service industry like insurance have been raised time and again as well as risk management techniques. Companies will need to leverage this sophistication backed by information technology to select good risks and rate them. On the other hand, insurance companies invest the funds of policy-holders and owned capital and accumulate surpluses and reserves. Companies try to earn the highest rate of return possible on investments consistent with risk objectives, because pre-eminence is related to investment performance. As the rate of return on investments increases, the insurance companies can lower the premiums they charge on new policies. Higher rate of return provides higher earnings on cash values and lesser the need for premium revenues. Premium rates are a competitive factor and high investment returns are crucial in maintaining and improving an insurance company's sales position. Strong investment performance supports growth in policy sales and sets aside the sense of helplessness among the employees and customers alike. Companies must realize this particularly in the emerging scenario of intense competition wherein customers will have a range of options for investments and insurance. At the same time, the regulators and companies will have to be cautious of customers who indulge in unethical practices by manipulating or hiding vital information in their dealings with companies and inflict losses, resulting in increase in cost of insurance. Ethics will have to be ensured in every activity of the company.

CURRENT SCENARIO OF INSURANCE INDUSTRY IN INDIA

Seventeen new players have entered the field of insurance, both life and non-life business, after opening up of insurance industry to private sector in India. Some of these are:

Tata AIG Life Insurance Company Ltd.
Birla Sunlife Insurance Company Ltd.
HDFC Standard Life Insurance Company Ltd.
Kotak Mahindra Old Mutual Life Insurance Company Ltd.
Reliance General Insurance Company Ltd.
ICICI Prudential Life Insurance Company Ltd.
Royal Sundaram Alliance Insurance Company Ltd.

Bajaj Auto Alliance Insurance Company Limited.
IFFCO Tokyo General Insurance Company Ltd.
ING Vysya Life Insurance Company (Pvt.) Ltd.
SBI Life Insurance Company Ltd.
Dabur CJU Life Insurance Company Ltd.
Max New York Life Insurance Company Ltd.

SBI Life Insurance has lunched three products Sanjeevan, Sukhjeevan and Young Sanjeevan and so far, it has sold more than 300 policies under its plans. Various insurance companies have tied up with banks to market their products, e.g. HDFC Standard Life has tied up with Indian bank and UCO Bank in the Eastern region. It has also entered into an MOU with Peerless Bank as the latter's branches will help a rural reach for insurance company. Proposed joint venture Dabur CJU Life Insurance where Dabur group holds 74% and UK-based CJU life's 26% stake would be started with an equity capital of Rs. 110 crore. CGNU group being UK's largest insurer and one of the world's sixty largest insurers with assets worth $ 300 Bn under its management and Dabur being India's leading FMCG Company, this venture may emerge as a leading player in insurance industry. Kotak Mahindra is likely to get approval for two more products, which include term insurance and equity linked policy in a bid to offer wider range of products.

In India, till now, only 20% of the insurable population is covered under insurance while the remaining population is yet to be insured. As the insurance sector has been opened up, the monopoly of government companies has broken and many new private players have entered into the insurance sector and thus the sector has become highly competitive, full of challenges. The insurance and the economic growth of the country mutually influence each other. As the economy grows, the standard of living of people also improves.

In fact, as the economy widens, the demand for insurance products emerges. A well developed insurance sector promotes economic growth by encouraging risk taking. The average annual rate of growth of the country in the first three decades after independence was 3.5%. In the nineties, the average annual rate of growth of income has been 5.8% per annum. Life expectancy has also increased from 32 years in fifties to 61 years now. As life expectancy increases, there will be a need to take care of long retired life. So, the Indian life insurance market alongwith general insurance market is full of potential. The only need is to frame suitable strategies to tap the whole market in more efficient and effective manner.

8

Concept of Asset-Liability Management for Ensuring Solvency of Insurers

INTRODUCTION

Traditionally and previously banks were concerned only with increasing the size of their balance sheets. They were focusing on few specific items of the balance sheet like deposits, credit to priority sector and reducing the size of NPAs—recovery of bad and doubtful loans and advances (Assets). After the introduction of prudential accounting norms, deregulation of interest rates, globalization and economic liberalization, Indian banks began facing serious problem of mismatch between their assets and liabilities due to volatility in the interest rates and foreign exchange rates. Emergence of new instruments, new players and new products at highly competitive rates in the market increased banks' risks. Now in a fairly deregulated environment, interest rates on all money market instruments are determined for most part, and often, by the market forces. All the banks are now allowed to determine own interest rates on domestic deposits and loans & advances over rupees 2 lakh.

The changes in interest rates affect the banks in two ways as under:

(1) Since assets (loans and advances) and liabilities (deposits and borrowings) are not realised simultaneously, the mismatch affects the interest income.
(2) It affects the market value of assets like treasury bills, commercial paper and certificate of deposits, etc.

Therefore, it is no longer the case that banks shall be asset-driven and primarily concerned to find resources to finance lending. Rather banks are moving progressively to the stage of not only adjusting liabilities in accordance with potential assets but also adjusting assets in accordance with potential liabilities.

MEANING OF ASSET-LIABILITY MANAGEMENT (ALM)

The various types of risks faced by the banks can be managed through the management process known as Asset-Liability Management (ALM). Asset-Liability Management refers to the policy of the banks with regard to mix of assets and liabilities. In the context of RBI guidelines to the banks, 'asset-liability' management can be defined as a continuous process of planning, organizing and controlling asset/ liability volume, maturities, yields and rates. In other words, asset-liability management can be defined as a function which involves planning, directing and controlling the flow, level, mix and rates on the bank assets and liabilities.

OBJECTIVES OF ASSET-LIABILITY MANAGEMENT (ALM)

An Effective Asset-liability management of banks should encompass:

(a) Review of interest-rate outlook.
(b) Fixation of interest, product pricing of both assets and liabilities.
(c) Review of credit-risk management and credit portfolio.
(d) Review of investment portfolio and risk management.
(e) Review of liquidity risk and management of liquidity risk.
(f) Review of policy of foreign exchange operations and Risk Management.

IMPLICATIONS FOR ASSET-LIABILITY MANAGEMENT (ALM)

The subject of assets (especially advances and investments) and liability (especially deposits and borrowings) management revolves around balance sheet. The ALM requires that assets and liabilities should be planned, organized and controlled so that profitability and liquidity are managed.

The analysis of balance sheet of a bank reveals that among the liabilities, a significant portion comes from deposits (savings, term deposits and current account deposits) and among these deposits, term deposits bear a fixed rate of interest for a specified period but carry a risk of pre-mature encashment. The savings bank deposits have no maturity period. Borrowings (from RBI and other banks) are also among liabilities which carry interest at market rate but repayment is generally known.

The analysis of assets side reveals that the most significant portion of advances is liked to prime lending rate (PLR) which is a floating rate. Once the PLR changes, the rate on the loans and advances would change instantly without any time lag. An overwhelming majority of the investment portfolio is in the form of fixed rate government and other securities.

BALANCE SHEET STRUCTURE

(A) Liabilities Side

(a) Deposits

Savings Fund Accounts and Current Accounts: The features of both the deposits are that there is no maturity date and the clients are free to deposit or withdraw any amount at any point of time.

Term Deposits: The term deposits may be in the form of cumulative term deposits, non-cumulative term deposits and recurring deposits. As regards liquidity, the client has the freedom to encash them at a pre-matured date if he needs money urgently. In case of recurring deposits, the installment amount may not be paid in time.

In case, interest rates increase, the customers can decide in their favour.

(b) Borrowing

Terms of Borrowings are clear as regards liquidity and interest rates.

(B) Assets Side

Investment: The investment may be for medium and long-term and there is little flexibility for reshuffling. Major portion of investments carries fixed rate of interest.

Advances: The repayment of advances by customers is no doubt pre-determined but repayment still depends upon host of factors. Some part of cash credit and overdraft may not be availed of by the borrowing units leading to uncertainty in liquidity management.

SCOPE OF ASSET-LIABILITY MANAGEMENT

Asset-liability management of a bank, earlier known as Treasury Management, is a part of overall risk management. Risk is defined as, "Risk is uncertainty as to the outcome of an event when two or more possibilities exist". The aim of asset-liability management is to manage risk exposures so that they are kept within the acceptable levels and at the same time help to generate income and maintain profitability. Efficient asset-liability management procedures should enable a bank to control and limit risks associated with maturity mismatching, Interest rate gaps and foreign exchange exposure and so on. ALM addresses the following risks:

Liquidity Risk; Interest Rate Risk; and Market Risk.

(1) Liquidity Risk

Liquidity Risk refers to the ability of a concern to meet its commitment when due and to undertake new transactions if profitable. Liquidity risk can emanate in any of the following situations:

(a) Conversion of contingent liabilities into fund-based commitment.
(b) Non-receipt of expected cash flows from recovery of loans.
(c) Increased availment of sanctioned limits.
(d) Disproportionate outflow of funds arising out of non-renewal/withdrawal of deposits.

Liquidity risk is categorised into two types:

(i) Trading Liquidity Risk, and (ii) Funding Liquidity Risk.

(i) **Trading Liquidity Risk:** Trading liquidity risk arises as a result of liquidity of securities in the trading portfolio of the bank. Liquidity and return are negatively correlated. So higher returns can be expected by accepting an illiquid investment in the portfolio and should be monitored on frequent basis. In reality, one of the important considerations for the inclusion of investment in the trading portfolio is on the basis of its liquidity status. As the trading portfolio is short-term in nature with regulator-constrained maximum holding period of 90 days, it is better to include only those securities which are not only liquid at the time of creation but are expected to be liquid over the holding period of portfolio.

(ii) **Funding Liquidity Risk:** Funding liquidity risk arises as a result of mismatch between the timing of the cash flow of assets and liabilities, funding liquidity risk that arises due to mismatch is the outcome of difference in balance sheet strategies followed by different institutions in the same industry. It is possible that a few banks may suffer from shortage of liquidity while others may have excess funding liquidity.

Measurement of Liquidity Risk

There are two approaches to measure liquidity risk at balance sheet level. These are:

(1) Liquidity Gap Analysis, and (2) Structural Balance Sheet Ratios.

(1) Liquidity Gap Analysis: The liquidity gap at a particular level of maturity is the difference between maturity of assets and maturing liabilities. When maturing liabilities exceed maturing assets, a negative gap is created and when maturing assets exceed maturing liabilities, a positive gap is created.

Reserve Bank of India, in its guidelines, has instructed the banks to classify maturing assets (cash inflows) and maturing liabilities (cash flows) in eight maturity periods (called the buckets). The cash flows from assets and liabilities include both principal and interest cash flows.

The liability gap analysis is illustrated through an example of "Liquidity Gap Statement" of PRS Bank:

Table 8.1: Liquidity Gap Statement of Angiras Goodwill Bank as on 25-06-2013

(*Rs. in crore*)

Maturity	*Assets*	*Liabilities*	*Gap*	*Cumulative Gap*
01 day-14 days	2,000	2,300	(300)	(300)
15 days-28 days	3,000	3,600	(600)	(900)
29 days-03 months	4,000	5,000	(1,000)	(1,900)
3 months-06 months	4,000	5,600	(1,600)	(3,500)
6 months-12 months	2,000	2,000	0	(3,500)
1 year-02 years	3,000	2,600	400	(3,100)
2 years-05 years	6,000	4,000	2,000	1,100
Over 5 years	2,000	3,100	(1,100)	0

It can be observed from the above statement that the liability maturing over the next three months from 25-06-2013 exceed maturing assets by Rs. 1900 crores (cumulative gap). The total maturing liabilities at Rs.10,900 crores (2300 + 3600 + 5000) over the first three months requires to be met by (a) fresh deposits, (b) renewal of deposits, and (c) borrowings from other banks and RBI. At the end, the liquidity gap will always be nil because assets always equal to liability plus equity.

Banks generally do not and can not maintain 'NIL' gap in all maturities. The objective of this liquidity gap analysis is to determine the tolerable gap. These gaps are also called mis-matches. The RBI desires that the gap in the maturity buckets of 1-14 days and 15-28 days should be limited to 20% of the maturing liabilities of cash outflows in the respective maturity buckets.

With the information available in the liquidity gap statement, the banks can evolve prudential limits for the gaps according to their risk taking capacities and as per guidelines/norms fixed by the RBI from time to time.

(2) **Structural Balance Sheet Ratios:** The liquidity position of the banks can be assessed through structural balance sheet ratios. Some of the ratios are discussed below:

Purchased Funds to Liquid Assets:

Purchased funds, for example, are call money borrowings including short-term refinance, etc. These funds should not constitute a significant portion of liquid assets. It is important and urgent to specify a tolerance limit for that purpose so that outflow of funds on account of purchased funds is controlled.

Core Deposits to Core Assets: Outstanding in loan books and the statutory reserves constituted core assets are considered for this ratio. The ratio of core deposits to core assets should be specified to maintain a stable liquid position.

Call Borrowing to Total Borrowing: This ratio reflects the dependence of a bank on call borrowings to honour its commitments. Call borrowings are generally costly.

Liquid Investment to Total Investments: Liquid investments are convertible into cash at any time. More the liquidity lesser the profits, so the banks are to trade-off between liquidity and profitability.

Liquid Assets to Total Assets: Extent of liquid assets available to meet outflows on account of deposits in normal/abnormal circumstances is shown by this ratio.

Liquid Assets to Total Assets: As banks deal in money, major part of money must be in the form of investment and liquid assets.

Liquidity Risk Management

A rational idea that emerges after liquidity analysis is liquidity risk management. The issues which are relevant in managing liquidity risks are:

To keep constant watch over the fact whether the liquidity-asset mis-match (surplus or deficit), under consideration, is within tolerable limits as per the policy of the management of the bank. If yes, it is OK. If not, what should be various measures or strategies to be employed to ensure that the imbalance is within the tolerance limit.

Financial experts suggest that even if liquidity mismatch is within the tolerance range, the management should adhere to strategies which maximize benefits in a given market environment. However, keeping in mind the tolerance limits to be strictly followed, the management must be proactive rather than passive. Among the numerous strategies available are: trading portfolio, refinance facilities, market borrowing, wholesale deposits, securitization, loan sales, etc. Every strategy has to be evaluated in terms of cost and the intended benefit before implementation for managing the A-L mismatch.

(2) Interest Rate Risk (IRR)

Interest affects all financial transactions. Banks' profits accrue from interest income more than non-interest income. The interest rate risk is the risk of decline of earnings owing to change in interest rates. The profitability of the bank is largely dependent on the interest spread (interest spread is the difference between interest earned and interest expended). A sizable chunk of banks' revenues and costs are indexed to interest rates. Since interest rates are unstable, so are the earrings.

The following kinds of risks will either individually or cumulatively result in interest rate risks:

Rate Level Risk: There is always a possibility of resetting interest rate levels either due to market forces or due to regulatory intervention. Suppose that RBI lowers Cash Reserve Ratio (CRR) by 2%, the result would be that the market would be flooded with excess liquidity which shall result in lowering interest rates.

Pre-mature Payment Risk: The decline in interest rates at times leads to pre-payment of loans. When interest rates are declining, customers who had taken loan at higher rates would like to substitute a cheaper debt or pre-pay the costly loan. The pre-paid cash in-flows will have to be re-deployed at a lower rate, which shall invariably affect profitability.

Basic Risk: It is quite possible to link liabilities and assets to two different bench-marks resulting in floating rate. Suppose that these two base rates do not move in tandem with each other, the net interest income either increases or decreases.

Real Interest Rate Risk: The level of inflation also plays a critical role in determining the real interest yield/cost.

Volatility Risk: The frequent changes in interest rates affect the business volume as well as pricing of the products. The effect or fluctuation in the short term will have a greater impact on cash flows since the adjustment period is very short.

Measurement of Interest Rate Risk

There are three approaches available to measure interest rate risk; these are:

Earnings Approach; Interest Rate Gap Analysis; and Economic Value Approach

Earning Approach to IRR: The earning approache which is an important top line performance indicator is expressed either as net interest income or net interest margin.

(a) Net Interest Income (NII): Net interest income is the excess of interest income over interest expenses. Mathematically, NII is expressed as:

$$\text{NII} = \text{Interest Income} - \text{Interest Expenses}$$

Interest income includes interest income from advances plus interest income from investment.

Note: Interest for the purpose of interest income also includes dividend received from equity portfolio of mutual fund investments, etc.

Interest Expenses include: Interest paid on deposits plus interest paid on borrowings.

(b) Net Interest Margin (NIM): When NII is expressed in percentage as the basis of total assets or earning assets, it is called as NIM. Mathematically, the formula is expressed as:

$$\text{Net Interest Margin} = \frac{\text{NII}}{\text{Earning Assets}} \times 100$$

$$\text{Or} = \frac{\text{NII}}{\text{Total Assets}} \times 100$$

Interest Rate Gap Analysis: Interest rate gap analysis technique is similar to liquidity gap analysis technique. In interest rate gap analysis, the assets and liabilities are placed in the buckets on the basis of timing of change or expected change in interest rates on the assets and liabilities and not on the basis of cash inflows and outflows as in the case of statement of liquidity gap. The RBI has prescribed a statement of interest rate sensitivity for regulatory reporting.

Table 8.2: Statement of Interest Rate Gap Analysis

(Amount Rs. in Crore)

Time Buckets	*Total Liabilities (A)*	*Total Assets (B)*	*Net Gap (C)*	*Cumulative Gap (D)*
1 day-28 days	4,198	4,324	126	126
29 days-3 months	5,186	2,960	(2,226)	(2,100)
3 months-6 months	21,860	21,302	(558)	(2,658)
6 months-12 months	5,460	2,850	(2,660)	(5,268)
1 year-3 years	13,202	5,972	(7,230)	(12,496)
3 years-5 years	7,584	7,786	202	12,296
Over 5 years	2,344	24,756	22,412	10,116
Non-sensitive	20,684	11,210	(9,474)	642
Total	80,518	81,160	642	-

Total liabilities and total assets, i.e. columns A and B refer to rate sensitive assets and rate sensitive liabilities.

All the assets and all the liabilities are categorized into rate sensitive and rate non-sensitivity groups. Equity capital on the liabilities side and cash on the assets side are non-sensitive. Any change in interest rates would not have any impact on cash and equity. Equity in itself is not sensitive to interest rate changes; it is sensitive through other liabilities and assets.

The assets and liabilities are rate sensitive if:

- The cash flows from them are on their maturity.
- The cash flows represent an interim, or part principal repayment.
- The interest rate applicable to the outstanding principal, changes contractually during the period under consideration.

The outstanding principal can be re-priced when some base rate or index changes.

Interest is payable on liabilities and interest is receivable on assets. If rate sensitive liabilities exceed assets, this will have negative effect on net interest income and *vice-versa.*

Economic Value Approach: The economic value approach takes into consideration the long-term impact of interest rate changes by covering the entire life of all rate sensitive assets and liabilities. Under this approach, the effect of interest rate changes are studied on an important variable called "Economic Value of Equity". Mathematically, Economic Value of Equity is:

Economic Value of Equity = Economic Value of Assets – Economic Value of Liabilities

It may be understood that the essence of the equation reflects the residuary nature of the claims of the equity shareholders who are the ultimate owners. The term economic value is preferred to the market value as number of assets and liabilities in the balance sheet of a bank do not have a ready market. Economic value of equity approach also removes the problem of different bases for valuation of items in the balance sheet. The balance sheet of a bank recognizes the changes in the value of few items while other assets and liabilities are reflected at historical cost despite the change in value. This approach is also superior to earnings approach. A higher accounting profit does not necessarily mean better performance unless the degree of risk attached to such profits is taken into considerations.

The economic value of equity approach is based on the present value of money which is the basic foundation of the subject of finance. The value of assets and liabilities is inversely related to the interest rates.

The interest rates receivable on assets and payable on liabilities influence the value as:

(a) When the rates of interest on assets and liabilities go up from the present level, the value of the assets would fall and *vice-versa.*
(b) When the value of assets increases or value of liabilities decreases, the economic value of equity increases and *vice-versa.*

(3) Market Risk

The Basel Committee on Banking Supervision (BCBS) in its publication "amendment to Capital Accord to incorporate Market Risks", published in January 1996, has defined market risk as, "The risk of losses in and off balance sheet position arising from movements in market price".

Market risks can arise out of the following:

Interest rate risk; Equity position risk; Foreign exchange risk; and Commodities risk.

Approaches to Measure Market Risk

Measures for market risk are broadly categorized as under:

(1) Factor Based Measures

(2) Volatility Based Measures

Factor Sensitivity Measures: Factor sensitivity measures assess the impact of change in the major factors on the market value of the portfolio. The most important factor sensitivity measure is the modified duration. Modified duration is the direct measure of sensitivity in value of a security or a portfolio of bonds for a change in interest rates. In duration method, the duration of an asset or liability is calculated as the weighted average maturity of the resultant cash flows, the weights being the present value of cash flows. Duration is less than the maturity of the coupon bond. Greater the duration of duration gap, higher is the interest rate risk exposure of the assets and liabilities.

One of the significant applications of the factor sensitivity measures is to use them for setting limits.

Example: A bank may set the maximum modified duration of its bond portfolio as (say) 8. This means that the price sensitivity that the bank is willing to accept in case of the bond portfolio is maximum 8% of the value of the portfolio for 1% change in interest rates. A loss more than 8% will not be tolerated by the bank. This limit is a caution to the trading manager in order to discourage them to earn higher commission (being percentage of trading profits) due to higher risk. There is higher risk if trading manager goes against the situation; it may lead to closure of banks as it has happened in case of Barings Bank of the U.K.

Volatility-based Measures: Volatility-based measure, popularly known as Value At Risk (VAR), has gained a lot of prominence. The most favourbale advantage of value at risk is its uniformity in measuring trading risk across various positions such as interest rates, equity, commodity and currency which is the weakest thing as far as factor sensitivity measures are concerned. As a result of uniformity of measurement, it is possible to aggregate risk across completely different positions (compare and contrast) among various positions to assess the relative riskiness.

The following examples will make the VAR clearer:

Market value of Security = Rs. 400 crores
Confidence Level used for VAR computation = 98%
Value at Risk = 8 crores
Holding period used for VAR competitions = 2 days
VAR = Rs. 8 crores

The example states that out of 400 crores of security Rs. 8 crores is value at risk. The maximum loss that bank will suffer on 2 trading days would not exceed Rs. 8 crores on 98% of the trading days (confidence level used for VAR computation is 98%). Only on 2% of the days, the loss would exceed the VAR of Rs. 8 crores. If we assume 200 trading days in a period, the above interpretation means that 196 trading days out of 200 days would have losses less than Rs. 8 crore. Only on 4 days out of 200 days, the losses would exceed the VAR computed.

Methods for Computation of Value At Risk (VAR): There are three main methods for the computation of VAR:

Historical Simulation: Historical simulation which is based on historical/past data is non-parametric in nature. The main assumption of this method is that the past trends and volatilities in price would repeat in future also.

Variance Co-variance Value at Risk (VAR): This is widely accepted and practised method at present. This method was popularized by the investment bank, J.P. Morgan, in the 90s. This method is parametric as it assumes that the prices follow normal distribution. This method is based on correlation, standard deviation, arithmetic mean and co-variance, etc. for the estimation of VAR.

Monte Carlo Value at Risk (VAR): The term Monte Carlo is a technique of research operation. This approach is not based on the assumption of distribution of properties or assets prices but involves empirical estimation and the statistical distribution from the prices which is then applied to simulate the prices leading to the estimation of VAR.

9

Concept of Regulation in Insurance

Human activities are many and varied; human behaviour is generally volatile. According to Thomas Hobbes of yester-years England, a great philosopher, "Man is basically selfish; his life is brutish and short. His life needs to be subject to oppressive control". Well, let us not rake up controversy but seeing various instances of deviant behaviour by many people round the globe, there is some truth in what Thomas Hobbes has said.

On the basis of the recommendations of Malhotra Committee, the Government of India constituted through resolution an Interim Insurance Regulatory Authority on 23rd January 1996. The relative Bill was introduced in the Parliament in 1996. The Bill was withdrawn and re-written as Insurance Regulatory and Development Authority Bill, 1999 and introduced again in 1999 alongwith three schedules containing amendments to the Insurance Act, 1938, Life Insurance Corporation of India Act, 1956 and General Insurance Corporation Act, 1972 and was passed as 'Insurance Regulatory and Development Act, 1999'.

Preamble of IRDA Act: Preamble of IRDA Act, 1999 reads, "an Act to provide for the establishment of an authority to protect the interest of holders of insurance policies, to regulate, promote and ensure orderly growth of the insurance industry and for matters connected therewith and incidental thereto".

The Act was enacted and it contains the following provisions:

STATEMENT OF OBJECTS AND REASONS

The insurance industry requires a high degree of regulation. The Insurance Act, 1938 provides for the institutions of the Controller of Insurance to act as a strong and powerful supervisory and regulatory authority with power to direct, advise, caution, prohibit, investigate, inspect, prosecute, search seize, fine, amalgamate, authorize, register and liquidate insurance companies. However, after nationalization of the life insurance industry in 1956 and the general insurance industry in 1972, the role of the Controller of Insurance diminished in its significance over a period of time.

In April 1993, the Government of India set-up a high-powered committee under the chairmanship of Sh. R.N. Malhotra, former Governor, Reserve Bank of India (RBI) to examine the structure of the insurance industry and recommend changes to make it more efficient and competitive, keeping in view the structural changes in other parts of the financial system of the economy. The Committee which submitted its report on the 7th January 1994 felt that the insurance regulatory apparatus should be activated even in the present set-up of nationalized insurance sector and recommended, *inter-alia*, the establishment of a strong and effective Insurance Regulatory Authority in the form of a statutory autonomous board on the lines of the Securities and Exchange Board of India (SEBI).

The recommendations of the committee were discussed at different forums including the Consultative Committee of the Parliament attached to the Ministry of Finance, Management of Life Insurance Corporation, the General Insurance Corporation and its subsidiary companies, trade unions, chambers of commerce and consumer interest groups. The recommendation to set-up an autonomous insurance regulatory authority found wide support. In view of the general support received, the Government of India decided to bring in a legislation to establish an independent regulatory authority for the insurance industry. Since enacting legislation for creating the insurance regulatory authority was to take time, the then government constituted through a Government resolution an Interim Insurance Regulatory Authority pending the enactment of a comprehensive legislation. The Chairman, Insurance Regulatory Authority was notified as Controller of Insurance under the Insurance Act, 1938. The said interim insurance regulatory authority at present is discharging certain functions and exercising powers of the Controller.

In pursuance of the Budget Speech in July 1996, the then Government introduced on the 20th December, 1996, the Insurance Regulatory Authority Bill, 1996 for establishment of an authority to protect the interest of holders of insurance policies and to regulate, promote and ensure orderly growth of the insurance industry and for matters connected therewith or incidental thereto. The Bill was referred to the department's Standing Committee of the Ministry of Finance. The Committee submitted its report on 9th May, 1997. However, the said bill incorporating therein the recommendations of the said Standing Committee was taken for consideration but could not be passed and the bill was withdrawn by the then government.

In order to provide better insurance coverage to our citizens and also to augment the flow of long-term resources for financing infrastructure, in the budget speech, 1998, the policy of the government was announced to open up the insurance sector and also to establish a Statutory Regulatory Authority. Accordingly, the Insurance Regulatory Authority Bill, 1998 was introduced in the Lok Sabha on the 15th December, 1998 providing for setting up a statutory insurance regulatory authority and containing three schedules incorporating amendments to the Insurance Act, 1938, the Life Insurance Corporation Act, 1956 and the General Insurance Business (Nationalization) Act, 1972. The Bill was referred to the Standing Committee on Finance on the 4th January, 1999 for examination and report. The Standing Committee, while recommending the Bill, suggested some amendments. These amendments were accepted by the government and amendments to the Bill were circulated on the 18th March, 1999. However, the Bill could not be taken up for consideration consequent on the dissolution of the Lok Sabha.

It was subsequently proposed to re-introduce a fresh Bill by incorporating the provisions of the Insurance Regulatory Authority Bill, 1998 and the amendments suggested by the Standing Committee on Finance. The Bill was titled Insurance Regulatory and Development Authority Bill on the basis of the recommendation of the Standing Committee. In the main text of the Bill, provisions were incorporated to give a statutory character to the interim Insurance Regulatory Authority and the three Schedules containing amendments to the Insurance Act, 1938, amendments to the Life Insurance Corporation Act, 1956 and the General Insurance Business (Nationalization) Act, 1972.

The proposed Authority shall be body corporate, having perpetual succession and a common seal with power to acquire, hold and dispose of property and to contract. It consists of a chairperson and other members not exceeding nine in number, of whom not more than five shall serve full time, to be appointed by the Central Government from amongst persons of ability, integrity and standing who have knowledge or experience of life insurance, general insurance, actuarial science, finance, economics, law, accountancy, administration or any other discipline which, in the opinion of the Central Government, shall be useful to the Authority. The chairperson and other whole time members shall hold office for a term of 5 years or until the age of 65 years in the case of chairperson and 62 years in the case of other whole time members whichever is earlier and they shall be eligible for reappointment subject to age consideration. A part time member shall hold office for a term not exceeding 5 years.

MAIN PROVISIONS OF IRDA ACT

Section 14 of IRDA Act lays the duties, powers and functions of the authority. Powers and functions of the authority shall include the following:

(a) Issue to the applicant a certificate of registration, renew, to review, modify, withdraw, suspend or cancel such registration.
(b) To protect the interest of policyholders in all matters concerning nomination of policy, assigning of policy, surrender value of policy, insurable interest, settlement of insurance claim, other terms and conditions of contract of insurance.
(c) Specifying requisite qualification and practical training for insurance intermediary and agents.
(d) Specifying code of conduct for surveyors and loss assessors.
(e) Promoting efficiency in the conduct of insurance business.
(f) Promoting and regulating professional regulation connected with the insurance and re-insurance business.
(g) Specifying the form and manner in which books of accounts will be maintained and statement of accounts rendered by insurer and insurance intermediaries.
(h) Adjudication of disputes between insurers and intermediaries.

(i) Specifying the percentage of life insurance and general insurance business to be undertaken by the insurers in rural or social sectors, etc.
(j) Section 25 provides that Insurance Advisory Committee will be constituted and shall consist of not more than 25 members.
(k) Section 26 provides that authority may, in consultation with Insurance Advisory Committee, make regulations consistent with this Act and the rules made hereunder to carry out the purpose of this Act.
(l) Section 29 seeks amendment in certain provision of Insurance Act, 1938 in the manner as set out in the First Schedule. The amendments to the Insurance Act are consequential in order to empower IRDA to effectively regulate, promote, and ensure orderly growth of the insurance industry.
(m) Sections 30 and 31 seek to amend LIC Act, 1956 and GIC Act, 1972.

CONTENTS OF THE ACT

Short title, extent and commencement as under:

This act may be called the Insurance Regulatory and Development Authority Act, 1999. It extends to the whole of India. It shall come into force on such date as the Central Government may, by notification in the official gazette, appoint. Provided that different dates as may be appointed for different provisions of this Act and any reference in any such provision to the commencement of this Act shall be constructed as a reference to the coming in force of that provision.

Definitions of various Terms used in the Act

In this act, unless the context otherwise requires, Appointee day shall mean the date on which the authority is established under sub-section (1) of Section 3. Authority will mean the Insurance Regulatory and Development Authority established under sub-division (1) of Section 3. Chairperson will mean the Chairperson of the Authority. Fund will mean the Insurance Regulatory and Development Authority Fund constituted under sub-section (1) of Section 16. Interim Insurance Regulatory Authority will mean the Insurance Regulatory Authority set-up by the Central Government through resolution No. 17(2)/94-Ins-V, dated the 23rd January, 1996. Intermediary will mean insurance intermediary and those will include insurance brokers, reinsurance brokers, and insurance consultants, surveyors and loss assessors. Member will mean a whole-time or a part-time member of the Authority and includes the Chairperson. Notification will mean a notification published in the official gazette of the Government of India, Prescribed will mean prescribed by rules made under this Act, and Regulations mean the regulations made by the Authority.

Words and expressions used and not defined in this act but define in the Insurance Act, 1938 or the Life Insurance Corporation Act, 1956 or the General Insurance Business (Nationalization) Act, 1972 shall have the same meaning, respectively, as assigned to them in those Acts.

BRIEF PROFILE OF IRDA ACT AND ITS FUNCTIONING

(a) Establishment and Incorporation of Insurance Authority: With effect from such date as the Central Govermet may, by notification, appoint, there shall be established, for the purpose of this act, an authority to be called 'The Insurance Regulatory and Development Authority'. The Authority shall be a body corporate by the name as foresaid having perpetual succession and a common seal with power, subject to the provisions of this Act, to acquire, hold and dispose of property, both movable and immovable, and to contract and shall, by the said name, sue or be sued. The head office of the authority shall be at such place as the Central Government may decide from time to time. The authority may establish offices at other places in India.

(b) Composition of Authority: The authority shall consist of the following members, namely, Chairperson, not more than five whole-time members, and not more than four part-time members, to be appointed by the Central Government from amongst persons of ability, integrity and standing who have knowledge or experience in life insurance, general insurance, actuarial science, finance, economics, law, accountancy, administration or any discipline which would, in the opinion of the Central Government, be useful to the authority.

Provided that the Central Government shall, while appointing the Chairperson and the whole-time members, ensure that at least the persons having knowledge or experience in life insurance, general insurance, general business or actuarial science, are appointed.

(c) Tenure of Office of Chairperson and other Members: In IRDA, the chairperson and every other whole-time member shall hold office for a term of five years from the date on which he enters upon his office and shall be eligible for re-appointment provided that no person shall hold office as a Chairperson after he has attained the age of sixty-five (65 years). A part-time member shall hold office for a term not exceeding five years from the date on which he enters upon his office. Notwithstanding anything contained in sub-section (1) or sub-section (2), a member may relinquish his office by giving in writing to the Central Government a notice of not less than three months, or be removed from his office in accordance with the provisions of relevant section.

(d) Removal of a Member from Office: In IRDA—(1) The Central Government may remove any member who is, or at any time has been, adjusted as an insolvent or has become physically or mentally incapable of acting as a member, or has been convicted of any offence which, in the opinion of the central government, involves moral turpitude, or has acquired such financial or other interest as is likely to affect particularly his functions as a member, or has so abused his position as to render his continuation in office detrimental to the public interest.

(2) No such member shall be removed under clause (d) or clause (c) of section (1) unless he has been given a reasonable opportunity of being heard in the matter.

(e) Salary and Allowances of Chairperson and Members: The salary and allowances payable to and other terms and conditions of service, of the members other than part-time members, shall be such as may be prescribed. The part-time members shall receive such allowances as may be prescribed. The salary, allowances, and other conditions of service of a member shall not be varied to his disadvantage after appointment.

(f) Restriction/Bar on Future Employment of Members: The Chairperson and the whole-time members shall not, for a period of two years from the date on which they cease to hold office as such, except with the previous approval of the central government, accept any employment either under the Central Government or under any State Government, or any appointment in any company in the insurance sector.

(g) Administrative Powers of Chairperson: The Chairperson shall have the powers of general superintendence and direction in respect of all administrative matters of the authority.

(h) Meeting of Authority: In IRDA—The Authority shall meet at such times and place and shall observe such rules and procedures in regard to transactions of business at its meeting (including quorum at such meetings) as may be determined by the regulations. The Chairperson, or if for any reason, he is unable to attend a meeting of the authority, any other member chosen by the members present from amongst themselves at the meeting, shall preside at the meting.

All questions which come up before any meeting of the authority shall be decided by a majority of votes by the members present and voting, and in the absence of unanimity emerging, the person presiding shall have a second or casting vote.

The authority may make regulations for the transaction of business at its meetings.

(i) Vacancies etc. not to Invalidate Proceeding of Authority: No act or proceeding of the authority shall be invalid merely by reason of:

> Any vacancy in, or any defect in the constitution of the authority, or any defect in the appointment of a person acting as a member of the authority, or any irregularity in the procedure of authority not affecting the merits of the case.

(j) Officers and Employees of Authority: In IRDA—The authority may appoint officers and such other employees as it considers necessary for the efficient discharge of its functions under this Act.

The terms and other conditions of service of officers and other employees of the authority appointed under sub section (1) shall be governed by regulations made under this Act.

(k) Transfer of Assets, Liabilities etc. of Interim Insurance Regulatory Authority: On the appointed day:

> All the assets and liabilities of interim insurance regulatory authority shall stand transferred to, and vested in the authority under this Act.

Explanation: The assets of the interim insurance regulatory authority shall be deemed to include all rights and powers, and all properties, whether movable or immovable, including, in particular, cash balance, deposits, all other interests and rights in or arising out of such properties as may be in the possession of the interim insurance regulatory authority and all books of accounts and other documents relating to the same, and liabilities shall be deemed to include all debts, liabilities and obligations of whatever kind,

(i) Without prejudice to the provision of clause (a), all debts, obligations and liabilities incurred, all contracts entered into or engaged to be done by, with or for the Authority,

(ii) All sums of money due to the interim insurance regulatory authority immediately before that day shall be deemed to be due to the authority, and

(iii) All suits and other legal proceedings instituted or which could have been instituted by or against the interim insurance regulatory authority immediately before that day may be continued or may be instituted by or against the authority.

(I) **Duties, Powers and Functions of Authority in IRDA:** IRDA provides as under:

(a) Subject to the provisions of this act and any other law for the time being in force, the Authority shall have the duty to regulate, promote and ensure orderly growth of the insurance business and re-insurance business.

(b) Without prejudice to the generality of the provision contained in sub-section (i), the powers and functions of the authority shall include: issue to the applicant a certificate of registration, renewal as well as modify, withdraw, suspend or cancel such registration; protection of the interests of the policyholders in matters concerning assigning of policy nomination by policyholders, insurable interest, settlement of insurance claim, surrender value of policy and other terms and conditions of contract of insurance; specifying requisite qualifications, code of conduct and practical training for intermediary or insurance intermediaries and agents; specifying the code of conduct for surveyors and loss assessors; promoting efficiency in the conduct of insurance business; promoting and regulating professional organizations connected with the insurance and re-insurance business; prompting and regulating professional organizations connected with the insurance and re-insurance business; levying fees and other charges for carrying out the purposes of this act; calling for information from, undertaking inspection of and conducting enquiries and investigations including audit of the insurers, intermediaries, insurance intermediaries and other organizations connected with the insurance business; control and regulation of the rates, advantages, terms and conditions that may be offered by insurers in respect of general insurance business not so controlled and regulated by the Tariff Advisory Committee under Section 44(u) of the Insurance Act, 1938 (4 of 1938). Other functions are as under:

> Specifying the form and manner in which books of account shall be maintained and insurers and other insurance intermediaries shall render statement of accounts; regulating investment of funds by insurance companies; enforcing regulation regarding maintenance of margin of solvency; adjudicating upon disputes between insurers and intermediaries or insurance intermediaries; supervising the functioning of the Tariff Advisory Committee; specifying the percentage of premium income of the insurer to finance scheme for promoting and regulating professional organizations referred to in clause (vi); specifying the percentage of life insurance business to be undertakes by the insurer in the rural or social sector, and exercising such other power as may be prescribed.

(i) **Grants by Central Government:** The Central Government may, after due appropriation made by parliament by law in this behalf, make to the authority grants of such sums of money, as the Government may think fit, for being utilized for the purpose of this act.

(i) *Constitution of Funds*—(1) There shall be constituted a fund to be called "The

Insurance Regulatory and Development Authority Fund" and there shall be credited thereto:

All government grants, fees and charges received by the authority; all such grants or moneys received by the authority from such other sources as may be decided upon by the central government; the percentage of prescribed premium income received from the insurers.

(2) The Fund shall be applied for meeting—The salaries, allowances and other remuneration payable to the members, officers and other employees of the authority, and the other expenses of the authority in connection with the discharge of its functions and for the purpose of this act.

(ii) *Accounts and Audit*—(1) The authority shall maintain proper accounts and other relevant records and prepare an annual statement of accounts in such form as may be prescribed by the Central Government in consultation with the Comptroller and Auditor General of India (CAG).

(2) The accounts of the Authority shall be audited by the Comptroller an Auditor General of India at such intervals as maybe specified by him and any expenditure incurred in connection with such audit shall be payable by the Authority to the Comptroller and Audit General.

(3) The Comptroller and Auditor General of India and any other person appointed by him in connection with such audit as the Comptroller and Auditor General generally has in connection with the audit of the government accounts and, in particular, shall have the right to demand the production of books of accounts, connected vouchers and other documents and papers and to inspect any of the offices of the authority.

(4) The accounts of the authority as certified by the Comptroller and Auditor General of India or any other person appointed by him in this behalf together with the audit report thereof shall be forwarded annually to the Central Government and that government shall cause the same to be laid before both houses of Parliament.

(m) Power of Central Government to Issue Directions: The Central Government is empowered to take action without prejudice to the foregoing provisions of this Act, the authority shall in exercise of its powers or the performance of its functions under this Act, be bound by such directions on questions of policy, other than those relating to technical and administrative matters, as the Central Government may give in writing to it from time to time.

Provided that the authority shall, as far a practicable, be given an opportunity to express its views before any direction is given under this sub-section. In this regard, the decision of the Central Government as to whether a question is one of policy or not, shall be final.

(n) Power of Central Government to Supersede Authority: (1) If at any time, the Central Government is of the opinion:

That, on account of circumstances beyond the control of the authority, it is unable to discharge the functions or perform the duties imposed on it by or under the provisions of this act, or that the authority has persistently defaulted in complying with any direction given by the Central Government under this Act or in the discharge of the functions of performance of the duties imposed on it by or under the provision of this act, and as a result of such default, the financial position of the authority or the administration of the authority has suffered, or that circumstances exists which render it necessary in the public interest to do so, the Central Government may, by notification and for reasons to be specified therein, supersede the Authority for such period, not exceeding six months, as may be specified in the notification and appoint a person to be the Controller of Insurance under section 2B of the Insurance Act, 1938 (4) of (1938), if not already done.

Provided that before issuing any such notification, the Central Government shall give a reasonable opportunity to the authority to make representations, if any, to the Central Government.

(2) Upon the publication of a notification under sub-section (1) superseding the authority:

The Chairperson and other members shall, as from the date of supersession, vacate their offices as such; all the powers, functions and duties which may by or under the provisions of this act, be exercised or discharged by or on behalf of the authority shall, until the authority is reconstituted under sub-section (3), be exercised and discharged by the Controller of Insurance, and all properties owned or controlled by the Authority shall, until the Authority is reconstituted under subsection (3), vest in the Central Government.

(3) On or before the expiration of the period of suppression specified in the notification issued under Sub-section (1), the Central Government shall reconstitute the Authority by a fresh appointment of its Chairperson and other members and in such a case, any person who had vacated his office under clause (a) of sub-section (2) shall not be deemed to be disqualified for reappointment.

(4) The Central Government shall cause a copy of the notification issued under sub-section (1) and a full report on the action taken, to be laid before each house of Parliament at the earliest.

(o) **Furnishing of Returns, etc. to the Central Government:** The authority shall furnish to the Central Government at such time and in such form and manner as may be prescribed, or as the Central Government may direct to furnish such returns, statements and other particulars in regard to any proposed or existing programme for the promotion and development of the insurance business during the previous financial year.

Copies of the reports received under sub-section (2) shall be laid, as soon as may be after they are received, before each House of Parliament.

(p) **Chairperson, Members, Officers and other Employees of Authority to be Public Servants:** The Chairperson, members, officers and other employees of the Authority shall be deemed, when acting or purporting to act in pursuance of any of the provision of this act, to be public servants within the meaning of section 21 of the Indian Penal Code (45) of 1860).

(q) **Protection of Action taken in Good Faith:** No suit, prosecution or other legal proceedings shall lie against the Central Government or any officer of the Central Government or any member, officer or other employee of the Authority for anything, which is done in good faith or intended to be done under this Act or the rules or regulations made thereunder:

Provided that nothing in this Act shall exempt any person from any suit or other proceedings, which might, apart from this Act, be brought against him/her.

(r) **Delegation of Powers:** The Authority may, by general or special order in writing, delegate to the Chairperson or any other member or officer of the authority subject to such condition, if any, as may be specified in the order, such of its powers and functions under this Act as it may deem necessary.

The Authority may, by a general or special order in writing, also form Committees of the members and delegate to them the powers and functions of the authority as may be specified by the regulations.

(s) **Power to make Rules:** The Central Government may, by notification, make rules for carrying out the provision to this Act.

In particular, and without prejudice to the geniality of the foregoing power, such regulations may provide for all or any of the following matters, namely:

The salary and allowances payable to and other terms and conditions of service of the members, other than part-time numbers, under sub-section (1) of Section (7);

The allowances to be paid to the part-time members under sub-section (2) of Section 7; such other powers that may be exercised by the Authority under clause (XVII) of sub-section (2) of Section 14;

The form of annual statement of accounts to be maintained by the Authority under sub-section (1) of Section 17;

The form and the manner in which and the time within which returns and statements and particulars are to be furnished to the Central Government under sub-section (1) of Section 20.

The matters under sub-section (5) of Section 25 on which the insurance Advisory Committee shall advise the authority, and

Any other matter which is required to be or may be, prescribed, or in respect of which provision is to be or may be made by rules.

(t) **Establishment of Insurance Advisory Committee:** The Authority may, by notification, establish with effect from such date as it may specify in such notification, a committee to be known as the insurance advisory committee.

The insurance advisory committee shall consist of not more than twenty-five members excusing *ex-officio* members to represent the interest of commerce, intermediaries, organizations engaged in safety and loss prevention, research bodies and employee's association in the insurance sector.

The chairperson and the member of the Authority shall be the *ex-officio* chairperson and *ex-officio*, members of the insurance advisory committee.

The object of the insurance advisor committee shall be to advise the authority on matters relating to the making of the regulations under Section 26.

Without prejudice to the provisions of sub-section (4) the insurance advisory committee may advise the authority on such other matters as may be prescribed.

(u) **Power to make Regulations:** The Authority may, in consultation with the Insurance Advisory Committee, by notification, make regulations consistent with this Act and the rules made thereunder to carry out the purposes of this Act.

In particular, and without prejudice to the generality of the foregoing power, such regulations may provide for all or any of the following matters, namely:

The time and places of meetings of the Authority and the procedure to be followed at such meetings including the quorum necessary for the transaction of business under sub-section (1) of section 10;

The transaction of business at its meeting under sub-section (4) of section 10;

The terms and other conditions of service of officers and other employees of the Authority under sub-section (2) of Section 12;

The powers and functions which may be delegated to Committees of the members under sub-section (2) of Section 23, and

Any other matter, which is required to be, or may be, specified by regulations or in respect of which provision is to be or may be made, by regulations, would be handled.

(v) **Rules and Regulations to be laid before Parliament:** Every rule and regulation made under the Act shall be laid as soon as may be after it is made, before each House of Parliament, while it is in session, for a total period of thirty (30) days which may be comprised in one session or in two or more successive sessions, and if, before the expiry of the session immediately falling the session or the successive session aforesaid, both Houses agree in making any modification in the rule or regulation or both Houses agree that the rule or regulation should not be made, the rule or regulation shall thereafter have effect only in such modified from or be of no effect, as the case may be. However, any such modification or annulment shall be without prejudice to be valid if anything previously done under that rule or regulation.

(w) **Application of Other Laws not Barred:** The provisions of this Act shall be in addition to, and not in derogation of the provision of any other law for the time being in force.

(x) **Power to Remove Difficulties:** If any difficulty arises in giving effect to the provisions of this Act, the Central Government may, by order published in the Official Gazette, make such provisions not inconsistent with the provisions of this Act as may appear to be necessary for removing the difficulty:

Provided that no order shall be made under this Section after the expiry of two years from the appointed day.

Every order made under this section shall be laid, as soon as may be, after it is made, before each house of Parliament.

SUMMARY

Insurance Regulatory and Development Authority (IRDA) has come to stay for the smooth management and control of insurance business in India. The performance of IRDA is being debated and appreciated both within and outside the nation. So far, IRDA has been trying very hard to streamline the business procedures in insurance section with an utmost caution on the quality of service by both new and old players in the field.

The emergence of IRDA has been widely appreciated by the insurance experts, professionals, and insurance business players. However, the success of IRDA may be tested in the long-term when the insurance policies sold by the private business players get matured.

10

Concept of Group Insurance

INTRODUCTION

Group insurance is a plan of insurance, which provides cover to a large number of individual sunder a single policy called the 'master policy". The individuals covered under the master policy are not parties to the contract. The contrast will be between the insurers and a body that represents the group of individuals covered. This body may be the employer who is interested in obtaining benefits for his employees, through insurance. The body may be an association of individuals through whom the collective interests of the individuals are safeguarded, like a trade or professional association. A bank or financier can make arrangements through a group policy to protect his interests against default securing because of the death of the debtors.

In India, the development of group insurance has taken place since the early 1960s, before that, the group insurance business was very little. Originally, group insurance was confined to employer employee groups only. Since then the scheme has been extended to cover different groups, provided they are identifiable by homogenous common attributes, like professions, membership of a cooperative society, etc. the number of person covered by group insurance policies is increasing at a faster rate than the individual policies. New insurers find that they can reach larger number of people easier through group insurance.

Group insurance schemes are used by the Government, as instruments of social welfare. Social security is a concern of Governments in all countries. But the dimensions of social security vary considerably. In some advanced countries, the entire living expenses of elderly persons are borne by the state as a social measure. In some countries, medical care is free. In some countries, benefits paid by the State during unemployment are more than the salaries of the employed. Social welfare measures are generally administered by the Governments out of funds generated through levies and taxations.

The costs of administering these schemes have been increasing over the years and

Government have found it expedient to use insurance companies to pursue these objectives. Insurers are seen as the natural instruments to take over these functions, because life insurance business has a powerful social dimension.

In India, the operations relating to social welfare are comparatively at an elementary level. The group insurance schemes of the LIC provide insurance cover of small amounts like Rs. 5000 or so to the poorer, sections of society like landless agricultural labourers, handloom workers, rickshaw pullers village artisans, etc.

As stated earlier, group insurance is a plan of insurance, which provides cover to a large number of individuals under a single policy called the "master policy". The issuance contract is with the body that represents the individuals, the employer or the association. Because the contract is with the body, that body is the policyholder. The individuals are the beneficiary, the amount and terms of insurance are negotiated by the policyholder and not by the individual beneficiaries. The benefits will be determined on bases that apply uniformly to all the individuals.

The premium will be paid to the insurer by the policyholder, who may, or may not, collect the same from the individuals concerned, if the individuals contribute to the premium, that maybe either full or partial. In many employer schemes, the entire premium is paid by the employer. Sometimes, employees are made to contribute part of the cost. If the premium is collected from the individuals concerned by an employer, the premium may be deducted from their salaries. That does not make this is policy under the salary savings schemes, because of two basic differences. One is that the ownership of the policy is that the employer and not the employee. Secondly, the extent of over and the terms are determined by the employers and to by the individual.

As many persons are covered under one single contrast, the administrative costs are low. Because the coverage is not at the choice of the individual concerned, the chance of an adverse selection is low, therefore, the rules of medical examination are more liberal in the case of group insurance policies.

ESSENTIAL FEATURES OF GROUP INSURANCE SCHEMES

The most important requirements is that the group must not have been formed for he proper of taking advantage of this scheme. The group must have some other bonding. Entry into or exit from the group must be for reason other than the availability of cover under the scheme. Also, there must a minimum number of members in the group. Twenty-five would be consider adequate. In many cases, the members would be in hundred's.

The individual beneficiary will not choose the amount of insurance cover. The amount will be determined on criteria, which are applied uniformly to all the members of the group. For example, the cover may depend on age or years of membership or income (in the case of employees) or rank. If the criterion is of age or rank, then all individuals of the same age or rank will get the same cover. If the criterion is of income, depending on output, maybe a suitable criterion, when the group consist of say, farmers or beedi workers or milkmen supplying milk to a diary.

The inclusion of members in the scheme also is a matter on which the member will have no choc. Everybody fulfilling specified criteria will have to compulsorily join the group. Usually, when the scheme is being introduced for the first time, the exiting members will be given a choice of joining or not joining the scheme. The choice, to be made within a specified period, will be final. In other words, if a member opts not to join, he cannot change his mind later. These are methods to avoid adverse selection.

Individual lives re not separately assessed for risks. The underwriting or selection is of the group as a whole. The health, morals or habits of any particular individual are not scrutinized.

The premium under a group insurance policy will change from year to year. This is so because the number of persons covered would change because of exist (deaths retirements, resignation) and new entrants. The amount of cover will also very because of changes in age, income rank, etc. of existing members.

The premium may also change according to the mortality experience of the group. If the experience is better than originally expected, the benefit of the favourable experience would be passed on to the policyholder, by way of reduction of premium/ this system is called profit sharing.

One of the earliest schemes is the One Year Renewable Group Term Insurance Schemes. Under this, the members are covered for specific amounts, payable on their death. This is the simplest and the cheapest of the shames. This is particularly helpful to relatives of employees, who die young and find that the amounts due under gratuity and Provident Fund Scheme are not adequate. This is also helpful to cover the liabilities of borrowers under mortgage or hire purchase agreements. The amount of over can be related to the outstanding loans.

Group Savings Linked Insurance Scheme are offered to employers of the benefit of the employees. Contributions from the employees are made up of two elements. Part of it is used as the premium for term insurance cover of the agreed amount. The balance is created to a savings scheme.

Group Gratuity Schemes are also offered to employers and are related to the gratuity of employees. Gratuity is paid to employees who retire or die after long years of service. Since 1972, payment of gratuity has been made compulsory by the Payment of Gratuity Act. The amount of gratuity is linked to the number of years of service and the salary drawn during the last few years.

The Group Gratuity Scheme provides two advantages. Firstly, it can guarantee a certain amount of gratuity, which would be more than what the rules provide, particularly for those who die young and with relatively lesser service. The second advantage is that it makes it easier to fund the gratuity liability of the employer. Actuarial advice is available from the insure about the adequacy of the funds.

In the absence of the arrangement with the group scheme with an insurer, the employer had three ways to pay gratuity. He could pay as and when the gratuity falls due out of his current revenues. This is not prudent business practice, because the amounts of gratuity payable can very considerably from year to year depending on the demographic profile of the employees, causing fluctuations in profits and also possibilities of delays or even defaults in gratuity payments.

Secondly, he could create an internal reserve for gratuity liabilities, this is better than the earlier method as the liability is being evened out. The risk here is that, if the management is not strict and disciplined, the reserved funds may be utilized for current requirements. Thirdly, he could set-up a gratuity fund as before and create a trust to administer the funds. The difference between this and the group gratuity scheme with an insurer is that, in the latter (a) the trustees hand over the funds to the insurer who will have better capabilities for managing the funds and also (b) there will be an insurance cover to provide additional funds for those who die young.

Group superannuating Scheme are also offered to employers and are related to the payment of pensions to employees. Pensions are increasingly becoming the preferred retirement benefit, mainly because of the increasing longevity of people. Lump-sum benefits like Provident Fund and Gratuity maybe inadequate to last the longer life span. Therefore, employers offer pension benefits. The group Superannuation schemes offered by insurers are intended to help employers administer the pension funds.

The employer can manage the pension liabilities in different ways, like the gratuity liabilities. The group scheme offered by insures has the advantage of easier administration and availability of actuarial and investment expertise. Further, it is possible to arrange for better benefits for those who die young.

The scheme can be managed in two ways. One way is to fix the contribution from the employer, generally as a percentage of salary. The benefit available to the employees would be equal to what this contribution can buy. The alternative is that the benefit to be given to the employees is fixed and the appropriate contribution is collected.

SPECIAL SCHEMES

The Employee's Deposit Linked Insurance (EDLI) scheme is applicable to all establishments and undertaking contributing towards provident fund under the Employee's Provident Fund and Miscellaneous Provisions Act, 1952, with effect from 1-8-1976, unless exempted under section 17(2A) of an employee linked to his balance in the provident fund account, subject to a maximum of Rs. 35,000. The Act empowers the Central Provident Fund Commissioner to exempt an employer from EDLI, if he opts for a group insurance scheme of LIC, which is more beneficial to the employees. The cover ranges from Rs. 11,000 to Rs. 37,000. The premium depends on the average age, occupations of members and the size of the group. The LIC's scheme has the advantage of low premium in many cases and the easy settlement of claims, compared to the Provident Fund.

Group Insurance is a convenient medium for Government to pursue its social security goals. For example, the LIC has introduced the Landless Agricultural Labourers' Group Insurance Scheme (LALGI) on behalf of the Government. It provides term insurance protection to the extent of Rs. 2000 each to families of landless agricultural labourers, who do not own land and do not have any inheritable rights to agricultural land. The entire cost (premium) is borne by the Government.

GROUP LEAVE ENCASHMENT SCHEME (GLES)

As per the amendments to the Companies Act, made in 1988, and the accounting standards, employers have to fund the liability in respect of the leave encashment facility. The LIC's scheme enables such funding (including medial leave cashment). In addition, the scheme provides for a sum assured ranging from Rs. 5000 to Rs. 25,000 payable to the families of employees who die while in service.

RETIREMENT SCHEMES

Studies show that the pensions paid by the Central and State Governments have increased from about Rs. 12,000 cores in 1996 to about Rs. 46,000 cores in 2002, Apart from the increase in wage rates and inflation, a major contributor factor for such exponential increase is the increasing life spans. The average expectation of life has gone up from 53 in 1980 to 63 in 2000. Employees, including Government, find it difficult to bear the increasing financial burden of retired employees.

Employers who have to pay pensions purchase annuities from a life insurer as and when they have to release the pension. After purchase, the annuities will be paid by the insurers directly to the pensioners. The benefits can be tailored to meet the requirements of the employer and the pensions. The purchase price would be decided by the employer, according to its policies and terms of employment. For a given purchase price, there could be various options as to how the annuity could be dispersed. The variations, as a in annuities, would be when to begin and when it should end. It could end on the pensioner's death or continue as long as the spouse is alive or be for not less than a specified period. These could be left to the preference of the pensioner.

Voluntary Retirement Schemes are very common these days. Employees receive substantial amounts from the employers. Group Insurance Schemes can help to channelise such funs to steady and assured flows of income.

HEALTH INSURANCES

Health insurance, is according to the laws in India, part of non-life business. Therefore, life insurers will not be catering to the insurance needs relating to sickness, except to a limited extent as riders to individual life insurance policies. It cannot become the subject matter of a group insurance policy. However, if the law changes in conformity with the provisions in other countries, life insurers will find a very big scope for a new line of business, both in individual and group policies.

AGENT'S ROLE

As mentioned earlier, group insurance has developed in India since the 1960s. The number of lives covered through group insurance policies is not much lower than the individual policies. The scope for this business is very vast. It is very practicable method to extent the benefits of insurance to the masses. Corporate can benefit from the insurer's expertise the agent who is conversant with the principles underlying group insurance might be able to innovate new ideas and develop schemes not tried so far.

11

Concept of Insurance Inclusion for Rural and Weaker Sections (Social Security-Net Concept)

INTRODUCTION

India has been struggling since centuries to fight two (never dying) demons—poverty and unemployment—and, therefore, the target for the present is necessarily the under-privileged sections—those with poverty of money income and poverty of deprivation. This chapter has focus on these sections though other sections too have to be brought under Insurance net (Inclusion).

LEGAL PROVISIONS

Vide paragraph 19 of the First Schedule of the Insurance Regulatory and Development Authority Act, 1999, undertake such percentage of life insurance business and general insurance business in the rural or social sector, as may be specified in the Official Gazetteer, by the Authority, in this behalf.

32B. **Insurance Business in Rural or Social Sector**—Every insurer shall, after the commencement of the Insurance Regulatory and Development Authority Act, 1999, undertake such percentages of life insurance business and general insurance business in the rural or social sector, as may be specified, in the official gazetteer, by the Authority, in this behalf.

32C. Obligation of insurer in respect of rural or unorganized sector and backward classes. Every insure shall, after the commencement of the insurance Regulatory and Development Authority Act, 1999, discharge the obligations specified under section 32B to provide life insurance or general insurance policies to the persons residing in the rural sector, workers in the unorganized or informal sector or for economically vulnerable or backward class of the society and other categories of persons as may be specified by Regulations made by the Authority and such insurance policies shall include insurance for crops.

The regulations made by the IRDA, in terms of these provisions, were notified in the official gazette on 19-7-2000. They were amended in October 2002 and notified in the Official Gazette dated 16-10-2002. Under these regulations:

- The rural sector has been defined as a place in which, as per the latest census, the population is less than 5000, the density of population is less than 400 per square kilometer and more than 25% of the male working populations are engaged in agricultural pursuits. (Agricultural pursuits are defined as cultivation, agricultural labour, work in livestock, forestry, fishing, hunting, plantation, orchards, and allied activities).
- The social sector is defined as including the unorganized sector, the informal sector, the economically vulnerable or backward classes and other categories of persons, both in rural and urban areas.
- The unorganized sector is defined as including self-employed worked such as agricultural labour, bidi workers, brick kiln workers, carpenters, cobblers, construction workers, fishermen, hamals, handicraft artisans, handloom and khadi workers, lady tailors, leather and tannery workers, papad makers, powerloom workers, physically handicapped self-employed persons, primary milk producers, rickshaw pullers, safai karmacharis, salt growers, sericulture workers, sugarcane cutters, tendu leaf collectors, toddy tappers, vegetable vendors, washerwomen, working women in hills or such other categories of persons.
- The informal sector is defined as the small scale, self-employed workers typically at a lower level of organization and technology, with the primary objective of generating employment and income with heterogeneous activities like retail trade, transport, repair and maintenance, construction, personal and domestic services, and manufacturing with the work being mostly labour-intensive, having often unwritten and informal employer-employee relationship.

People below the poverty line are included in the expression economically vulnerable or backward classes. The expression other categories of person includes person with disability as defined in the person and disabilities (equal opportunities, protection of rights and full participation) Act, 1995, and who may not be gainfully employed and also includes guardians who need insurance to protect spastic person with disability.

These sections of society are normally neglected by insurers. They are difficult to reach and the scope for insurance is limited. But, they need insurance more than the other segments need. The insurers who began to transact life insurance business in the year 2000 or later, are required by these regulations to write, in the rural sector:

- At least 5% of the total policies written direct, in the first financial year, going up to
- 9% in the second financial year,
- 12% in the third financial year,
- 14% in the fourth financial year, and

- 16% in the fifth financial year.

With regard to the social sector, the obligations are laid down as:

- 5000 lives in the first financial year,
- 7500 lives in the second financial year,
- 10,000 lives in the second financial year,
- 15,000 lives in the second financial year, and
- 20,000 lives in the second financial year.

It has also been provided that in the first year, if the period of operation is less than twelve moths, the obligation of live sin the social sector, could be proportionality less. It is also provided that the IRDA may normally revise the obligations once in five years.

With regards to existing insurers, the regulations provide that obligations would be decided by the IRDA after consultation, but the quantum would not be less than what had been recorded for the year ended 31-3-2002.

The insurers would develop appropriate policies to comply with the obligations under the act. The extent of the compliance will depend on the vigour with which the agents will carry forward the efforts in these sectors. Reports at the end of the year 2001-02 are that all the insurers have exceeded the limits laid down by the IRDA.

RURAL SECTOR

There are more than 5 lakh villages in India with a total population of nearly 75 crores. This represents a vast potential. But nearly 25% of them are below the poverty line compared to only about 7% in the urban areas; they are scattered and not continuous as in the urban areas. Therefore, to contact people, one has to travel long distances, along roads that are not well constructed. Only 60% of the villages are connected by all weather roads. There my not be convenience pleas for visitors to stay or to eat food. Agents may find it more profitable to spend their efforts in the urban areas. That is why there would be tendencies to avoid the rural market, unless compelled by the law or by the IRDA through Regulations.

Apart from the large numbers in the rural areas, there are also indicators that show increasing prosperity in the rural areas nearly 1.5 crore households in the rural area are considered to have an annual income of Rs. 50,000 or above. More than 3500 branches of commercial banks operate in the rural areas, apart from the banks exclusively concerned with agricultural development. The consumption of various consumer items like biscuits, chocolates, soaps, detergents, washing powers, toothpastes, motorcycles, TV sets, radios, pressure cookers, etc. are more in the rural areas than in the urban areas. The FMCG producers find that the rural markets will be the main areas for the growth in future.

The LIC's business from the rural area had been increasing steadily. In 1997-98, the business was more than 53% in number of policies and more than 42% in sum assured. This is part from the business covered under group schemes in the social sector. The awareness about life insurance is not as low as it used to be some thirty years ago. The LIC had been doing intensive publicity through the mobile vans and other traditional as well as non-traditional media. The radio and television broadcasts reach almost every village through community sets.

Despite the long distances and the inconvenient infrastructure for travel and staying, the effort may be rewarding. The rural folk are simple people, but not ignorant of worldly matters. If an agent can win their trust, selling insurance would be an easy proposition. He can be almost sure that no other agent would be able to make an entry into that village. But the agent will have to take care that the interest of the prospects are not jeopardized in any manner whatsoever. Policies may not be of big amounts, but the numbers would be large. The impact of these policies, particularly when the claims are paid, would be much more valuable than in the urban areas. The story of insurance would travel far.

SOCIAL SECTOR (PARTICULARLY LOWER DENOMINATIONS OF POPULATION)

In the earlier paragraphs, reference was made to the obligations of the insurers in the special sector, the benefits of life insurance are need most by people in this sector, the benefits of life insane are needed most by people in this sector, as they are relatively poor and have very little savings, if at all. Any loss of income through early death would make the surviving family poorer than before. The conditions would be worse if the deceased had not repaid loans, taken for the purpose of his work f=or for personal requiremetns.

Soon after nationalization of life insurance, this need was recognized and efforts were made to introduce what was called 'mass' insurances. The concept was to cover very larger number of poor people in one scheme. The difference between such plans under the social sector and group insurance policies is that the former are not policies taken voluntary by any employer or organization or association, but are part of the schemes of the government being implemented through the business of life insurance.

Till early 2000, there were social security group insurance schemes (SSGIS) separately for recognized occupations, 24 occupations had been approved and as at the end of 1999, these schemes covered nearly 50 lakh persons for a total sum assured of nearly Rs. 1750 crores. This averaged out to nearly Rs. 1750 crores. This averaged out to nearly Rs. 3500 per head. In fact, the SA differed from scheme to scheme. The benefit on death by accident was Rs. 25,000. The premium for the crore was paid by the state or from the social security fund set-up by the LIC in 1988-89, for this purpose.

There was also the Rural Group Life Insurance Scheme (RGLIS), whereunder persons aged between 20 and 50 years were covered for sums of Rs. 5000 payable on death before the age of 60. The scheme was administered through elected panchayats.

A new scheme was launched in July 2000, called the Janashree Bima Yojana. It was meant to cover all the rural and urban poor who were aged between 18 and 60 years and are bread winners of the family. The persons to be covered are recommended by a nodal agency, which is a statutory body or voluntary organization recognized for this purpose. It acts as the sole point of contact for the insurer, giving data about its members, collecting premia and making the claims as and when they arise. The sum assured under this scheme is Rs. 20,000 (Rs. 50,000 in the case of death by accident). The minimum number in the group has to be 250. Half the premium is paid by the social security fund and the other half by the members or the nodal agency or the State Government.

The beneficiaries of the Integrated Rural Development Programme are covered by the Swaranjayanti Gram Swarozgar Yojana. A separate fund has been set-up by Government of India for funding the scheme. The scheme is administered through district rural development agency coming under Zilla Parishad. All the persons between 18 and 60 years and receiving subsidy/financial assistance/loan under IRDP after 1-4-1988 are eligible to join the scheme. The premium is fully borne by the Government of India. The insurance cover is provided for a period of 5 years from the date of disbursement of subsidy/financial assistance/loan. In the event of death before age 60 a sum assured of Rs. 5000 becomes payable to the nominee. In case of death due to accident, an amount of Rs. 10,000 becomes payable.

Details of the Landless Agricultural Labourers Group Insurance Scheme (LALGI) have been given in earlier chapter. This scheme provides insurance cover of Rs. 2000 without accident benefit.

The Krishi Shramik Suraksha Yojana, introduced in 2001, provides periodical lump-sum survival benefits and pension to agricultural workers. The member has to pay Rs. 90 at the beginning of every quarter and double the amount is contributed from the social security fund. Agricultural workers between 18 and 50 years of age are covered. On death before age 60, and SA of Rs. 20,000, along with accumulated amount with interest, is payable to the nominee. In case of death by accident, the insurance cover is for Rs. 50,000. PDB benefits are provided. On the life assured surviving 60 years, if the period of contribution is 10 years or more, a lump-sum will be paid, depending on his contribution. A minimum pension of Rs. 100 per month will be paid during this lifetime.

The Shiksha Sahayog Yojana, also introduced in 2001, is designed to provide, at an additional cost, an educational allowance of Rs. 300 per quarter to students studying in classes 9 to 12, whose parents are below the poverty line (BPL) and are members of Janashree Bima Yojana. The payments will be made out of the social security fund of the Government through the educational institutions concerned.

12

Publicity and Advertising Tools for Insurance Inclusion

INTRODUCTION

The purpose of all business is to create and retain customers. Without customers, there can be no business. Often, in the modern context, customers do not come on their own. They have to become aware of the availability of the goods or services on offer. Awareness is not enough. It must be convenient to access the offer. The cost must be seen to be reasonable for the benefit offered. An excellent product does not guarantee that sales will happen, unless people interested in that product come to know about it and find that the effort to get it is not too taxing they will continue as customers when they are satisfied with what they have got. Business, therefore, has to inform the likely customers through media that reach them, make the goods and services available at convenient outlets and ensure that the customers experience satisfaction while using them. Marketing is the activity that comprises of all these. It focuses on the customers. Insurance, particularly life insurance, is a matter of solicitation.

The marketer asks questions like what do people buy, why do they buy (what are the needs), when and where do they buy, how do they buy, how much are they prepared to pay, what are their preferences and priorities, what do they look for while buying, what are their concerns, etc. the products, and the distributions are then designed in ways that try to match these requirements. Studies over the years have developed ideas and concept that help marketers become more effective in their functions.

Marketing concepts relevant to tangible products like motor cars, refrigerators and cosmetics are not entirely applicable to the service businesses, like hotels, finance, health care, credit cards or travel. Every service is different. The needs of their customers are different. The ways of producing the services are different. Even service is catering to a different kind of need and is different in the internal dynamics of making the service available. Those entering a disco parlour are totally different from those entering a casualty department of a hospital. The two places cannot have the same ambience, even in insurance, life is different from general, this chapter deals with some of the important concepts relating to marketing of life insurance, keeping in mind the responsibilities and functions of agent.

DISTRIBUTION CHANNEL

A distribution channel is the route by which the product (or offer) prepared by the producer reaches the ultimate consumer (or buyer). The distribution channel bridges the distance between the producer (point of manufacturer) and the consumer (point of sale). In the case of goods, the product manufactured in the factory passes through wholesalers, stockiest and retailers, before it reaches the consumer. In the case of life insurance, the agent is the primary component of the distribution channel. He is the equivalent of the retailers. The supervisor or agent, by whatever name called, is an important part, because it is he who, by training as agent, makes the channel effective. New agents widen the channel.

Equally important would be the other intermediaries, like brokers and insurance consultants. Some life insurers are trying to eliminate intermediaries to save costs. Direct contacts are made to eliminate intermediaries to save cost. Direct selling is one such attempt. This is increasing in foreign countries. In India, people, by and large, know about life insurance, but still have many wrong notions about it. Personal contacts by agents may continue to be necessary for quite some time.

Another method being attempted is the use of the extensive network of branches of banks. The customers of both banks and life insurers are practically from the same segments of population. Through the same contact, the prospect can be helped to arrange for both bank deposits and life insurance. There would be saving in infrastructure costs and overheads. New insurers find this an easy way to access vast areas. It may be possible to develop composite products having the elements of both life insurance and banking. These trends have to develop.

LIFE INSURANCE IS SOLD NOT BOUGHT

Life insurance is not bought practically by anybody. General insurance is often bought because there are compulsions under the Law (as in case of motor vehicles) or from the financiers (who seek thereby to hedge their risk) asking for insurance as collateral security. In the case of life insurance, there is very little compulsion. The tendency is to defer the decision. The possibility of death is either ignored or not considered imminent. The requirements of today take priority over the requirements of tomorrow. Even if not absolutely essential, the requriemetns of today seem to be more compelling. Tomorrow never comes for many.

Superstitious beliefs and cultural or religious backgrounds often interfere with the process of considering the usefulness of life insurance. There is also a tendency to leave everything to fate. There are notions about life insurance not being a good investment (yields are low, the money after 20 years is worth much less) and so on. By the time someone realizes himself the need for life insurance, the chances are that he may not be in the best of health and the insurer may have doubts about the insurability. Life insurance has to be had when in the best of health. Otherwise, the insecure will refuse to grant the insurance cover, in this complex milieu, people need to be persuaded that there is need to be concerned about the future and that life insurance is a necessity, not an option. Insurance has to be sold.

That person is a better risk who meets an agent at his normal place of work or at his residence than the one who comes to the office himself and asks for insurance. The agent who is the primary underwriter can study and report on the circumstances and motivations of the former. The latter is likely to be a case of moral hazard and must be looked at more discreetly and carefully.

THE CUSTOMER (POLICYHOLDER/BENEFICIARY)

The quality of service of life insurance business can be found out at the time of claim when people will experience how the promises are being kept. Until then, it is a hope of a promise the significance of which is vague. The customer in life insurance is not only the person who bought the policy, but also the person who is making the claim (beneficiary). He is the one experiencing the service. This difference is not only in death claim cases. Even in the case of a maturity claim, where the claimant is the same person as the policyholder or life insured, the two mind-sets are different. At the start, at the buying stage, the mind-set is one of anxiety and fear at the possibility of death and welfare of the family. At the end, there could be satisfaction that nothing untoward had happened, but also there could be disappointment that the moneys could have been utilized elsewhere better.

Claimants of the death benefits are person different from the one who had taken out the policy and perhaps know little about the circumstances and conditions under which the policy was taken or had been looked after. They may not be familiar with their entitlement sunder the policy; they are also troubled people, coming to terms with the loss of an important member of the family. The insurer will be asking for information and documents of various kinds to decide on the admissibility of the claim. There could be discrepancies in the records of the insurers. Anybody from the insurance company, who helps the claimant in finding the right information and in completing the formalities, will be providing great satisfaction. If the agent who sold the policy is not available for any reason, the office can depute another person or another agent.

MANAGEMENT OF RELATIONSHIPS

The agent is the main intermediary between the customers and the insurers. The customer-agent link is stronger than the agent-company link (this tends to be impersonal), which in turn is stronger than the customer-company link. Customer loyalty to the insurer depends on how strong the agent's link with the customer is. A death claim provides a tremendous opportunity to strengthen this link.

The agent is expected to keep in constant touch with his policyholders to become aware of the changes in his situation including marriages, death of relatives, and release of mortgages. Anyone of them may necessitate some changes like title to policy moneys or more insurance. The contact conveys a message that the agent cars for the policyholder and the family. An agent who is seen only at the time the policy was being bought, is likely to be perceived as selfish, not concerned about the policyholder's interest and therefore, not believed. The agent's concern could also be interpreted as not genuine and, therefore, his promises not very dependable.

A study made by the Insurance Institute of India in1987, by interviewing 2510 policyholders in 26 cities, had the following observations:

- Agents do not maintain regular contact with policyholders, although they are seen as available whenever necessary.
- 50% said that if they had any work to be done, they would go to the office directly rather than get in touch with the agent.
- Agents are perceived as knowledgeable, but also as concerned more with their own benefits than those of policyholders.

These observations reflect badly on the agents.

ROLE AND FUNCTIONS OF AN AGENT

The agent's main function is to solicit and procure life insurance business for the insurer, which has appointed him for that purpose. At the same time, he is trusted by the prospect to advise him suitably keeping his circumstances and needs in mind. He is thus in the unique role of a person trusted by both parties to the transaction. His functions would include—

- Understand the prospectus's needs and persuade him to buy a plan of life insurance that suits his interest best.
- Complete the formalities (paper work, medial examination) necessary to get the policy expeditiously.
- Keep in touch to ensure that changing circumstances are reflected in the arrangements relating to premium payments, nomination and other necessary alternations.
- Facilitate quick settlement of claims.
- Be totally honest with both the prospect and the insurers.

The Regulations framed by the IRDA lay down a code of conduct, which incorporates some of these concepts. The code says *inter-alia* that the agent shall:

- Identify himself and the insurance company of which he is an agent.
- Disclose the licence to the prospect on demand.
- Explain all available options to the prospect.
- Recommend a suitable plan taking into account the needs of the prospect.
- Disclose the scales of commission, if asked for by the prospect.
- Explain the nature and importance of the information required in the proposal form.
- Impress upon the prospect the need to disclose all information.
- Make all enquiries about the prospect.
- Inform the insurer about any material fats, including habits that could adversely affect the underwriting decision.
- Convey the prospect about the acceptance or rejection of the proposal.
- Render necessary assistance to policyholder or claimants or beneficiaries in complying with requirements asked for by the insurer.

- Advise policyholder to effect nomination.
- Make every attempt to ensure remittance of premiums by the policyholders within the stipulated time, by giving notice orally and in writing.
- Not to induce prospects to submit wrong information
- Not to interfere with the proposals introduce by other insurance agents.
- Not demand or receive from beneficiary, share of proceeds under an insurance contact.
- Not cause the termination of an existing policy with a view to effect a new proposal.

ADVERTISING

Life insurance is rarely bought as a response to advertisements. It is a matter of solicitation. Advertisements are otherwise effective marketing tools.

- As reminders to intimate change of address, pay premium, make nomination, etc.
- As information on bonus declaration, special reveal schemes, concessions, new plans, etc.
- To build corporate image as financially strong, as responsible social citizen, etc.

The Regulation framed by the IRDA have made some stipulations about advertisements by insurers as well as by intermediaries like agents. These stipulations apply to all messages in the print and electronic media, hoardings, internet, leaflets, business cards, etc. that urge other to buy life insurance. These stipulations, *inter-alia,* state that:

- Claims made about the benefits should not be beyond the ability of the policy to deliver.
- Benefits described should match policy provisions.
- Words or phrases should not be used in such a way as to hide or minimize the cost of hazards.
- Important exclusion, limitation and conditions of the contract should be disclosed sufficiently.
- Information should not be misleading.
- Illustrations about future benefits or assumptions should not be unrealistic or unrealizable in the light of current performance.
- Benefits that are not guaranteed should not be referred to in ways that they are not noticed.
- There should be no implication of sponsorship, affiliation or approval that does not exist.
- These should not be any unfair or incomplete comparisons with products of competitors.

Those who have received policy moneys on the death of the life insured are the best endorsement for a life insurer. They are the ones who have experienced what life insurance means and know what it can do differently from other financial arrangements. They know how it feels when a previously determined amount comes in at a time when the future looks bleak with debtors threatening to foreclose mortgages and attach property. Satisfied claimants are powerful and effective as word of mouth media. Their stories persuade strongly. In all services, the word of mouth is the most effective endorsement. In insurance it is particularly so. The word of mouth is an endorsement, not only for the need for life insurance, but also for the insurer and the agent in particular.

HAPPY CUSTOMERS ARE LOYAL

A customer is satisfied when the product meets his needs. In life insurance, this happens at the time of the claim, which is a long way off. It is important to keep him happy during this period, to avoid what is called 'Cognitive Dissonance'. This arises because of doubts about the decision to buy. In the case of life insurance, such doubts may easily arise because others (friends and agents) will talk about better alternative plans, better insurers, and so on. The only way to counter these possibilities is to be in touch with the prospect and reassure him at every possible opportunity that the purchase he made was not a mistake. In other words, the agent will be effectively repeating the sales talk, overcoming objections, till the benefits are seen through claims.

Studies show that people are happy when they are recognized and respected and not taken for granted. Recognition happens when one's feeling, requirements, etc. are understood and not ignored. Agents can do a lot in terms of recognizing people. One way is to be available whenever the prospect or the policyholder has a point for clarification. These may happen during the policy term itself, when a change in job or place may raise doubts as to the effects on the policy. Another way is to avoid denying the validity of his thoughts. There is nothing more meaning than to be discredited for one's idea. This is important while handling objections during a sale. Recognition is high when the thoughts of the other persons are anticipated and attended to.

Two other factors which make customers happy are Responsiveness (willingness to help) and Ease of Access. On both counts, agents can do much more than what the insurer's office can do. It is difficult for an office to be warm and personalized when dealing with anybody. The agent can. Some agents do not let the policyholders go to the office at all. They get everything done. Such agents are reinforcing the impression that the agent is trustworthy and can be depended upon to fulfil his promises. The image of the insurer remains high.

13

Concept of Organic Linkage (Role of an Insurance Agent)

INTRODUCTION

An insurance agent is defined in the Insurance Act. He requires a licence to be able to function as an agent. He is remunerated by way of commission on the premium paid under policies procured through his efforts. Insurers designate agents differently like consultants, advisors and so on. The designations do not matter. He is the main component of the distribution channel for the life insurance business.

A life insurance agent would be required to solicit and procure new life insurance business, in a manner that is consistent with the interests of the policyholders and of the insurance company. For this purpose, he would have to do the following:

- Contact prospects for life insurance, study their needs and persuade them to buy.
- Complete all related formalities, including filling up proposal forms, collecting premium, arranging medial examination, collecting proofs (of age or income), reports and other information required by the underwriter.

After having sold a new insurance policy, the agent has to ensure that the policy continues, without a lapse, till it becomes a claim. The conservation of the policy is in the interest of all the three persons concerned, the insurer, the policyholder and the agent. For this purpose, he has to:

- Keep in touch with the policyholder to make sure that renewal premiums are paid in time.
- Ensure that nominations are made or changed according to changing circumstances.
- Assist in settlement of the claim, by helping the claimants to complete the necessary formalities and requirements.

The other function is to be of assistance to the policyholder in case he needs a loan under the policy or wants to make an assignment. These services strengthen the relationship between the agent and the policyholder.

PRE-REQUISITES FOR AGENTS FOR SUCCESS

In order that he may perform all these tasks well, the agent has to be familiar with:

- The benefits under the various plans of insurance offered by his insurers.
- The office procedures for various matters including the forms and documents. The forms and procedures will vary between one insure and another.

As stated earlier, the insurance agent is an agent of the prospect as well. He is looked upon as a knowledgeable person, who can be trusted to give the right advice. To be able to match these expectations, the agent must be familiar with the benefits and advantages of other financial instruments suitable for savings and investments and also the laws, particularly on taxation mattes, relevant to these instruments. The variety of instruments available for an individual, is very vast and it is difficult for anyone to master the details of all of them. Some agents, who do not have the necessary knowledge, give answers on the basis of guess work or hearsay. Others admit that they do not know enough and promise to come back after checking out the details. The latter are respected and trusted more.

The important legal provisions relating to the business of life insurance are explained in a subsequent chapter. The tax implications of life insurance transactions are also explained in a subsequent chapter.

PERSONAL SELLING OF INSURANCE

The first requirement is to have a continually expanding list of prospects, persons who can be approached for insurance. These are names of people within reach, obtained from acquaintance, newspapers reports, directories, contact at parties meetings, seminars, etc. These names have to be qualified, which means that some preliminary work should be done to collect details about them. These details may indicate whether it may be worth approaching them for insurance. The work of 'qualifying' is done to ensure that the prospect is not apparently unfit for insurance like being sick, or with great moral hazard.

Those in the qualified prospect list have to be met. A sale results when the salesman takes the prospect through well defined steps. The steps are not separate and clear cut but blend into one integrated process. The steps are:

- Pre-approach
- Approach
- Interview
- Objections
- Close

PRE-APPROACH (HOMEWORK)

Pre-approach means preparing to approach the prospect. This requires forming some idea as to how the interview could be held and proceeded, for which you require basic information regarding his income, his habits, his concerns, his interests, his saving capacity, his family position, etc. These facts can be had from a variety of sources, and you may even have to make a personal call on the man himself, and get from him the facts you need to persuade him in taking decision. If such a call is made, the proposal for insurance is not made at that stage, although in some circumstances a pre-approach call may develop further and end with the proposal and the cheque.

The information collected during pre-approach will provide a reasonable idea of the prospects financial position and his needs and concerns, and help to make a tentative recommendation of a plan. If you make the sale first in your mind, you will find it easy to make the sale to the prospect.

It is advisable to write down the proposal. The advantages of a written proposal are:

- Details are not missed by either the agent or the prospect.
- The impression is more lasting.
- The prospect can go back to earlier data on his own.
- The prospect can understand, at his own pace.
- It is easy to stop at any point, clarify questions and continue further without losing the trend.

APPROACHING THE PROSPECT

When you knock at the prospect's door and are face to face with him, the dynamic phase of sale begins. You should make known to the prospect, at the very earliest, that you are calling on him for life insurance. There is no need to hesitate on this or to feel apologetic. The agent has to believe that he is calling on the prospect to render him the valuable service of ensuring financial security for him and his family.

The agent should open the talk by explaining the purpose of his call in such a way so as to arouse enough interest in the prospect. It is an art how to open the dialogue and how well to explain details from the prospect's point of view. Otherwise, he may not pay attention to the proposal. In most of the cases, the situation may arise where the prospect will come out with a 'No'; the agent at this stage should not be in hurry to convert the 'No' into 'Yes'. The purpose of the approach stage is not to sell insurance, but to sell an interview, which gives him the opportunity to talk about what he wants the prospect to think about, and that too with seriousness the subject deserves. The Agent will tell that a man is a social being; he wants to remain happy and with all his relations; both these are required by man in continuity and for that to happen, the person needs prosperity, and prosperity also in continuity—not one time action/achievement. He can go further to explain that death is certain but its timing is not certain. Insurance, therefore, serves all the three view-points (purposes) in one go.

INTERVIEW FOR AROUSAL OF INTEREST

The interview should, first of all, make the prospect listen. This happens if the agent refers to things which interest him, his needs, or things that matter to him, without making it appear like patronizing or flattering. Any hint that the prospect's decision of the past (relating to insurance or investment) were not appropriate or need to be changed, will have the opposite effect. The proposal being made by the agent should be seen as beneficial and complimentary to the existing arrangement.

The agent should follow some simple rules like the ones mentioned below:

- Do not talk more than necessary.
- Ask questions, and make the prospect talk, make it interactive.
- Create doubts and get him to ask questions for clarification.
- Listen to the prospect's point of view carefully. Do not interrupt, contradict or argue. People feel good when they are listened to and then they listen better.
- Make your talk interesting. Tell a true story of how life insurance has helped families in various situations and how families have suffered without it. Make the story have a personal appeal. Use names of his children or relatives. That will make the story more appealing.
- Use pictorial aids, graphics, and written presentations. If you have a lap top use Power Point presentation.
- Let the prospect write down the figures of his needs, of his liabilities, of benefits of the insurance plan and of the premium. This ensures concentrated attention.
- Let your advice be in the best interest of the prospect, not your interest.

Successful agents prepare their presentations carefully every time. They rehearse in their minds the way the interview should proceed. This ensures that they do not fumble for ideas or the right words. The ideas, too, come in the most natural and logical sequence. Lastly, a prepared sales talk conveys more enthusiasm and conviction than a talk without preparation. A well prepared approach ensures a favourable interview.

OBJECTIONS

Prospects will raise objections, one after another. Objections are a part of every sale. If prospects did not object, there would be no need for salesmen. People would buy on their own. Also, if the prospect remained silent, you will not know how his mind is working; the objection is his way of referring to the further information that he needs.

The entire selling process is, therefore, interspersed with objections. At the stage of approach itself the prospect may say 'I do not believe in life insurance', 'I do not need life insurance', and the like. Such objections are not against life insurance but rather against the agent whom he wants to put-off gracefully, or sings of indecision, or of a fear of being 'forced' into buying.

Then, there are objections during the interview, like, "I pay more than what I get back, it is advantageous only if I die. Meet me after six months". Such objections, which come up during the main discussion are real objections. However, their intention is not to put you off. It is quite the contrary. The prospect wants you to convince him. He wants you to give him detailed information that will remove his fear and doubts and to back up his latent or unstated desire to buy. Every objection tells you about the prospect's thinking and gives you an opportunity to remove his mental block. Indeed, a prospect, who puts forward an objection, is actually asking you to give him one more reason to buy. A true agent should, therefore, welcome objections.

Then there are objections raised at the closing stage, such as, 'I will think it over', 'I will consult my father', 'See me next month when I get my confirmation/increment/ promotion, etc'. These objections reveal an inability to take a major decision.

Objections cannot be treated in a summary manner. The answers must be complete and convincing to the prospect. He needs help to make the decision to buy. His doubts or difficulties need to be removed or clarified. The agent, while answering the objections, should never get into an argument. The 'yes ... but' method is the most effective. You agree (say, yes) in principle with what the prospect says under circumstances assumed buy him, but, you say, "the actual circumstance are different" and then convey you point. The prospect is bound to be receptive to such an open 'give and take' in discussion. For example, you may say "Mr. Prospect, I agree that conditions are hard and people have difficulty in saving, but imagine how much more difficult it will be if your family has to carry on without you". The secret of successful selling is to make the prospect feel that he has taken the decision you only help him in the process by answering his objections. Agents should remember that an objection is a 'blessing in disguise'. It is also a stepping stone to a sale.

Closing the Interview

The 'close' has to be sensed and timely, because very few prospects will, of heir own accord, say 'I will insure'. The agent sensing the close takes the prospect's positive decision for granted by asking for his implied (not direct) consent. "Will you pay the premium by cash or cheque"?, "do you have your school certificate at hand now or can you give it tomorrow" (affirmative response)?. A positive answer to any of these questions is an indication to go ahead. If the interview does not end with a close and is put-off to another time, the interview will have to be gone through all over again.

In selling life insurance, an appeal to the heart of the prospect is more useful than an appeal to the head. Life insurance is both for the prime reason of protecting the loved ones, affording a good start in life to the children, duty to aged parents, or perhaps a desire for self-preservation in old age. So, a sale can be accomplished only when an appeal is made to one of these motives, and appeal to sentiments of love, of affection and of concern. The agent need not be an expert in psychology to do this.

Service

The prospect becomes a policyholder with the sale of a life insurance policy. The agent's relationship with the policyholder thereafter depends on the service that he renders. Service assumes more importance in life insurance, because unlike other savings or investment plans, a contract of life insurance is a long-term commitment. People are often quite late in paying premium. If the premium is not paid, the policy becomes a useless piece of paper. The agent's attention to service (including monitoring premium payments, nominations, revivals, if they become necessary, help in settling claims, etc.) will ensure that the insurance policy does not suffer from such neglect.

Every servicing call gives an opportunity to the agent to review the insurance programme. The insurance already sold may become inadequate because of changes in the policyholder's financial position or family. Perhaps, he may need more insurance or he may suggest insurance of his relatives and friends, service benefits the policyholder. But it benefits the agent more by conveying messages about his liability and trustworthiness. This is his competitive advantage over other agents, of the same insurer and of other insurers.

ETHICAL BEHAVIOUR

Of late, serious concerns are voiced about the properties in business, because increasingly there are reports of improper behaviour. Some of the world's biggest companies have been found to have cheated through false accounts and dishonest audit certification. The funds of banks have been misused by their managements to bolster the greed of some friends. Officials have used their authority to promote personal benefits. Courts of Justice have failed to render justice. Increasingly, people who are trusted by the community to perform their tasks are seen tc have betrayed the trust. Personal aggrandizement and greed prevail.

The insurance agent is in a position of trust. On his assurance, the policy-holders entrust their small savings to an insurer, trusting it to look after these funds and look after their dependants in later years. Issues of propriety and ethics are extremely important in this business of insurance.

Unethical behaviours happen when the benefit of self are considered more important than of the others. The code of ethics spelt out by the IRDA in the Agent's Regulations, and referred to earlier, is directed towards ethical behaviour while it is important to know every clause in the code of conduct to ensure that there is no violation of the code, compliance would be automatic if the agent always kept the interest of the prospect in mind. Things go wrong when the agent becomes concerned with the commission that he will earn from the policy, rather than the benefits to the prospect.

The LIMRA, which is the premier international organization on matters concerning life insurance marketing, has found that ethics in life insurance selling consists mainly of putting the interest of the prospect/policyholder first. The research studies show that such an approach helps the agent through:

- Improved business and earnings.
- Business remaining in the books longer, without lapsation.
- Stronger relationships with the clients.
- More referrals and word of mouth recommendations.

Some agents think that they are doing the prospect a good turn, when they do not reveal some vital information in the proposal form, for fear of the underwriter raising awkward queries. In fact, they are doing harm to the prospect, because if there happens to be an early claim who can guarantee that this will not happen again? The claim may be repudiated. The loser at that time is the prospect's family. The commission collected by the agent is not affected. The loser is also the creditability of the entire life insurance industry, both agent and the insurers. Stories will circulate that insurers do not pay claims, the truth will not be known.

Some of characteristics of good ethical behaviour are:

- Placing the best interest of the client above one's own direct or indirect benefits.
- Holding in the strictest confidence and considering as privileged, all business and personal information pertaining to the client's affairs.
- Making full and adequate disclosure of all fact so to enable clients make informed decisions.

There could be a likelihood of ethics being compromised in the following situations:

- Having to choose between two plans, one giving much less commission than the other.
- Temptation to recommend discontinuance of an existing policy and taking out a new one.
- Becoming aware of circumstances, that if known to the insurer, could adversely affect the interest of the client or the beneficiaries of the claim.

14

Consumer Protection Concept

CONSUMER PROTECTION ACT, 1986 (COPRA)

This legislation is aimed at protecting the consumer/customer or service client against unscrupulous practices in trade and services. Brief description of this Act is given hereafter:

In the past several decades, there had been a movement to safeguard the interests of the customer. This has become known as consumerism and developed as a reaction to business ignoring the rights of consumers and exploiting them. Issues of safety were raised, particularly in the case of motor cars. The following four consumer rights have been accepted as basic:

A) The right to safety
B) The right to be informed
C) The right to choose
D) The right to be heard (redressal)

Under this Act, a consumer, as an individual or along with other individuals, or through a consumer organization, can approach the various forums prescribed under the Act for redress, in case he is not satisfied with the gods or service provided. He has to allege a defect in the goods or service. A defect or deficiency is a fault, imperfection, shortcoming or inadequacy in the quality, nature or manner of performance, which is required to be maintained by or under any law or in pursuance of a contract or undertaking in relation to that service.

In order to attend to complaints under this act, consumer dispute redressal forums are to be established in each District and for each state. The forum at the district level will hear complaints up to the value of Rs. 20,00,000 and the forum at the State level will hear complaints up to the value of Rs. 1 crore. There is a provision also for the constitution of a National Commission, which will attend to matters beyond the jurisdiction of the state forums and also appeals agents the decisions of a state forum.

The COPRA applies to the insurance business as well. Policyholders have the right to seek redress against unfair practices or unsatisfactory service from insurers and from agents. The majority of disputes relating to insurance arise out of repudiation and delays in claims. On all these matters, agents can help a great deal to mitigate the complaint or grievance. A written presentation is a sure method of ensuring that the correct information is given. Delays in office procedures can be avoided through the agent's personal intervention. Such delays occur often due to non-compliance with requirements or ambiguity in title. If due care is taken at the time of proposal and all material information supplied, there cannot be a repudiation of a claim.

THE OMBUDSMAN

In exercise of the powers conferred by sub-section (1) of Section 114 of the Insurance Act, the Central Government has framed rules known as Redressal of Public Grievances Rules, 1998, whereby Ombudsmen are appointed. Ombudsmen are appointed by the Governing body of the Insurance council. Their function is to resolve complaints in respect of deputes between policyholder and insurers in cost effective, efficient and impartial manner.

The complaints to the ombudsman may relate to (a) partial or total repudiation of claim, (b) any dispute regarding premium paid or payable in terms of the policy, (c) any dispute on the legal construction of the policy relating to claims, (d) any dispute regarding premium paid or payable in terms of the policy, (c) delay in settlement of claims, and (d) non-issue of any insurance document to customers after receipt of premium.

The Ombudsman shall act as counsel and mediator in matters within its terms of reference. It is not a judicial authority. It has no right to summon witnesses. It has to make its decision on the basis of documents submitted to it. The complainant and the insurer are allowed to make personal submission. But lawyers are not permitted to argue the case.

Complaints to the ombudsman lie only when the insurer had reject the complaints or no reply was received within one month of the complaint or the reply was not satisfactory. A complaint can be made within one year after the insurer had rejected the representation. The subject matter should not be already before any court or consumer forum or arbitration.

The ombudsman is expected to make a recommendation within one month from the date of receipt of complaint. If the complainant accepts this recommendation, the insurer has to comply within 15 days and inform the Ombudsman accordingly. If the complainant does not accept the Ombudsman's recommendation, the Ombudsman shall pass an award in writing, stating the amount awarded which shall not be in excess of what is necessary to cover the loss suffered by the complainants as direct consequence of the insured peril or for an amount not exceeding Rs. 10,00,000, whichever is lower. The award has to be passed within 3 months. The complainants has to intimate his acceptance of the award within one month by a letter of acceptance to the insurer and the insurer has to comply within 15 days and inform the Ombudsman. If the complainant does not intimate acceptance, the award cannot be implemented.

OTHER LAWS

Income Tax Act

The tax laws in India have always encouraged people to save through life insurance or other instruments, by providing relief from tax liabilities. The details provided herein are, as on a date when the book was being written. These could change at any time, through budget provisions or otherwise. The agent should keep himself up-to-date with the changes. Offices of the insurance companies would normally communicate the effect of such changes for the benefit of the agents. Knowledge of tax provisions is essential for an agent as it affects the benefits under a policy.

Any sum received under a life insurance policy, including the bonus additions is exempt from income tax. That means that income tax does not have to paid on policy claim amounts. There are some exceptions to this rule. One is the amount to be refunded under 'Jeevan Aadhaar' a plan of the LIC, meant for the handicapped dependents. The other is a claim under a key man insurance policy.

Deductions (from taxable income) to the extent of Rs. 10,000 are allowed to an individual in respect of amounts paid or deposited into the Jeevan Suraksha annuity plan for receiving pension (from a fund set-up by the LIC). Similarly, an amount not exceeding Rs. 40,000 deposited with LIC under Jeevan Aadhaar plan for maintenance of handicapped dependent is eligible for deduction from total income. This position has changed with amendment proposed in the budget for 2003-04, whereby maturity claims payments will be taxable if the premium paid in any one year exceeds 20% of the SA.

The amount of income tax payable on the total taxable income is reduced by a percentage of the aggregate amount paid towards insurance premiums (on life of self, spouse or children), contribution to Provident Fund or approved Superannuating Fund, National Savings Certificates, etc. the percentage of deduction was a flat 20% of the aggregate subject to limits. Most of the assessees could get the rebate to the extent of Rs. 15,000. Some could get more. This position has changed since 2002. the deduction reduces as the income slab goes up.

The Wealth Tax Act exempts life insurance policies totally provided premiums are payable for a period of 10 years or more. If the policy term is less than 10 years, proportionate value of the right or interest of the assessed in the policy will be exempted. Hence, such policies will have to be included in the net wealth as on the date of valuation.

Insurance premiums paid under partnership or keyman's insurance are allowed as expense.

Married Women's Property Act, 1874

Section 6 of the WWP Act provides hat a policy of issuance effected by any married man on his own life and expressed on the face of it for the benefit of his wife and children shall be deemed to be a trust for the benefit of his wife and children and shall not be subject to the control of the life assured or his creditors or form part of his estate.

FINANCIAL PLANNING AND TAXATION

Savings and Investment Schemes

Life insurance is often equated with savings and investments schemes. They are not the same. Savings schemes are plans whereby you can part your surplus money and are paid interest for the same. These deposits can be small amounts. In an investment scheme, one puts in a lump-sum of money to produce income, perhaps to increase the capital. Income is mostly not guaranteed. The capital may rise or may go down. But before one can invest such a lump-sum, one must possess it. One must first create it by saving systematically in well selected savings schemes. Many savings plans have both the elements of saving as well as investment combined.

A good savings plan should score high when following tests are applied:

(a) It should be safe.
(b) It should be flexible.
(c) It should have incentives to help save continuously without default.
(d) It should help in saving tax.
(e) It should fulfil the financial objectives, even if one dies.

An ideal investment scheme should answer favourably to the following tests:

(a) Safety
(b) Liquidity (easily encashable)
(c) A high rate of interest yield
(d) Capital growth
(e) Beneficial to save tax.

If the above tests are applied, one may be tempted to look around for some 'most perfect' investment from which to expect everything. There is not a single investment, which has all those attributes together. One cannot have the opportunities of windfall gains of the stock market with the safety or the life cover and tax concessions of life insurance, all in one. A sacrifice has to be made for the sake of one or the other attributes. A prudent person should look for those investments, which offer the best solutions to his personal needs, under his own set of circumstances.

The 'highest' returns and the 'best' returns are also not necessarily the same thing. High returns may be offset by risk to capital. The best return should be determined by the advantages an investment offers to achieve one's financial objectives under one's unique circumstances.

Banks offer 3 main types of accounts:

(a) The current account paying no interest.
(b) The savings bank account paying relatively low interest.
(c) The term deposit account paying varying rates of interest, rarely exceeding 10% p.a.

Interest earned is subject to income tax.

LIQUIDITY

The amount invested in current account or savings bank account can be withdrawn and the moneys obtained at any time. In case of term deposits, one has to wait till maturity of the term or the amount can be withdrawn earlier but at a loss of some interest. These amounts do not exceed what was put in and therefore there is no question of any capital gains tax on it.

UNIT TRUST AND MUTUAL FUNDS

Unit trust and mutual funds are based on the principle that a large number of individuals pool their moneys collectively in a single fund. These funds through the expertise of professional managers invest the collected amounts in shares and securities of a large number of companies. Thus, they establish a direct link between savings and the capital market. The investments made in these funds are divided into segments called 'units' normally, the units have face value of Rs. 10 each. One can buy or sell any number of units at current market prices, which may be more or less than Rs. 10.

The tax benefits are not the same for all investments in mutual funds. The income distributed is sometimes completely tax-free. Contributions to specified mutual funds are aggregated with insurance premia for tax rebates. The value of the unit is not protected. The net asset value can vary a lot. In several cases, it is less than the face value.

SHARES

Shares are the most popular kind of investment. But only person with adequate savings can find investment in shares worthwhile. They are bought mostly for appreciation. Earnings are neither guaranteed nor high in the short-term. Dividends may not be declared even if the company is making profits. Dividends declared on face value may not be significant as a return on the purchase price. The share prices fluctuate, being sensitive to trends in the US markets, rumours, company results, political crises, etc. They can be sold at any time, but the price will depend on market value. The chances of making losses are as great as the chances of making gains. There are no tax advantages.

The table below shows safety, liquidity and return on various investments.

Table 14.1: Safety, Liquidity and Return on various Investments

	Safety	*Liquidity*	*Return*
Savings bank account	High	High	Low
Fixed deposits with banks	-	Moderate/High	Moderate
Life insurance	High	Low	Moderate
Shares	Low	High	Moderate/low
Provident fund/PPF	High	Low	High

COMPARISONS BETWEEN DIFFERENT INSURANCE PLANS

Comparisons are often unfair. Even while comparing two different insurance plans of the same insurer, it would be wrong to compare only the premiums payable under the plans. A whole life plan is not to be chosen just because the premium is lower than that of an endowment plan. The choice of plan must depend firstly on the requirement of the prospects. That which does not meet the needs is costly. If the plan identified according to needs requires a premium larger than what the prospect is in a position to spare, one might begin to think of lower sum assured within the same plan, rather than a cheaper plan.

While comparing plans of insurance, one must also take into account, the manner in which the benefits are payable, the ease with which death claims can be settled, ease of alteration, availability of loans. Some policies have restriction on all of these.

15

Information Technology: Tool for Catching up with the Emerging World (Accuracy and Speed Concept)

INTRODUCTION

Computer (high computing power), Telecommunication Technology (Satellite Communication and Digital Technology) and Information Technology have converged to invade home, hearth and work-place. There is instant connectivity and real time messaging service on offer, and being availed. Mobile telephone has very many features including camera, computer and Internet, among other novelties. Salient features are discussed below:

The developments in the information technology (IT) are working wonders in all fields of activity. It has become possible to send and receive information almost instantaneously. If circulars do not reach the agents on time or doubts are not cleared quickly, or the agent does not have details of new plans announced in the press, the agent may face awkward situations with the prospects. These problems can be totally avoided with the use of IT. Insurers traditionally, have been quick to adapt latest advances in technology. This is happening in the areas of IT as well. The extent of IT application will vary between insurers. The broad possibilities are discussed in this chapter.

INTRANET AND INTERNET

The Internet is a worldwide system, accessible through computers. Information travels through the Internet at incredible speeds. It cuts across national and international boundaries. Information posted on a 'website' is available to anybody from anywhere in the globe, at no cost, unless the access is protected and made available only to specified individuals, such individuals will be identified by a password. Sometimes, they may be required to pay a fee for the information. The availability of the required information will become known to all.

While the Internet allows access for anybody from anywhere, the intranet is an in-house network, working on the same principle. The difference is similar to the difference between a national newspaper and in-house newsmagazine, which is for private circulation. If an insurer has an intranet system, the information in the intranet will be available only to its offices and personnel. The policyholder will not be able to access the data in the intranet. Circulars meant for internal circulation can be posted on the intranet, and everybody will have immediate access to it, however, far away he may be located. In the intranet also, it is possible to restrict some information to certain categories of persons, who will be identified through passwords.

Both internet and intranet enable users to do the following at any time (24 hours, 365 days)

- Send and receive letters, which are called e-mail. Every person will have an 'e-mail id', which is his address in the net.
- Search, read and retrieve (download) data, files, pictures.
- Exchange letters and discuss with individuals.
- Join discussion groups, including video conferences.
- Communicate in real time (without any delay whatever) across long distances.
- Display information for whoever is interested.
- Buy and sell (e-commerce).

BENEFITS TO AGENTS

If the insurer has an intranet, the agent can, sitting at his place of work, be attending the insurer's office, making enquiries about status of proposals or claims or discussing with any officers or other agent, for clarification or advice, whenever he wants to do it. The physical distance between the agent and the office will not be of any consequences at all. The benefits to the agents will be:

- He can receive all circulars and instructions issued by any office. All delays on account of postal transmission, being forwarded from one level to another, dispatch department, absence of peons, wrong addresses, misplaced through oversight, lost in transit, etc. are avoided.
- Any doubts with regard to proposal, benefits, premium, taxation, medical examination, insurability, etc. can be discussed and got clarified directly from the person concerned.
- Communications to and from the office will be immediate through e-mail and at low cost.

BENEFITS TO POLICYHOLDERS/PROSPECTS

Prospects can benefit through the internet in the following ways:

- They can get details of the various policies, the benefits thereunder, the premiums payable, etc.
- Prospects can get advice on the suitable insurance plan for themselves.
- Policyholders can get information with regard to the status of the policy, the

premiums due, the bonuses attached, the surrender values or loans available, revival possibilities, nearest office for any further transaction.

- Details can also be had about housing loans or other benefits available to policyholders.
- Premiums can be paid without having to go to the office of the insurers, by direct debit to the policyholder's credit card or bank account.

The LIC has included in its websites, for the benefit of the prospects and the policyholders, information relating to health issues.

KIOSKS

Kiosks are unmanned information centres, placed strategically at public places. They are called interactive touch screen kiosks. A kiosk is a self contained unit that combines hardware and software to blend all current media including graphics, video, text and quality sound. It consists of a touch sensor and a monitor on which the sensor can be fitted. The user is expected to touch the relevant sensors, according to the choices offered by the kiosk visually on the monitor. The kisk then takes him through various interactive screens to provide him the required information or to transact the required business.

The railways have kiosks located at various stations to help passengers find out about the reservation status of their tickets. The kiosk responds to the touch of the passenger. The passenger makes an enquiry by touching the number that constitute the PNR No. on the ticket. The reservation status will be shown on the display panel. He does not have to go to the reservation office, which in big cities, could be miles away.

The LIC has installed kiosks in more than 100 locations covering its Divisional headquarters. The kiosks provide information on policy status, product information about all products including group insurance products. These can be used by persons, who do not have their own computers and cannot access the internet. They can be operated 24 hours a day and do not require any supervision like the ATMS of banks.

IT in the Rural Areas

According to experts, the growth of the economy in the future will be faster in the rural areas than in the urban areas. The income levels and life styles are changing. As and when the business houses move into the rural areas, they will also bring in the necessary infrastructure. The normal channels of communication are slow, because of the distances involved, the lack of good roads and infrequent transport services. The telephone which has penetrated deep into the rural areas, is not good enough to transmit detailed reports on consumptions, stocks, etc. with retailers, which help the companies plan their logistics better.

But the telephone system is a good base for building the internet. ITC, the cigarette company, with interest in the agricultural economy of the rural areas, has taken a lead in this matter. Called 'choupals' the system had covered nearly a thousand villages by the end of the year 2001. It will expand to many more villages in the years to come. If insures find it possible to work with the ITC or others who may also build such systems in the villages, it will also become easier to extend the services to the policyholders in the rural areas.

16

Risk Management in Banks: Concept of Provisioning for Non-Performing Assets

In line with international practices and moving towards greater consistency and transparency in the published accounts, the Committee on Financial System (CFS) set-up under the Chairmanship of M. Narasimham, had recommended the prudential guidelines, which were implemented from April 1, 1992.

Guidelines focused on the following:

(a) A policy of income recognition should be objective and based on record of recovery and not on subjective considerations;
(b) The classification of assets has to be done on the basis of objective criteria which would ensure a uniform and consistent application of norms; and
(c) The provisions should be made on the basis of classification of assets into four different categories namely, Standard Assets, Sub-Standard Assets, Doubtful Assets and Loss Assets.

INCOME RECOGNITION

As per RBI, income should be recognized on the basis of objective criteria i.e., 'realization' basis, keeping in view the record of recovery of principal and interest. Hence un-recovered interest on all assets should not be charged and taken to income account.

NON-PERFORMING ASSETS (NPAs)

NPAs are those assets, which do not yield income or cease to generate income for the bank. The parameters for terming different credit facilities as NPAs are as follows:

(A) Term Loans: An a/c in which interest and/or instalment of principal remain overdue for a period of 90 days.

(B) Cash Credit/Overdraft: A Cash Credit/Overdraft account remains 'out of order' for a period of 90 days.

(C) Account Out of Order: An account is treated as out of order:

(a) When outstanding balance remains continuously in excess of sanctioned limit or drawing power; or

(b) When there are no credits continuously in the account or the credits are there but they are not sufficient to cover the entire interest or other charges debited in the account; or

(c) When the stock statement is overdue for a period of 3 months, even if account is running regular; or

(d) When the limit is overdue for renewal/review for a period of 6 months, the account is to be treated as NPA.

(D) Bills Account: When the bill purchased or discounted remains overdue/ unpaid for a period of 90 days, it is treated as NPA.

(E) Other Accounts: When an amount to be received remains overdue for a period of more than 90 days, it is treated as NPA.

(F) Agriculture: *Short Duration Crop* (Crop season up to one year)—If the instalment of principal or interest thereon remains overdue for two crop seasons.

Long Duration Crop (Season longer than one year)—If the instalment of principal or interest thereon remains overdue for one-crop season, the account is treated as NPA.

In respect of agricultural loans given to non-agriculturists, identification of NPAs would be done on the same basis as non-agricultural advances, i.e., 90 days delinquency norm.

(G) Infrastructure Finance: Infrastructure Projects financed after 28th May, 2002, should be classified as Sub-standard if the date of commencement of commercial production extends beyond a period of one year (it was two years earlier).

NPA ON ACCOUNT OF EROSION IN VALUE OF SECURITY

When the realizable value of security has eroded and has become less than 50% of the value assessed by the bank or accepted by RBI at the time of last inspection, such an account has to be straightaway classified under doubtful category.

If the realizable value of security has become less than 10% of the outstanding in the borrowal accounts, the existence of the security is to be ignored and the account to be straightaway classified as loss asset.

ASSET-CLASSIFICATION

In line with the RBI norms, Banks classify the advances into four broad groups namely: (i) Standard assets, (ii) Sub-standard assets, (iii) Doubtful assets and, (iv) Loss assets by compressing the existing eight health codes taking into consideration the degree (and extent) of well defined credit weaknesses and extent of dependence on collateral security/or realization of dues.

SPECIAL MENTION ACCOUNTS (SMA)

RBI has also instructed banks to identify accounts, which are overdue/out of order but not yet so for 90 days and maintain a special watch on those accounts. Banks are free to fix the number of days (30, 45 as desired) for identifying SMAs as NPAs for the purpose of provisioning; SMAs are clubbed with Standard Assets only.

Table 16.1: Asset-Classification

Group	*Definition*
Standard	Accounts which are in order
Sub-standard	Accounts which have been classified as NPAs for a period not exceeding 12 months
Doubtful	Sub-standard accounts, which have remained NPAs for a *period exceeding* 12 months
Loss assets	Accounts which have become unrealizable, where losses have been identified by the bank/internal/external auditor/RBI Inspectors.
SMA	Special mentioned assets: RBI has instructed banks to identify accounts which are overdue/out of order but not NPA & maintain a special watch.

Category	*Provision Requirements*				
Standard assets	Direct Agri. & SME sectors		All other loans & Advances	Commercial Real Estate	Teaser Rate—Housing Loan
	0.25%		0.40%	1%	2%
Sub-standard assets	Secured Sub-standard		Unsecured Sub-standard : Where the value of security is not more than 10% right from the beginning i.e. *ab-initio*		
	15% of outstanding dues		25% of outstanding dues		
Doubtful assets	D1		D2		D3
	First 12 months		Next 24 months		Over 36 months
	RVS	Shortfall in Security	RVS	Shortfall in Security	100% Uniformly
	25%	100%	40%	100%	
Loss assets	The entire assets should be written-off. If permitted to remain in the books for any reason, 100% of the outstanding should be provided for.				

Standard Assets provisions are covered under Tier II capital under the head 'Other liabilities and provisions (Schedule 5)'.

As per the Income recognition norms, interest is recognized on realization/cash system basis.

State Government-guaranteed advances—90 days norm with effect from 31-3-

2006. The Central Government guaranteed advances are treated as NPAs when the government repudiates its guarantee.

Accounts with Stock Statement submission overdue for 3 months are to be treated as 'Out of Order'.

Accounts in which Renewal/revival is overdue for six months are to be treated as NPAs.

Classification of accounts is borrower-wise and not account-wise. In case of consortium advances, each bank has to classify the account on the basis of its own record of recovery.

The provisioning on Teaser Rate Housing Loans to be reduced to .40% after one year from the date on which the rates are reset higher if the account remains 'Standard'.

Restructured accounts classified as standard advances will attract a provision of 2% in the first 2 years from the date of restructuring, or in cases of moratorium on payment of interest/principal after restructuring, for the period covering moratorium and 2 years thereafter (as against existing provision of 0.25-1.00%, depending upon the category of advances).

Restructured accounts classified as non-performing advances, when upgraded to standard category will attract a provision of 2% in the first year from the date of upgradation (as against existing provision of 0.25-1.00%, depending upon the category of advances).

SALE AND PURCHASE OF NPAs

Background: The past a few years have witnessed several financial and economic crises world wide, crippling economies and affecting the health of financial Institutions. Such instances invariably culminate in increase in the level of Non-Performing Assets (NPAs) of financial institutions and Banks.

Worldwide, prudential guidelines prevent Banks from recognizing income on Non-performing assets. Apart from such obvious setbacks, high-level NPAs affect the Banks in other ways as well. Financial and Human resources of the banks become engaged (often with scant results) in recovery and resolution of NPA related problems. There is also an opportunity loss as these resources could have been employed in more useful and income generating activities instead of handling NPAs. Capital adequacy becomes an issue due to locking up of essential capital in such bad assets. Decision-makers too become risk averse in granting new loans, particularly to small and medium sized companies. Thus, large scale NPAs when left unattended, cause economic and financial degradation. This results in a credit slow-down signaling adverse investment climate.

Giving due importance to this phenomenon, Governments engage themselves in resolving the problem of high NPAs in their financial systems. A feasible solution to a system-wide clean up of NPAs is the creation of Asset Reconstruction Companies (ARCs), which are typically publicly/Government owned. These Institutions act as debt aggregators and engage in acquisition of NPAs. They take away the NPAs from the banking system and act as "bad banks". This leaves rest of the banking system free to act as "good banks" and return to normal banking business unlocking funds and human energy. Governments then proceed to encourage transfer of assets to ARCs through creation of supportive environment. They also provide special powers to ARCs that are not otherwise available to banking system at times to enable them to become efficient and effective.

INTERNATIONAL EXPERIENCE

ARCs have been used worldwide, particularly in Asia, to resolve bad-loan problems, and have had a varying degree of success. In 1980s, U.S.A. used government sponsored ARC-Resolution Trust Corporation (RTC) to overcome thrift crisis. RTC acted as a "bad bank" and functioned as an effective sales mechanism for disposal of assets. In early 1990s, Mexico and Sweden demonstrated successful use of ARC mechanism as a "bad bank" and to clean and re-privatize/re-capitalize the banks. Korea, Malaysia, Taiwan, have all used ARC models to help their Financial Institutions to clean up their balance sheets. Japan, China, Thailand & Indonesia used ARC mechanism during the South-East Asian crisis.

INDIAN SCENARIO

The problem of recovery from NPAs, in the Indian banking system, was recognized by the Government of India long ago. The Narasimham Committee Report mentioned that an important aspect of the continuing reform process was to reduce the high level of NPAs. It was expected that with a combination of policy and institutional development, new NPAs in future could be lower; however, the problem of the huge backlog of existing NPAs still remained. This problem affected Banks' performance and profitability severely. The Report envisaged creation of an "Asset Recovery Fund" to take the NPAs off the lender's books at a discount. In this background ARCs were formed in India.

ASSET RECONSTRUCTION COMPANY OF INDIA LIMITED (ARCIL)

ARCIL, the first ARC in India, was promoted by SBI, ICICI; IDBI and PNB. The sale of the financial assets to ARCIL enables the NPA to be taken off the loan books of the Bank/FI and unlocks capital. Notable among the deals were the sale of bad assets to the tune of Rs. 1400 crores by ICICI and assets worth Rs. 1750 crores by Indian Banks. Sale of NPAs on a portfolio basis enables loss on sale of any one asset to be set-off against capital gains on another, subject to RBI guidelines on provisioning/valuation norms.

RESERVE BANK OF INDIA (RBI) GUIDELINES

The guidelines are applicable to banks, FIs and NBFCs purchasing/selling Non-performing financial assets, from/to other Banks/FIs/NBFCs (excluding Securitization companies/Reconstruction companies). A financial asset, including assets under multiple/consortium banking arrangements, is eligible for purchase/sale if it is a Non-performing asset/investment in the books of the selling bank.

PROCEDURE INCLUDING VALUATION AND PRICING ASPECTS

(1) A bank which is purchasing/selling Non-performing financial assets should ensure that the purchase/sale is conducted in accordance with a policy approved by the Board.

The Board shall lay down policies and guidelines covering: Non-performing financial assets that may be purchased or sold; Norms and procedure for purchase/sale of such financial assets; Valuation procedure to be followed to ensure that the economic value of financial assets is reasonably estimated based on the estimated cash flows arising out of repayments and recovery prospects.

(2) Delegation of powers of various functionaries for taking decision on the purchase/sale of the financial assets.

(3) The Board should satisfy itself that the bank has adequate skills to purchase Non-performing financial assets and deal with them in an efficient manner which will result in value addition to the bank. The Board should also ensure that appropriate systems and procedures are in place to effectively address the risks that a purchasing bank would assume while engaging in this activity.

(4) At least 10% of the estimated cash flows should be realized in the first year and at least 5% in each half year thereafter, subject to full recovery within three years (earlier the estimated cash flows were expected to be realized within a period of three years and not less than 5% of the estimated cash flows should be realized in each half year).

(5) A bank may purchase/sell Non-performing financial assets from/to other banks only on "without recourse" basis, i.e., the entire credit risk associated with the Non-performing financial assets should be transferred to the purchasing bank. Selling bank shall ensure that the effect of the sale of the financial assets should be such that the asset is taken off the books of the bank and after the sale there should not be any known liability devolving on the selling bank.

(6) Banks should ensure that subsequent to sale of the Non-performing financial assets to other banks, they do not have any involvement with reference to assets sold and do not assume operational, legal or any other type of risks relating to the financial assets sold. Consequently, the specific financial asset should not enjoy the support of credit enhancements/liquidity facilities in any form or manner.

(7) Each bank will make its own assessment of the value offered by the purchasing bank for the financial asset and decide whether to accept or reject the offer.

(8) Under no circumstances can a sale to other banks be made at a contingent price whereby in the event of shortfall in the realization by the purchasing banks, the selling banks would have to bear a part of the shortfall.

(9) A Non-performing asset in the books of a bank shall be eligible for sale to other banks only if it has remained a Non-performing asset for at least two years in the books of the selling bank.

(10) Banks can sell Non-performing financial assets to other banks only on cash basis. The entire sale consideration should be received upfront and the asset can be taken out of the books of the selling bank only on receipt of the entire sale consideration.

(11) NPA—financial asset should be held by the purchasing bank in its books at least for a period of 15 months before it is sold to other banks. Banks should not sell such assets back to the bank, which had sold the NPA.

(12) Banks are also permitted to sell/buy homogeneous pool within retail Non-performing financial assets; on a portfolio basis provided each of the Non-performing financial assets of the pool has remained as Non-performing financial asset for at

least 2 years in the books of the selling bank. The pool of assets would be treated as a single asset in the books of the purchasing bank.

PRUDENTIAL NORMS FOR PURCHASE/SALE TRANSACTIONS

(A) Asset Classification Norms

(a) The Non-performing financial asset purchased, may be classified as "Standard" in the books of the purchasing bank for a period of 90 days from the date of purchase. Thereafter, the asset classification status of the financial asset purchased should be determined by the record of recovery in the books of the purchasing bank with reference to cash flows estimated, while purchasing the asset.

(b) The asset classification status of an existing exposure (other than purchased financial asset) to the same obligor in the books of the purchasing bank will continue to be governed by the record of recovery of that exposure and hence may be different.

(c) Where the purchase/sale do not satisfy any of the prudential requirements prescribed in these guidelines the asset classification status of the financial asset in the books of the purchasing bank at the time of purchase shall be the same as in the books of the selling bank. Thereafter, the asset classification status will continue to be determined with reference to the date of NPA in the selling bank.

(d) Any restructure/reschedule/rephrase of the repayment schedule or the estimated cash flow of the Non-performing financial asset by the purchasing bank shall render the account as a Non-performing asset.

(B) Provisioning Norms: Books of Selling Bank

(a) When a bank sells its Non-performing financial assets to other banks, the same will be removed from its books on transfer.

(b) If the sale is at a price below the net book value (NBV) (i.e., book value less provisions held), the shortfall should be debited to the profit and loss account of that year.

(c) If the sale is for a value higher than the NBV, the excess provision shall not be reversed but will be utilized to meet the shortfall/loss on account of sale of other Non-performing financial assets.

BOOKS OF PURCHASING BANK

The asset will attract provisioning requirement appropriate to its asset classification status in the books of the purchasing bank.

RECENT DEVELOPMENTS

Reserve Bank has observed that in some cases NPAs have been sold for much less than the value of available securities and no justification has been given.

RBI's DIRECTIVE/ADVICE TO BANKS

Banks should, while selling NPAs, work out the net present value of the estimated cash flows associated with the realizable value of the available securities net of the cost of realization. The sale price should generally not be lower than the net present value arrived at.

Same principle should be used in compromise settlements. As the payment of the compromise amount may be in instalments, the net present value of the settlement amount should be calculated and this amount should generally not be less than the net present value of the realizable value of securities.

FORWARD CONTRACTS AND FUTURES

Swaps, caps, and floors are recent innovations in the derivatives markets. The derivatives market traditionally included forward contracts in addition to options (puts, calls, warrants). A forward contract involved a commitment to trade a specified item at a specified price at a future date. For example, if an American company will have need of 1 million British pounds six months from now they may avoid exposure to exchange rate risk by entering into a forward contract for the pounds now. The forward contract takes whatever form the two parties agree to. There is also a market for standardized forward contracts, which is called the futures market. The standardization makes possible a wider market with greater liquidity and efficiency. Often the futures markets eliminate the ties between specific parties, the party and the counter-party, and the risk that the other might not fulfil the contract. In the futures market everyone deals with the clearinghouse who guarantees fulfilment.

OPTIONS

In the options market there has developed some terminology that is somewhat intimidating to the uninitiated. A *call option* is the right to buy a share of a stock, the underlying security, at a specified price, called the exercise price or the strike price. A *put option* is the right to sell a share of a stock at a specified price, the exercise price or the strike price.

There is a limited time for the exercise of the call option. An American option can be exercised at any time up to and including the expiration date. A European option can only be exercised on the expiration date. The value of a call option at any time depends upon.

17

Concept of Licensing of Corporate Agents—IRDA (Licensing of Corporate Agents) Regulations, 2002

IMPORTANT PROVISIONS

These Regulations are as per the IRDA (Licensing of Insurance Agents) Regulations, 2002. The important provisions are as follows:

(1) A corporate agent can be a firm, a company under the Companies Act, a banking company, a corresponding new bank, a regional rural bank, a cooperative society, a panchayat, a local authority, a non-government organization, a micro-lending finance organization, a non-banking finance company, a or any other organization that may be approved by the IRDA.

(2) The partnership deed or the Memorandum of Association or any other document that states the objectives of the person wanting to be the corporate agent, must state clearly that soliciting and procuring insurance business is one of its objectives.

(3) The corporate agent has to nominate its partner (in the case of a firm), director (in the case of a company), or one or more of its officers or employees, as a 'corporate insurance e executive'. The issue of licence to the corporate agent is subject to the insurance executives satisfying the requisite educational and other qualifications, as in the case of an individual agent. He is also required to undergo the minimum training requirements and pass the examination conducted by the insurance institute of India, as in the case of individual agents.

(4) The corporate agent also has to nominate one or more of its partners, directors or employees as 'specified person', who will be responsible for soliciting insurance business on behalf of the corporate agent. The specified person must have a minimum educational qualification on the same lines

as individual agents, and must also not suffer from any of the disqualifications like being insane, being confided for a criminal offense, etc., he must obtain a certification, which will be given to him after he undergoes the prescribed training and passes an examination. The fees for the certification are Rs. 500. The certification will be valid for 3 years and can be renewed.

(5) Both corporate insurance executives and specified persons are bound by the code of conduct for agents, as applicable to individual agents. A violation of the code can result in the cancellation of the licence of the corporate agent, the corporate insurance executives or certification of the specified persons.

18

Bancassurance: A Novel Concept

INTRODUCTION

Banks have large clientele in all countries. In Europe, banks were allowed to do marketing for Insurance companies for fee. In India, the banking regulations did not permit any direct connection or financial stake in insurance. Of late, Banks in India have been permitted to float subsidiaries to do Insurance business. For those subsidiaries, canvassing is permitted and business is directed from depositors and others without any legal impediment. This is bancassurance. A brief discussion of Bancassurance is given below:

In terms of the Regulations issued by the Insurance Regulatory and Development Authority (IRDA), agents for insurance companies have to obtain licenses, such licenses may be issued to individuals or to corporate bodies, like banks, firms, cooperative societies, etc. in the case of corporate agents, the licences will be issued to person who are designated by the corporate bodies as 'corporate Insurance Executives'. In addition, the corporate agent may avail of the services of 'Specified persons' who will have to obtain certificates. This supplement is written for the benefit of those who are working in banks and seek to qualify for the licences and certificates.

This supplement is to be studied along with the main course, which is the basis of the training and examination for individual agents. So far, there is no such supplement for other corporate agents. It is not expected that there may be any issues affecting all such corporate agent in an uniform manner. In the case of banks, however, there is likely to be such common issues. That is the justification for this special supplement.

WHAT IS BANCASSURANCE?

Bancassurance is a word coined in the western world, when banks began to get involved in the marketing of insurance business. The involvement took different forms in different countries. In some countries, the same institution would offer both banking and insurance products, separately or together as the customers may need, managing both the businesses themselves. This was possible when the institution was allowed to transact both insurance band banking businesses. This was permitted in certain countries. The product or service offered to the customer was the product of the bank and had in it some elements of insurance. This strictly is bancassurance. In practice, however, there are variations.

One variation was that the bank might offer both service-combines, but having done the business, pass on the insurance part of the funds to an insurance company, with whom it had an alliance or a business arrangements. Both of them may be under the same industrial group. For example, when the Unit Trust of India offered Unit linked life insurance policies, it had an arrangement with the Life Insurance Corporation to the extent of the term insurance component. The 'Peerless' used to offer its account holders insurance cover on accidental death. This was done by arrangement with a general insurance company. Although marketed as one product, the business remained separate. The funds were accounted for and managed separately by separate institutions.

The third method that is the pattern emerging in India is that the bank undertakes marketing activities for the insurance products for a fee None of the bank's services are modified or enhanced by the insurance services. Also, the benefits offered are not in any manner modified or enhanced by the association with the bank. The product is in no way different from what any other agent of the insurer may offer. The bank is only an agent of the insurer.

BANCASSURANCE ABROAD

For years together world over, insurance and banking businesses were considered to be separate and regulated as such. The principles of managing the funds were different in the two businesses. The risk profiles and the capital needs are different. They have different time horizons, while making investment decision. Even within the banking business, development banking was different from merchant banking, which was again different from commercial retail banking.

The 1970s and 1980s saw these barriers crumbling. The financial sector was becoming one. There was need for a one stop delivery for all financial services. Financial institutions transacting different businesses began to work together in strategic alliances or merged into one entity. Banks could offer insurance policies and insurers could offer banking services.

In 1997, the Credit Suisse bought over the Winterthur, the second largest insurer in Switzerland. Such mergers happened in the Netherlands, Belgium, Germany, France and Spain. This was not permitted in the USA because of the Glass Steagall Act (passed in 1933). This act was recently repealed and some insurance companies and banks have merged.

In Europe, bancassurance seems to have made the greatest impact in France. It is claimed that 55% to 60% of the life insurance business in France had come through banks. In the U.K., the figure is about 15%. In Portugal and Spain, it was over 70%. In Argentina, Brazil, Chile, Colombia and Mexico, bancassurance is popular. Big international banks have got into the business of insurance and pension funds. In

Brazil, ,the online banking systems are used. Everywhere, the contribution for non-life insurance is low, less than 10%.

The potential impact of bancassurance is much more than what these figures of shares represent. If the Royal bank of Canada and the London Insurance Co. were to merge or the Chase Manhattan Bank in the US were to merge with the AIG, (the third largest insurer in the US) the impact would be as huge as the State Bank of India and the LIC merging in India. These are not hypothetical, but real possibilities in Canada and in the US. These also raise issues relevant to anti-trust laws. In Canada, the Competition Bureau as well as the Superintendent of Financial Institutions have expressed concern about mega mergers between banks having reduced competition. They also see possibilities of conflict of interests.

VALUE PROPOSITIONS

The services offered by banks as well as insurance companies, are related to assets and risks. They have to be managed. These institutions manage risks and assets for the customers, reducing and taking over the risks and transforming the assets. The core of the businesses is similar, though not same. The basic distinctions in the values offered by banks insurance companies and other financial institutions are indicated below.

Banks offer to its customers liquidity (while at the same time making long-term loans), safety, trust (managing estates on behalf of beneficiaries), collections of interests or dividends, payment of commitments (rentals and insurance premiums, for example) and annuities. Insurers primarily protect clients from risks (political, financial, commercial, business, and human). In life insurance, there is a major component of management of an asset which is created by the policy. The benefits of the insurer's expertise in asset management, passes on to the clients by way of premiums levels and bonuses the liquidity concerns of insurers are different from the liquidity concern of banks.

Securities firms primarily provide information and advice. They also act as brokers or agents for the customers, but do not take responsibility for risk on assets. Pension funds manage the savings made directly or through employers and help the pensioners manage the risk of loss of income in the old age. Mutual funds are asset transformers, providing small savers easy access to complex portfolios of capital markets and protecting them from the vagaries of the capital market, without sacrificing the needs of liquidity.

Most customers, big and small, individuals and companies, are all interested in all these services. That is the justification for the concept of a single window for all financial services. Bancassurance is a step in this evolution.

THE INDIAN CONTEXT

In India, no company is allowed to transact both insurance and banking business. They are kept separate. In fact, even a company, registered as an insurer has to choose between life and non-life business. It cannot do both. Therefore, the banks in India cannot have the advantages, which are available in the European context.

There are joint ventures in India between banks and foreign insurers. State Bank of India, HDFC, ICICI and Vysya Bank are examples. But apart from a greater willingness to help each other, the joint venture will not give either party a greater advantage in the other's business. The joint venture is an entirely independent unit of operation, with separate personnel and funds, and subject to different regulations.

The only way in which banks can be associated with the insurance business in India is by becoming a corporate agent for remuneration. The bank can do so for a particular life insurer and/or particular non-life insurer. The bank can not, on its own, develop any insurance product. It can, of course, make suggestions on the basis of its intimate contacts with the customers. Since 2000, many banks and insurers have agreed to arrangements for mutual benefit. The LIC has tied with more than one bank. So also have other insurers.

For more than a hundred years, insurance business had been sold through insurance agents and their supervisors. This system had not been very satisfactory. The LIC inherited this system. The efforts to make the agents more professional had not yielded very satisfactory results, despite incentives and training programmes. Many of them continued to treat the agency business casually, as just as source of additional income. The turnover had been high and the efforts of replenishing the strength, costly. The banks have skilled staff, to whom the procurement of insurance, can be assigned as a duty. This was an opportunity made available after the regulations of the IRDA.

Benefits to the Insurer

The main benefits to the insurer are as follows:

> The market for insurance is very heterogeneous, with customers of widely varying profiles and needs. Therefore, they have to use multiple channels for distribution, to match the different segments. As an additional channel, the banks have a good match with certain segments of the market.

It gets the advantage of the existing infrastructure of the bank.

In India, the public banks have 70000 branches, of which more than 35000 are in the rural areas and 17000 in the semi urban areas. The LIC, the biggest life insurer in the country, had, after nearly 57 years of existence, less than 2700 branches all over the country including the metro cities. The four general insurance companies also had a similar number of branches.

Access is easily available to a huge client-base. The customers of the banks are similar to the customers for insurance. Where the general banks have 19 crore accounts, the number is a large reservoir of potential customers for insurers.

There is a relationship of loyalty and trust between the bank and its customers which can become a valuable base for selling insurance. Banks have much more intimate contacts with their customers than insurers, because (i) the frequency of contact is more, and (ii) they meet under more pleasant circumstances.

Customers tend to have more trust in the banks than in insurers, with whom their contacts are comparatively much less.

There is a complimentary between insurance and banking. Loans are given by banks on security and credit of persons and of assets. Insurance ensures that the security is not lost.

Banks constitute a readily available, competent, trusted, educated distribution channel for the insurer.

Particularly for new insurers, the association with the banks helps them penetrate the markets much faster and also to give themselves some credibility. They can get some leverage from the bank's branch image.

Banks can leverage their contact with commercial clients for developing personal lines of insurance, which are relatively neglected, particularly in non-life business.

Premium can be paid by debit to the account with the bank.

Employees bound by the discipline of the banks are easier to be monitored and controlled than independent agents are.

BENEFITS TO THE BANK

Banks are under pressure because of falling/fluctuating interest rates and increasing costs of administration. Competition from global players, is to making it easy. All banks are looking for fee-based incomes. Insurance commissions provide an excellent avenue for such income, it is expected that banks would be looking for fee-based (non-interest) incomes of the order of Rs. 15,000 to Rs. 20,000 crores over the next five years. In India, the fee is only through the commission received on the business placed with the insurer.

Banks can help to develop insurance products, which are relevant to its business, particularly in the areas of international trade, with risks on account of political upheavals, exchange fluctuations, etc.

There is no risk in the business. The bank cannot lose. The only risk is if the chosen insurer gets into trouble or is poor in service. The customer is likely to blame the bank for the problem. This is, however, a remote risk.

The other benefits include:

- Better customer retention and stronger relationship.
- Clear competitive advantage in the rural areas.
- Possibility that the insurer's accounts as well as the accounts from the claimants will remain with the bank.
- Insurance products can augment the value of the banking products and services.
- Banks are in a better position to offer complete integrated financial solutions.

THE LEGAL REQUIREMENTS

Any scheduled commercial banks or its subsidiary can become a corporate agent. To float a joint venture, the bank must have according to RBI regulations:

- Net worth of at least Rs. 500 crores.
- Reasonably low Non-Performing Assets.
- Net profit for the last three years.
- Record of satisfactory performance by its subsidiaries, if any, should be recorded.
- Capital to Risk weighted Ratio of not less than 10%.
- A share in the insurance company's capital not exceeding 50%. Exceptions may be considered by the RBI.
- Limit share of capital of foreign partner, if any, to 49% (being raised to 74%).

Unlike in foreign countries, the banks in India are required to maintain separate staff for doing insurance business. These persons will be exclusively dealing with insurance business. The overhead expense will, therefore, remain high until the business increases adequately.

The banks will be entitled to receive commission on the insurance business only if it is licensed to act as an agent and the specified person, who procured the business is an employee of the bank. It will not be entitled to receive any commission, if the business is procured by a person who is employed, by the insurers, but is allowed to occupy space or other facilities of the bank.

THE PROBLEMS

Any bank getting into the business of selling insurance cannot afford to have a casual approach to it. The staff, if deputed from within the existing bank staff, will have to be specially trained in the intricacies of insurance and the art of salesmanship. These skills will be required at levels different from the requirements in banking operations. They will have to be persons who have an external orientation.

The amount of business acquired through the bank depends entirely on the persons skills of the specified persons and the corporate insurance executives. An effective and successful specified person, might perhaps find it more remunerative to branch of as an insurance agent on his own, instead of being tied to the bank. The options available to the bank to prevent this, may lie in developing attractive compensation packages. The relevant issues will be the restrictions imposed by the insurance act as well as the relative pressures within the unions of the bank employees.

The commitment of the senior management is crucial to the success of the person deputed for the insurance work. The priorities for the managers may depend on the criteria by which they will be appraised at the end of the year. If the progress in insurance is not an important criterion, the support to the insurance activities may be reduced. They would see mainstream banking activities as more important for their own future growth. The appraisal and reward systems of the bank have to be appropriately aligned.

CONCEPT OF UNIVERSAL BANKING

Traditionally, development banking was separate from commercial or retail banking. A development bank would evaluate the proposed projects of a company and help it to acquire long-term finance, either as equity or as loans. It may provide these funds by itself, or in conjunction with other financial institutions or give confidence to investing public that the project was sound, by declaring its support. The Industrial Development Bank of India (IDBI), the Industrial Finance Corporation of India (IFCI), the Industrial Credit and Investment Corporation of India (ICICI) were such organizations specializing in developing banking. There were many other institutions in the States as well.

Current thinking is that there is no need for such division of activities and that commercial banks can take upon themselves the responsibility of all kinds of banking activities. The ICICI has merged with ICICI bank. The IDBI and the IFGCI are also looking at similar options. The Narasimham Committee has recommended that the banking system should move towards universal banking.

Universal banking means that there is full integration of the financial businesses, including securities, insurance, mortgages, etc. Banks in India are already into the business of long-term financing of companies, mortgages, individual loans, hire-purchase, investments etc. Banks are also involved in performing tasks on behalf of government, like collecting taxes and paying pensions. Insurance is still kept out but may not remain so for too long.

Studies abroad have shown that banks prefer to have their own insurance companies. Instead of working for other insurance companies as agents for the latter, they prefer to do insurance business independently. The reasons given are of the following kinds:

- Efficient operation and good products come only when they are built by themselves, not through buying from some other producer.
- There could be differences in the cultures of the two institutions, particularly with regard to customer orientation.
- They do not want to compete with the insurer's distribution channel, which may include other banks.

19

Concept of Hedging Foreign Exchange Transactions

FOREIGN EXCHANGE CONTRACTS

An Exporter in India contracts to sell to a firm in London items of Machinery at a price of GBP 10,000. Before agreeing to this price, the exporter calculates his cost of production, adds a reasonable margin for profit and satisfies that the proceeds of GBP 10,000 would cover this amount. He bases his calculations on the exchange rate prevailing as on the date of his quotation. For example, if the exchange rate on the date is Rs. 80 per pound sterling (GBP), he expects to receive Rs. 8,00,000 on execution of the contract.

The exchange rate, however, is not stable. It is changing every day. By the time the exporter executes his contract and his bill is realised, which may occur after a lapse of three months or six months, the rate of exchange might have turned adverse for him. For example, if the rate prevailing on the date the bill is realised or purchased by his banker is Rs. 75 per GBP, he would receive only Rs. 7,50,000 thus incurring loss of Rs. 50,000 as against his estimate of Rs. 8,00,000. He may have to bear a shortfall of Rs. 50,000. Alternately, the exchange rate may turn favourable to him and bring him unexpected profits. But the fact remains that the amount that he would receive on execution of the contract remains uncertain.

The uncertainty about the rate that would prevail on a future date is known as the 'exchange risk'. For the exporter, the exchange rate is that the foreign currency in which the transaction is designated may depreciate in future and may bring less than the expected realisation in local currency terms.

The importer too faces exchange risk when the transaction is designated in a foreign currency. The risk is that the foreign currency may appreciate in value and he may be compelled to pay in local currency an amount higher than that was originally contemplated. Importers generally make arrangements for loans for payments for the imports. If the foreign currency appreciates subsequent to the arrangement of the loan, the importer may find that the resources are not sufficient to meet the import bill putting him in a difficult position.

FEATURES OF A FORWARD EXCHANGE CONTRACT

Forward Exchange Contract is a device which can afford adequate protection to an importer or an exporter against exchange risk. Under a Foreign Exchange Contract, a banker and a customer or another banker enter into a contract to buy o sell a fixed amount of foreign currency on a specified future date at a pre-determined rate of exchange. An exporter, for instance, instead of groping in the dark or making a wild guess about what the future rate would be, enters into a contract with his banker immediately. He agrees to sell foreign exchange of a specified amount and currency at a specified future date. The banker on his part agrees to buy this currency at a specified rate of exchange. The exporter is thus assured of his price in the local currency. In our example (mentioned before), the exporter may enter into a forward contract with the bank for three months delivery at Rs. 59.50. This rate on the date of the contract is known as 3 months forward rate. When the exporter submits his bill under the contract, the banker would purchase it at the rate of Rs. 59.50 irrespective of the spot rate then prevailing.

When Indian Rupee (INR) was devalued by about 18% in 1991, many importers found that their liabilities had increased overnight. The devaluation of the 'Rupee', had the effect of appreciation of foreign currency in terms of Rupees. Those importers who had booked forward contracts to cover their imports were obviously a happy lot.

DATE OF DELIVERY

According to Rule 7 of FEDAI, a 'forward contract' is deliverable at a future date, duration of the contract being computed from the spot value date of the transaction. Thus, if a 3 months forward contract is booked on the 15th March, the period of three months should commence from 14th March and the forward contract will fall due on the 14th June.

Date of delivery under the forward contract will be:

(a) In case of bills/documents negotiated, purchased or discounted: date of negotiation/purchase/discount and payment of Rupees to the customer.

(b) In case of bills/documents sent for collection: date of payment of Rupees to the customer on realisation.

(c) In case of retirement/crystallization of Import Bills/documents: the date of retirement or crystallisation of liability, whichever is earlier.

FIXED CONTRACT AND OPTION FORWARD CONTRACTS

The forward contract under which the delivery of foreign exchange should take place on a specified future date is known as 'fixed forward contract'. For instance, if on the 5th March, a customer enters into a 3 months forward contract with the bank to sell GBP 10,000, it means that the customer would be presenting a bill or any other instrument on the 7th June to the bank for GBP 10,000. He can not deliver foreign exchange prior to or later than the determined date.

We saw that forward contract is a device by which the customer tries to cover the exchange risk. The purpose will be defeated if he is unable to take delivery or surrender foreign exchange exactly on the due date. In real situations, it is not possible for any exporter to determine in advance the precise date on which he will be tendering export documents. Besides internal factors relating to production, many other external factors also decide the date on which he is able to complete shipment and present documents to the bank. At the most, the exporter can only estimate the probable date around which he would be able to complete his commitment.

With a view to eliminating the difficulty in fixing the exact date for delivery of foreign exchange, the customer may be given choice of delivering the foreign exchange during given period of days. An arrangement whereby the customer can sell or buy foreign exchange from the bank on any day during a given period of time at a pre-determined rate of exchange is known as 'Option Forward Contract'. The rate at which the deal takes place is the option forward rate. For example, on the 15th September, a customer enters into two months forward sale contract with the bank with option over November. It means that the customer of the bank can sell foreign exchange specified in the contract on any date from the 1st day of November to the 30th day of November. The period from the 1st November to the 30th November is called the 'option period'.

RULE REGARDING OPTION FORWARD CONTRACTS (RULE 7 OF FEDAI)

1. The option period of delivery should be specified as a calendar week (i.e. 1st to 7th; 8th to 15th; 16th to 23rd; 24th to the last working day of the month) or a calendar fortnight (i.e. 1st to 15th or 16th to the last working day of the month).

2. The option of delivery can not exceed a period of one calendar month. Calendar month here means the period between any two corresponding dates in consecutive months. Illustratively, the option period can be 1st May to the 31st May or 15th May to the 14th June, or 20th May to the 19th June.

3. As between a bank and a customer, the option is that of customer. So, the bank can not force the customer to deliver foreign exchange on any specific date. It is up to the customer to choose any date within the option period.

It is worth noting at this point that in the free trade regime that is going to be in place, foreseeable in the next ten years, the phasing is already planned to progress to that end and beyond, to establish world market for free competition and as integrated world economy under one supervisory and regulatory body. In such a situation, option to break free from the option contract, or at least to exercise option of delivery of foreign exchange, not only selling but even buying it, will be available to the other party to the option forward contract, the bank.

EXCHANGE CONTROL REGULATIONS

While booking forward contracts for customers, the banks are required to observe that the Exchange Control Regulations are complied with. The regulations relating to forward contracts are summarised below:

1. Forward contracts can be booked for resident customers who are exposed

to exchange risk in respect of genuine transactions permitted under current regulations.

2. Before entering into forward contract, it should be ensured that the customer is, in fact, exposed to exchange risk in a permitted currency in the underlying transaction. The choice of currency in which the forward contract is entered into is left to the customer. The implication of this provision is that the forward contract need not be booked in the same currency as that of the underlying transaction. Thus, a customer who has an export order for Japanese Yen (JPY) 1 million may book any of the following forward contracts:

   (a) Forward purchase (by the bank) of Yen against Indian Rupees.
   (b) Forward purchase (by the bank) of US Dollar (USD) against Indian Rupee.
   (c) Forward purchase (by the bank) of Yen against US Dollar (USD).
   (d) Forward purchase (by the bank) of Mark against US Dollar (USD).

   Any contract other than Yen (Yen) against Indian Rupee will keep the customer open on the other leg of the transaction, which will be done at the spot rate. For example, under (b) when the bill is tendered, it will be converted into US Dollar at the forward rate and the equivalent US Dollar will be converted into Indian Rupees at the spot rate.

3. While booking forward contracts, the bank should verify suitable documents to ensure the authenticity and the amount of permitted foreign currency of the underlying transaction. The amount, date and number of the forward contract should be marked on such documents under the stamp and signature of the bank/authorised signatory in order to ensure that more than one forward contract is not booked in respect of the same underlying transaction. Copies of the documents so marked should be retained by the bank for its record.

4. Forward Contract may be booked for the whole or part amount of the underlying transaction. Ordinarily, the maturity of the forward contract should match that of the underlying transaction. Thus in case of Exports, the maturity of the Forward Contract should match with the due date of the bill expected to be drawn under the relevant Export Order. Contracts may, however, be booked for shorter maturities with a view to reducing costs to the customer.

5. The bank may permit the customer to substitute an export/import order under a forward contract provided it is satisfied after verifying the documentary evidence that a genuine exposure to the extent of the amount of the original forward contract subsists under the substituted order.

6. A forward contract booked for exports may be cancelled if so desired by the customer. The exposure can again be covered by the customer with the same or another bank. Bank concerned will have to ensure that a genuine exposure to the extent of the amount of the forward contract in respect of a permissible transaction continues to exist. Cancellation of forward contracts of US Dollar 1,00,000 and above should be reported on a weekly basis to Reserve Bank of India.

7. A forward contract booked for Import may be rolled over on or before maturity. The contract my be cancelled if so desired by the customer.. However, once cancelled, it can not be re-booked. While booking a forward contract for an Import transaction, the bank concerned should ensure that the underlying exposure had not been hedged earlier and cancelled.

BOOKING OF FORWARD CONTRACTS

The stage involved in booking and utilization of a forward contract may be summarised as under:

1. The transaction of booking of a forward contract is initiated with the customer enquiring of his bank the rate at which the required foreign currency is available. Before quoting a rate, the bank should get details about (i) the currency involved, (ii) the period of forward cover, including the particulars of option, and (iii) the nature and tenor of the instrument. For instance, when the customer says simply 'Dollar', the bank should ascertain whether it is US Dollar or Canadian Dollar or Australian Dollar. Similarly, if it is a bill transaction, it should be ascertained whether it is the sight bill or 30-day bill, etc. In the case of Usance Bills, whether the due date is calculated from sight or from the date of bill of lading. Differences on these counts would vary the rate applicable.
2. The bank-branch may not be fed with forward rates of all currencies by the Dealing Room. Even for major currencies, forward rates for standard delivery periods may only be available to the branch. If the rate for the currency and/or delivery period is not available, the bank-branch should contact the Dealing Room over phone or telex or E-mail and obtain the rate.
3. If the rate quoted by the bank is acceptable to the customer, he is required to submit an application to the bank along with documentary evidence to support the application, such as the sale contract.
4. After verification of the particulars in the application and the documentary evidence submitted, the bank prepares a 'Forward Exchange Contract'.
5. While preparing the contract, the following points are to be noted:
   (a) The bank-branch may give a serial number to the contract, so that further reference to it becomes easy.
   (b) Contracts must state the first and last dates of delivery. It is not permissible to state in contracts 'delivery one week' or 'delivery one month' or 'delivery three months forward', etc.
   (c) When more than one rate for bills with different deliveries are mentioned, the contract must state the amount and delivery against each rate.
   (d) No Usance option may be stated in any contract for the purchase of bills. That is, the contract should not give option to the customer to tender sight bill or, in the alternative, 30-day bill, etc. It can be either sight bill or a Usance bill of a specified Usance as mentioned in the contract.

(e) The first portion of the contract is relevant for booking of the contract. The second portion is used for recording deliveries under the contract.

(f) The contract should be complete in all respects.

6. The number of copies of the contract to be prepared will depend upon the requirements of the bank concerned. The original of the contract duly signed by the bank, along with the duplicate, is sent to the customer. The duplicate, signed by the customer, is returned to the bank for its records.
7. The details of the contract are entered in a 'Forward Contracts Register'. The register also provides for recording of details of documentary evidence verified.
8. The documents are verified and marked with the Bank stamp and signature of authorised signatory of the bank, after entering the particulars of the forward contract booked. It is then returned to the customer.
9. The due date of the contract should be diarised in a register and followed upon the due date.
10. A minimum of Rs. 1,000 is recovered (this fee varies from bank to bank and from time to time; it was Rs. 250 about 10-12 years back) from the customer as charge for booking the forward contract.
11. When the customer delivers Foreign Exchange on the due date, the transaction is done at the rate agreed.

EXCHANGE DEALINGS BY BANKS/BUSINESS CONCERNS

When the foreign currency-denominated assets and liabilities are held by the banks or the business concerns, two types of risks are faced. First, the risk that the exchange rates may vary and the change may affect the cash flows/profits. This is known as 'exchange risk'. Secondly, the interest rate may vary and it may affect the cost of holding the foreign currency assets and liabilities. This is known as 'interest rate risk'.

Foreign Exchange is a sensitive commodity; it is subject to wide fluctuations in price that the bank which deals in it would like to keep the balance always near zero. The bank would endeavour to find a suitable buyer whenever it purchases so as to dispose of the foreign exchange acquired and be free from exchange risk. Likewise, whenever it sells, it tries to cover its position by a corresponding purchase. But, in practice, it is not possible to match purchase and sale for each transaction. So, the bank tries to match the total purchases of the day-to-day's total sales. This is done for each foreign currency separately.

(i) If the amount of sales and purchases of a particular currency is equal, the position of the bank in that currency is said to be square.

(ii) If the purchases exceed sales, then the bank is said to be in 'overbought' or 'long' position.

(iii) If the sales exceed purchases of a currency, then the bank is said to be in 'oversold' or 'short position'.

The bank's endeavour would be to keep its position square. If it is in 'overbought' or 'oversold' position, it is exposing itself to exchange risk.

There are two aspects of maintenance of dealing position. One is the total of purchase or sale or commitment of the bank to purchase or sell, irrespective of the fact whether actual delivery has taken place or not. This is known as 'exchange position'. The other is the actual balance in the bank's account with its correspondent abroad, as a result of the purchase or sale made by the bank. This is known as the 'cash position'.

EXCHANGE POSITION

Exchange position is the net balance of the aggregate purchases and sales made by the bank in particular currency. This is thus an overall position of the bank in a particular currency. All purchases and sales, whether spot or forward, are included in computing the exchange position. All transactions for which the bank has agreed for a firm rate with the counter-party are entered into the exchange position when such commitment is made. Therefore, in the case of forward contracts, they will enter into the exchange position on the date the contract with the customer is concluded. The actual date of delivery is not considered here. All purchases add to the balance and all sales reduce the balance. The exchange position is worked out every day so as to ascertain the position of the bank in that particular currency. Based on the position arrived at, remedial measures as are needed may be taken.

CASH POSITION

Cash position is the balance outstanding in the Bank's 'Nostro' account abroad. The stock of foreign currency is held by the bank in the form of balances with correspondent bank in the foreign centre concerned. All foreign exchange dealings of the bank are routed through these 'Nostro' accounts. The balance in the 'Nostro' account is kept in current account which does not earn any interest for the bank. Therefore, keeping the balances in these accounts will be wastage of foreign resources of the bank. On the other hand, if insufficient balance is kept in the account, deliveries that take place may render the account to be overdrawn for which the bank has to pay interest. The endeavour of the bank would, therefore, be to keep just adequate balance in the account to meet the obligations as and when they arise.

EXCHANGE AND CASH POSITIONS COMPARED

The exchange position is concerned with the overall position of the bank with respect to a particular currency. Transactions enter into the exchange position on the date of purchase/sale or on the date the bank commits itself to purchase/sell, quoting a firm rate.

FOREX RISK MANAGEMENT

The Dealing Room is rightly identified as a profit centre for a bank. In these days of reducing spread between the lending and borrowing rates, banks have to look to other sources to improve their bottom lines. Foreign Exchange is one area where the potential is vast. However, banks have to take calculated risks in booking forex transactions. Unbridled enthusiasm has to be monitored so that the bank does not expose itself to unduly huge risks. The following are the major risks in foreign exchange dealings:

Open Position Risk; Cash Balance Risk; Maturity Mis-match Risk; Credit Risk; Country Risk; Over-trading Risk; Fraud Risk; and Operational Risk.

EXPORT CREDIT INSURANCE

Consequent upon the movement towards free trade regime under the WTO, International Trade is highly competitive. An Exporter has to offer good quality material/products/services at competitive prices and extend longer and liberal terms of credit to the foreign importers to be successful. Also, selling in international markets is highly risky. Some of the risks are in common with those involved in internal/ domestic trade. However, some risks are aggravated in or are peculiar to international trade.

Two major risks in International trade are: (i) Risk of loss of or damage to the goods, and (ii) risk of non-realisation of Export proceeds. While former is a risk which is covered by general insurance (under marine insurance), the latter risk is financial risk or credit risk which is not covered by the general insurance.

Commercial Risk: When export proceeds are not realised due to the failure of the buyer to accept and/or pay for the goods, the risk is called commercial risk. Non-realisation of the export proceeds may also be due to the reasons beyond the control of the buyer; such difficulties may be attributed to the political and economic changes. There can be outbreak of war, hostilities between countries or unfriendly relations for various reasons. As exports are in the interest of the country, loss of hard-to-get business opportunities may adversely affect the country's 'balance of payment' position—imports are paid out of exports, or else raise loans abroad. Ultimately, loans have also to be repaid out of export proceeds.

The need, therefore, obviously arises for a scheme of export credit insurance designed to protect exporters from the consequences of export-payment risks, both political and commercial and to enable them to expand their overseas business without fear of loss. In India, the Export Risks Insurance Corporation (ERIC) was set-up by the government of India in July 1957 to undertake this function. While the policies issued by ERIC provided adequate cover to exporters, it was thought that its functions should be extended. Encouragement to exporters consisted not only of affording protection against credit risks but also in facilitating their getting timely and adequate credit on liberal terms from the banks. The availability of insurance policies to the exporter was an indirect benefit to the banks and should encourage the banks' lending to the exports sector. But, it was subsequently found that this incentive was not thought to be sufficient to prompt the flow of bank finance to the exporters. As a measure of direct encouragement to banks, guarantees were begun to be issued in their favour. The guarantee, fundamentally, protects the bank against failure of the exporter to repay the bank advance. Consequently, the ERIC was transformed into Export Credit and Guarantee Corporation Limited, in 1964. It has since been renamed 'Export Credit Guarantee Corporation of India Limited'. ECGC is a company owned by the Government of India. It functions under the administrative control of Ministry of Commerce and is managed by a Board of Directors representing the Government, Banking, Insurance, Trade, Industry, etc. It has evolved various kinds of policies for Exporters—standard and specific—and similarly many types of guarantees for the bankers. Since it is a separate and vast subject to explain all these policies, it has been kept out of the scope of this book—only concept has been given in this book.

20

Fundamental Concept of Risk Management

CONCEPT OF RISK MANAGEMENT

Risk management, as a concept, operates on a set of principles, and there have been several attempts to define these principles. British Standard BS 31100 sets out 11 risk management principles and the international standard ISO 31000 also includes a detailed list of the suggested principles of risk management. The following list is a consolidated version of these principles. It is suggested that a successful risk management initiative will be:

- Proportionate to the level of risk within the organization;
- Aligned with other business activities;
- Comprehensive, systematic and structured;
- Embedded within business processes; and
- Dynamic, iterative and responsive to change.

This provides the acronym PACED and provides a very good set of principles that are the foundations of a successful approach to risk management within any organization. A more detailed description of the PACED principle of risk management is set out in Table 20.1. The approach to risk management is based on the idea that risk is something that can be identified and controlled.

The above statement of principles relates to the essential feature of risk management. These principles describe what risk management should be in practice. Some lists of principles also include information on what risk management should do or deliver. It is useful to separate the principles of risk management into two separate lists, what risk management should be, as listed above, and what it should deliver, as listed below:

- Compliance with laws and regulations;

- Assurance regarding the management of significant risks;
- Decisions that pay full regard to risk considerations; and
- Efficiency, Effectiveness and Efficacy in operations, projects and strategy.

This provides the acruyonym CADE3 and confirms that outputs from risk management will lead to less disruption to normal efficient operations, reduction of uncertainty in relation to change and improved decisions in relation to evaluation and selection of alternative strategies. In other words, a key part of risk management is improved organizational decision-making.

The resources available for managing risk are finite and so that aim is to achieve an optimum response to risk, prioritized in accordance with an evaluation of the risks. Risk is unavoidable and every organization needs to take action to manage it is a way that it can justify to a level that is acceptable. The appropriate range of responses to a risk will depend on the nature, size and complexity of the risk.

Figure 20.1: Principles of Risk Management

Principle	*Description*
Proportionate	Risk management activities must be proportionate to the level of risk faced by the organization.
Aligned	Risk management activities need to be aligned with the other activities in the organization
Comprehensive	In order to be fully effective, the risk management approach must be comprehensive.
Embedded	Risk management activities need to be embedded within the organization.
Dynamic	Risk management activities must be dynamic and responsive to emerging and changing risks.

IMPORTANCE OF RISK MANAGEMENT

There are a number of examples that illustrate the importance of risk management. Risk management has become increasingly high profile in recent times, because of the global financial crisis and the number of high profile corporate failures across the world that preceded it. Also, risk management has become more important because of increasing stakeholder expectations and the ever increasing ease of communication.

As well as assisting with better decision-making and improved efficiency, risk management can also contribute to the provision of greater assurance to stakeholders. This assurance has two important components. The directors of any organization need to be confident that risk have been identified and that appropriate steps have been taken to manage risk to an appropriate level.

Also, there is greater emphasis on accurate reporting of information by organization, including risk information. Stakeholders require detailed information on company performance, including risk awareness. The Sarbanes Oxley Act of 2002 (SOX) in the United States has accuracy of financial reporting as its main requirement. SOX brings the issue of the accurate reporting of results to a higher authority (section 404), whilst also requiring full and accurate disclosure of all information about the organization (section 303).

Sarbanes Oxley is a specific piece of legislation that only applies in certain circumstances. The principles that it contains are vitally important to all risk management practitioners. Accordingly, later parts of this book consider risk assurance and accurate reporting as integral parts of the overall risk management process.

RISK MANAGEMENT ACTIVITIES

Risk management is a process that can be divided into several stages. The IRM Risk Management Standard provides one representation of the stages involved in the risk management process. Alternative illustrations of the risk management process can be found in the British Standard BS 31100, the International Standard ISO 31000 and in other publications.

There are some stages in the (hazard) risk management process. The terminology that is used to describe the stages in the risk management process has been deliberately selected, so that the process can be represented the 7Rs and 4Ts of hazard risk management.

ISO Guide 73 and British Standard BS 31100 describe the risk management process as the systematic application of management policies, procedures and practices to the tasks of communicating, consulting, establishing the context, identity, analysis, evaluation treating, monitoring and reviewing risk. However, it could be argued that the setting of policies, procedures and practices, together with the tasks of communicating, consulting and establishing that context are actually part of the risk management framework, rather than the risk management process itself.

Within this book, the risk management processes taken as a narrow set of activities, described above as identifying, analyzing, evaluating, treating, monitoring and reviewing risk. This provides a clear distinction between the risk management process and the framework that supports this process. Descriptions of the risk management process together with the risk management framework are required in order to produce comprehensive risk management standards.

There has been much discussion about whether a single risk management process and/or diagram can be used to describe the management of hazard risks, control risks and opportunity risks. This book uses different terminology to describe the three types of risks.

There are a number of options when responding to hazard risk. There are often represented as the 4Ts of hazard risk management. The options for responding to hazard risks are: tolerate, treat, transfer and terminate.

EFFICIENT, EFFECTIVE AND EFFICACIOUS

Insurable or hazard risks can have an immediate impact on operations. Therefore, the initial application of risk management principles was to ensure continuation of normal efficient operations.

As risk management has developed, emphasis has been placed on project management and the delivery of programmes to provide enhancement to business processes.

Strategic decisions are the most important that an organization has to make. Risk management delivers improved information so that strategic decision can be made with greater confidence. The strategy that is decided by an organization must be capable of delivering the results that are required. Such a strategy may be described as efficacious. There are many examples of organizations that selected an incorrect strategy or failed to successfully implement the selected strategy. Many of these organizations suffered corporate failure.

Strategy should be designed to take advantage of opportunities. For example, a sports club may identify the possibility of selling more products to its existing customer base. Some clubs will establish a travel agency for fans of the club who travel overseas, together with the provision of associated travel insurance. Also, there is the possibility of creating a club credit card that will be managed by a new finance subsidiary.

Having identified these possibilities, the club will need to look at the risks associated with these potential opportunity investments and devise a suitable programme of projects to implement the selected strategies. Ensuring that adequate account is taken of risk during all of these activities will increase the chances of selecting the correct efficacious strategy, designing the appropriate effective processes and, ultimately, ensuring efficient and profitable operations.

Organizations that have efficient operations and effective processes but an incorrect overall strategy will fail. This will be the case, however good the risk management processes are at operational and project level. Incorrect strategy has resulted in more corporate failures than inefficient operations or ineffective processes.

PERSPECTIVES OF RISK MANAGEMENT

In a rapidly developing discipline like traditional risk management, there is scope for different practitioners to become intolerant towards the approach adopted by others. Internal control specialists who believe that risk management is all about the management of uncertainty and the achievement of corporate objectives should not become intolerant of the more traditional insurance risk management approach. There is no value in one group of specialists being dismissive of the approach adopted by others and being unwilling to utilize the expertise that is available in another group.

In any case, there is no single style of risk management or approach to risk management that offers all the answers. Clearly, the various styles that can be adopted should operate as complementary approaches within an organization. The integrative approach to risk management accepts that the organization must tolerate certain hazard risks and must have an appropriate appetite for investment in opportunity risks. Risk management tools and techniques should be brought to achieve the following:

- Hazard management makes outcomes less negative.
- Control management reduces the spread of possible outcomes.
- Opportunity management makes outcomes more positive.

Hazard management will make the outcome of any hazard event less negative. Within the context of hazard management, insurance represents the mechanism for restricting the financial cost of losses when a risk materializes. Risk control and loss management techniques will reduce the expected losses and should ensure that the overall cost is contained. The combination of insurance and risk control/loss management will reduce the actual cost of hazard losses and this will inevitably (and correctly) cause the hazard tolerance of the organization will then be available for opportunity investment.

Control management reduces the range of possible outcome from any event. Control management is based on the established techniques of internal financial control, as practiced by internal auditors. The main intention is to reduce losses associated with inadequate control management at the same time as reducing the range of possible outcomes. This is the contribution that internal control should make to the overall approach to risk management within an organization.

Opportunity management seeks to make positive outcomes more likely and more substantial. As part of the opportunity management approach, the organization should also look at possibilities for increasing the revenue from the product or service. In not for profit organization, opportunity management should facilitate the delivery of better value for money.

These reward enhancement options can be discussed at strategy meeting and some options may be adopted, including the introduction of bonus and incentive schemes for staff and management. Clearly, in light of the lessons learnt from the global financial crisis, these incentive schemes should be balanced and should not reward excessive risk taking.

21

Concept of Risk Management in Insurance

INTRODUCTION: KINDS OF RISK

Risk is the basis of insurance. Everybody wants to get his activities insured in order to cover the losses arising out of uncertainties. The term 'insurance' is a general term. Everybody is quite familiar and uses the term knowingly or unknowingly. Insurance may be understood as a way of reducing uncertainty of occurrence of an event. The basic purpose of the insurances is to counteract the financial loss due to some unfavourable event. It is the financial mechanism through which the persons who are exposed to a similar risk contribute money to a common pool. The unfortunate a few people of this group who faces the loss, are compensated out of the pool. Hence, insurance is based on the principle of the co-operation. The persons who are fortunate and do not suffer a loss, share the burden of unfortunate suffers.

MEANING OF RISK

By risk we mean 'uncertainty'. In other words, it refers to 'possibility' or 'chance' of meeting a danger or suffering or change of exposure to adversity or danger. The risk due to uncertainty of an event can be positive or negative to human life. It is blessing as it give rise to hope, a curse as it give rise to dispute, fear, defense, tactics, failure and retrogression.

DEFINITION OF RISK

As the subject of Insurance is still evolving, there is no single universally accepted definition of the word 'Risk'. It is used to describe the different situations. Some of the definitions on the definition on the 'Risk' given by different authors are as follows:

According to Frank Knight, "Risk is a measurable uncertainty".

According to A.H. Willet, "Risk is an objectified uncertainty regarding the occurrence of an undesirable event".

According to Federation Invariance Institute, "The risk can be thought of as the degree of variation in the possible outcome from an uncertainty event, or as the variation in the possible outcomes".

Considering the above definitions, it may be concluded that 'Risk' may be defined as the phenomenon which is closely associated with uncertain event or peril to which the object is exposed and may cause loss or injury to something of value.

CHARACTERISTICS OF INSURABLE RISKS

The concept of 'risk' in insurance refers to only those uncertainties which are related to economic matters. Non-economic risks such as risk of respect, reputation, insult, prestige, or love, are not insurable risks. There is no specific criterion to decide whether any risk is insurable or not. However, the following can be considered as the main features that should be present in any risk to be insurable:

Figure 21.1: Characteristics of Insurance Risks

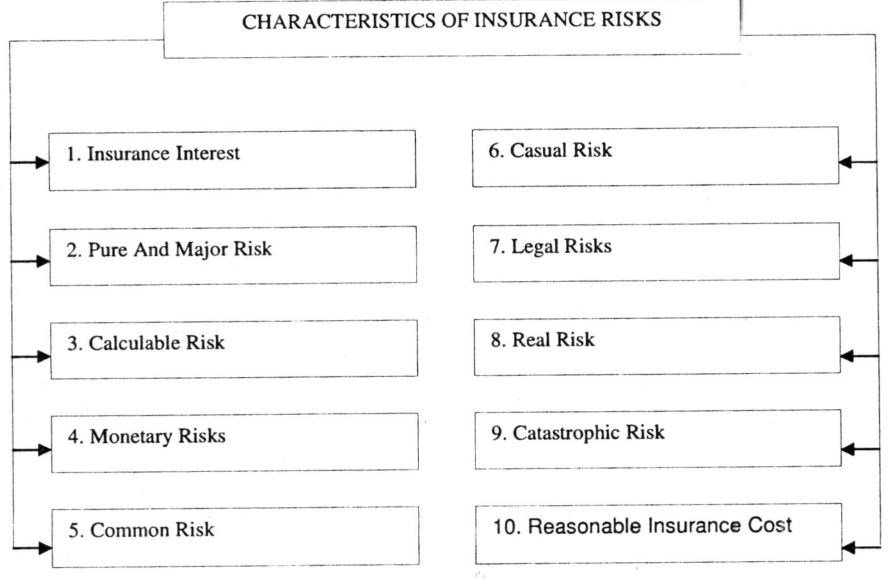

INSURANCE (OR INSURABLE) INTEREST

It is a settled fact that no "Risk" can be insured unless one has insurable interest in its object or in a person life. Stated in simple words, insurable interest is understood to exist when one is financially benefited by its existence and is prejudiced by the damage on its non-existence. Essentially, insurable interest is in the nature of pecuniary or financial interest in a life or thing. It follows that one can have an insurable interest only when one would stand to benefit financially by the continuance of the life or object insured, or when, in other words, one would be put to financial loss through the happening of the event against which the thing, or the life of a person has been insured. It is pecuniary interest and it follows that the loss caused by the risk insured against must be capable of estimation in terms of money.

Pure and Major Risk

One risk is pure (i.e. casual, uncertain and non-speculative) and the other is major (i.e. involving huge amount of loss). Both categories of risks are insurable. Insurance is concerned with only pure risk. Only in case of pure risks, the outcome of the event is uncertain. Speculative risks may produce two outcome either profit or loss. Pure risk can produce only one outcome i.e. loss. There is question of loss of profit. In insurance only those risks need to be insured which cause large amount of loss; small risks do not prove to be advantageous if insured at high costs; cost is called premium.

Quantifiable Risks

Estimation or approximate assessment of possibility of risk is the basis of insurance. Some risks are capable of being measured quantitatively but some are not. Only those risks which are capable of quantitatively measured are insured.

Risks in Money Terms

Only those risks that are payable in money are insurable whenever there is occurrence of loss. The losses which cannot be paid in terms of money are net insurable.

Risks that are Common

Risks must be such by which many persons are affected at the same time. In other words, there must be a large number of persons who are affected at the same time. In other words, there must be a large number of persons who are affected by or rather likely to be affected by the common risk. Risk affecting a minority section of society are not feasible to be insured because spread of risk distribution will be among a fewer persons and in such a case, cost will be more to the insured since the corpus formed out of the accumulated aggregate premia would be small, not enough to pay for the loss or damage to those affected by the uncertainty insured against.

Risk must be Causal

It is settled principle in insurance that Risk must be uncertain and not expected, certain or capable of being insured. Risks, in which the loss is certain, are not insurable. For example, in life insurance, death is certain but the time of death cannot be predetermined.

RISKS WITH LEGAL OBJECTIVE

Insurable risk must possess a valid object. Any risk whose object is against the public policy or public interest (i.e. acts of smugglers, thieves, dacoits, etc.) is not insurable. In the same way, the act/behaviour of a person while driving a vehicle, not following the traffic rules, resulting in an accident and causing a loss, is not insurable.

Risk must be Real

It is another principle that Risk being insured need to be real and not imaginary. Therefore, the risks arising on account of theft, death, fire and accident are only insurable. For example, if a person plans to commit a suicide and does it, the loss caused by his death is not a real risk and it cannot be insured.

Catastrophic Risk

Risks of catastrophic nature (i.e. affecting a large number of persons) e.g. war, earthquake, floods, storms, typhoon, cyclone, tsunami, etc. are not insurable due to their high cost of insurance. A risk to be insurable must repeat or revisit after a short interval and affect only a small number of persons insured, e.g. accidents, fire, theft, etc. (not all).

Risk having Reasonable Insurance Cost

In general, only those risks are insured which carry low premium/insurance cost. In case the premium is high, few persons will purchase the insurance policy and it will not be feasible rather economically viable for the insurance companies to carry such polices. Therefore, the risk must have widespread effect, and magnitude of risk (loss) and the possibility of occurrence should be less. Premium or insurance cost shall be low on such risks.

Figure 21.2: Causes of Risk

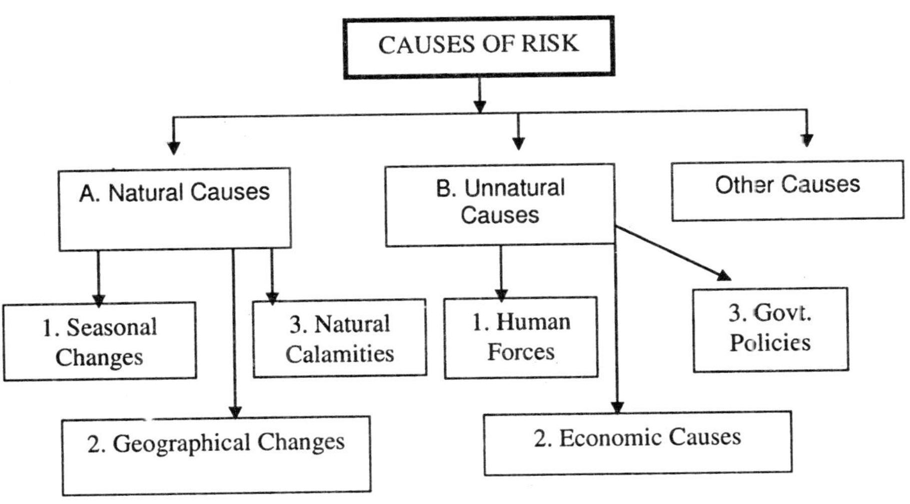

Causes of Risks

The theory of 'cause' and 'effect' equally applies to risk also. Generally, all risks are caused by certain factors or forces, and concentration of these factors causes a loss. The major causes of risk are shown in the Figure 21.2.

As depicted in the above figure, the risks are caused by certain factors. These factors are explained in brief below:

(1) **Natural Causes:** The risks caused by the natural factors such as floods, earthquake, storms, draughts, etc. are known as natural causes. These causes can be further sub-divided into the following groups:
   (a) *Seasonal Changes:* These risks are caused by excessive heat in summer, snowfall in winter, heavy rains in the rainy season, etc.
   (b) *Geographical Changes:* These are the risks that occur due to changes in earth like earthquake, etc.
   (c) *Natural Calamities:* The risks which occur due to natural calamities like storm, dusty winds, hail stones, snowfall, earthquake, etc. are sub-classified under natural calamities.

(2) **Unnatural Causes:** Unnatural causes of risk include the following categories:
   (a) *Human Forces:* There are Risks caused by changes in people's preference, taste of customers, lock-outs by Industrial managements, strikes or pens downs by workers or by the anti-social elements.
   (b) *Economic Causes:* Such Risks are caused by the changes in trade cycle, demand and supply situations, market competition, etc.
   (c) *Government Policy:* Risks are caused by the changes in Government policy like fiscal policy, monetary policy, credit policy, Export-Import (Exim) policy, industrial policy, etc. and affect the common man and business adversely.

(3) **Other Causes:** The above list is illustrative, not exhaustive. Therefore, in addition to the above mentioned natural and unnatural causes, sometime causes like inefficient management, adulteration in food articles, lower quality of product, etc. may cause loss.

Types of Risks: Risks can be classified into the following categories:

- Financial and Non-financial Risks.
- Pure and Speculative Risks
- Dynamic Risks and Static Risks
- Fundamental and Particular Risks

Financial and Non-financial Risks: Financial risks are those risks outcomes of which can be measured in terms of money. For example, loss of property due to theft, loss of property due to fire, loss of profits in case of consequential loss policy, personal injury to a person in case of accident insurance policy are such risks. In all these situations, the outcome of risky situations can be measured in terms of money.

But in case of non-financial risks, the outcome cannot be measured in terms of money. For example, when one buys a car or a person chooses a career or a person chooses to marry a woman who is having children, risks cannot be measured in monetary terms. These events may or may not involve any financial implications. These are better governed by human criteria. But in the business world, we are primarily concerned with risks having financially measurable outcome only.

Pure and Speculative Risks: Risks which can produce only loss are known as pure risks. There is no chance of profit in such risks. Pure risks either cause a loss or at the best break-even situation. Therefore, the outcome can only be unfavourable or can leave us in the same position as before the event had taken place. These types of risks can be further classified into the following:

Personal Risks: Personal risks are those risks which are related to persons. Human life is surrounded by a number of uncertainties, such as illness, unemployment, death, old age, bodily injury, etc. Such risks cause a financial loss either to the concerned human or his dependent.

Property Risks: Outcome of the risks which cause a loss to the property, are classified as property risks. For example, fire may destroy houses, godown, factory, or a ship may sink on high seas or loss to the property may be caused by earthquake, floods, war, riots, etc.

Liability Risks: The risks which create a financial liability on a person on the occurrence of some uncertain event are known as liability risks. For example, when a person is injured in an accident, the owner of the vehicle may be held liable to compensate the injured person for the damage or loss.

When there is a possibility of loss or break-even or gain as an outcome of an event, such risks are known as speculative risks. For example, investment of money in shares of certain companies may result into a profit or loss or break-even (no profit no loss). Although these types of transactions are undertaken with the objective of earning profits, yet there always remains a risk of loss. These speculative risks are not insurable.

Dynamic and Static Risks: Dynamic risks are the risks in the nature of speculative risks. These risks are the outcome of the changes taking place in the society due to economic, social, technology, environment and political changes. Static risks are those risks which exist in the absence of dynamic situations. These are similar to pure risks.

Fundamental and Particular Risks: Fundamental risks are those risks that arise outside the control of any individual or even a group of individuals; the effect of such risks is felt by a large number of people. This includes the loss caused by earthquake, floods, famines, volcanoes and other natural disasters. Even the social changes (upheavals), political intervention under the provisions of UN Charter/International Law and war are also sometimes included in the fundamental risks.

In contrast to the fundamental risks, the personal risks are more of personal nature both in their cause and effect. These include many types of risks such as fire, theft, work-related injury and motor accidents. All these risks arise from individual causes and affect individuals in their consequence.

It is interesting to note that the above mentioned classifications of risks are not water tight classifications. The risk classification may undergo a change due to legislative measures taken by the government or from country to country. For example, in many parts of the world, fundamental risks are regarded as not insurable, but in the United Kingdom, they are insurable.

RISK MANAGEMENT OR CONTROL OVER RISK

Risk management is not a static concept; it is a continuous effort to be aware of operational uncertainties to minimize the loss potential to a company. Risk management is a plan to prevent happening of such events that destroy company's assets or contributing resources. The fiscal integrity and current position of the company is adversely affected by unplanned incidents or losses. Risk management provides a precise plan to handle various types of contingencies. In other words, risk management includes all efforts made by a company to minimize the outcome of uncertain events or risks. For example, Banks in India make provisions out of annual profits for possible losses due to Non-Performing Assets (Doubtful Loan Assets) in their investment portfolios.

We are now in a position to define risk management. It is as: The identification, analysis and economic control of those risks that can threaten the assets or earning capacity of an enterprise are part of risk management.

This articulated definition is important as it highlights the approach through which risks in the operating business environment are to be managed. These are as follows:

Risks must be identified before they can be measured, and only after their impact has been evaluated can we decide on the most effective control of risks.

To decide to control risk, it must be 'economic' preposition. There is no point in spending Rs. 100 to control a risk which can only save Rs. 40. There will always be a point where spending on risks control has to stop.

The definition mentions the assets and earning capacity of an organization.

These assets can be physical or human. Both are important, and risk management has a part to play in both of them.

Even so, risks do not only strike at assets directly and for this reason the definition also mentions the earning capacity of an enterprise.

Finally, the word in the definition uses enterprise rather than a more restrictive word such as company or manufacturer.

The principles of risk management are applicable in the services sector just as they are in the manufacturing sector.

Control of Speculative Risks: Speculative risks can be controlled by adopting the modern management techniques, conducting market research, forecasting government policies, diversification of product portfolio, etc. A producer who manufactures more than one product is in a better position to face loss caused by uncertain market conditions.

Moreover, the application of all concepts and principles of risk management are equally applicable to all types of speculative risks in the same way as they are applicable in case of pure risks, which call for their identification, quantification and control. In practice, each speculative risk needs different areas of knowledge and skills and needs to be tackled as a part of respective specialized managerial function.

Control of Pure Risk: Affects or outcome of the pure risks can be controlled only through the techniques of risk management. The techniques of controlling the pure risks are different from that of speculative risks. However as a whole risk management is a specialized managerial function and therefore risks manager must take the following steps to minimize uncertainties and loss:

Step in Risk Management are the following: Identification of source of risk; Measurement of impact of risk; Treatment of risk; Selection of suitable methods of risks handling; Implementing the selected method; and Feedback and review.

Identification of source of Risk: The risk manager is to locate the source or causes of risks. He is to determine where the source of risks for company lies. This includes fixed assets and property, other areas of potential loss like property borrowed, business interruption, natural risks like flood, earthquake, etc.; these risks may involve financial loss and may create financial liability to injured or affected third party.

Measurement of Risk: The risk manager makes a loss study using historical data to eliminate future losses. The past experience and historical data enable a manager to decide in advance how many and to what size of losses may occur in future as a result of outcomes of an uncertain event. It also helps all the parties to calculate volume of insurance, premium amount, etc.

Treatment of Risk: After the completion of the risk analysis, the next step is to decide what risks may be retained and what will be transferred onward to others.

Selecting suitable method of risks handling: There are various techniques of risks handling such as avoidance, prevention, assumption, reduction, transfer or assurance of risk. It is essential to select an appropriate method to take care of risk.

Implementing the selected method: The selection of a suitable method to cover the risks is important. It is necessary to implement it. This will be done after taking into consideration all important factors that would affect its successful implementation. Various factors like cost of insurance, required information amount of periodical premium, financial condition, amount of loss require proper attention while implementing the selected (appropriate) method.

Evaluation: Feedback process helps in evaluation of results of selected method. It is appropriate that evaluation of result of adopted method is done after a certain interval and corrective actions or measures must be taken to eliminate the bad results or effects of implementation.

Risk Handling Techniques: Risk is the happening of an uncertain event, which causes a loss. The following are the important technique available to avoid the problem of risk:

Avoiding Risk: Some human activities are full of risk. Risk varies, however, from activity to activity. The activities may increase the possibility of loss. So, the best method to avoid risk is not to undertake such type of activity. For example, if there is certainty of accident while driving a car, best method to avoid accident is, not to buy a car or not to drive it yourself. Similarly, a risk of damage by floods may be avoided by moving to another place, less prone to recurring floods.

Risk Reduction: Another important method of risk handling is risk reduction. Risk reduction includes all those efforts made by company management to reduce the risk creating events. There are a number of ways to handle risk, e.g. to avoid fire by using fire-proof materials, slogans/notice boards prohibiting smoking like 'no smoking', etc.

Assumption of Risk: As risk is unavoidable to the full extent, we must assume some risk. It is the best method to retain the risk with self by creating some contingency reserves or funds to meet losses arising from those risks. The non-insurable risks are covered by maintaining funds (reserves) at own level.

Transfer of Risks: Some of the methods of shifting non-insurable risks are as under:

Hedging: One of the most important methods of shifting non-insurable risks (e.g. changes in prices) is hedging by entering into future contract. It involves shifting of the existing risk incurred in the cash or spot market by entering into another contract in the future market.

Therefore, hedging transaction involves two transitions simultaneously, one in the spot market and the other in the futures market.

Sub-Contracting: The general and original contractor may shift most of his risk to other contractors by entering into sub-contract with them for the work contracted for. It is mostly applicable in case of building industry. The main contractor, after getting a contract, enters into sub-contract with other person(s) for the supply of raw material, labour or even for the construction of most of the parts of the building. Thus, original contractor shifts most of his risk to the sub-contractors.

Surety Bond: This is an arrangement under which third party steps into the shoes of the person who furnishes surety bond. If the main person fails to meet the liability, the surety will have to meet the liability.

Limited Company: Company form of business has a large number of shareholders. Total risk of failure of a business is divided among three large number of members of the company.

Insurance: The unavoidable, insurable risks may be transferred to an insurance company by purchasing suitable/appropriate policy. Modern insurance system is capable of taking over the largest possible risks relating to business, property and other kinds of liability. This is the most widely used device of risk avoidance.

A business may adopt all or any of the methods of risk avoidance in the light of its organizational planning, policies and objectives and financial considerations.

REASONS FOR RISE OF RISK: RISK MANAGEMENT PRACTICES

In the present era, there is a great increase in the amount and variety of risk due to industrial development and other economic factors. The main reasons for rise in risk management are as follows:

- Industries and business have grown in size, diversification, process and strategic alliances.
- Complication of evaluating risk of each and every aspect has increased.
- Increase in business relations with suppliers, consumers, employees and government.

- Physical hazards have increased and changed in shape due to raw material quality and sources, manufacturing processes, range of products, technology, etc.
- Increased trend in movement of large investments has also increased the importance of protection and prevention measures.
- Business operations face many contingencies due to tough competition between enterprises.
- Globalised economy has brought in many complications due to e-commerce, e-banking, global tendering, economic co-operation, technology transfers, increasing inter-dependence of nations for various goods and services.

22

Development of Risk Management

ORIGINS OF RISK MANAGEMENT

Risk Management has a variety of origins and is practiced by a wide range of professionals. One of the early developments in risk management was in the United States out of the insurance management function. The practice of risk management became more widespread and better co-ordinated because the cost of insurance in the 1950s had become prohibitive and the extent of coverage limited. Organizations realized that purchasing insurance was insufficient, if there was also inadequate attention to the protection of property and people. Insurance buyers therefore became concerned with the quality of property protection, the standards of health and safety, product liability issues and other risk control concerns.

This combined approach to risk financing and risk control developed in Europe during the 1970s and the concept of total cost of risk became important. As this approach became established, it also became obvious that there were many risks facing organizations that were not insurable.

The range of different approaches to risk management is illustrated by the definitions of risk management as set out in Table 22.1.

The increasing importance of risk management can be explained by the list of issues set out in Table 22.2. Many of these issues demonstrate that the application of risk management has moved a long way from the origins in the insurance world, nevertheless, the insurance origins of risk management remain vitally important and are still the part of the approach to hazard management.

Risk Management has well-established stages that make up the risk management process, as described in Table 22.3. These stages build up to valuable risk management activities, each of which makes an important contribution. There are many ways of representing the risk management process, and each of the standards mentioned later in this part provides a slightly different description.

Table 22.1: Definitions of Risk Management

Organization	*Definition of Risk Management*
ISO Guide 73 BS 31000	Coordinated activities to direct and control an organization with regard to risk.
Institute of Risk Management (IRM)	Process which aims to help organizations understand, evaluate and take action on all their risks with a view to increasing the probability of success and reducing the likelihood of failure.
HM Treasury	All the processes involved in identifying, assessing and judging risks, assigning ownership, taking actions to mitigate or anticipate then, and monitoring and reviewing progress.
London School of Economics	Selection of those risks a business should take and those which should be avoided or mitigated, followed by action to avoid or reduce risk.
Business Continuity Institute	Culture, processes and structures that are put in place to effectively mange potential opportunities and adverse effects.

Table 22.2: Importance of Risk Management
Managing the Origination

- Variable cost or availability of raw materials.
- Cost of retirement/pension/social benefits.
- Desire to deliver greater shareholder value.
- Greater transparency required from organizations.
- Pace of change in business ever increase.
- Impact of e-commerce on all aspects of business life.
- Increased reliance on information technology (IT) system.
- Increasing importance of intellectual property (IP).
- Greater supply-chain complexity/dependency.
- Reputation becomes more and more important.
- Reputation damage—especially to world-wide brands.
- High profile losses and failures ruin reputations.
- Regulatory pressures continue to increase.
- Changes/variation in national legislative requirements.
- Joint ventures becoming more common.

Table 22.3: Changes in the Marketplace

- Changing commercial and marketplace environment.
- Globalization of customers, suppliers and products.
- Increased competition in the marketplace.
- Greater customer expectations, often led by competitors.
- Need to respond more rapidly to stakeholder expectations.
- More volatile markets with less customer loyalty.
- Diversification leads to working in unfamiliar areas.
- Constant need to make bold strategic decisions.

- Short-term success required, without long term detriment.
- Product innovation and continuous improvements.
- Rapid changes in (consumer) product technology.
- Threats to world/national economic.
- Threat of influenza or other pandemics.
- Potential for international organized crime.
- Increasing occurrences of civil unrest/political risks.
- Extreme weather events resulting in population shift.

7 Rs AND 4 Ts OF (HAZARD) RISK MANAGEMENT

(1) Recognition or identification of risks and identification of the nature of the risk and the circumstances in which it could materialize.

(2) Ranking or evaluation of risk in terms of magnetite and likelihood to produce the 'risk profile' that is recorded in a risk register.

(3) Responding to significant risks, including decision on the appropriate action regarding the following options:
   - Tolerate;
   - Treat;
   - Transfer; and
   - Terminate.

(4) Resourcing controls to ensure that adequate arrangement are made to introduce and sustain necessary control activities.

(5) Reaction planning and/or event management. For hazard risks, this will include disaster recovery or business continuity planning.

(6) Reporting and monitoring of risk performance, actions and events and communicating on risk issues, via the risk architecture of the organization.

(7) Reviewing the risk management system, including internal audit procedures and arrangement for the review and updating of the risk architecture, strategy and protocols.

Figure 22.1 provides a simple diagrammatic representation for the risk management process. This basic explanation of the risk management process is referred to as the **7 Rs and 4 Ts** of hazard risk management. The activities associated with risk management are as follows:

- Recognition of risks;
- Ranking of risks;
- Responding to significant risks;
- Resourcing controls;
- Reaction (and event) planning;
- Reporting of risk performance; and
- Reviewing the risk management system.

Risk management can improve the management of the core processes of an organization by ensuring that key dependencies are analyzed, monitored and reviewed. Risk management tools and techniques will assist with the management of the hazard risk, control risks and opportunity risks that could impact these key dependencies.

Figures 22.1: 7 Rs and 4 Ts of (Hazard) Risk Management

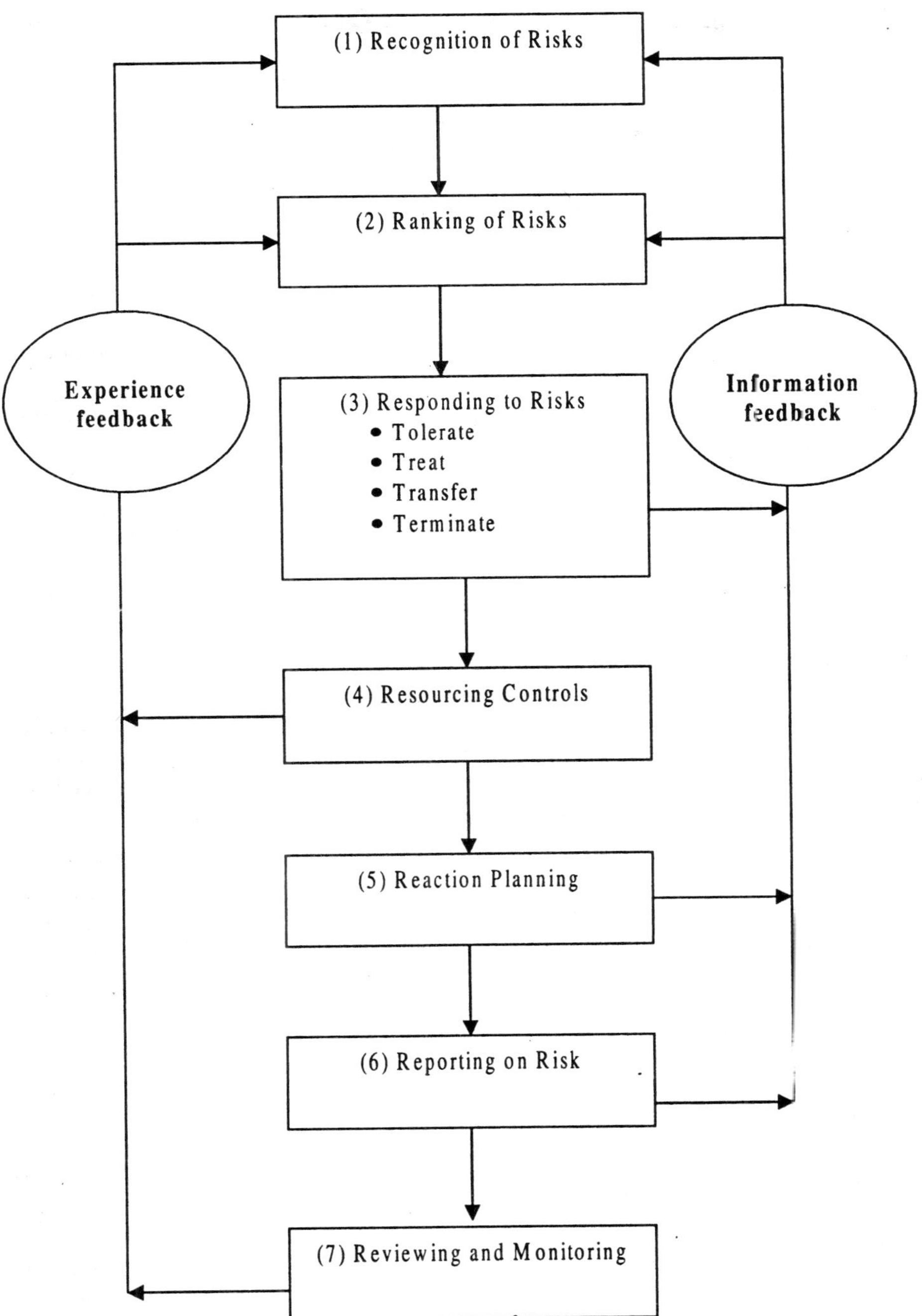

SPECIALIST AREAS OF RISK MANAGEMENT

Risk management is a constantly developing and evolving discipline. As well as its origins in the insurance industry and in other branches of hazard management, risk management has strong connections with the credit and treasury functions. Additionally, other specialist areas of risk management have developed over the past four decades, including:

- Project risk management;
- Clinical/medical risk management;
- Energy risk management; and
- Operational risk management.

All of the above specialist areas of risk management have contributed considerably to the development and application of risk management tools and techniques. Project risk management is an area where the application of risk management tools and techniques is particularly well developed.

Clinical risk management has been developing for some time. This area of risk management is primarily concerned with patient care, especially during surgical operations. The cost of medical malpractice claims and the inevitable delay in making insurance payments has resulted in risk management systems being introduced. Particular aspects of clinical risk management include greater attention to making patients aware of the risks that may be associated with the procedure they are about to undertake.

It is also important that surgeons report incidents that occur during the surgery. Considerable emphasis has placed on clinical risk management on the need to report, in an accurate and timely manner, details of any incidents that occur in the operating theatre. There are many publications available on clinical risk management, and a great deal of work has been put into establishing the necessary system and procedures to cover this specialist area of the management.

Project and Clinical risk management, risk management tools and techniques have also been applied in a range of specialist industries. In particular, risk management techniques have been applied in the finance and energy sectors. Risk management in the finance sector focuses on operational risks, as well as market, credit and other types of financial risks. It is in the finance sector that the title Chief Risk Officer was first developed.

The energy sector has also seen an increase in the attention paid to risk management tools and techniques. For some organizations in the energy sector, risk management is mainly concerned with the future price of energy and with exploration risk. Therefore, there risk management approach is similar to the activities of the treasury function, where hedging and other sophisticated financial techniques form the basis of the risk management effort.

ENTERPRISE RISK MANAGEMENT

Another area where the risk management discipline has developed in recent time is the approach that is referred to as enterprise or Enterprise-wide Risk Management (ERM).

A good example of the ERM approach is the pharmaceutical industry. If a person reliant on a particular medication, then it is vitally important that the medication is constantly available. From the point of view of the pharmaceutical company, this means that a core process for the organization must be the constant availability of medication process.

If the pharmaceutical company takes this approach, it will look at the risks that could affect this core process or stakeholder expectation on an enterprise-wide basis. This will involve analysis of the supply-chain, evaluation of manufacturing activities and analysis of the delivery arrangements. The overall question that needs to be answered is what could prevent the continuous supply of medication. Risks to the continuous supply will include unavailability of ingredients, disruption to manufacturing activities, contamination of the product, breakdown in supply transportation arrangements and disruption to distribution.

This enterprise-wide approach has considerable advantages, because it analyses the potential for disruption to the overall stakeholder expectation. Health and safety, for example, is then viewed as a component in ensuring that staff are always available so that the overall process will not be disrupted, rather than (or perhaps as well as) a separate hazard management issue coming up.

LEVELS OF RISK MANAGEMENT SOPHISTICATION

At first, an organization may be aware of a new risk and the need to take appropriate action. In that case, there will be a need for the organization to reform in response to the hazard risk. As the organization responds to the risk, it will seek to conform with the appropriate risk control standards. After this stage, the organization may realize that there are benefits to be obtained from the risk. The organization will then have the ability to perform and view the risk as an opportunity risk.

There is a danger that organization will become obsessed with risk management to the point that important decisions are not taken. At this point, it may be said that too much attention and concern about risk and risk management will cause the organization to deform its operations. In summary:

- Awareness of non-compliance—REFORM;
- Actions to ensure compliance—CONFORM
- Achieve business opportunities—PERFORM;
- Inactivity caused by obsession—DEFORM.

As the level of sophistication increases and risk management professionals become aware of the alternative approaches to risk management, they should value the contribution that can be made by other approaches. The development in risk management approach can be summarized as follows:

- Hazard management specialists may find that there has been a trend towards a desire to retain more insurable risks (and buy less insurance) as a result of more holistic approach to risk management.
- Control management specialists must not squeeze entrepreneurial spirit and effort out of the organization.

- Strategic planners must recognize that risk management tools and techniques can contribute to better strategic decision and the successful exploitation of business opportunities.

RISK MATURITY MODELS

Increases in risk management effectiveness can also be measured by the use of risk maturity models. The level of risk management sophistication provides an indication of the benefits that can be achieved from risk management. The level of risk maturity in the organization is a measure of the quality of risk management activities and the extent to which they are embedded within the organization.

Risk maturity models can be used to measure the current level of risk culture within the organization. The greater the level of risk maturity, the more embedded risk management activities will become within the routine operations undertaken by the organization.

Risk maturity models will be dealt with in more detail in a later chapter. Risk maturity is not the same as considering the level of sophistication that an organization achievers in respect to risk management. An organization may have limited expectation of risk management, but nevertheless have a very mature approach to the way in which it seeks to obtain the available benefits.

The level of risk maturity within an organization is an indication of the way in which risk processes and capabilities are developed and applied. In an immature organization, informal risk management practice will take place. However, there is likely to be a blame culture in existence when things to wrong and a potential lack of accountability for risk. Also, resources allocated to manage risks may be inappropriate for the level of risk involved.

When explicit risk management is in place, there will be attempts to keep the processes dynamic, relevant and useful. There is likely to be open dialogue and learning so that information is used to inform judgement and decisions about risk. There will be confidence that innovation and risk taking can be managed, with support when things go wrong.

When an organization becomes obsessed with risk, there will be over-dependence on process and this may limit the ability to manage risk effectively. There will be over reliance on information at the expense of good judgement and dependence on process to define the rationale behind decisions. Individuals may become risk averse for fear of criticism and procedures are followed only to comply with requirements, not because benefits are sought.

23

Various Types of Risks: Fundamental Concepts

INTRODUCTION

We shall see in this Chapter the different types of losses covered under general insurance. We shall also discuss in detail the different types of insurances available in the market as of now. The insurance policies are grouped and explained the way they are used both in the Indian and international contexts. In view of the rapid changes expected in the market as a result of de-tariffing and the introduction of 'File and Use' approval systems, product innovations are expected sooner than later. It is possible that products of a different composition replace many of the insurance products existing in the market today. This possibility has been taken into account while discussing the types of insurance in this Chapter. The readers, students and insurance counsellors are provided with the necessary conceptual clarity to understand the products despite the changes.

TYPES OF LOSSES COVERED UNDER INSURANCE

We have seen that insurance contract aims at mitigation of financial hardships due to losses. Losses can be of various types, based on the risk insured and its exposure to various perils. As insurance contracts are designed to indemnify losses, different risks with different kinds of exposure have to be distinguished and given appropriate covers, terms, etc. Contracts are, therefore, worded suitably. Understanding losses and classifying insurance products into different loss types helps the insurers in dealing more professionally with the varied requirements of the insurance market.

Losses are broadly grouped as losses from damage or destruction of property, losses due to liabilities, losses of income and personal losses. The first type erodes the insured assets, the second increases his liabilities, the third chokes up his sources of income, and the fourth hurts him by way of physical hardship or death.

Property Losses: Property losses can be direct or real losses, as used in real estate. These include loss or damage sustained by land, buildings, structures, appurtenant attachments, machinery, equipments, stock-in-process and the like. This property is considered more prone to perils, such as fire, earthquake, lightning, flood, storm, tempest, inundation, landslide, accidents in the processing phase, etc. Personal property is not attached to land. It is movable and can be stolen, accidentally dropped or damaged by fire. Property losses can be indirect as well. These are also losses to property but not direct losses. Damage to a refrigerator can cause loss of medicines kept within. Seepage of rain water through the wall can cause an electrical short circuit leading to a fire loss in the factory. A person falling on the road and fracturing himself can lose his watch in the process.

Liability Losses: These are losses that arise from a legal obligation cast on the insured to pay. Liabilities can arise when one's vehicle accidentally hits someone or something on the road. If one's tree falls on the neighbourer's house, a liability can arise. If one's sewerage drips and falls while at work, liability can arise. An injury or a disease contracted by a worker due to certain conditions in a factory can cause a liability to the factory owner. Liability can arise out of deficiency of services rendered, defects of products sold, by negligence or by oversight. In the Indian social set-up, liabilities are not normally enforced as the victims are generally tolerant. In the western markets and the USA, however, as people are more aware of their rights and less tolerant of others' faults, liability is perceived a major risk. Consequently, there is a large demand for liability insurances.

Income Losses: Net income losses are those that are caused by increased expenses or reduced income. Losses can be caused as a consequence of one's sources of income getting dried up. A daily wage worker who can not go to work due to ill health is one such example. Retrenchment is another cause of loss of personal income. When one's house is damaged by flood, one may have to vacate it and stay in a rented house.

When a factory is gutted by fire, it may not be able to complete pending orders or realize sales proceeds from its customers, while it would continue to pay interest on borrowed capital, and pay fixed costs on rent and electricity for the building and salary to its employees. It may have to pay demurrages to third parties, pay its suppliers, and repay loans and advances already availed of. Losses due to business interruption or consequential loss fall under this category.

Personal Losses: Personal losses are those faced by a person, such as death, sickness, accident, unemployment and superannuating. In the organizational context, losses to the business entity relating to performance of key persons, business discontinuation, losses due to death or disablement of a customer, all these are collectively grouped as personal losses. Some authors call these losses as personnel losses.

However, these categorizations are not water-tight. There are many areas where the loss types so overlap and policies are issued covering different types of losses, depending on the market demand. Innovative products and products that are tailor-made for corporate requirements may be of a dumpsite type (all inclusive) or hybrid types (chopped and put together from different groups). However, all these are for the consumption of the insured. For the insurer who bears the risk, each and every component of the contract is appropriately researched and accurately priced. The insurer is in business and has to run his business productively and professionally. Like the clothes—seller who gifts a silk tie to a customer who buys a designer shirt, knows his costing well enough not to gift a designer shirt to a customer who buys a silk tie. An insurer is expected to know his costing well enough to make his product appear attractive as a bundle but not to sell his product at a loss.

TYPES OF PROPERTY INSURANCE

Property insurances deal with the 'real' risks that include exposure to perils such as fire, earthquake, lightning, flood, storm, tempest, inundation, landslide, or personal property that can be stolen, accidentally dropped, damaged by fire, etc. These insurances are designed to cover loss or damage sustained by buildings, factories, shops, multiplexes, roads, buildings under construction, bridges, goods stored at site, etc. The cost of covering the risk would depend on various physical attributes of the risk such as the geographical location, strength of the building, hazardous nature of the processes carried out in the premises, fire protection systems, burglar alarms, electrical installations, nature of material stored, etc.

FIRE INSURANCE (STATIC PROPERTY)

Fire insurance design is based on the All India Fire Tariff effective from 31-3-2001 issued by the Tariff Advisory Committee, a Statutory Body. The product has been de-tariffed from January 1, 2007 in respect of rates, but the cover is expected to continue for some time. The product composition is expected to change once the cover is also allowed to be insurer-designed.

In any market situation, a basic fire policy would exist the way it is today and operate as a commercial policy covering buildings, offices, machinery, contents and personal belongings in the office. The fire policy mitigates the risk of losses of the insured arising from fire breakout.

Salient features of the Standard Fire and Special Perils policy are given below:

Cover available

Losses due to:

(1) Fire, lightning, explosion and implosion.
(2) Aircraft damage, riot, strike, malicious damage and terrorism.
(3) Storm, tempest, flood and inundation.
(4) Impact damage and subsidence.
(5) Landslide/rockslide.
(6) Bursting and/or overflowing of water tanks, apparatus and pipes.
(7) Missile testing, leakage from automatic sprinkler instilations and bush fire.

Sum Assured

The value of the property is considered while fixing the sum insured. The property can be insured on depreciated cost (market value) or replacement cost basis. (Some insurers recommend reinstatement (replacement) basis for full protection).

Basis of Premium Computation

Premium rate will depend on construction of building and occupancy. Discounts/ loadings on premium are given based on past claims experience for risks exceeding Rs. 50 corers sum insured at any location and installation of fire extinguisher appliances. The amount of premium depends on a number of actors based on the underwriting policies of different insurers.

Condition of Excess

5 per cent of every claim resulting from lightning, storm, tempest, flood and inundation, subsidence, and landslide is treated as excess. The insurance policy doesn't cover the first Rs. 10,000 (or as applicable) of each and every claim.

Significant Exclusions

Losses arising out of perils of war and allied perils, theft, wilful act or gross negligence, loss of earnings, loss of bullion, documents, currency, etc. for an amount exceeding Rs. 10,000 unless expressly stated.

Main Extensions

(1) Earthquake (fire and shock).
(2) Spontaneous combustion.
(3) Deterioration of stocks in cold storage.
(4) Impact damage due to own vehicle(s).
(5) Omission to insure additions.
(6) Architect/surveyor/consulting engineer's fees in excess of 3 per cent of claim amount.
(7) Debris removal, in excess of 1 per cent of claim amount.

General Conditions

The insured should take all possible steps to minimize the loss.

Salient Features: Salient features of a Home Insurance Policy are given below:

Policy Coverage

Coverage damages to the structure and contents of one's home from natural and man-made calamities. Choice is allowed to buy insurance for only the building (structure), or only the contents (belongings), or both.

Calamities Covered

(1) Fire, earthquake and lightning.
(2) Riot, strike and malicious damage.
(3) Explosion and implosion.
(4) Storm, cyclone, tempest, tornado, hurricane, flood and inundation.
(5) Damage due to impact by vehicles.
(6) Missile testing operation.
(7) Subsidence, landslides and rockslides.
(8) Leakage from automatic sprinkler installations.
(9) Aircraft damage.
(10) Bursting and/or overflowing of water tanks, apparatus and pipes.

Burglary Cover (only for contents)

The contents of one's home are also covered against loss due to burglary or an attempted burglary. It also covers loss of jewellery, silver articles and precious stones kept under lock and key, up to 25 per cent of the total content sum insured or Rs. 1 lac, whichever is lower.

Optional Covers Available

(1) Terrorism cover: Covers any damages and losses to the structure and/or contents of your home due to acts of terrorism.

(2) Additional expenses of rent for alternative accommodation: If you are forced to shift into an alternative accommodation because your home is destroyed or damaged by any insured peril, the policy will cover you against the additional rent. The maximum coverage is up to Rs. 1,00,000 for up to 6 months. The cover is available only if you are insuring the structure of your home.

Policy Exclusions

(1) Wilful destruction of property.

(2) Loss, damage and destruction caused by war, wear and tear, atmospheric conditions, etc.

(3) Losses if the home has been unoccupied for more than 30 days.

(4) Cash, bullion, painting, works of art and antiques.

(5) Loss to the structure and/or contents of your home due to acts of terrorism.

How to calculate the sum insured for?

(1) Home Structure: The home insurance policy insurers the structure of the home for its reconstruction value (and not for market value). Reconstruction value is defined is the cost incurred to reconstruct the home if it is damaged in the other hand, market value is a combination of cost of land, demand and supply scenario, etc.

Sum insured is calculated by multiplying the built-up area of the home with the construction rate per sq. feet (e.g. if the built-up area of your home is 1000 sq. feet and the construction rate is Rs. 800 per sq. feet the sum insured for the home structure is Rs. 8,00,000). However, this value can be revised appropriately if expensive material such as marble flooring, etc. has been used in construction. If the home has lawn/garden surrounded by a perimeter wall, the construction rate can be revised to include the cost of construction of this wall in home structure sum insured.

(2) Home Contents: The contents of the home furniture, durables, clothes, utensils, jewellry, etc. are to be valued on market value basis, i.e. the current market value of similar items after deprecation. Depreciation does not apply for jewellry.

Examples of benefit offered by some Insurers: For comprehensive cover covering both structure and contents of the home, 15 per cent discount on a 3 year home insurance policy and 25 per cent discount on 5-year policy.

ENGINEERING INSURANCE (WORKS IN PROGRESS)

Engineering insurance basically covers property risks while work is in progress.

The insurance can cover completed sites for operations as in the case of Machinery Breakdown, Boiler and Pressure Vessel Plant or Electronic equipment insurance; engineering insurance covers works that are under construction process, such as contactors all risks, eruption all right, etc.

Salient features of a Machinery Breakdown Policy (Engineering) are given below:

Scope of Cover

The insurance policy broadly covers loss due to all kinds of accidental, electrical and mechanical breakdowns due to internal and external causes. Cover is granted during the time the machinery is in operation or rest, or in the process of dismantling, overhauls or during subsequent re-erection at the same premises.

Sum Assured

Value proposed for insurance should be equal to new replacement cost including freight, erection costs, and custom duty, if any.

Rate of Premium

Rate of premium depends upon the type of machinery. Discounts are offered in respect of stand by facility, availability of spares, and favourable claims experience, subject to rules laid down in the tariff.

Significant Exclusions

The insurance policy does not cover loss and or damage from:

(1) Fire and allied perils,
(2) Theft,
(3) Overloading experiments,
(4) Willful acts or gross negligence,
(5) Gradually developing flaws, and
(6) Deterioration from normal use.

Excess

Policy is subject to a compulsory excess, which depends upon the value of the machinery.

Main Extensions

(1) Air freight,
(2) Express freight (excluding air freight) overtime and holiday wages,
(3) Insured's own surrounding property, and
(4) Third party liability.

SALIENT FEATURES OF A BOILER AND PRESSURE VESSELS POLICY

Scope of Cover

The policy broadly covers boilers and other pressure vessels, both fired and unfired against losses due to explosion or collapse.

Sum Assured

Sum insured should be reinstatement cost of the boiler.

Premium Charged

The premium chargeable depends on the type of boiler type of fuel and the age of equipment. Discount is allowed for seasonal factories and stand by facilities.

Significant Exclusions

The policy does not cover loss and/or damage arising from:

(1) Fire and allied perils,
(2) War and nuclear perils,
(3) Losses arising out of overload experiments,
(4) Gradual wear and tear of parts,
(5) Failure of individual tubes, loss due to chemical reactions,
(6) Wilful acts or gross negligence,
(7) Loss which is manufacturer's or repairer's responsibility, and
(8) Consequential loss from explosion or collapse.

Main Extensions

(1) Surrounding property of the insured (including the property held in trust or on commission),
(2) Legal liability for third party bodily injury and property damage,
(3) Express freight,
(4) Air freight, and
(5) Additional customs duty can also be covered by payment of additional premium.

SALIENT FEATURES OF AN ELECTRONIC EQUIPMENT INSURANCE POLICY

(1) Material damage to electronic equipment (which can include systems software) due to sudden and unforeseen events, under Section I (details given below).
(2) Cost of external data media, including cost of reconstruction of data under Section II, as also increased cost of working under Section III (details given below).
(3) While Section I is compulsory, Section II and Section III are optional.

Sum Assured

(1) Section I: New replacement cost of the insured property including freight, erection cost, and customs duty, if any.
(2) Section II: Cost of restoring the external data media by replacing lost or damaged data media by new material and lost information.
(3) Section III: Sum insured should represent the hiring charges per hour for substitute equipment for ensuring continued data processing for the period of indemnity specified, including personnel and transportation charges.

Rate of Premium

Rate of premium is 1 per cent for equipment valued more than Rs. 1,00,000, and a valid maintenance agreement is required to be in force, failing which 100 per cent loading is attracted.

Significant Exclusions

The Policy does not cover losses/damages due to:

(1) Wear and tear,

(2) War, wilful act or wilful negligence, and

(3) Aesthetic defects and consequential loss.

Excess

The policy is subject to compulsory excess. Excess depends upon value of equipment. Separate excess applies to Winchester Drive. Higher voluntary excess qualifies for reduction in premium level.

There are policies such as contractors. All risks Insurance, Contraltos Plant and Machinery insurance, civil engineering construction risks insurance, erection All risks Insurance, Deterioration of stocks Insurance, etc., which are similar in nature. These are not being discussed in detail.

TRANSIT INSURANCE

Losses of property and merchandise while in transit are historically important for insurance transactions. Goods in transit include those sent by airplanes, ships, railways, roadways and waterways. Goods can be sent by own vehicles, containers, ships or airplanes, or by chartered vessels. Very often, goods shift between multiple modes of transits with multiple trans-shipments and storages at various stages of the transit. Between the consignor and consignee of goods, there are various parties involved, such as port authorities, forwarding agents, cargo handlers, for lift operators and others.

Goods in transit are exposed to perils of the sea, loss of the ship, water damages, contamination from other cargo, pilferage, theft, breakage of roads/bridges, road accidents, overturning/derailment of land conveyance, etc. the mode of sending the cargo. Such as break bulk, full container road, packed in cartons, shrink wrapped, fully pressed bales, etc. are also relevant for the insurance.

MARINE CARGO POLICIES

Internationally, marine cargo policies are generally issued based on institute Cargo clauses framed by the Institute of London Underwriters (ILU). The inland transit policies also are largely guided by the ILU framework.

Salient features of a marine Cargo (import/Export) insurance policy are as under:

Introduction: The coverage is generally defined by reference to clause known as institute clauses, known as institute clauses. The ICC (C), ICC (B) and ICC (A) clauses define different levels of coverage (detailed below) against marine risk and the cargo may be covered subject to any one of these clauses. The type of policy available is the specific policy to cover single consignment or an open policy.

Scope of Cover

There are three types of covers:

(1) Institute Cargo Clause (C) named peril basis.
(2) Institute Cargo Clause (B) named peril basis.
(3) Institute Cargo Clause (A) offers the widest form of cover under Marine Cargo Insurance in so far as it relates to the perils covered.

ICC (A) is unnamed perils clause.

Sum Assured

This is an agreed value policy, normally insurance is taken for CIF +10%.

Rate of Premium

Rate depends on factors such as:

(1) Nature of cargo,
(2) Scope of cover,
(3) Packing,
(4) Mode of conveyance,
(5) Distance, and
(6) Past claim experience.

Significant Exclusions

(1) Wilful misconduct,
(2) Ordinary leakage,
(3) Improper packing,
(4) Delay,
(5) Inherent vice, and
(6) War, strike, riot and civil commotion.

Main Extensions

On payment of additional premium, the insured can opt for certain extensions to the cover provided under the policy.

Extensions available include war, strike, riot and civil commotion, and delay insurance cover.

INLAND TRANSIT POLICIES

Inland transit policies by and large follow the framework of the marine cargo policies with due changes to cover rail, road and associated risks.

Salient features of a marine cargo (inland transit) insurance policy are as under:

Introduction

This policy broadly covers the risk of physical loss or damage to the insured's goods (machinery, raw materials, finished goods, etc.) during transit under a contract of affreightment.

Scope of Cover

There are two types of covers:

(1) *Basic Risk Policy:* It covers loss or damage to specified goods caused by fire, lightning, breakage of bridges, overturning of vehicles, and collision with or by carrying vehicle, subject to specified exclusions.

(2) *All Risks Policy:* It covers all risks of loss or damage to specified goods subject to exclusions.

Sum Assured

This is an agreed value policy. Normally insurance is taken for amount equal to CIF + 10%.

Rate of Premium

Rate depends on factors such as nature of cargo, scope of cover, packing mode of conveyance, distance and past claims experience.

Significant Exclusions

This policy does not cover loss or damage due to:

(1) Wilful misconduct,
(2) Ordinary leakage,
(3) Improper packing,
(4) Delay,
(5) Inherent vice, and
(6) War, strike, riot and civil commotion.

Main Extensions

Extensions available include strike, riot and civil commotion.

There are other segments of inland transit insurance covering inland waterways, storage cover incidental to transit, goods sent by hand cart, bullock cart and camel cart, postal insurance, etc. These are relatively small segments used only in a very limited manner and hence are not being discussed in this unit.

ACCIDENT INSURANCE

Accident insurance is a large area of insurance covering a large number of small value policies such as scooters and auto rickshaw, and medium value such as cars, vans, buses and commercial vehicles. At the other end of the spectrum, airplanes, helicopters, ships, yachts and customized limousines are there with very high claims. While the high value segment cases infrequent involving high value claims, those cases are treated differently by the insurers.

MOTOR VEHICLE INSURANCE

Vehicle insurance in India was de-tariffed with effect from January 1, 2007. The policy terms are still frozen to those fixed by the Tariff Advisory Committee. The insurers are allowed to fix rates for the Own Damage part themselves. As third party liability insurance is mandatory under the Motor Vehicle Act, IRDA has fixed rates for the third party cover so that the policy is kept affordable of the users of motor vehicles.

The insurance available are mainly (1) policy covers only limited liability to third parties (TP) as per the Motor Vehicles Act, 1988, (2) policy covers own damage (OD) or damage to the vehicles, (3) personal accident cover for owner driver, and (4) under a comprehensive package policy, increased cover for third party liability for bodily injury and/or death, damage to property of third parties and loss or damage to the vehicle insured (Own Damage or OD).

Salient features of a comprehensive motor vehicle (Private Car) insurance policy.

Policy Coverage

Motor Insurance policy wordings are governed by the Indian motor tariff. It covers you against any loss or damage caused to your vehicle or its accessories due to the following natural and man-made calamities:

(1) *Natural Calamities:* Fire, explosion, self-ignition or lightning, earthquake, flood, typhoon, hurricane, storm, tempest, inundation, cyclone, hailstorm, frost, landslide, rockslide.

(2) *Man-made Calamities:* Burglary, theft, riot, strike, malicious act, accident by external means, terrorist activity, and any damage in transit by road, rail, inland waterway, lift, elevator or air.

Rates

(1) *Personal Accident Cover:* The motor insurance provides compulsory personals accident cover of Rs. 2 lac for individual owners of the vehicle while driving. You can also opt for a personal accident cover for passengers.

(2) *Third Party Legal Liability:* This protest you against legal liability arising due to accidental damages, such as any permanent injury/death of a person, and any damage caused to the property.

Policy Exclusions

Under this policy, you are covered against:

(1) Normal wear and tear, and general aging of the vehicle.

(2) Depreciation or any consequential loss.

(3) Mechanical/electrical break down.

(4) Wear and tear of consumables such as tyres and tubes.

(5) Vehicles being used otherwise than in accordance with limitations as to use.

(6) Damage to/by a person driving the vehicle without a valid license.

(7) Damage to/by a person driving the vehicle under the influence of drugs or liquor.

(8) Loss/damage due to war, mutiny or nuclear risk.

Key Benefits

(1) You can claim towing charges up to Rs. 1,500.

(2) Cashless claim settlement is available across India. Refer all India cashless Charge List.

Avail of the following Bonuses and Discounts

(1) *No Claim Bonus* (*NCB*): If you do not make a claim during the policy period, a No. 50 per cent (NCB) is offered on renewals. This discount can go as high as 90 days of the expiry date of the previous policy.

(2) *Transfer your NCB*: You can transfer full benefits of No Claim Bonus when you shift your motor insurance policy from another company to another.

The discount rate remains the same provided you show evidence that you are entitled to No Claim Bonus from your previous motor insurance company.

Evidence

It can be in the form of a renewal notice or a letter confirming the NCB entitlement from the previous insurer or a written declaration.

No Claim Bonus (NCB) Declaration

I/We declare that the rate of NCB claimed by me/us is correct and that no claim has arisen in the expiring policy period. I/we further undertake that if this decision is found to be incorrect, all benefits under the policy will stand forfeited.

Voluntary Excess Discount

A further discount on the premium is available if you opt for a voluntary excess in addition to the compulsory excess. (Compulsory excess is the amount of loss that the insured has to bear in each and every claim).

Additional Discount

You can also avail of additional discounts if you are a member of a recognized Automobile Association in India.

ARAI Device

(1) Cover yourself and your family: You can also opt for personal accident cover of Rs. 2 lac for other unnamed passenger in your car. For example, your family, friends, relatives, etc. can be covered.

(2) Customer your insurance with additional cover: Electrical and/or non-electrical items fitted to the vehicle can be insured separately. For example, fog lights, music system, seat covers, etc.

Bio-fuel Kit

In case of vehicles fitted with bio-fuel systems such as petrol/diesel and CNG/LPG, permitted by the concerned RTO, the CNG/LPG kit fitted to the vehicle is to be insured separately at an additional premium of 4 per cent of the value of such kit. You need to specifically declare this in the proposal form.

Sum Assured

The vehicles are insured at a fixed value called the insured's declared value (IDV), which is the sum insured for motor OD. IDV is calculated on the basis of the manufacture's listed selling price of the vehicle (plus the listed price of any accessories) after deducting the depreciation for every year as per the schedule provided by the Indian motor tariff. If the price of any electronic and/or electrical item installed in the vehicle is not included in the manufacturer's listed selling price, then the actual value (after depreciation) of this item can be added to the sum insured over and above the Insured's Declared Value (IDV).

The Schedule of Depreciation for Fixing IDV of the Vehicles

Age of the Vehicle	*% of Depreciation*
Not exceeding 6 months	5
Exceeding 6 months but not exceeding 1 year	15
Exceeding 1 year but not exceeding 2 years	20
Exceeding 2 years but not exceeding 3 years	30
Exceeding 3 year but not exceeding 4 years	40
Exceeding 4 year but not exceeding 5 years	50

Salient features of a Motor (Goods Carrying Commercial Vehicle) third Party Liability Insurance Policy are as follows:

Policy Coverage

This cover is applicable to Public and Private Carriers including Motorized Three-Wheelers and Motorized Pedal Cycles. The Indian Motor Tariff defines goods carrying commercial vehicle as:

(1) Public carriers (other than three-wheelers).
(2) Private carriers (other than three-wheelers).
(3) Goods Carrying Motorized Three-wheelers and motorizes Pedal Cycles (Public Carriers).
(4) Goods Carrying Motorized Three-wheelers and Motorized Pedal Cycles (Private Carriers).

Cover

The policy covers:

(1) Personal injury, and
(2) Property damage.

Third Party Insurance Cover for Personal Injury

Liability for deaths or injury to third parties means that you are insured against death or injury (caused by your vehicle) to pedestrians, occupant of other vehicles, and outsiders other than passengers.

Factors Determining Rate of Premium

The premium for Commercial Vehicles Insurance is calculated on:

(1) Carrying capacity or gross vehicle weight, and
(2) Value of the vehicles.

Accessories will be charged extra, as specified. If you do not make a claim during the policy period, a No Claim Bonus (NCB) is offered on renewals.

Sum Assured

The vehicles are insured at a fixed value called the insured's Decelerated Value (IDV). IDV is calculated on the basis of the manufacturer's listed selling price of the vehicle (plus the listed price of any accessories) after deducting the depreciation for every year as per the schedule provided by the Indian Motor Tariff.

If the price of any electrical and/or electronic item installed in the vehicle is not included in the manufacturer's listed selling price, the actual value (after depreciation) of this item can be added to the sum insured over and above the IDV.

Exclusions

Under this policy, you are not covered against:

(1) Own damage losses.
(2) Any claim arising out of persons accident.
(3) Third party legal liability cover for commercial vehicles other than goods carrying commercial vehicles.
(4) Any accidental loss damage and/or liability caused, sustained or incurred outside the geographical area.
(5) Any claim arising out of any contractual liability.
(6) Any accidental loss, damage or liability due to war, mutiny or nuclear risk.
(7) Any employee(s) of the insured other than the owner driver of the goods carrying vehicle.
(8) Damage to any bridge and/or way bridge and/or via duct and/or to any road and/or any thing beneath by vibration or by the weight of the insured vehicle and/or load carried by the insured vehicle.

MARINE HULL INSURANCE

Ships involve heavy capital and a loss can be crippling even to big steamer companies. A ship is insured according to the value of the ship's hull or body, its machinery and other integral attachments, freight, and disbursements against marine perils. Ocean going vessels, sailing vessels, trawlers, barges, fishing vessels, etc. are conventionally covered under hull. Vessels are generally classified as mechanically self-propelled vessels of steel construction, which are further classified, and smaller crafts built of steel, wood, etc. not subject to any classification.

Ships are insured as per the Institute Voyage Clauses for a particular voyage or for the Institute Time Clause for a specific period. There are specific clauses designed for different types of vessels such as sailing vessels, barges or tugs, and for different specific covers including ship building, ship breaking and ship repairing. Oil drilling rigs and off-shore oil platforms, fixed off-shore pipelines and jet ties are also covered under hull insurance.

Salient features of a marine hull insurance policy are as follows:

Scope of Cover

The purpose of hull insurance is to cover ship owners against various incurable interests and these include:

(1) Hull and Machinery Insurance.
(2) Insurance of Freight.
(3) Loss of Hire Insurance.
(4) Loss of Profit Insurance.

The Institute Time Clause forms the basis for most policies used for insurance of vessels and their machinery.

Sum Assured

It is an agreed clause policy.

Premium Rate

The premium will depend on the following factors:

(1) Types of vessel, trading limits, age, tonnage and technical aspects of machinery.
(2) Management and ownership considerations.
(3) Past claims experience.
(4) Valuation of vessel.
(5) Type of cover required.
(6) Size of the deductible.

Significant Exclusions

The exclusions will depend upon the type of cover availed and would be governed by the Institute Time Clauses and the Institute Voyage Clauses.

Excess

The policy will be subject to deductible, which will depend on the type of cover availed.

Aviation Hull Insurance

Insurance of Aviation Hull covers different types of customized products based on international wordings. The aviation portfolio encompasses the following types of covers:

(1) *Hull All Risk Insurance Policy*: This policy is suitable for small aircraft operators belonging to flying clubs, companies engaged in agricultural spraying operations, aircraft especially designed for VIPs and business executives, and for those engaged in industrial aids. The policy scope includes all physical loss or damage sustained by the insured aircraft including total loss and disappearance. All loses are paid subject to deductibles.
(2) *Spares All Risk Insurance Policy*: Covers loss or damage to spares, tools, equipments and supplies owned by the insured or the property for which the insured is responsible whilst on ground or in transit by land, sea, air, including in own aircraft or whilst on the premises of other for storage only.
(3) *Hull/Spares War Risk Insurance*: Indemnity is provided to the aircraft as well as spares on damage caused by war, invasion, acts of foreign enemies, hostilities, civil war, rebellion, revolution, resurrection, martial law, strikes, riots, civil commotion, malicious acts and sabotage.
(4) *Aviation Personal Accident (Crew Member) Insurance*: This policy is designed to cover the insured person against injury, disablement or death, arising as a result of an accident that is generally granted on annual basis. The cover operates while mounting or dismounting from and whilst traveling an aircraft, while the aircraft is being used within the geographical scope as per its permitted usage. This cover can also be on 24 hours basis. The capital sum insured varies according to the status of the insured or his/her earning capacity and fixed by the insurers.

(5) *Loss of License Insurance*: Operating crews of the aircraft are required to have valid license. License is liable to be suspended either temporarily or permanently on medical grounds. Consequential financial loss is covered by the loss of license policy. Cover provided is in respect to incapacity causing permanent total disablement or temporary total disablement duet to bodily injury or illness.

Besides the aforesaid general aviation policies, various other tailor-made insurance as per specific requirements of the insured also exists.

Some of the basic aviation insurance models are discussed below:

Salient features of Aircraft Hull and Spares/All Risks/Aviation Liability Insurance are as under:

Covered Risks

(1) Accidental physical loss or damage to the aircraft/aircraft spares.
(2) Legal liability to third parties towards bodily injury/death and property damages, passengers(s) bodily injury/death baggage, cargo and mail, premises, hangar-keepers.
(3) Catering and vehicle liability on airports can also be covered.

Major Exclusions

(1) Wear and tear.
(2) War risk.
(3) Radioactive contamination.
(4) Illegal use.
(5) Noise pollution.
(6) Insured's own property, etc.

Salient features of Aircraft Hull/Liability Insurance Policy are as under:

Brief Description

This policy is meant for the owners/operators of smaller aircraft being used for the purpose of private pleasure, training, industrial aid, business, commercial, off-shore operations, etc.

Covered Risks

(1) Accidental Physical loss or damage to the aircraft,
(2) Bodily injury/death of the passenger(s),
(3) Loss of passenger's baggage, and
(4) Bodily injury/death and property damage to the third parties.

Major Exclusions

(1) Wear and tear,
(2) War risk,
(3) Radioactive contamination,
(4) Illegal use,
(5) Noise pollution, and
(6) Insured's own property, etc.

INCOME INSURANCE

While the regular property insurance cover material losses, there are other losses that an insured would suffer due to the interruption of business. We have seen that a fire and special perils policy compensates only for material damage to the insured property. It specially excludes any consequential loss. In case of major loss caused by fire, there could be an interruption in business operation leading to reduction in turnover, finally resulting in possible loss of profits. However, standing or fixed charges continue to accrue regardless of whether there is any production or not. Such loss cannot be covered under the policy. Losses of this type would include the following:

(1) Net profit of the business venture.
(2) Standing of fixed charges (overhead expense) such as salaries, wages, taxes and interest, which have to be paid despite the loss.
(3) Increased costs of working or the abnormal expenses incurred post loss to keep the venture afloat.
(4) Losses due to failure of electricity, gas and water supply.
(5) Interpretation of business at other locations, such as suppliers and customs premises.

Insurance of this loss of income is called by different names—consequential loss, business interruption, loss of profits, etc. A consequential loss policy compensates for the revenue loss suffered by the enterprise. Hence, for complete protection to the business enterprise and its profitability, consequential loss policy is very essential in addition to fire insurance policy.

BUSINESS INTERRUPTION/LOSS OF PROFITS INSURANCE

This type of policy offers a solution by covering profit lost due to reduction in turnover arising from interruption of business following damage to the property insured. This policy can be taken only in conjunction with the fire policy or the machinery breakdown policy. This policy is also known by various names such as consequential loss policy or business interruption policy or loss of profit policy.

Salient features of a consequential loss (fire) insurance policy are:

Scope of Cover

The policy broadly covers loss of net profit on account of interruption of business consequential upon maturely damage to property due to fire or any other insured peril under the standard fire and special perils policy.

It also covers standing charges that continue to be incurred during the period of interruption and the increase in cost of working, necessarily and reasonably incurred to maintain the business as far as possible at its normal level, so that loss under net profit and standing charges is avoided or at least minimized.

Sum Assured

Sum to be insured under this policy is the estimated gross profit of the indemnity period, the maximum period beginning with the occurrence of the damage, for which cover of loss of gross profit is required, and should reflect the maximum period anticipated for reinstatement of the damaged property. The maximum indemnity period permissible under the policy is 3 years.

Premium Rate

Basis rate depends on fire and special perils rate. Final rate is influenced by the indemnity period chosen. At inception, gross profit is taken on an estimated basis and is subject to declaration of the actual figures after expiry of policy, based on final audited account.

Excess

Claims are payable in full without any deduction.

Significant Exclusions

The insurance policy does not cover.

(1) Loss of gross profits, which is not consequent upon property damage due to an insured peril.
(2) Loss due to material damage to property.
(3) Difference between value of stock at the time of fire and the value at the time of subsequent replacement, deterioration of undamaged stock after fire.
(4) Cost of preparing fire and/or loss of profits claim.
(5) Third party claims and loss of goodwill.

Main Extension

Policy can be extended to suppliers and customers premises or public utilities, on which the business is dependent and cost of auditors' fees for making the claim on the insurers.

ADVANCE LOSS OF PROFITS INSURANCE

The Advance Loss of Profit (ALOP) policy is taken by the principal of an erection all risks policy or a contractor All Risks Policy as he stands to lose in case of any delay in the commissioning of the project. A marine-*cum*-erection/storage-*cum*-erection or contractor's All Risk Policy covers only physical damage to property, which at best, covers the expenses incurred for repairing or replacing the damaged property.

Salient features of an Advance loss of profits insurance policy are as under:

Scope of Cover

The advance loss of profit policy is designed to cover:

Loss of Gross Profit = Net Profit + Standing Charges

or

Loss of Gross Earnings = Turnover – Specified Working Expenses

or

Fixed Operation and Management Costs (Debt Service Charges, increased Cost of Working, and Special Expenses such as Penalties).

The policy pays for the actual loss of gross profit incurred during the period of delay, commencing from the scheduled date of commencement of commercial operation till the actual date of commencement of commercial operation, subject to a time excess and indemnity period selected. The delay, however, should have occurred due to a claim payable under marine-*cum*-erection policy, storage-*cum*-erection policy or contractor's all risks policy.

Special Exclusions

The policy does not cover delay due to:

(1) Inventory Losses,
(2) Delay in shipment of supplies,
(3) Normal project schedule slippages,
(4) Non-availability of funds for repairs/replacement to damaged items, and
(5) Cancellation of licenses or government restriction, etc.

Sum Assured

The sum insured should represent the anticipated gross profit (i.e. Net Profit + Standing Charges) for the indemnity period selected.

Net Profit is the business profit before taxation.

Standing Charges are the fixed charges incurred even in the absence of business activity (e.g. interest charges, salary and wages, director's fees, O&M costs, liquidated damages, etc.).

Indemnity period should be selected keeping in mind the maximum period required for re-importing, re-erecting and/or re-testing any part of the project.

Credit Guarantee Insurance

Credit Guarantee Insurance provides a business with protection against failure of its customers to pay their debts. Like any form of insurance, credit insurance is purchased to protect a business from a large loss that could impair its performance.

Despite company's best efforts, large or catastrophic losses occur due to:

(1) One large long-term buyers unexpectedly failing.
(2) A significant change in the market (or economy) where a number of buyers become distressed and are unable to meet their obligations in time.
(3) A sudden shift in the political or economic conditions of a buyer's country (in the case of exports).

It is also a risk management tool that can provide concrete solutions for the trade expansion issues being considered. The credit insurance policy is an insurance product, rather it sets in motion an ongoing process of partnership between you and the insurer. The insurer vets a debtor's credit worthiness and monitors his financial position to identify possible problems if a debt goes bad and cannot be collected (or collected only partially), a claim is paid.

Salient features of a credit guarantee insurance policy are the following:

Coverage

(1) Declared insolvency of the buyer, i.e. the buyer is declared bankrupt.
(2) He has made a valid assignment/compositions/arrangement for the benefit of his creditors.
(3) A receiver has been appointed.
(4) Order has been made for compulsory winding up.
(5) An effective resolution has been passed for voluntary winding up.

(6) An arrangement binding on all creditors has been sanctioned by the court or equivalent conditions.

Protracted Default

Protracted default is the non-payment for (specified number of) days after the expiry of the due date for payment, of any undisputed invoice submitted by the insured (suppliers) to his buyer.

Political Risks (for Exports only)

Political risk is the risk undertaken on non-payment of the buyer caused by a political act such as war or civil war, sabotage, embargo, cancellation of import/export contract, and imposition of import/export restrictions.

Major Exclusions

(1) Disputed debts.
(2) Default of agents/employees.
(3) The insured accepting an arrangement with the buyer, without prior approval of the insurer.
(4) If the rights under the policy are assigned by the insured without prior approval.
(5) Interest, taxes, consequential losses, etc.
(6) Dishonesty and fraud.
(7) Disregard of agreed credit management procedures.
(8) Sales made to subsidiaries/associates/public/government bodies.
(9) Claims in excess of discretionary/sanctioned credit limits.

Basis of Indemnity

(1) The basis of indemnity will be the invoice value excluding interest and taxes.
(2) Up to 85 per cent of the insured loss.
(3) Payment will be the insured percentage of the insured loss, for sales made during the policy period, net of excess and subject to the overall indemnity limit under the policy.

Risk Monitoring

(1) The insurer assesses the creditworthiness of buyers for fixing credit limits.
(2) An extensive information database and constant monitoring provides an early warning to the insured that the buyer is in financial difficulty.
(3) Enables the insured to withdraw from the relationship on a structured basis.

Procedure for Obtaining Cover

(1) Completion of proposal form.
(2) Submission of proposal form along with payment of processing fees.
(3) Issue of quotation by the insurer.
(4) Payment of premium by the client.
(5) Issue of policy.
(6) Credit limit-applications for new buyers.

Premium Payable

(1) Premium rate is the amount obtained by applying a rate per cent on the annual insured credit sales turnover.
(2) Provisional premium to be paid in advance, on estimated turnover, subject to adjustment on actual turnover.

FIDELITY GUARANTEE INSURANCE

The term fidelity guarantee insurance embraces policies indemnifying employers against financial loss on account of forgeries, deflection, embezzlement and fraudulent conversion by employees. The object is to provide protection in respect of the default of an individual acting in capacity, such as cashier, accountant, store-keeper, etc. The cover may be required in respect of a single employee or a number of employees. There are three types of policies normally issued for this class of business, viz. individual policy, collective policy and floating policy. The insurers find it necessary to obtain the private reference and/or former employer's report forms in addition to the completed employer and employees application form, as appropriate.

Scope of Cover

The commercial fidelity guarantee policy provides indemnity against loss of money or goods as a result of acts of fraud or dishonesty on the part of the employees.

Covered Risks

The policy covers direct pecuniary loss caused by an act of fraud or dishonesty committed by any salaried person employed by the insured. This loss should have occurred in connection with the employee's duties during the period of his emplacement, and should be discovered within six months of his/her death, dismissal or retirement, or within six months after the policy ceases to exist, whichever is earlier.

The policy covers direct pecuniary loss caused by an act of fraud or dishonesty committed by any salaried person employed by the insured.

Individual Policy

The policy covers one individual only for a stated amount.

Collective Policy

A schedule is included in the policy. The insured decides the amount of guarantee required for each individual according to his/her responsibilities and position.

Floater Policy

A single amount is shown in the policy, which represents the company's liability in respect of any one individual and its total liability in respect of all the employees guaranteed who are individually named in the schedule. Such policies can be granted where the number of persons to be guaranteed is not less than five.

Blanket Policy

It is possible to issue, in certain selected cases, blanket policies without the names of the guaranteed persons being shown, in respect of all employees who are grouped according to categories such as employees handling cash, other clerical staff, etc. They are issued only to large well established business houses conducted on sound lines.

Premium Rating

Rates vary from 0.50 per cent to 1.50 per cent per annum on the amount of guarantee, depending upon the merits of each case.

LIABILITY INSURANCES

Liabilities can arise from a legal obligation on the insured to pay. Liability can occur from many day-to-day activities. There are many examples of liability ranging from workmen's compensation, third party liability on road accidents, professional liability, product liability, and many other liabilities. There is a large demand for liability insurances in the developed markets.

MOTOR TRANSPORT INSURANCE

As per the Motor Vehicles Act, 1988, it is mandatory for every owner of a vehicle plying on public roads to take an insurance policy to cover the amount that the owner becomes legally liable to pay as damages to third parties as a result of accidental death, bodily injury or damage to property. A certificate of insurance must be carried in the vehicle as a proof of such insurance.

Cover Available

The policy covers the vehicle owner's legal liability to pay compensation for:

(1) Death or bodily injury to a third party person.
(2) Damage to third party property.

Personal accident cover for owner driver is also included.

Liability is covered for an unlimited amount in respect of death or injury and damage to third party property for Rs. 7.5 lac for a commercial and private vehicle, and Rs. 1 lac for scooter/motor cycle.

Additional Cover

(1) Legal liability to employees.
(2) Legal liability to non-fare paying passengers in commercial vehicles.

PUBLIC LIABILITY INSURANCE

Legal liability under the law of tort can arise under several circumstances in the insured's premises, such as collapse of building structure, accidental falling of fixtures, bad maintenance or poor house-keeping resulting in accident to visitors on the premises, and accidental leakage of toxic substance that pollutes the atmosphere and injures or kills people.

The term liability means responsibility and legal liability means responsibilities that can be enforced by law. Legal liability may be classified into Criminal Liability and Civil Liability. Only civil liability claims are payable. Civil liability claims will arise if there is *prima facie* evidence of negligence by the insured resulting in injury or death to any third party or resulting in damage to property belonging to a person other than the insured, or in the insured's custody.

Negligence will be proved only when the following conditions are satisfied.

(1) Existence of duty of care.
(2) Breach of this duty.
(3) Injury suffered by a person, or property damaged as a result of that breach.

Salient features of a Public Liability Insurance Policy are as under:

Highlights

This policy covers the amount that the insured becomes legally liable to pay as damages to third parties as a result of accidental death, bodily injury, and loss or damage to the property belonging to a third party. The legal cost and expense incurred in defending the case with prior consent of the insurance company are also payable subject to certain terms and conditions.

One can insure more than one unit situated in different locations under a single policy.

The policies offers a benefit of retroactive period on continuous renewal of policy, whereby claims reported in subsequent renewal, but pertaining to earlier period after first inception of the policy, also become payable.

Scope

Three types of public liability policies are issued—

(1) *Public Liability Non-Industrial Risk:* For offices, hotels, cinema houses, hospitals, schools, etc.
(2) *Public Liability Industrial Risk:* For godowns, warehouses and factories.
(3) *Public Liability Insurance Act, 1991:* This is a mandatory policy to be taken by the owners, users or transporters of hazardous substances as defined under the Environment (Protection) Act, 1986 in excess of the minimum quantity specified under the Public Liability Insurance Act, 1991.

Add on Covers

The Public Liability Policy can be extended to cover the following risks on payment of an additional premium:

(1) Natural calamities such as flood, earthquake, etc.
(2) Pollution risk subject to NOC from Pollution Control Board.
(3) Transportation risk.

Sum Insured

In Public Liability Policy, the sum insured is referred to as Limit of Indemnity. This limit is fixed according to per accident and per policy period, which is called Any One Accident (AOA) limit and Any One Year (AOY) limit, respectively. The ratio of AOA limit to AOY limit can be on the basis of (a) 1:1, (b) 1:2, (c) 1:3 or (d) 1:4.

The AOA limit, which is the maximum amount payable for each accident, should be fixed taking into account the nature of activity of the insured, the maximum number of people who could be affected and the maximum property damage that could occur in the worst possible accident in the insured's premises.

In case of the Public Liability Insurance Act, 1991, the AOA limit should represent the paid up capital of the company subject to maximum of Rs. 5 crore/the AOY limit is fixed at 3 times the AOA limit (max. Rs. 15 crore).

In case of the Public Liability Insurance Act, 1991, any award that exceeds the AOA limit will be paid by the government through Environment Relief Fund to which the insured has to contribute an amount equivalent to the premium paid under policy issued under the Public Liability Insurance Act.

Exemptions

The policy will not pay for claims arising out of:

(1) Contractual liability,
(2) Intentional non-compliance of any statutory provisions,
(3) Loss of goodwill,
(4) Slander,
(5) Fines and penalties,
(6) Libel,
(7) False arrest,
(8) Defamation, and
(9) Mental injury, etc.

PRODUCT LIABILITY INSURANCE

Policy indemnifies the insured against legal liability to third parties in consequence of death/bodily injury arising from the use of product sold to them.

Salient features of a Product Liability Insurance Policy are as under:

Scope of Cover

Policy indemnifies the insured all sums that the insured shall become legally liable to pay as damages in consequence of accidental death/bodily injury or disease to third party or damage to their property arising out of any defect in the products manufactured and covered under the policy after such products have left the insure's premises.

Excess

The policy is subject to compulsory excess, i.e. in the event of a claim, the insured must bear 0.50 per cent to 1 per cent of the limit of indemnity.

Premium

The premium will depend on the kind of product produced by the insured, i.e. the insured's classification as per the risk group, turnover, ratio of any one accident limit to any one year limit, etc.

Exports

The export of products to the USA, Canada, Europe and other countries can also be insured under the policy.

Vendors' Legal Liability

The policy can be extended to include the liability of vendors.

Technical Collaborator Liability

The liability arising out of any agreement of technical collaboration can be covered as an extension.

Main Exclusions

(1) Product recall.
(2) Deliberate, wilful or international non-compliance of any statutory provision.
(3) Loss of goodwill, and loss of market.
(4) Fines, penalties, and punitive/exemplary damages.
(5) War and war like situations.
(6) Any loss occurring prior to the retroactive date mentioned in the policy.

PROFESSIONAL LIABILITY INSURANCE

The cover granted under the Professional Liability Insurance Policy provides indemnity for legal liability to third parties, arising out of errors and omissions or negligence in professional service rendered by the insured.

Policies will be issued for a period of 12 months (1 year). These policies are usually issued for Doctors, Medical Establishment, Engineers, Architects, Chartered Accountants, Lawyers and other professionals.

Salient features of a Professional Liability (Medical Practitioners) Insurance Policy are the following:

Salient Features

This insurance covers legal liability arising from errors and omissions on the part of Registered Medical Practitioners while rendering professional service.

Scope of Cover

The policy indemnifies any act committed by the insured, who shall be a Registered Medical Practitioner, giving rise to any legal liability to third parties. The insured includes the policyholder and his qualified assistant or employees, as named in the proposal form.

It applies to claims arising out of bodily injury and/or death of any patient caused by or alleged to have been caused by error, omission or negligence in professional service rendered, or which should have been rendered by the insured or qualified assistants named in the schedule or any nurse or technician employed by the insured.

(1) Legal liability as fixed by courts in India to pay compensation.
(2) Defence costs and expense. This means all costs, fees and expenses incurred with the prior consent of the insurer in the investigation, defense or settlement of any claim made against the insured, provided the claim falls within the ambit of the policy.

The amount of payment under (a) and (b) will not exceed the amount insured for in the policy under the limit of any one accident (AOA) in respect of any or all claims made against the insured arising out of any one accident.

Special Benefit

(1) *Retroactive Benefit:* This means that the insured will be covered for any professional act or omission occurring during the period of insurance, starting from the first date of the first policy, provided that the policy is renewed without interruption and is in force when the claim arising out of the act or omission is made in writing against the insured during the policy period, policy period means the period incepting from the date and hour mentioned in the policy schedule and terminating at midnight on the expiry date indicated in the policy schedule.

(2) *Notification Extension clause:* If the insured notifies during the policy period any special event or circumstance that the insurer accepts may give rise to a claim, the acceptance of such notification means that the insurer will deal with the claim as if it has been made during the policy period.

(3) *Extended claim Reporting Clause:* In the event of non-renewal or cancellation of the policy, the insurer will allow a time limit of up to 90 days, provided another policy does not exist, for notification of claims for accidents that had taken place during the period of insurance.

Meaning of Any One Accident (AOA) : Any One Year (AOY)

AOA means Any One Accident, which may include on or more or a series of claims arising out of the same cause or error or omission relating to professional service. AOY means Any One Year. The insured can choose an indemnity limit that can be in the ratio of 1:1, 1:2, 1:3, or 1:4 of AOA : AOY, and the premium will be charged on AOY limit.

Main Exclusions

(1) Liability arising from any criminal act or act in violation of any law or ordinance.
(2) Service rendered under the influence of intoxicants or narcotics.
(3) Dental treatment under general anesthesia, except in a hospital.
(4) Use of drugs for weight reduction.
(5) Plastic surgery, except for repair of scar being the result of previous surgery, or in connection with burns or other traumatic injury.
(6) AIDS-related conditions.
(7) Liability arising due to intentional non-compliance of statutory provisions.
(8) Personal injuries caused by x-ray and radioactive substances.
(9) Liability caused by intentional disregard of technical or administrative management of the need to take all care to prevent claims.
(10) Liability to employees/apprentices/contractors/general third party public.
(11) Fines, penalties, punitive or exemplary damages.
(12) Any loss of goodwill, loss of market, etc.

Important Condition

(1) Early written notice of any claim to the insurer. Sending of any claim, writ, summons or process and all documents to the insurer.
(2) No admission offer promise or payment to be made without the consent of the insurer.

(3) The insurer has the right to take over and conduct in the name of the insured, the defense/settlement of the claim.
(4) The insured shall give all such information and assistance that the company may reasonably require.
(5) No short period policy is permitted, i.e. all policies will be for 12 months.

Indicative Premium Rate

Varies between 0.30 to 0.50 per cent or per thousand rupees depending upon:
(1) Category of Doctor, and
(2) AOA : AOY ratio chosen.

WORKMEN'S COMPENSATION INSURANCE

This liability policy covers employers' liability towards his workmen. An employer, as a principal or contractor, engaging workmen as defined in Workmen's Compensation Act, 1923, would need to cover his liability to them under statue and at common law. The worker's compensation policy cover the employer's liability towards his employees who come within the definition coverage employment-related injury (including death). The employer can cover employees who do not qualify as workmen under a separate table.

SALIENT FEATURES OF A WORKMEN'S COMPENSATION INSURANCE POLICY

Scope of Cover

The policy provides for two forms of insurance viz.
(1) Table A: Indemnity against legal liability to all employees (whether or not coming within the definition of the term workmen) under the Workmen's Compensation Act, 1923 and subsequent amendment to the said Act prior to the date of issue of the policy, the Fatal Accident Act, 1855 and the Common Law.
(2) Table B: Indemnity against legal liability under the Fatal Accident Act, 1855 and the common Law. (Table B policies may not be issued to cover employers who fall within the definition of workmen under the Workmen's Compensation Act, 1923 as amended) (Code Misc. 10).

Sum Assured

The policy does not have a sum insured the estimated earning sof the workmen for the policy period are mentioned on the policy.

Premium

The premium rate depends on the occupation of the workmen and their annual earnings.

Significant Exclusion

The insurance policy does not cover losses arising out of war and allied perils, nuclear activities, and contractual liabilities.

Main Extensions

(1) *Medical Expenses:* On extra premium, medical, surgical and hospital expenses, including the cost of transport to hospital for accidental employment injuries.

(2) *Occupational Disease:* Liability in respect of diseases mentioned in Part C schedule III of the Workmen's Compensation Act, on additional premium which arise out of and in the course of employment.

Apart from above, there are other types of liability policies—Director and Officers' Liability Policy, Lift (Third Party) Insurance, Employer's Liability Policy, Carrier's Liability Insurance, Golfer's Indemnity Insurance, etc. The above five types of liabilities are indicative of the different types of liabilities that can arise and can be covered by insurance.

PERSONAL INSURANCES

Personal lines of insurance relate to losses faced by a person, such as death, sickness, accident, unemployment and superannuation.

HEALTH INSURANCE

Health care costs are high and getting higher. Payment of hospital bills relating to a serious accident or major illness is scary for many. Health or Medical policies protect a person and his/her family in case they need expensive medical care. Some health insurances offer cashless benefit at hospitals, meaning that the insurer will make the payment directly to the hospital. Some policies are of medical reimbursement types. Variations of health insurance policies offer lump-sum payment on a per day/per event basis, instead of paying the hospital bills in lieu of reimbursing hospitalization expenses.

Salient Features of a Health Insurance Policy are the following:

Scope

Expense incurred by the insured for hospitalization for illness/diseases or injury sustained (domiciliary hospitalization also payable as per policy) these include hospital charges (room, boarding and operation theatre), fees for surgeon, anaesthetize, nursing, specialist, etc., cost of diagnostic tests, medicines, blood, oxygen, etc., cost of appliances such as pacemaker, artificial limbs, etc.

Cover

Illness/disease, accidental injury sustained leading to one or more class(es) of expenses listed above are covered.

The Insured

(1) Any person in the age group of 5 to 75 years.

(2) Children between 3 months to 5 years can be covered only along with parents.

(3) Institutions (Government or Private) for their employees.

(4) Clubs/associations for their members in the said age group.

(5) Group schemes for homogeneous groups of more than 50 persons.

Other Benefits

(1) Domiciliary hospitalization benefits can be excluded under group med claim policy and a premium discount can be availed.

(2) A discount of 10 per cent of total premium for coverage of family under a single policy.

Policy Will Pay

(1) Actual hospitalization expenses of various types listed above, subject to a maximum of Rs. 15,000 to Rs. 5,00,000 are reimbursable depending upon the sum insured chosen at the inception of the policy (sum insured is maximum liability under the policy).

(2) Actual domiciliary hospitalization expenses limited to Rs. 30,000 to Rs. 50,000, depending on the sum insured chosen at inception.

(3) Cost of health check-up reimbursable at the end of four continuously claim free underwriting years limited to 1 per cent of average sum insured of four claim free years.

(4) The sum insured will be increased by 5 per cent, cumulative bonus, for every claim free year. If there is a claim in a policy with cumulative bonus of 10 per cent the sum insured will be reduced from the earned bonus.

(5) Maternity expenses incurred in hospital/nursing home as in patient, subject to limit of sum insured or Rs. 50,000, whichever is lower, on payment of extra premium and the policy being extended to cover maternity benefits. This benefit is only available in-group policies.

(6) All terms, benefits and conditions of the cover are subject to the definitions of various terms under the policy.

Exclusions

Broadly, there would be no claim under the policy under the following circumstances:

(1) Domiciliary hospitalization.

(2) Pre- and post-hospitalization treatment.

(3) Treatment of Asthma, Chronic Nephritis and Nephritis Syndrome, Gastroenteritis, Diabetes Mellitus and Insipidus, Epilepsy, Hypertension, Influenza, Cough and Cold, all Psychiatric or Psychosomatic Disorders, Pyrexia of Unknown Origin for less than 10 days. Tonsillitis and URT(I), Arthritis, Rheumatism, etc. (the list is not exhaustive).

(4) Any treatment relating to any illness/disease already in existence at the time of proposal.

(5) Any disease/injury during first 30 days of commencement of policy (accidental injury is not an exclusion).

(6) During first year of cover of Cataract, Benign Prostatic Hypertrophy, Hysterectomy for Hemorrhagic on Fibromyoma, Hernia, Hydrocele, Congenital Internal Disease, Fistula in Anus, Sinusitis and related disorder.

(7) Any pre-existing disease/illness is not covered of during renewal also.

(8) Vaccination, inoculation circumcision or change of life or cosmetic or aesthetic treatment, and plastic surge and dental treatment unless requiring

hospitalization necessitated due to accident or as a part of any illness.

(9) Cost of spectacles, contact lenses, and hearing aids.

(10) Convalescence, general debility, rundown conditions, sterility, venereal disease, intentional self-injury and use of intoxicants.

(11) Any variation of deficiency syndrome or AIDS.

(12) Hospital/nursing home charges not consistent with or included in the diagnosis and treatment.

(13) Vitamins and tonics not forming part of any treatment.

(14) Any treatment related to pregnancy, childbirth and voluntary medical termination of pregnancy during the first 12 weeks of pregnancy.

(15) Nuclear perils and war group of perils.

(16) Naturopathy treatment.

PERSONAL ACCIDENT INSURANCE

Personal accident insurance policy covers a person against accidental death, permanent total disablement (PTD) and permanent partial disablement (PPD). There are many Personal Accident Plan options (Accidental Death and Permanent Total Disablement Cover) with different sum insured.

Salient features of a Personal Accident Insurance Policy are mentioned below:

Policy Coverage

A comprehensive personal accident plan usually would cover the insured for an agreed amount of cover, say Rs. 20,00,000.

(1) *Death of the Insured Personal:* In case of death of the insured due to an accident (including on account of terrorism or acts of terrorism) whiten the policy period, the nominee (mentioned in the policy) is compensated with the sum insured.

(2) *Permanent Total Disablement (PTD)*: Personal accident plan pays compensation against the permanent and total loss of limbs, sight, etc. (including on account of terrorism or acts of terrorism) due to an accident.
Note: If any such injury as mentioned above shall result in the inability to remain gainfully employed then the capital sum insured payable will be 100 per cent.

(3) *Permanent Partial Disablement (PPD)*: Personal accident covers total and/ or partial loss of use of the defined body parts or loss by actual physical separation (including on account of terrorism or acts of terrorism).

(4) *Carriage of Dead Body*: Reimbursement of expenses incurred for transportation of the insured person's dead body to the place of residence subject to a maximum of 2 per cent of capital sum insured or Rs. 2,500 whichever is less.

Key Benefits

(1) Covers against accidental death or permanent total disablement (PTD) on account of an accident, with option to cover permanent partial disablement (PPD).

(2) Flexible plan options, with sum insured of Rs. 3, 5, 10 and Rs. 20 lac.

(3) Covers claims arising out of terrorism or acts of terrorism.
(4) Choice of cover 3, 4, or 5 years.
(5) No health check-up required.
(6) Renewable till the age of 70 years.

Eligibility

(1) Age criteria at entry minimum 18 years, maximum 70 years.
(2) The application can buy the policy for his spouse aged between 18-70 years.
(3) The policy cover is renewed till the age of 70 years.

Policy Exclusions

The company shall not be liable under this policy for:

(1) Compensation/claim under more than one of the categories specified in the policy coverage in respect of the same period of disablement of the insured person.
(2) Claims arising from sickness/illness.
(3) Death, injury or disablement of the insured person:
    (a) From intentional self-injury, suicide or attempted suicide;
    (b) Whilst under the influence of intoxicating liquor or drugs;
    (c) Whilst engaging in aviation or ballooning, or whilst mounting into or dismounting from or traveling in any balloon or aircraft other than as a passenger (fare paying or otherwise) in any duly licensed standard type of aircraft anywhere in the world;
    (d) Directly or indirectly caused by venereal disease or insanity;
    (e) Arising or resulting from the insured committing any breach of the law with criminal intent;
    (f) War, invasion, act of foreign enemy, hostilities (whether war be declared or not), civil, war, rebellion, revolution, insurrection, mutiny, military or usurped power, seizure, capture, arrests, restraints and detainment of all kinds;
    (g) Nuclear weapon induced treatment; and
    (h) Childbirth or pregnancy, or in consequence thereof.

LIFE INSURANCE

Life insurance is a personal insurance, may be the most personal of them all. Life insurance covers one's own life and the lives of one's close relatives, premature death, disability and dependency during old age are some of the greatest risks people are willing to cover. This is one of the most common types of insurance cover and is designed to payout to loved ones in the event a person dies. There are certain restrictions in place with this types of cover, for instance, suicide is not covered. The subject being so vast, it is the topic of a separate book and hence not dealt with in this unit.

SPECIALISED INSURANCES

We have by now seen that the categorizations are broad and indicative of certain basic characteristics. Many of the areas are overlapping, as over segmentation and mutual exclusiveness are difficult to achieve when loss and related hardship is the subject matter.

There are many policies that may not exactly fall in a specific category or where such categorization may be practically meaningless. Some of such insurances are discussed below:

Agriculture Insurance

Indian agriculture is heavily dependent on natural factors, particularly rainfall. Rainfall variations cause variability in crop yields. Again, rainfall is increasingly unpredictable and uncertain. Although there are no ways of controlling weather factors, agriculture insurers strive to mitigate the adverse financial effects that rainfall can have on the rural economy, particularly farm incomes. While going through the salient features, you will realize how the products are different from the other insurances, and the points of comparison as well.

Salient features of Varsha Bima (an Agriculture Insurance Policy) are as under:

Scope

Varsha Bima covers anticipated shortfall in crop yield on account of deficit rainfall. It is voluntary for all classes of cultivators who stand to lose financially upon adverse incidence of rainfall and can take insurance under the scheme. Initially, Varsha Bima was meant for cultivators for whom National Agricultural Insurance Scheme (NAIS) was voluntary.

Period of Insurance

The insurance operates during June to September for short duration crops, June to October for medium duration crops, and June to November for longer duration crops. Further, these periods (and subjects) are state-specific. In case of the sowing failure option, the period covered is from June 15 to August 15.

Insurance Buying Period

A cultivator can buy Varsha Bima only upto June 15 for the sowing failure option and June 30 for other options.

Coverage Options

(1) **Option I: Seasonal Rainfall Insurance:** Coverage is against negative deviation of 20 per cent and beyond in actual rainfall (in mm) from normal rainfall (in mm) for the entire season. Actual rainfall is the monthly cumulative rainfall from June to November (with June to September or October for short and medium duration crops). The pay out structure is designed in such a way that the yield is correlated to various ranges of adverse deviation in rainfall.

The sum insured per hectare is the maximum pay out corresponding to the maximum potential loss. The claim pay out shall be on a graded scale (in slabs), corresponding to different degrees of adverse deviation in actual rainfall).

(2) **Option II: Rainfall Distribution Index:** Coverage is against adverse deviation of 20 per cent and beyond in actual rainfall index from normal rainfall index for the entire season. The index is constructed to maximize the correlation for weekly rainfall within the season. The indices vary from India Metrological Department

(IMD) station-to-station and crop-to-crop. The sum insured per hectare is the maximum pay out corresponding to the maximum potential loss. The claim pay out shall be on a graded scale (in slabs), corresponding to different degrees of adverse deviation in actual rainfall index.

(3) **Option III: Sowing Failure:** Coverage is against adverse deviation in actual rainfall (in mm) from normal rainfall (in mm) beyond 40 per cent between June 15 and August 15. The sum insured per hectare is the maximum input cost incurred by the cultivator till the end of the sowing period and is pre-specified the claim pay out shall be on a graded scale, corresponding to different degrees of rainfall deviation. The maximum payout of 100 per cent of sum insured is available at deviations of 80 per cent and above.

(4) **Option IV: Vegetative Phase:** Coverage is against adverse deviation in actual rainfall (in mm) from normal rainfall (in mm) beyond 20 per cent between August 1/August 16 and September 30/October 31 to November 30. The sum insured per hectare is the maximum payout corresponding to the maximum potential loss. The claim pay out will be on a graded scale, corresponding to different degrees of rainfall deviation. The maximum pay out of 100 per cent of sum insured is available at deviation of 80 per cent and above.

Sum Insured

The sum insured is pre-specified and is normally between cost of production and vale of production. In case of the sowing failure option, it is the maximum input cost incurred by the cultivator till the end of the sowing period, which again is pre-specified.

Premium

The premium may vary from option to option and crop to crop. The premium rates have been optimized *vis-a-vis* benefits, and starts from 1 per cent.

Time Schedule and Procedure of Claim Payment

The procedure for working out claims is automated, i.e. there shall be no necessity for submission of loss information or claims intimation by the insured cultivator. Normally, claims are paid on the basis of actual rainfall data within a month from end of the indemnity period.

Salient Features of a Horticulture (Agriculture Insurance) Policy

Cover

Trees/plants/shoots/vegetative parts only for crop duration or 12 months, whichever is shorter.

The Insured

They are farm owners/lessees cultivating the plantations and horticulture.

Risks Covered

Coverage and indemnity to the insured to the extent of loss or damage to the crop by operation of any one of the following perils:

(1) Fire including forest fire and bush fire,

(2) Lightning,
(3) Riot, strike, and acts of terrorism, and
(4) Storm, hailstorm, cyclone, hurricane, flood and inundation.

Benefits

The input costs or recurring expense incurred for raising the crop (establishment and maintenance) till the date of the loss. Limits of indemnity on input cost basis are fixed at each stage of the crop. Claims are subject to franchise and excess deductibles.

Exclusions

The policy excludes to pay for loss or damage to crop arising due to:
(1) Theft, malicious damage, and negligence,
(2) Natural mortality
(3) War and nuclear perils,
(4) Insects, pests and diseases,
(5) Drought, earthquake, climatic variations,
(6) Water logging,
(7) Inconsequential losses, and
(8) Damage to structures, capital items, irrigation systems, agricultural implements, and harvested produce.

Salient Features of Weather Insurance (an agriculture insurance) Policy

Scope of Cover

Whether insurance is an indemnity for losses that may arise due to abnormal weather conditions. These abnormal weather conditions can be events such as excess of rainfall, shortfall in rainfall or variations in temperature, wind speeds and humidity.

Product Structure

(1) *Peril Identification:* Peril identification involves appreciation of agronomic properties of the crops or nature of the economic activity. Detailed correlation analysis is carried out to ascertain the manner in which the weather impacts yields of the crops output of other economic activities.
(2) *Index Setting:* In weather insurance, the claim is settled on the basis of a transparent index. The index is created by assigning weights to critical time periods of crop growth. The past weather data is mapped on to this index to arrive at a normal threshold index. The actual weather data is then mapped to the index to arrive at the actual index level. In case there is a material deviation between the normal index and the actual index, compensation is paid out to the insured on the basis of a pre-agreed formula.
(3) *Back testing for Payouts:* In order to ensure the robustness of the structure, the normal index is extensively tested based on historical data, to ascertain if the payouts made on the basis of the chosen indices would have adequately indemnified the loss in the past or not.
(4) *Pricing:* Pricing is determined based on components of expected loss, volatility of historical losses and management expense.

(5) *Monitoring:* This claim related weather data is collected during the policy period and concurrent assessment of the ground conditions.

(6) *Claims Settlement:* The claim settlement is a hassle free process, as the beneficiary is not required to file a claim for loss to receive a payout. Instead, some companies compensate the beneficiary at the end of the crop season for any deviations from the normal conditions on the basis of the data collected from an independent source accessible to all, such as a local weather station, thus removing the need for carrying out field surveys.

PROMOTIONAL LOW VALUE INSURANCE

These are policies intended to provide social support to the underprivileged sectors and those segments of the economy that are not commercially viable due to their low turnover, geographically not easily/less accessible, and possibly, economically and educationally backward. In essence, these relate to the country's rural and social sectors.

SALIENT FEATURES OF POULTRY INSURANCE POLICY

Brief Description

This provides indemnity to poultry birds, which includes layers, broilers and hatchery birds (breeding stock) which are exotic and cross bred. Indigenous and non-descriptive birds will not be insured.

The scheme is applicable to poultry farms consisting of a minimum 100 birds under scheme category and 500 birds under non-scheme category, and under general broilers, 100 per batch, layers 500 per batch and hatching 2000 birds per batch.

Covered Risk

The policy shall provide indemnity against:

(1) Death of birds due to accident (including fire, lightning, flood, cyclone, strike, riot and civil commotion, and terrorism), or

(2) Diseases contracted or occurring during the period of insurance.

Major Exclusions

(1) Wilful injury,

(2) Transit by an mode,

(3) Theft and clandestine sale,

(4) Intentional slaughter,

(5) Avian Leucosis complex disease,

(6) War and nuclear perils,

(7) Improper management,

(8) Undergrowth,

(9) Cannibalism,

10) Predators action,

(11) Permanent and partial disablement,

(12) Loss of production, and

(13) Standard exclusions

SALIENT FEATURES OF HONEY BEE INSURANCE POLICY

Brief Description

This policy is to cover beehives and/or colonies belonging to individual, cooperative societies, and those sponsored and subsidized under various projects of respective State and the Central Government. This cover is only for Indian Honeybee and Italian Honeybee.

Covered Risks

Total loss damage to beehives and/or bee colonies as a result of an accident caused by fire, flood, inundation, storm, tempest, cyclone, hurricane and tornado. Additional covers are theft, specified viral disease, and transit loss during migration.

Major exclusions are partial loss/damage of whatsoever nature, loss of production wax moth and ectoparasitic termites, and loss of bee colony resulting from death of queen bee.

SALIENT FEATURES OF FAILED WELL INSURANCE POLICY

Brief Description

The scheme is applicable only to those wells financed by banks where re-financing by NABARD is involved. This is applicable to shallow tube well, filter point, dug wells, bore wells and dug-*cum*-bore wells.

Covered Risks

Risk of failure of well due to failure of guaranteed yield and the expenditure actually incurred by farmers towards boring or digging of wells.

Major Exclusions

(1) Cessation of work, whether total or partial,
(2) Negligence,
(3) War and allied perils,
(4) Quality of water and structure failure,
(5) Exclusions are as per NABARD scheme,
(6) Flood, earthquake and other convulsions of nature, and
(7) Riot and strike risk.

SALIENT FEATURES OF ANIMAL DRIVEN CART/ TONGA INSURANCE POLICY

Brief Description

This insurance covers all types of animal driven carts, driven by any animal, such as bullock, male buffalo, castrated bullock, camel, horse, mule, donkey, yak, etc. This policy has four sections. Sections I and II are compulsory. Sections III and IV are optional. Section I covers the animal driven cart, Section II covers the animal pulling the cart. Section III covers the third party liability. Section IV indemnifies the driver. The values of the animal and carriage are to be declared separately. The sum insured shall be 100 per cent of the market value of the animal and carriage. If the animal is insured for the purpose of pulling or driving the carriage by a separate policy, the cart/tonga/coach alone can be insured keeping on the record the particulars of the animals insured. In case of normal cover offered by the policy, no veterinary examination is required. However, if full death cover for the animal is required by the proposer, a Veterinary Certificate is to be obtained at the cost of the proposer. The animal should be identified by ear tagging or branding with hot iron or tattooing, as per Cattle Insurance Market Agreement.

Covered Risk

(1) *Section I:* Loss or damage to the cart/tanga/coach by:

(a) Accidental external means, or

(b) Fire, explosion, lightning, storm, tempest, flood, inundation, earthquake, burglary or theft.

(2) *Section II:* This section provides indemnity against death or permanent total disablement of the animal used for pulling or driving the carriage.

(3) *Section III:* Third party liability arising out of an accident caused by cart. Tonga/coach insured, including passengers liability up to Rs. 5,000 per accident and Rs. 10,000 for all accidents.

(4) *Section IV:* This section indemnifies the driver against death or disablement due to driving the cart or whilst mounting into or dismounting from the cart.

COMPREHENSIVE INSURANCE

There are many areas where policy types overlap in scope. Similarly, there are products covering different types of loses bunched together depending on the need of a customer. A home insurance policy is a common example of such a policy that covers certain aspects of fire insurance, engineering insurance (break-down of an air conditioner or refrigerator), persons accident insurance, travel insurance, and liability insurance, all rolled into one. In an industrial scenario, products are tailor-made for corporate requirements as composite types (all inclusive) or hybrid types (chopped and put together from different groups). Examples of a few such products are provided for enabling the student to understand such products.

SALIENT FEATURES OF INDUSTRIAL ALL RISKS INSURANCE POLICY

Brief Description

This policy is a comprehensive package policy that covers almost all risk and perils, which a large industry may face during its operation. This policy covers building, machinery, furniture, fixtures, fitting and electrical installation on reinstatement value, while the stock is covered on market value basis. Underinsurance on each item of the schedule will be ignored if it does not exceed 15 per cent of the sum insured. Policy also covers equipments and machinery sent for repairs outside the premises for a period of 60 days. Transit risk inside the compound of an industry is also covered.

Covered Risks

(1) Bursting and overflowing of water tanks, apparatus and pipes;

(2) Deterioration of stocks due to power failure following damage to premises of public power stations and electric service feeders (for cold storages);

(3) Forest fire, leakage and contamination covers;
(4) Spoilage material damage cover;
(5) Sprinkler leakage cover;
(6) Subterranean fire;
(7) Spontaneous and landslide cover;
(8) Burglary (other than larceny);
(9) Machinery breakdown/boiler explosion/electronic equipment; and
(10) Business interruption following fire or machinery breakdown.

Major Exclusions

(1) Damage to the property caused by faulty or defective design materials, or workmanship, inherent vice, wear and tear, etc.
(2) Interruption of water supply, gas, electricity or fuel systems.
(3) Collapse or cracking of the building.
(4) Wilful act or gross negligence.
(5) War, invasion, mutiny, rebellion, revolution, etc.
(6) Damage (direct or indirect) by nuclear weapons material.
(7) Contamination by radioactivity.

Salient features of Office Insurance Policy are the following:

Scope of Cover

Office Insurance Policy is a comprehensive insurance policy for the office. The policy covers:

(1) *Fire (Building and Contents):* Losses to the building and contents against (a) fire, lightning, riot, strike, storm, cyclone, flood, and terrorism. (b) Loss or damage due to terrorism can also be covered as an add-on cover.
(2) *Burglary:* This cover protects the contents of your office against any loss or damage caused by burglary or an attempted burglary.
(3) *All Risk Functional Equipments:* This cover provides of the damage caused to the equipment in the office.
(4) *Cost of Data Reinstatement:* This covers the cost incurred in restoring the data lost because of an insured peril.
(5) *Cash-in-Safe:* This covers provides for losses resulting due to burglary of cash kept in safe.
(6) *Cash in Transit:* This covers losses due to burglary of cash while it is being carried from the bank/ATM to your office.
(7) *Glass Breakage:* This covers for loss or damage to any fixed plain glass caused by any accident, external and mobile phones.
(8) *All Risks Non-functional Items:* This cover provides for damage or loss to mobile equipment such as laptops and mobile phones.
(9) *Fidelity:* It covers direct financial losses sustained due to fraud or dishonest acts by salaried employees.
(10) *Cheque Forgery:* This covers for losses caused by forgery or alteration of cheques, drafts or any other negotiable instruments issued by you or in your favour.
(11) *Personal Accident:* Body injuries sustained due to an accident, resulting in

death or permanent/total disability, ambulance charges of up to Rs. 2000 for carriage of the dead body, in the event of death.

(12) *Mediclaim:* According to the terms and conditions of the Mediclaim section.

(13) *Public Liability:* This cover provides for legal liability on behalf of the proposer for: (a) Accidental Death or bodily injury to a third party, excluding resident employees or domestic staff. (b) Accidental damage to third party property.

(14) *Professional Indemnity:* It provides for legal liability to your employees.

(15) *Employer's Liability:* It provides for legal liability to your employees.

(16) *Tenant's Legal Liability:* This cover provides for legal liability imposed on the proposer, due to unintentional property damage for the loss or damage to the property caused by a fire, explosion or water damage to the premises. It could be in the form of a building or contents owned by or belong to another and used by the insured in the capacity of a tenant or a person holding them in custody for which the proposer is legally responsible.

Exclusions

(1) *Under Insurance:* In case the actual value of the insured property at the time of loss under the Fire Policy is found to be greater than the sum insured chosen by you then the claim would be proportionally reduced.

(2) *Wilful Destruction:* Loss, damage or destruction of property caused by war perils, wear and tear, and atmospheric conditions, wilful destruction.

(3) *Loss:* If the dwelling is unoccupied for more than 30 days.

(4) *Any item:* Covered under Contents for fire and Burglary, whose value is more than Rs. 10,000, unless specified in the proposal form.

Premium Rates

The premium depends on the construction of the asset, the occupancy and the accident prevention measures implemented in the office. Appropriate discounts/ loading are given, based on past claims history.

SPECIALTY INSURANCE (EXAMPLES OF HYBRID COVER)

There are various specialty covers for some specific sectors.

Films and Television

Making a film involves heavy investment and consequently involves significant risks. With film production in India getting an industry status, the burning need of the hour for production houses is insurance coverage. This insurance cover is tailor-made for all aspects of the film industry, such as films and documentaries, television serials, advertising films, etc.

Sports Tournaments

The policy provides specific coverage for sporting tournaments, such as cricket, hockey, golf, athletics, football, swimming, etc.

Events

With the advent of professional event managers, there is now a more professional approach to the business of event management. Bajaj Allianz offers insurance covers for various events, such as musical evens, award ceremonies, product launches, fashion shows, exhibitions, etc.

Scope of Coverage

The insurance coverage is highly customized to suit specific requirements; the basic coverage includes the following:

(1) Event cancellation,
(2) Cast insurance,
(3) Extra expenses,
(4) Film negative,
(5) Fire (allied peril),
(6) Personal accident,
(7) Money (in transit and in safe),
(8) Hospital cash,
(9) Burglary, and
(10) Public Liability.

Though these are suggested, the insurance covers are practically enhanced or modified to suit specific requirements.

Other Specialty Insurances include

(1) Oil and Gas Insurance that covers drilling and pipeline risks.
(2) Satellite insurance that covers infrequent events, such as the pre-launch phone, launch phase and in orbit phases of satellites.
(3) Title insurance that insures against loss from defects in title to real property and from the invalidity or unenforceability of mortgage liens. It is meant to protect an owner's or lender's financial interest in real property against loss due to title defects, lines or other matters.

SUMMARY

From this unit, you should be able to understand the main types of loss categories covered by insurance and familiarise yourself with the different types of insurances.

You must be able to have a reasonable degree of familiarity about the various policies in use in the insurance industry, and appreciate the basic structure and underlying loci of the major product types so that the insured deal within the insurance market.

(1) Physical losses or damages to real or personal property are property losses.
(2) Loss to building by earthquake, and loss to machinery by fire are examples of property losses.
(3) Legal losses are ones that arise from a legal obligation on the insured to pay.
(4) Death, sickness, disability are examples of personal losses.
(5) Fire, lightning, explosion and implosion are some of the perils included in a fire policy.

(6) Theft, wilful act or gross negligence, and loss of earnings are some of the exclusions of a fire policy.
(7) Terrorism cover and additional expenses of rent for alternative accommodation are two of the optional covers provided under a Home insurance policy.
(8) Machinery breakdown policy broadly covers loss due to all kinds of accidental, electrical and mechanical breakdown due to internal and external causes.
(9) The boiler and pressure vessel's policy does not cover loss and/or damage arising from:
    (a) Fire and allied perils,
    (b) War and nuclear perils,
    (c) Losses arising out of overload experiments, and
    (d) Gradual wear and tear of parts.
(10) Electronic Equipment Insurance Policy covers loss or damage in the form of:
    (a) Material damage to electronic equipment (which can include systems software) due to sudden and unforeseen events,
    (b) Cost of external data media, including cost of reconstruction of data, and
    (c) Increased cost of working.
(11) Marine Cargo Export/Import Policy includes:
    (a) Institute Cargo Clause (C): named peril basis.
    (b) Institute Cargo Clause (B): named peril basis.
    (c) Institute Cargo Clause (A): offers the widest form of cover under Marine Cargo Insurance in so far as it relates to the perils covered. ICC (A) is an unnamed perils clause.
(12) An inland Transit Policy includes:
    (a) Basic Risk Policy that covers loss or damage to specified goods caused by fire, lightning, breakage of bridges, overtrumping of vehicles, and collision with or by carrying vehicle, and is subject to specified exclusions.
    (b) All Risks Policies that covers all risks of loss or damage to specified goods, and is subject to exclusion.
(13) Natural Calamities covered under a comprehensive Motor Policy are:
    (a) Fire, explosion, self-ignition or lightning
    (b) Earthquake, flood, typhoon, hurricane storm, tempest, inundation, cyclone, hail storm, frost, landslide or rockslide.
(14) A comprehensive Motor Policy does not cover against:
    (a) Normal wear and tear and general aging of the vehicle,
    (b) Depreciation or any consequential loss,
    (c) Mechanical/electrical breakdown, and
    (d) Wear and tear of consumables such as tyres and tubes.
(15) The vehicles are insured at a fixed value called the insured's declared value (IDV), which is the sum insured for motor OD.

(16) The Motor Liability Policy excludes the following:
   (a) Own damage losses,
   (b) Any claim arising out of personal accident,
   (c) Third party legal liability covers for commercial vehicles other than goods carrying commercial vehicles,
   (d) Any accidental loss damage and/or liability caused, sustained or incurred outside the geographical area, and
   (e) Any claim arising out of any contractual liability.

(17) Hull insurance covers various interests such as:
   (a) Hull and machinery insurance,
   (b) Insurance of freight, and
   (c) Loss of hire insurance.

(18) The premium will depend on the following factors:
   (a) Type of vessel, trading limits, age, tonnage, and technical aspects of machinery,
   (b) Management and ownership considerations,
   (c) Past claims experience,
   (d) Valuation of vessel,
   (e) Type of cover required, and
   (f) Size of the deductible.

(19) Some policies used under Aviation insurance are:
   (a) Hull all risk insurance policy,
   (b) Spares all risk insurance policy,
   (c) Hull/spares, wares, risk insurance,
   (d) Hull deductible insurance, and
   (e) Aviation personal accident (crew member) insurance.

(20) The loss of profits insurance policy does not cover.
   (a) Loss of gross profit, which is not consequent upon property damage due to an insured peril,
   (b) Loss due to martial damage to property,
   (c) Third party claims, and
   (d) Loss of goodwill.

(21) The ALOP policy does not cover delay due to:
   (a) Inventory losses,
   (b) Delay in shipment of supplies,
   (c) Normal project schedule slippages,
   (d) Non-availability of funds for repairs/replacement of damaged items,
   (e) Cancellation of license, or
   (f) Government restrictions, etc.

(22) The Credit Guarantees Policy cover include:
   (a) Declared insolvency of the buyer, i.e. the buyer is declared bankrupt,
   (b) He has made a valid assignments/composition arrangement for the benefit of his creditors,
   (c) A receiver has been appointed, and
   (d) Order has been made for compulsory winding up,
   (e) An effective resolution has been passed for voluntary winding up.

(23) Some of the exclusions of a credit guarantee policy are:
   (a) Disputed debts,
   (b) Default of insured's agents/employees,
   (c) Interest, taxes, consequential losses, etc.,
   (d) Dishonesty and fraud, and
   (e) Disregard of agreed credit management procedures.

(24) The Commercial Fidelity Guarantee Policy provides indemnity against loss of money or goods as a result of acts of fraud or dishonesty on the part of the employees.

(25) The motor TP Liability Policy covers the vehicle owners' legal liability to pay compensation for:
   (a) Death or bodily injury to a third party person, and
   (b) Damage to third party property.

(26) The public liability policy covers the amount that the insured becomes legally liable to pay as damages to third parties as a result of accidental death, bodily injury, and loss or damage to the property belonging to a third party.

(27) In a public liability policy, the sum insured is referred to as limit of indemnity. This limit is fixed per accident and per policy period, which is called Any One Accident (AOA) limit and Any One Year (AOY) limit, respectively.

(28) The public liability policy will not pay for claims arising out of:
   (a) Contractual liability,
   (b) Intentional non-compliance of any statutory provision,
   (c) Loss of goodwill,
   (d) Slander, fines, penalties, and
   (e) Libel, false arrest, defamation, mental injury, etc.

(29) A Product liability policy indemnifies the insured all sums which the insured shall become legally liable to pay as damages in consequences of accidental death/bodily injury or disease to third party, or damage to their property arising out of any defect in the products manufactured and covered under the policy, after such products have left the insured's premises.

(30) The professional liability policy indemnifies any act committed by the insured, who shall be a registered medical practitioner, giving rise to any legal liability to third parties. The insured includes the policyholder and his qualified assistants or employees, as named in the proposal form.

(31) Retroactive benefit cover means that the insured will be covered for any professional act or omission occurring during the period of insurance which means from the first date of the first policy, provided that the policy is renewed without interruption and is in force when the claim arising out of the act or omission is made in writing against the insured during the policy period.

(32) Some exclusions of a professional liability policy are:
   (a) Liability arising from any criminal act or act in violation of any law or ordinance,
   (b) Services rendered under the influence of intoxicants or narcotics,
   (c) Use of drugs for weight reduction, and

(d) Due to intentional non-compliance of statutory provisions.

(33) According to a workmen's compensation policy, an employer, as a principal or contractor engaging workmen, as defined in the Workmen's Compensation Act, would need to cover his liability to them under statute and the common law. The workmen's compensation policy covers the employer's liability towards his employees who come within the definition, covering employment related injury (including death). Employer can cover employee who do not qualify as workman under a separate table.

(34) The Workmen's Compensation Policy does not have a sum insured but the estimated earnings of the workmen for the policy period are mentioned on the polity.

(35) A health insurance policy covers the expense incurred by the insured for hospitalization for illness/diseases or injury sustained (domiciliary hospitalization also payable as per policy). These include:
(a) Hospital charges (room boarding and operation theatre),
(b) Fees for surgeon, anaesthetize, nursing, specialist, etc.,
(c) Fees for diagnostic tests, cost of medicines, blood, oxygen, etc., and
(d) Cost of appliances such as pacemaker, artificial limbs, etc.,

(36) The exclusions under a health insurance policy are:
(a) Domiciliary hospitalization,
(b) Pre- and post-hospitalization treatment,
(c) Any treatment relating to any illness/disease already in existence at the time of proposal,
(d) Any disease/injury during first 30 days of commencement of policy (accidental injury is not excluded),
(e) Any pre-existing disease/illness is not covered during renewal also, and
(f) Cost of spectacles, contact lenses, and hearing aids.

(37) The Personal Accident Insurance Policy covers a person against:
(a) Accident death,
(b) Permanent total disablement (PTD), and
(c) Permanent partial disablement (PPD).
There are many personal accident plan options (Accidental Death and Permanent Total Disablement cover) with different sums insured.

(38) The Varsha Bima Policy covers anticipated shortfall in crop yield on account of deficit rainfall. It is voluntary for all classes of cultivators who stand to lose financially upon adverse incidence of rainfall and can, thus, take insurance under the scheme.

(39) The benefits payable under the Horticulture insurance policy include:
(a) The input costs or recurring expenses incurred for raising the crop (establishment and maintenance) till the date of the loss, and
(b) Limits of indemnity on input costs basis are fixed at each stage of the crop.

(40) The Horticulture Insurance Policy excludes to pay for loss or damage to crop arising due to:
(a) Theft, malicious damage, and negligence,
(b) Natural mortality,

(c) War and nuclear perils,
(d) Insects, pests and diseases,
(e) Drought, earthquake, and climatic variations,
(f) Water logging,
(g) Inconsequential losses, and
(h) Damage to structures, capital items, irrigation systems, agricultural implements, and harvested produce.

(41) Weather Insurance Policy covers losses that may arise due to abnormal weather conditions. These abnormal weather confusions can be events such as excess of rainfall, shortfall, or variations in temperature, wind speeds and humidity.

(42) The aviary insurance policy provides indemnity against death of birds due to accident (including fire, lightning, flood, cyclone, strike, riot and civil commotion, and terrorism), diseases contracted or occurring during the period of insurance.

(43) The Honey Bee Insurance Policy provides cover for total loss/damage to beehives and/or bee colonies as a result of an accident caused by fire, flood, inundation, storm, tempest, cyclone, hurricane and tornado. Additional covers are covered against theft, specified viral disease, and transit loss during migration.

(44) The Animal Driven Cart/Tonga Insurance Policy covers all types of animal-driven carts driven by such animals as bullock, male buffalo, castrated bullock, camel, horse/mule, donkey, yak, etc.

(45) The animal should be identified by ear-tagging or branding with hot iron or tattooing as per the cattle insurance market agreement.

(46) The IAR policy provides cover against:
(a) Bursting and overflowing of water tanks, apparatus and pipes,
(b) Deterioration of stocks due to power failure following damage to premises of public power stations and electric service feeders (for cold storages),
(c) Forest fire,
(d) Leakage and contamination cover,
(e) Spoilage material damage cover,
(f) Sprinkler leakage cover,
(g) Subterranean fire,
(h) Spontaneous and landslide cover,
(i) Burglary (other than larceny),
(j) Machinery breakdown/boiler explosion/electronic equipment,
(k) Business interruption due to fire, and
(l) Business interruption due to machinery breakdown.

(47) The IAR Policy does not cover:
(a) Damage to the property caused by faulty or defective design materials or workmanship, inherent vice, wear and tear, etc.,
(b) Interruption of water supply, gas, electricity of fuel systems,
(c) Collapse or cracking of the building,
(d) Wilful act or gross negligence,

(e) War, invasion, mutiny, rebellion, revolution, etc.,
(f) Damage, direct or indirect, by nuclear weapons material, and
(g) Contamination by radioactivity.

(48) The Office Insurance Policy covers the following:
(a) Fire (building and contents),
(b) Burglary,
(c) All risk functional equipment,
(d) Cost of data reinstatement,
(e) Cash in safe,
(f) Cash in transit,
(g) Glass breakage,
(h) All risk non-functional items,
(i) Fidelity,
(j) Personal accident, and
(k) Public Liability, etc.

(49) The exclusions under an Office Insurance Policy are:
(a) Under Insurance,
(b) Wilful destruction of property,
(c) Loss, damage or destruction caused by war perils,
(d) Wear and tear, and
(e) Atmospheric conditions, etc.

REFERENCES

An open policy or a Floating policy in marine cargo insurance denotes a continuous insurance cover for a year for an estimated yearly sum insured. It is usually granted to insured having a large number of dispatches to be covered.

Brief description, this policy is designed for scheduled airlines.

In case of films and television serials.

Indicative only, need not be uniform.

Projected by a private insurance company.

24

Benefits of Enterprise Risk Management

INTRODUCTION

A string of large and highly public organizational and Governmental failures over the past 10 years (Woolworths, Golden Wonder, Northern Rock, Citigroup, Enron and even the entire banking system of Iceland) has focused the attention of inventors, customers and regulators on the way in which directors, managers and boards are managing risk. This has led to a greater appreciation of the wider scope of risks facing organizations, which in turn has led to risk management becoming a core management discipline.

Risk is everywhere and derives directly from unpredictability. The process of identifying, assessing and managing risks brings any business full circle back to its strategic objectives: for it will be clear that not everything can be controlled. The local consequences of events on a global scale, such as terrorism, pandemics and credit crunches, are likely to be unpredictable. However, they can also include the creation of new and valuable opportunities. Many of today's household names were born out of times of adversity.

Risk management provides a framework for organizations to deal with and to react to uncertainty. Whilst it acknowledges that nothing in life is certain, the modern practice of risk management is a systematic and comprehensive approach, drawing on transferable tools and techniques. These basic principles are sector independent and should improve business resilience, increase predictability and contribute to improved returns. This is particularly important given the pace of change of life today.

Risk management involves a healthy dose of both common sense and strategic awareness, coupled with an intimate knowledge of the business, an enquiring mind and most critically superb communication and influencing skills.

The institute of Risk Management's International Certificate in risk management is an introductory qualification, which reflects the changing and global nature of risk management. Recognizing both the enterprise-wide (for 'ERM') importance of comprehensive risk management and the growing use of international standards (such as ISO 31000), this qualification equips future professional risk managers with the fundamental knowledge and tools to make invaluable contributions to long-term organizational growth and prosperity.

NATURE OF RISK

Recent events in the world have brought risk into higher profile. Terrorism, extreme weather events and the global financial crisis represent the extreme risks that the societies are facing and equally the commerce, too. These extreme risks exist in addition to the daily, somewhat more mundane risks mentioned above.

Evaluating the range of risk responses available and deciding the most appropriate response in each case is at the heart of risk management. Responding to risks should produce benefits for us as individuals, as well as for the organizations where we work and/or are employed.

Within our personal and domestic lives, many of the responses to risk are automatic. One way of avoiding fire and road traffic accidents is based on well-established and automatic responses. Fire and accident are the types of risks that can only have negative outcome and they are often referred to as hazard risks.

Certain other risks have established or required responses that are imposed on us as individuals and/or on organizations as mandatory requirements. For example, in our personal lives buying insurance for a car is usually a legal requirement, whereas buying insurance for a house is often not, but is good risk management and very sensible.

Keeping your car in good mechanical order will reduce the chances of a breakdown. However, even vehicles that are fully serviced and maintained do occasionally break down. Maintaining your car in good mechanical order will reduce the changes of breakdown, but will not eliminate them completely. These types of risks that have a large degree of uncertainty associated with them are often referred to as control risks.

As well as hazard and control risks, there are risks that we take because we desire (and probably expect) a positive return. For example, you will invest money in anticipation that you will make a profit from the investment. Likewise, placing a bet or gambling on the outcome of a sporting event is undertaken in anticipation of receiving positive payback.

People participate out of choice in motor sports and other potentially dangerous leisure activities. In these circumstances, the return may not be financial, but can be measured in terms of pride, self-esteem or peer group respect. Undertaking activities involving risk of this type, where a positive return is expected, can be referred to as taking opportunity risk.

RISK MANAGEMENT

Organizations face a very wide range of risks that can impact the outcome of their operations. The desired overall aim may be stated as a mission or a set of corporate objectives. The events that can impact an organization may inhibit what it is seeking to achieve and overcome (hazard risks), enhance that aim (opportunity risks), or create uncertainty about the outcomes (control risks).

Risk management needs to offer an integrated approach to the evaluation, control and monitoring of these three types of risk. This book examines the key components of risk management and how it can be applied. Risk management also has an important part to play in the success of not for profit organizations such as charities and (for example) clubs and other membership bodies.

The risk management process is well established, although it is presented in a number of different ways and often uses differing terminologies. The different terminologies that are used by different risk management practitioners and in different business sectors are explored in this book. In addition to a description the established risk management standards, a simplified description of risk management that sets out the key stages in the risk management process is also presented to help with understanding.

The risk management process cannot take place in isolation. It needs to be supported by a framework within the organization. Once again, the risk management framework is presented and described in different ways in the range of standards, guides and other publications that are available. In all cases, the key components of a successful risk management framework are the communications and reporting structure (architecture), the overall risk management strategy that is set by the organization (strategy) and the set of guidelines and procedures (protocols) that have been established. The importance of the risk architecture, strategy and protocols (RASP) is discussed in detail in this book.

The combination of risk management processes, together with a description of the framework in place for supporting the process, constitutes risk management standards. There are several risk management standards in existence, including the IRM Standard and the recently published British Standard BS 31100. There is also the American COSO ERM framework. The latest addition to the available risk management standards is the international standards, ISO 21000, published in 2009. The well-established and respected Australian Standard AS 4360 (2004) was withdrawn in 2009 in favour of ISO 31000. AS 4360 was first published in 1995 and ISO 31000 includes many of the features, and offers a similar approach to that previously described in AS 4360.

RISK MANAGEMENT TERMINOLOGY

Most risk management publications refer to the benefits of having a common language of risk within the organization. Many organizations manage to achieve this common language and common understanding of risk management processes and protocols at least internally. However, it is usually the case that within a business sector, and sometimes even within individual organization, the development of a common language or risk can be very challenging.

BENEFITS OF RISK MANAGEMENT

There are a range of benefits arising from successful implementation of risk management. These benefits are summarized in this book as compliance, assurance, decisions and efficiency/effectiveness/efficacy (CADE3). Compliance refers to risk management activities designed to ensure that an organization complies with legal and regulatory obligations.

The board of an organization will require assurance that significant risks have been identified and appropriate controls put in place. In order to ensure that correct business decisions are taken, the organization should undertake risk management activities that provide additional structured information to assist with business decision-making.

Finally, a key benefit from risk management is to enhance the efficiency of operations within the organization. Risk management should provide more than assistance with the efficiency of operations. It should undertake risk management activities that provide additional structured information to assist business decision-making.

Finally, a key benefit from risk management is to enhance the efficiency of operations within the organization. Risk management should provide more than assistance with the efficiency of operations. It should also help ensure that business processes (including process enhancements by way of projects and other change initiatives) are effective and that the selected strategy is efficacious, in that it is incapable of delivering exactly what is required.

Risk management inputs are required in relation to strategic decision-making, but also in relation to the effective delivery of projects and programmes of work, as well as in relation to the routine operations to the organization. The benefits of risk management can also be identified in relation to these three time scales of activities within the organization. The outputs from risk management activities can benefit organizations in three timescales and ensure that the organization achieves:

- Efficacious strategy;
- Effective processes and projects; and
- Efficient operations.

To achieve a successful risk management contribution, the intended benefits of many risk management initiatives have to be identified.

Therefore, good risk management must have a clear set of desired outcomes benefits. Appropriate attention should be paid to each stage of risk management process, as well as to details of the design, implementation and monitoring of the framework that supports these risk management activities.

FEATURES OF RISK MANAGEMENT

Failure to adequately mange the risks faced by an organization can be caused by inadequate risk recognition, insufficient analysis of significant risks and failure to identify suitable risk response activities. Failure to set a risk management strategy and to communicate that strategy and the associated responsibilities may result in inadequate management of risks. It is also possible that the risk management procedures or protocols may be flawed, such that these protocols may actually be incapable of delivering the required outcomes.

The consequences of failure to adequately manage risk can be disastrous and result in inefficient operations, projects that are not completed on time and strategies that are not delivered, or were incorrect in the first place. In order to be successful, the risk management initiative should be proportionate, aligned, comprehensive, embedded and dynamic (PACED).

Proportionate means that the effort put into risk management should be appropriate to the level of risk that the organization faces. Risk management activities should be aligned with other activities within the organization. Activities will also need to be comprehensive, so that any risk management initiative covers all the aspects of the organization and all the risks that it faces. The means of embedding risk management activities within the organization are discussed in this book. Finally, risk management activities should be dynamic and responsive to the changing business environment faced by the organization.

FUTURE FOR RISK MANAGEMENT

As the global financial crisis has unfolded, there is an increasing tendency for news reports to indicate that risk is bad and risk management has failed. In reality, neither of these two statements is correct. Organizations have to address the risks that they face because many of them have to undertake high risk activities, either because these activities cannot be avoided, or because the activities are undertaken in order to produce a positive outcome for the organization and its stakeholders.

The global financial crisis does not demonstrate the failure of risk management, but rather the failure of the management of organizations to successfully address the risk that they faced. Achieving benefits from risk management requires carefully planned implementation of the risk management process in the organization, as well as the design and successful embedding of a suitable and sufficient risk management framework.

GLOBAL FINANCIAL CRISIS

The extract below offers a summary of the actions that would help to avoid a repeat of the global financial crisis. Many organizations lack a common risk management framework across the enterprise. This has many elements, each of which is required to help avoid similar disasters in the future:

- First, there should be common processes, terminology and practices for managing risk of all kinds.
- Second, it is essential that risk tolerance be fully understood, communicated and monitored across the enterprise.
- Third, risk management practices should be incorporated into all key business processes and decisions.
- And, fourth, management should make risk-related decision using dedicated high quality risk information.

APPROACHES TO DEFINING RISK: DEFINITIONS OF RISK

The Oxford English Dictionary definition of risk is as follows: 'a chance or possibility of danger, loss, injury or other adverse consequences and the definition of at risk is exposed to danger'. In this context, risk is used to signify negative consequences. However, taking a risk can also result in a positive outcome. A third possibility is that risk is related to uncertainty of outcome.

Take the example of owning a motorcar. For most people, owning a motorcar is an opportunity to become more mobile and gain the related benefits. However, there are uncertainties in owning a motorcar that is related to maintenance and repair costs. Finally, motorcars can be involved in accidents, so there are obvious negative outcomes that can occur.

Definitions of risk can be found from many sources and some key definitions are set out in Table 24.1 An alternative definition is also provided to illustrate the broad nature of risk that can affect organizations. The Institute of Risk Management (IRM) defines risk as the combination of the probability of an event and its consequences. Consequences can range from positive to negative. This is a widely applicable and practical definition that can be easily applied.

The international guide to risk-related definition is ISO Guide 73 and it defines risk as effect of uncertainty on objectives. This definition appears to assume a certain level of knowledge about risk management and it is not easy to apply to everyday life. The meaning and application of this definition will become clearer as the reader progressed through this book.

Guide 73 also notes that an effect may be positive, negative, or a deviation from the expected. These three types of events can be related to risks as opportunity, hazard or uncertainty, and this relates to the example of motorcar ownership outlined above. The guide notes that risk is often described by an event, a change in circumstances, a consequence, or a combination of these and how they may affect the achievement of objectives.

Table 24.1: Definitions of Risk

Organization	*Definition of Risk*
ISO Guide 73 ISO 31000	Effect of uncertainty on objectives. Note that an effect may be positive, negative, or a deviation from the expected. Also, risk is often described by an event, a change in circumstances or a consequence.
Institute of Risk Management (IRM)	Risk is the combination of the probability of an event and its consequence. Consequences can range from positive to negative.
"Orange Book" from HM Treasury	Uncertainty of outcome, within a range of exposure, arising from a combination of the impact and the probability of potential events.
Institute of Internal Auditors	The uncertainty of an event occurring that could have an impact on the achievement of the objectives. Risk is measures in terms of consequences and likelihood.
Alternative Definition by Paul Hopkin	Event with the ability to impact (inhibit, enhance or cause doubt about) the mission, strategy, projects, routine operations, objectives, core processes, key dependencies and/or the delivery of stakeholder expectation.

The Institute of Internal Auditors (IIA) defines risk as the uncertainty of an event occurring that could have an impact on the achievement of objectives. The IIA adds that risk is measured in terms of consequences and likelihood. Different disciplines define the term risk in very different ways. The definition used by health and safety professionals is that risk is a combination of likelihood and magnitude, but this may not be sufficient for more general risk management purposes.

Risk in an organizational context is usually defined as anything that can impact the fulfilment of corporate objectives. Risk is best defined by concentrating on risk as event, as in the definition of risk provided in ISO 31000 and the definition provided by the Institute of Internal Auditors, as set out in Table 24.1.

Types of Risks as in the Guide 73 definition, risks are divided into three categories:

- Hazard (or pure) risks;
- Control (or uncertainty) risks; and
- Opportunity (or speculative) risks.

There is no 'right' or 'wrong' sub-division of risks, readers will encounter other sub-divisions in other texts and these may be equally appropriate.

There are certain risk events that can only result in negative outcomes. These risks are hazard risks or pure risks, and these may be thought of as operational or insurable risks. In general, organizations will have a tolerance of hazard risks and this need to be managed within the levels of tolerance of the organization. A good example of a hazard risk faced by many organizations is that of theft.

There are certain risks that give rise to uncertainty about the outcome of a situation. These can be described as control risks and are frequently associated with project management. The management of control risks will often be undertaken in order to ensure that the outcome from the business activities falls within the desired range.

At the same time, organizations deliberately take risks, especially market place or commercial risks, in order to achieve a positive return. These can be considered as opportunity or speculative risks, and an organization will have a specific appetite for investment in such risks.

There are risks/dangers associated with taking an opportunity, but there are also risks associated with not taking the opportunity. Opportunity risks may not be visible or physically apparent, and they are often financial in nature. Although opportunity risks are taken with the intention of having a positive outcome, this is not guaranteed. Opportunity risk for small businesses include moving a business to a new location, acquiring new property, expanding a business and diversifying into new products.

Computer Viruses: An Example

In order to understand the distinction between hazard, control and opportunity risks, the example of the use of computers is useful. Virus infection is an operational or hazard risk and there will be no benefit to an organization suffering a virus attack on its software programs. When an organization installs or upgrades a software package, control risks will be associated with the upgrade project.

The selection of new software is also an opportunity risk, where the intention is to achieve better results by installing the new software, but it is possible that the new software will fail to deliver all of the functionality that was intended and the opportunity benefits will not be delivered. In fact, the failure of the functionality of the new software system may substantially undermine the operations of the organization.

INTERNET LEVEL OF RISK

Identifying the inherent level of the risk enables the importance of the control; measures in place to be identified. The institute of internal auditors (IIA) has the view that the assessment of all risks should commence with the identification of the inherent level of the risk. The guidance from the IIA states that in the risk assessment, we look at the inherent risk before considering any controls. The new international risk management standard, ISO 31000, recommends that risks are assessed at both inherent and current levels.

Often, a risk matrix will be used to show the inherent level of the risk in terms of likelihood and magnitude. The reduced or current level of the risk can then be identified, after the control or controls have been put in place. The effort that is required to reduce the risk from its inherent level to its current level can be clearly indicated on the risk matrix.

Terminology varies and the inherent level of risk is sometimes referred to as the absolute risk or gross risk. The example below provides an example of how inherently high risk active are reduced to a lower level of risk by the application of sensible and practical risk response options.

CROSSING THE ROAD: INHERENT RISK (AN EXAMPLE)

Crossing a busy road would be inherently dangerous if there were no controls in place and many more accidents would occur. When a risk is inherently dangerous, greater attention is paid to the control measures in place, because the perception of risk is much higher. Pedestrians do not cross the road without looking and drives are always aware that pedestrians may step into the road. Often, other traffic control measures are necessary to reduce the speed of the motorists or increase the risk awareness of both motorists and pedestrians.

LIKELIHOOD OF RISKS AND THEIR MAGNITUDE

Risk likelihood and magnitude are best demonstrated using a risk map, sometimes referred to as a risk matrix. Risk maps can be produced in many formats. Whatever format is used for a risk map, it is a very valuable tool for the risk management practitioner. The basic style for a risk map, is a very valuable tool for the risk management practitioner. The basic style of risk map plots the likelihood of an event against the magnitude or impact should the event materialize.

The vertical axis is used to indicate magnitude in Figure 24.1. The word magnitude is used rather than severity, so that the same style of risk map can be used to illustrate hazard, control and opportunity risks. Severity implies that the event is undesirable and is, therefore, related to hazard risks.

As a practical example of risk management in action at strategic level, consider the uncertainties embedded in the merger involving Delta Airlines and Northwest Airlines. This illustrates that organizations take strategic decision that involve high levels of risk and uncertainty. There will be considerable uncertainties relating to whether all of the benefits outlined below can be delivered in practice.

Figure 24.1: Risk Likelihood and Magnitude

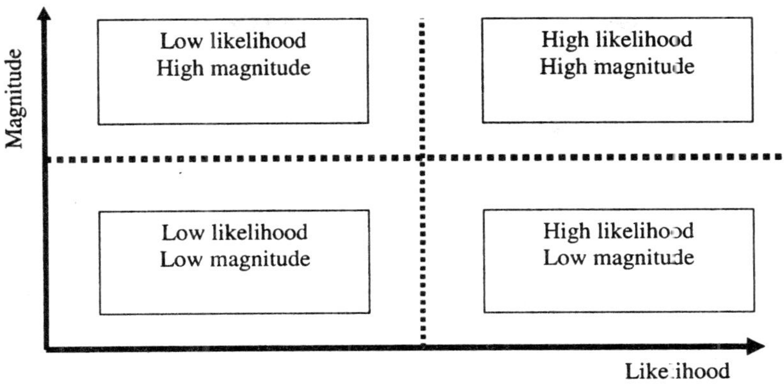

Magnitude

Low likelihood
High magnitude

High likelihood
High magnitude

Low likelihood
Low magnitude

High likelihood
Low magnitude

Likelihood

UNCERTAINTY IN STRATEGIC DECISIONS (EXAMPLE)

An agreement has been reached and, barring any roadblocks from antitrust authorities, Delta Airlines and Northwest Airlines decided merge to and would operate under the Delta Airlines name. Delta Airlines released information outlining the basic elements of the deal and the ramifications it foresaw for the new airline and its passengers.

THE LIST OF BENEFITS IT SAW BY MERGING

- Combining Delta and Northwest created a global US carrier that can compete with foreign airlines that continued to increase service to the United States.
- Customers and communities benefited from access to a global route system and a more finically stable airline.
- More destinations resulted in more schedule options and more opportunities to earn and redeem frequent flyer miles.
- Delta customs benefited from Northwest's routes to Asian markets and Northwest's customer would benefit from Delta's routers to other markets.
- Delta and Northwest complementary common membership in the sky Team alliance eased the integration risk that had complicated some airline mergers.

25

Impact of Risk on Organizations (A Concept)

RISK IMPORTANCE

Following the events in the world financial system during 2008, all organizations are taking a greater interest in risk and risk management. It is increasingly understood that the explicit management of risks brings benefits. By taking a proactive approach to risk and risk management, organizations will be able to achieve the following three areas of improvement.

- Operations will become more efficient because events that can cause disruption will be identified in advance and action taken to reduce the likelihood of these events occurring, reducing the damage caused by these events and containing the cost of the events that can cause disruption to normal efficient production operations.
- Processes will be more effective, because consideration will have been given to selection of the processes and the risks involved in the alternatives that may be available. Also, process changes that are delivered by way of projects will be more effectively and reliably delivered.
- Strategy will be more efficacious in that the risk associated with different strategic options will be fully analyzed and better strategic decisions will be reached. Efficacious refers to the fact that the strategy that will be developed will be fully capable of delivering the required outcomes.

It is no longer acceptable for organizations to find themselves in a position whereby unexpected events cause financial loss, disruption to normal operations, damage to reputation and loss of market presence. Stakeholders now expect that organizations will take full account of the risks that may cause disruption within operations, later delivery of projects or failure to deliver strategy. The exposure presented by an individual risk can be defined in terms of the likelihood of the risk materializing and the impact of the risk when it does materialized.

IMPACT OF HAZARD RISKS

Hazard risks undermine objectives, and the level of impact of such risks is a measure of their significance. Risk management has its longest history and earliest origins in the management of hazard risks. Hazard risk management is closely related to the management of insurable risks. Remember that a hazard (or pure) risk can have only a negative outcome.

Hazard risk management is concerned with issues such as health and safety at work, fire prevention, damage to property and the consequences of defective products. Hazard risks can cause disruption to normal operations, as well as resulting in increased costs and poor publicity associated with disruptive events.

Hazard risks are related to business dependencies, including IT and other supporting services. There is increasing dependence on the IT infrastructure of most organizations and IT system can be disrupted by computer breakdown or fire in server rooms, as well as virus infection and deliberate hacking or computer attacks.

Theft and fraud can also be significant hazard risks for many organizations. This is especially true for organizations handling cash or managing a significant number of financial transactions. Techniques relevant to the avoidance of theft and fraud include adequate security procedures, segregation of financial duties, and authorization and delegation procedures, as well as the vetting of staff prior to employment.

ATTACHMENT OF RISKS

Most standard definitions of risk referred to risk as being attached to corporate objectives. There are options for the attachment of risk as depicted in Figure 25.1. Risks are as being capable of impacting the key dependencies that deliver the core processes of the organization. Corporate objectives and stakeholder expectations help define the core processes of the organization. These core processes are key components of the business model and can relate to operations, projects and corporate strategy.

The intention is to demonstrate that significant risks can be attached to features of the organization other than corporate objectives. Significant risks can be identified by considering the key dependencies of the organization, the corporate objectives and/or the stakeholder expectations, as well as by analysis of the core processes of the organization.

In the build up to the recent financial crisis, banks and other financial institutions established operational and strategic objectives. By analysing these objectives and identifying the risks that could prevent the achievement of them, risk management made a contribution to the achievement of the high-risk objectives that ultimately led to the failure of the organization. The example illustrates that attaching risks to attributes other than objectives is not only possible but may well have been desirable in these circumstances.

It is clearly the case explaining that risks are greater in circumstances of change. Therefore, linking risks to change objectives is not unreasonable, but the analysis of each objective in turn may not lead to robust risk recognition/identification. In any

Figure 25.1: Attachment of Risks

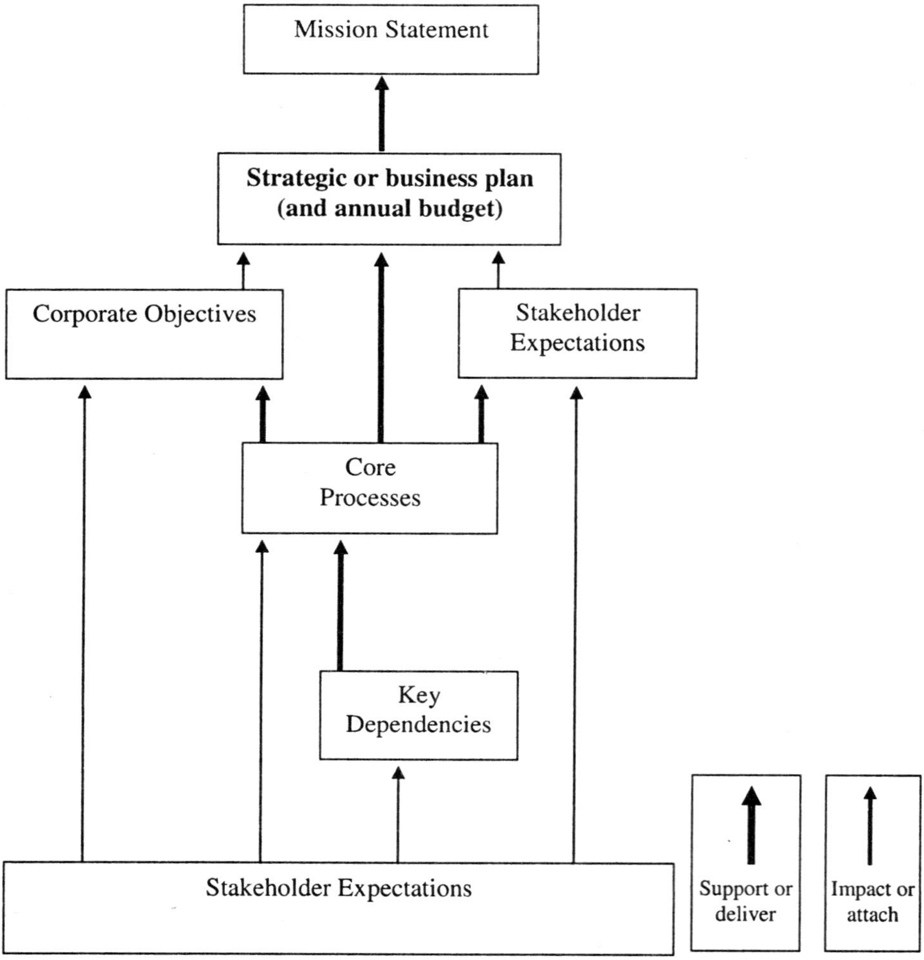

Mission Statement

Strategic or business plan (and annual budget)

Corporate Objectives

Stakeholder Expectations

Core Processes

Key Dependencies

Stakeholder Expectations

Support or deliver

Impact or attach

case, business objectives are usually stated at too high a level for the successful attachment of risks.

To be useful to the organization, the corporate objectives should be presented as a full statement of the short, medium and long-term aims of the organization. Internal, annual, change objectives are usually inadequate, because they may fail to fully identify the operational (or efficiency), the change (or competition) and the strategic (or leadership) requirements of the organization.

The most important disadvantage associated with the objectives driven approach to risk and risk management is the danger of considering risks out of the context that gave rise to them. Risks that are analysed in a way that is separated from the situation that led to them will not be capable of rigorous and informed evaluation. It can be argued that a more robust analysis can be achieved when a dependencies driven approach to risk management is adopted.

It remains the case that many organizations continue to use an analysis of corporate objectives as a means of identifying risks, because some benefits do arise from this approach. For example, using this objective-driven approach facilitates the analysis of risk in relation to the positive and uncertain aspects of the events that may occur, as well as facilitating the analysis of the negative aspects.

If the decision is taken to attach risks to the objectives of the organization, then it is important that these objectives have been fully and completely developed not only do the objectives and to be challenged to ensure that they are full and complete, but the assumptions that underpin the objectives should also receive careful and critical attention.

Core processes will be discussed later in this book and may be considered as the high level processes that drive the organization. In the example of a sports club, one of the key processes is the operational process, delivering successful results on the pitch; risks may be attached to this core process, as well as being attached to objectives and/or key dependencies.

Although risks can be attached to other features of the organization yet, the standard approach is to attach risk to corporate objectives. One of the standard definitions of risk is that it is something that can impact (undermine, enhance or cause doubt) the achievement of corporate objectives. This is useful definition, but it does not provide the only means of identifying significant risks.

RISK AND REWARD

Another feature of risk and risk management is that many risks are taken by an organization in order to achieve a reward. Figure 25.2 illustrates the relationship between the level of risk and the anticipated size of reward. A business will launch a new product because it believes that greater profit is available from the successful marketing of the new product. In launching a new product, the organization will put resources at risk because it has decided that a certain amount of risk-taking is appropriate. The value put at risk represents the risk appetite of the organization with respect to the activity that it is undertaking. When an organization puts value at risk in this way, it should do so with the full knowledge of the risk exposure and it should be satisfied that the risk exposure is within the appetite of the organization. Even more important, it should ensure that it has sufficient resources to cover the risk exposure. In other words, the risk exposure should be quantified, the appetite to take the level of risk should be confirmed and the capacity of the organization to withstand any foreseeable adverse consequences should be clearly established.

Not all business activities will offer the same return for risk taken. Start-up operations are usually high risk and the initial expected return may be low. Figure 25.2 demonstrates the probable risk return development for a new organization or a new product. The activity will commence in the bottom right hand corner as a start up operation, which is high risk and low return.

As the business develops, it is likely to move to a higher return for the same level of risk. This is the growth phase for the business or product. As the investment matures, the reward may remain high, but the risks should reduce. Eventually, an organization will become fully matures and move towards the low risk and low return quadrant. The normal expectation in very mature markets is that the organization

Figure 25.2: Risk and Reward

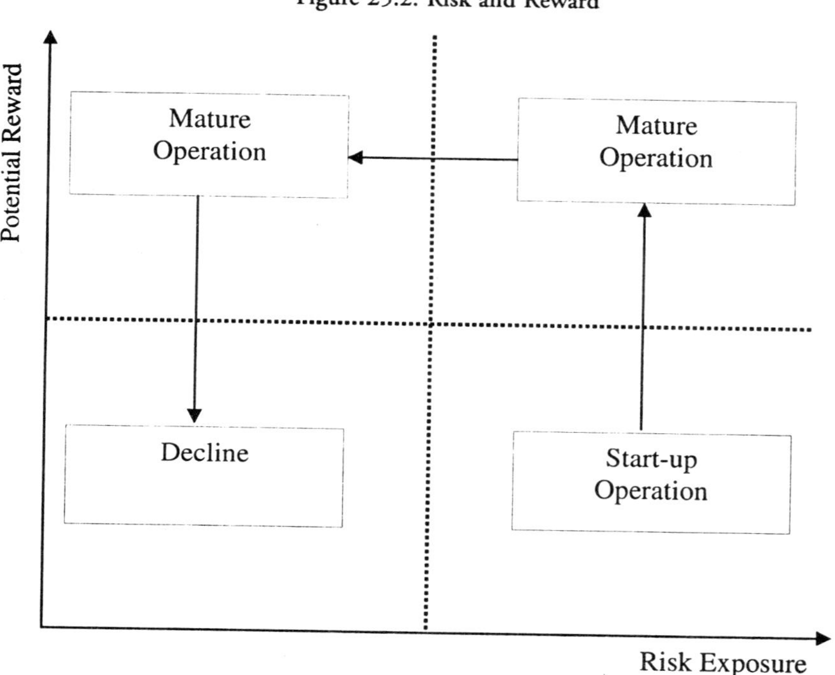

or product will be in decline.

The particular risks that the organization faces will need to be identified by management or by the organization. Appropriate risk management techniques will then need to be applied to the risks that have been identified. The nature of these risk responses and the nature of their impact will be considered in a later chapter.

RISK AND UNCERTAINTY

Risk is sometimes defined as uncertainty of outcomes. This is a somewhat technical, but nevertheless useful definition and it is particularly applicable to the management of control risks. Control risks are the most difficult to identify and define, but are often associated with projects. The overall intention of a project is to deliver the desired outcomes on time, within budget and to specification.

For example, when a building is being constructed, the nature of the ground conditions may not always be known in detail. As the construction work proceeds, more information will be available about the nature of the ground conditions. This information may be positive news that the ground is stronger than expected and less foundation work is required. Alternatively, it may be discovered that the ground is contaminated or the ground is weaker than expected or that other potentially adverse circumstances exist, such as archaeological remains being covered.

Given this uncertainty, these risks should be considered to be control risks and the overall management of the project should take account of the uncertainty associated with these different types of risk. It would be unrealistic for the project manager to assume that only adverse aspects of the ground conditions will be discovered. Likewise; it would be unwise for the projects manager to assume that conditions will be better than he has been advised; just because he wants that to be the case.

Because control risks cause uncertainty; it may be considered that an organization will have an aversion to these risks. Perhaps, the real aversion is to the potential variability in outcomes. A certain level of deviation from the project plan can be tolerated; but it must not be too great. Tolerance in relation to control risks can be considered to have the same meaning as in the manufacture of engineering components where the component must be of a certain size; within acceptable tolerance limits.

ATTITUDES TO RISK

Different organization will have different attitudes to risk. Some organizations may be considered to be risk averse; whilst other organization will be risk aggressive. To some extent, the attitude of the organization to risk will depend on the sector and the nature and maturity of the marketplace within which it operates as well as the attitude of the individual board members.

Risks cannot be considered outside the context that gave rise to the risks, it may appear that an organization is being risk aggressive; when in fact the board has decided that there is an opportunity that should not be missed. However, the fact that the opportunity is high risk may not have been fully considered.

One of the major contributions from successful risk management is to ensure that strategic decisions that appear to be high risk are actually taken with all of the information available. Improvement in the robustness of decision-making processes is one of the key benefits of risk management.

Other key factors that will determine the attitude of the organization to risk include the stage in the maturity cycle, as shown in Figure 25.2. For an organization in the start-up phase, a more aggressive attitude to risk is required than for an organization that is enjoying growth or one that is a mature organization in a mature marketplace. Where an organization is operating in a mature marketplace and is suffering from decline, the attitude to risk will be much more risk averse.

It is because the attitude to risk has to be different when an organization is in the start up operation, compared with a mature organization; it is often said that certain high profile businessmen are very good at entrepreneurial start up, but are not as successful in running mature businesses. Different attitudes to risk are required at different parts of the business maturity cycle.

CHICKEN FARMER: AN ILLUSTRATION

Consider the example of a very successful breeder and reseller of chicken in a mature marketplace involving little risk and manageable growth prospects. The CEO saw an opportunity to transform his family's company. Overturning the family tradition of avoiding debt, he borrowed $ 500,000 and set about fundamentally changing the operation from a chicken farmer and reseller to a fully automated chicken raising and retail operation.

It is not surprising that many great CEOs and founders had a strong propensity for risk without taking at least some calculated risks, the business would not have flourished and more importantly lasted. Some had nothing to lose, but for others, there was a tremendous amount at stake both personally and professionally.

Like vision, an appetite for risk taking it considered almost a prerequisite for success. Knowing when to be a risk taker and opportunistic is critical to being able to the successfully take advantage of the times. It can also be disastrous when the context of the times changes sharply. The same act performed too soon or too late or in the wrong scene may make a person a fool rather than a hero. That analysis fully applies to risk taking in business.

TIMESCALE OF RISK IMPACT

Risks can be classified in many ways. Hazard risk can be divided into many types of risks, including risks to property, risks to people and risks to the continuity of the business. There are a range of formal risk classification systems.

The classification of risks as long, medium and short-term impact is a very useful means of anglicizing the risk exposure of an organization. These risks will be related to the strategy, tactics and operations of the organization, respectively. In this context, risks may be considered as related to events, changes in circumstances, actions or decisions.

Long-term risks will impact several years, perhaps up to five years, perhaps up to five years, after the event occurs or the decision is taken. Long-term risks therefore relate to strategic decisions. When a decision is taken to launch a new product, the impact of that decision (and the success of the product itself) may not be fully apparent for some time.

Medium-term risks have their impact some time after the event occurs or the decision is taken and typically this will be about a year later. Medium-term risks are often associated with projects or programmes of work. For example, if a new computer software system is to be installed, then the choice of computer system is a long term or strategic decision. However, decisions regarding the project to implement the new software will be medium-term decision with medium-term risk attached.

Short-term risks have their impact immediately after the event occurs. Accidents at work, traffic accidents, fire and theft are all short-term risks that have an immediate impact and immediate consequences as soon as the event has occurred. These short-term risks cause immediate disruption to normal efficient operations and are probably the easiest types of risks to identify and manage.

Insurable risks are quite often short-term risks, although the exact timing and magnitude/impact of the insured evens is uncertain. In other words, insurance is designed to provide protection against risks that have immediate consequence. In the case of insurable risks, the nature and consequences of the event may be understood, but the timing of the event is unpredictable. In fact, whether the event will occur at all is not known at the time the insurance policy is taken out.

An example: consider the operation of a new computer software system in more detail. The organization will install the new software in anticipation of gaining efficiency and greater functionality. The decision to install new software and the choice of the software involves opportunity risks. The installation will require a project, and certain risks will be involved in the project. The risks associated with the project are control risks. The new software would be exposed to hazard risks. It may not deliver all of the functionality required and the software may be exposed to various risks and virus infection. These are the hazard risks associated with this new software system.

HAZARD, CONTROL AND OPPORTUNITY RISKS

Risks can be divided into three categories:

- Hazard risks;
- Control risks; and
- Opportunity risks.

A common language of risk is required throughout the organization if the contribution of risk management is to be maximized. The use of a common language will also enable the organization to develop an agreed precipitation of risk. Part of developing this common language and perception of risk is to agree on a risk classification system or series of such systems.

For example, consider people reviewing their financial position and the risks they currently face regarding finances. It may be that the key financial dependencies relate to achieving adequate income and managing expenditure. The review should include an analysis of the risks to job security and pension arrangements, as well as property ownership and other investments. This part of the analysis will provide information on the risks to income and the nature of those risks (opportunity risks).

Regarding expenditure, the review will consider spending pattern to determine whether cost cutting is necessary (hazard risks). It will also consider leisure time activities, including holiday arrangements and hobbies, and there will be some uncertainties regarding expenditure and the cost of their activities (control risks).

Hazard risks are the risks that can only inhibit achievement of the corporate mission. Typically, these are insurable type risks or perils, and will include fire, storm, flood injury and so on. The discipline of risk management has strong origins in the management and control of hazard risks. Normal efficient operations may be disrupted by loss, damage, breakdown, theft and other threats associated with a wide range of dependencies, as shown in Figure 25.1 and these may include (for example):

- People;
- Premises;
- Assets;
- Suppliers;
- Information Technology (IT); and
- Communications.

Control risks are risks that cause doubt about the ability to achieve the mission of the organization. Internal financial control protocols are a good example of a response to a control risk. If the control protocols are removed, there is no way of being certain about what will happen.

Control risks are associated with uncertainty, and examples include the potential for legal non-compliance and losses caused by fraud. They are usually dependent on the successful management of people and successful implementation of control protocols.

Opportunity risks are the risks that are (usually) deliberately sought by the organization. These risks arise because the organization is seeking to enhance the achievement of the mission, although they might inhibit the organization if the outcome is adverse. This is the most important type of risks for the future long-term success of any organization.

Many organizations are willing to invest in high-risk business strategies in anticipation of a high profit or return. These organizations may be considered to have a large appetite for opportunity investment. Often, the same organization will have the opposite approach to hazard risks and have a small hazard tolerance. This may be appropriate, because the attitude of the organization may be that it does not want hazard-related risks consuming corporate resources, when it is putting so much value at risk investing in opportunity.

HAZARD TOLERANCE

Organizations face exposure to a wide range of risks. These risks will be hazard risks, control risks and opportunity risks. Organization need to tolerate a hazard risk exposure, accept exposure to control risks and invest in opportunity risks.

In the case of health and safety risks, it is generally accepted that originations should be intolerant of these risks and should take all appropriate actions to eliminate them. In practice, this is not possible and organizing will manage safety risk to the lowest level that is cost effective and in compliance with the law.

For example, an automatic braking system fitted to trains to stop them passing through red lights is technically feasible. However, this may represent an unreasonable investment for the train operating company. The consequences of trains going through red lights may be regarded as the risk exposure or hazard tolerance of the organization but the cost of introducing the automatic braking system may be considered to be prohibitively high.

Less emotive example is related to theft. Most organizations will suffer a low level of petty theft and this may be tolerable. For example, businesses based in an office environment will suffer some theft of stationery, including paper, envelopes and pens. The cost of eliminating this pretty theft may be very large and so it becomes cost effective for the organization to accept that these losses will occur. The approach to theft in shops may be very different in different retail sectors, as illustrated by the example below:

SECURITY STANDARDS

An example can be seen in the operation of a security conscious jewellery shop. Customers are allowed into the shop one at a time. They are recorded on CCTV as they wait to enter. Items are held securely, and customers are invited to ask to see specific items under the suspicious gaze of the shop assistants of course, some customers are put off, but equally the shops suffer negligible rates of shoplifting.

Contracts this with a supermarket, where there are no barriers on entry and customer are allowed to handle all of the items. There is CCTV monitoring the shops, and there are likely to be store detectives patrolling but the object of the security is to deter rather than to prevent shoplifting. Shoplifting does occur, but at rates that are acceptable to the ship owners. Conversely, few potential customers are put off visiting the shop because of the measures.

MANAGEMENT OF HAZARD RISKS

The range of hazard risks that can affect an organization needs to be identified by the organization. Hazard risks can result in unplanned disruption for the organization. Disruptive events cause inefficiency and are to be avoided, unless they are part of for example, planned maintenance or testing of emergency procedures.

These events are divided into several categories, such as people, property, assets, suppliers, information technology and communication. For each category of hazard risks, the organization needs to evaluate the types of incidents that could occur, the sources of those incidents and their likely impact on normal efficient operations.

UNCERTAINTY ACCEPTANCE

When undertaking projects, and/or implementing change, an organization has to accept a level of uncertainty. Uncertainty or control risks are inevitable part of undertaking a project.

The nature of control risks and the appropriate responses depend on the level of uncertainty and the nature of the risk. Uncertainty represents a deviation from the required or expected outcome. When an organization is undertaking a project, such as a process enhancement, the project has to be delivered on time, within budget and to specification. Also, the enhancement the project has to be delivered on time, within budget and to specification. Also, the enhancement has to deliver the benefits that were required. Deviation from the anticipated benefits of a project represents uncertainties that can only be accepted within a certain range.

Control management is the basis of the approach to risk management adopted by internal auditors and accountants. The UK Turnbull Report will be mentioned later in this boo, and it concentrates on internal control with little reference to risk assessment. Control management is concerned with reducing the uncertainty associated with significant risk and reducing the variability of outcomes.

There are dangers if the organization becomes too concerned with control management. The organization should not become obsessed with control risks. Because it is sometimes suggested that over focus on internal control and control management suppresses the entrepreneurial effort.

OPPORTUNITY INVESTMENT

Some risks are taken deliberately by organizations in order to achieve their mission. These risks are often marketplace or commercial risks that have been taken in the expectation of achieving a positive return. These opportunity risks can otherwise be referred to as commercial, speculative or business risks. Opportunity risks are the type of risks with potential to enhance (although they can also inhibit) the achievement of the mission of the organization. These risks are the ones associated with taking advantage of business opportunities.

All organizations have some appetite for seizing opportunities and are willing to invest in them. There will always be a desire for the organization to have efficient operations, effective processes and efficacious strategy. Opportunity risks are normally associated with the development of new or amended strategies, although, opportunities can also arise from enhancing the efficiency of operations and implementation change initiatives.

Every organization will need to decide what appetite it has for seizing new opportunities and the level of investment that is appropriate. Foe example, an organization may realize that there is a requirement in the market for a new product that its expertise would allow it to develop and supply. However, if the organization does not have the resources to develop the new product, then it may be unable to implement that strategy and it would be unwise for the organization to embark on such a potentially high-risk course of action.

Opportunity management is the approach that seeks to maximize the benefits of taking entrepreneurial risks. Organizations will have an appetite for investing in opportunity risks. There is a clear link between opportunity management and strategic planning. The desire is to maximize the likelihood of a significant positive outcome from investment in business opportunities.

26

Risk Management Policy (A Concept)

RISK, ARCHITECTURE, STRATEGY AND PROTOCOLS (RASP)

This part provides information on the risk, architecture, strategy and protocols (RASP) for an organization. The most important component of the RASP is the risk management policy. The RM policy will set out the overall strategy of the organization towards risk management, define risk management roles and responsibilities and set out the protocols that should be followed.

The risk architecture, strategy and protocols create the risk framework that supports the risk management process. British Standards BS 31100 provides notes on the risk management framework that state that it should include the objectives, mandate and commitment to mange risk (strategy) and the organizational arrangements that include plans, relationships, accountabilities, resources, processes and activities (architecture), and that the framework should be embedded within the organization's overall strategic and operational policies and practices (protocols).

Most large organizations will document their risk protocols as a set of risk management guidelines. The range of guidelines that are required will very according to the size and complexity of the organization. The types of documents that will need to be kept are as follows:

- Risk management administration records;
- Risk response and improvement plans;
- Event reports and recommendations; and
- Risk performance and monitoring reports.

RISK MANAGEMENT ARCHITECTURE

The risk management structure of an organization can be described as the risk architecture. The risk architecture sets out lines of communication for reporting on risk management issues and events. It is vital that the risk architecture reinforces the fact that the responsibility for managing risks remains with the owners of that risk. Management can be fully embedded into the processes and operations of an organization; a clear statement of risk management responsibilities is required. Also, as part of the analysis of each significant risk, risk management responsibilities need to be clearly allocated to the following aspect of managing that risk:

- Development of risk strategy and standards;
- Implementation of the agreed standards and procedures; and
- Auditing compliance with the agreed standards.

The risk architecture can be represented diagrammatically as a means of identifying the committees with risk management responsibilities and the relationship between those committees. The importance of the risk architecture of an organization will be discussed later in this part and example of typical risk architectures will be provided.

- Committee structure and terms of reference,
- Roles and responsibilities,
- Internal reporting requirements,
- External resorting controls, and
- Risk management assurance arrangements.

RISK MANAGEMENT STRATEGY

It is important for an organization to have a clearly establish strategy in relation to risk management. The strategy needs to be based on the overall approach of the organization to risk and risk management. An important component of that risk strategy will be the arrangements for censuring risk management input into strategy, projects and operations.

In order to establish the risk management strategy, important decision will need to be made about the risk appetite of the organization. Risk appetite will be discussed in more detail in a later chapter. The risk appetite will be based on the opportunity investment, control acceptance and the hazard tolerance of the organization.

It is important that the risk appetite is within the total risk capacity of the organization. Decisions will need to be taken on how the risk capacity will be calculated. Also, though will need to be given to how the total risk exposure of the organization will be recorded and used in decision-making processes. Measurement of the total risk exposure of an organization is an important feature of operational risk management, as discussed in a later chapter.

There are important decisions to be made in relation to the risk processes that will be adopted by the organization, as well as decision about the design and implementation of the risk management initiative that will be undertaken in order to fulfil the requriemetns of the risk strategy.

- Risk management philosophy,
- Arrangements for embedding risk management,
- Risk appetite and attitude to risk,

- Benchmark tests for significant,
- Specific risk statements/policies,
- Risk assessment techniques, and
- Risk priorities for the present year.

RISK MANAGEMENT POLICY FOR A COUNCIL

The council is aware that some risks will always exist and will never be eliminated. It recognizes that it has a responsibility to manage risk (both positive and negative) and supports a structured, systematic and focused approach to managing them by approval of the risk management strategy.

In this way the council will:

- Demonstrate effective corporate governance;
- Better achieve its corporate objectives; and
- Enhance the value of services it provides to the community.

The Objectives of the Council's Risk Management Strategy are to:

- Integrate risk management into the culture of the council;
- Manage risk in accordance with best practice;
- Anticipate and respond to changing social and legislative requriemetns;
- Prevent injury, damage and losses, and reduce the cost of risk; and
- Raise awareness of risk with all involved with delivery of council service.

These Objectives will be Achieved by:

- Establishing clear roles, responsibilities and reporting lines;
- Providing opportunities for shared learning on risk management;
- Offering a framework to direct resources to identified priority risk areas;
- Reinforcing the importance of risk management as part of every task;
- Increasing awareness of employees by offering training;
- Incorporating risk management into business planning;
- Incorporating risk considerations into partnerships and projects; and
- Monitoring risk management arrangements on an ongoing basis.

RISK MANAGEMENT POLICY

The risk management policy sets out the risk strategy The risk management policy should facilitate successful implementation of risk management in the organization. The policy should confirm the protocols for undertaking the activities, as set out in the risk guidelines for the organization. The risk guidelines may be produced as separate set of documents, so that they can be more easily updated.

A risk management policy should include the following sections:

- Risk management and internal control objectives;
- Statement of the attitude of the organization to risk (risk strategy);
- Description of the control environment;
- Level and nature of risk that is acceptable;
- Risk management organization and arrangements (risk architecture);

- Arrangements for communicating risk information;
- Standard procedures for risk recognition and rating (risk assessment);
- List of documentation for analyzing and reporting risk (risk protocols);
- Risk mitigation requirement and control mechanisms;
- Allocation of risk management roles and responsibilities;
- Criteria for monitoring and benchmarking risks;
- Allocation of appropriate resources;
- Risk priorities and performance targets; and
- Risk management calendar of the coming year.

The risk management policy should set out the strategy that the organization is seeking to achieve with respect to risk management, together with the systems and procedures that will be put in place to monitor performance, as well as the means for reporting and communicating on risk management. It will, in effect, define the context within which risk management activities take place.

A range of risk management guidelines will need to be produced. The risk guidelines provide more information on how the risk protocols should be interpreted and how they should be delivered. The detailed risk guidelines will set out:

- Risk assessment procedures;
- Risk control objectives;
- Risk resourcing arrangement;
- Reaction planning requirement; and
- Risk assurance systems.

RISK MANAGEMENT PROTOCOLS

The working relationship between risk management and internal audit is critically important. Risk management expertise rests in the assessment of risk and the identification of existing and additional controls. Internal audit has its expertise in the evaluation of controls and the testing of their efficiency and effectiveness. Successful implementation of a risk management initiative will require close co-operation and understanding between risk management and internal audit. The RASP should set out the details of how this close co-operation will be achieved in practice.

The risk architecture defines how information on risk is communicated throughout the organization. The risk strategy defines the overall objectives that the organization is trying to achieve with respect to risk management. The risk protocols are the systems, standards and procedures that are put in place in order to fulfil the defined risk strategy.

(1) Risk Assessment Procedures

- Turnbull procedures
- Response to significant risks
- Projects and CapEx approvals
- Procedures for strategy and budgets

(2) Risk Control Objectives

- Brand management guidelines

- Health and safety at work
- Environmental protection
- Contract risk management

(3) Risk Resourcing Arrangements
- Opportunity management
- Project resource allocation
- Insurance programme
- Captive insurance company

(4) Reaction Planning Requirements
- Loss and claims management
- Disaster and recovery planning
- Cost containment procedures
- Risk management record-keeping

(5) Risk Assurance Systems
- Maintenance of risk register
- Corporate RM committee
- Terms of reference for audit committee
- Control self-certification arrangements.

The framework or risk architecture that has been set-up to achieve adequate management of risk should also be presented in the risk management policy. It will then to be for the individual companies within the group to operate within the established framework and arrange their own additional policies, procedures and protocols as necessary. Specifically, the risk management policy should include details of at least the following:

- The board member responsible for risk management;
- Language and perception of risk in the organization;
- Framework for identifying significant risks;
- Role of the risk manager and internal auditors;
- Terms of reference for the risk management committees; and
- Risk management structure or architecture.

Many organizations find that it is necessary to update the risk management policy each year. This is undertaken for a number of reasons, including the desire to ensure that risk management activities and the overall risk management approach is in line with current best practice. Updating the risk management policy every year also gives the organization the opportunity to identify the risk priorities for the coming years and ensure that appropriate attention is paid to the significant risks.

The risk management policy will set out responsibilities for risk as well as the arrangements for implementing the policy. Risk management protocols will be set out in a series of risk guidelines and these are described in a later chapter.

Procedures and protocols for undertaking the assessment of risk to strategy, project and operations will need to be established in writing. The organization will also need to produce guidance on the frequency and nature of risk reports and who is responsible for compiling the information.

Typically, the risk management protocols will need to be reviewed on an annual basic, so that they are kept up-to-date. The risk protocols should also describe the extent of record-keeping that is required. The range of risk management documentation that may be necessary is extensive.

Risk Administration

- Risk management policy (and priorities)
- Specific risk statements (health and safety policy)
- Terms of reference of the risk/audit committees
- Risk protocols; and procedures
- Risk awareness training records.

Risk Response

- Results of risk assessments (risk register)
- Risk control standards
- Risk improvement recommendations
- Risk assurance reports
- Business continuity plans/disaster recovery plans.

Event Reports

- Loss/claim reports and recommendations
- Legal and litigation reports
- Enforcement action/customs complaints
- Incident and near miss-investigations
- Business performance report/key performance indicators.

Risk Performance

- Control risk self-assessment (CRSA) returns
- Audit procedures and protocol
- Internal audit reports
- Unit risk management reports
- External disclosure reports

RISK MANAGEMENT GUIDELINES

There are risk management guidelines that may need to be produced by an organization. This should not be seen as an exhaustive list and other types of guidelines may be necessary, depending on the exact nature of the organization and the risk strategy that it is following.

Preparation of a risk management policy is good opportunity for an organization to establish detailed procedures on a range of risk management topics, as well as setting out the risk management priorities for the following year. For example, many organizations produce an annual health and safety and/or environmental policy and this should be an integral part of the risk management documentation.

The structure reinforces the importance of the activities involved in the risk management process. Ach of these activities produces several outputs, and the required outputs can be discussed in the risk guidelines.

The guidelines need not include a set of risk control or loss control standards, but should describe how risk control decision will be taken, implemented and audited. In fact, the risk guidelines for a diverse group of companies cannot include physical control requirement and stands. Each unit, division or department should set its own standards for risk control, including health and safety, fire safety, physical security, information security and environmental protection. This may be appropriate because of the diverse nature of the diffident units within the organization.

The risk guideline should define the means by which embedded risk management is to be achieved in the organization. The setting of strategy, standards and procedures need to be undertaken within the framework of the risk guideline. The format for the risk guidelines will depend on the organization and the nature of the risks that it faces. Typically, these guidelines will contain information on at least the following:

- Financial and authorization procedures;
- Insurance arrangement;
- Managers' control responsibilities;
- Project risk managements;
- Incident reporting and investigation;
- Event and reaction planning; and
- Physical risk control objectives and responsibilities.

27

Risk Management Documentation Practices

DESIGNING A RISK REGISTER

A risk is defined in the ISO Guide 73 as the 'document used for recording risk management process for identified risks. The guide adds that the purpose of the risk register is to facilitate ownership and management of each risk. Typically, the risk register will cover the significant risks facing the organization or the project. It will record the results of the risk assessment related to the process, operation, location, business unit or project under consideration.

When a risk assessment is undertaken of strategic options, it is more usual for the risk assessment to be used as part of the decision-making process. Typically, this information will not be recorded in the format of risk register, but will be presented to the decision-maker as part of the full range of information available for making that strategic decision.

The purpose of the risk register is to form an agreed record of the significant risks that have been identified. Also, the risk register will serve record of the control activities that are currently undertaken. It will also be a record of the additional actions that are proposed to improve the control of the particular risks.

Other information about risks will also be included in the risk register. Although there is no fixed format for this document yet Table 27.1 provides an outline of basic format for a risk register. It may not be necessary to include all of the risk description information set out in the table in the risk register, as this could make it a complex and clumsy document.

Risk registers can be compiled in a number of formats, depending on the type of risk assessment that is being recorded. Table 27.2 provides an example of a partially completed risk registered for a sports club and Table 27.3 provides an example of a risk register for a hospital

Table 27.1: Format for a Basic Risk Register

Risk index	*Risk description*	*Current level of risk*			*Controls in placing*
		Likelihood	*Magnitude*	*Overall rating*	
1.	Serious traffic accident involving the transport of fuel/explosive. Anticipate fatalities and evacuation of 1 km radius, depending on substances involved. Potential for release of up to 30 tonnes of liquid fuel into local environment.	Low	High	Medium	• Police emergency plan • Highway agency plans • Local authority emergency plan • Company emergency response • Liaison with the family of staff • Notification to customers.
2.	Storm force winds affecting transport routes for up to 6 hours. Anticipate that most roads in the vicinity will be closed or restricted. Journey times will be extended and late deliveries probable.	Medium	Medium	Medium	• Police emergency plans • Highway agency plans • Investigate weather forecast • Liaison with the family of staff • Notification to customers

Table 27.2: Risk Register for a Sports Club

Risk Index	*Risk Description*	*Existing control measures*	*Current level*	*Further actions planned*	*Owners*
Financial Risk					
1.1	Insufficient funds for suitable new players		High		
1.2	Pension fund inadequate to meet liabilities		Medium		
Infrastructure Risks					
2.1	Loss of highly respected young manager		High		
2.2	Building of the new stadium is delayed		Low		
Reputational Risks					
3.1	Complaints that merchandise is too expensive		Low		
3.2	Club supporters riot at an away game		Medium		
Marketable Risks					
4.1	New range of merchandise is unattractive		High		
4.2	Fans favour other activities rather than club attendance		Low		

At its most simple, the risk register can be stored as a document held on computer. However, there are many more sophisticated forms of risk registers, including records of significant risks held on databases. Where quantification of exposure is required, then a simple risk register held as document in unlikely to be sufficient. This is true of systems for recording operational risks, where quantification of risk exposure is required.

Table 27.3: Risk Register for a Hospital

Risk index	*Risk description*	*Current level of risk*			*Risk Rating*
		Likelihood	*Magnitude*	*Overall rating*	
1.	The roofs on operating theatres 3 and 4 are leaking because of poor condition, resulting in disruption to the surgery lists and non-achievement of waiting times.	High	High	High	• Ingress of water can lead to loss of theatre facility, with cancelled operations, lows of key activity and threat to waiting time targets. • With high incidence of rain, it is likely that between 1 and 7 days surgery time will be lost. Problems in the last 2 years suggest that the failure will occur twice per year.
2.	Progress towards achievement of standards in children's care will remain unsatisfactory due to failure to implement action plan for improved facilities, resulting in children receiving care below the national standards.	Medium	Medium	Medium	• The perception of patients of the current environment is good and the level of care provided is good. • Robust action needs to be taken to ensure that standards do not become unsatisfactory.

USING A RISK REGISTER

A well-constructed and dynamic risk register is at the heart of a successful risk management initiative. However, there is danger that the risk register may become a static document that records the status of risk management activities at any moment in time. The practical implications of this are that senior management may consider that attending a risk assessment workshop and producing a risk register fulfils their risk management obligations and no ongoing actions are required.

Risk control activities should be described in sufficient detail for the controls to be auditable. This is especially important when the risk register relates to the routine operations undertaken by the organization. Risk registers should also be produced for projects and to support strategic decision.

A project risk register has to be very dynamic document. Details of the risks faced by the project, as recorded in the risk registered, should be discussed at every project review meeting. As well as risk registers being relevant to projects, they should also support business decisions. In this case, the precise format of a risk register may be less formal. When a strategic decision has to be taken at board level, the risk assessment of that strategy should be attached to the proposal. This risk assessment could include both the risks of undertaking the strategy and an analysis of the risks associated with not undertaking the proposed strategy.

Table 27.4: Project Risk Register

Risk index	*Risk description*	*Current level of risk*			*Action to be taken*
		Likelihood	*Magnitude*	*Overall rating*	
1.	Project management arrangement unable to deliver project	High	High	High	• Clear project management structure in place, with executive team established to oversee project. • Smaller project team runs project on day-to-day basis with expert support, as required. Clear links between various management functions to ensure co-ordinated approach.
2.	Project resources inadequte with insufficient staff to support project.	Medium	Medium	Medium	Project management team established with support from other staff departments, including HR and Finance.
3.	Project resource has insufficient funds for the necessary external professional technical advice.	Low	High	Medium	Sufficient budget identified to fund external advice.
4.	Project not co-ordinate with other developments in organization.	Low	Low	Low	Project management team also oversees related projects with cross representation on other groups.

Finally, a risk register should be attached to a business plan as a record of the risks that could impact the achievement of that business plan.

Table 27.5: Risk Register Attached to a Business Plan

Risk Index	*Circumstances*	*Assessment and Controls*	*Current Level of Risk*			*Action and Assurance*
			Likelihood	*Magnitude*	*Overall rating*	
1.1.	Loss of grant funding		High			Negotiations are in hand and final settlement figure should soon be notified.
1.2.	Job upgrade costs			Medium		Provisions have been made in reserves and any additional costs will be met from existing budgets.

1.3.	Overtime claims	Medium	Heads of department should enforce the rules concerning overtime payments as a result of job upgrades
1.4.	Mileage claims	Low	Heads of department should ensure that only essential journeys are undertaken.

For example, a sports club may wish to record risks to reputation in the risk register. There could be particular concerns regarding the reputation of the club, so that the board will require a detailed evaluation of the reputational risks related to:

- Success on the pitch;
- Legal compliance; and
- Supply of ethical goods at a fair price.

When considering reputational issues, the level of control that is required will be evaluated, together with responsibility for managing the brand. The club will so make sure that existing controls and any additional controls are described in a way that will ensure that implementation of the controls can be fully audited.

The board will probably wish to see the risk register on at least a quarterly basis and more frequently if significant changes occur. This will ensure that the risk register remains a dynamic document and is kept fully up-to-date. This will also ensure that necessary actions are taken and reported to the board.

28

Risk Management Standards (Practices)

SCOPE OF RISK MANAGEMENT STANDARDS

There are a number of established risk management standards and framework. The first such standard was developed by the standards body in Australia in 1995, which has been followed by those being developed in Canada, Japan, the UK and the United States. Standards have also been developed by other national standards bodies, as well as by government departments across the world.

The overall approach of each of these standards is similar. The standard that had the widest recognition was the Australian Standard AS 4360 (2004). AS 4360 was withdrawn in 2009 in favour of ISO 31000. The ERM version of the COSO standard is also widely applied in many organizations. British Standards BS 31100:2008 'Risk Management—Code of Practice' was published in October 2008.

The latest addition to the available standards is the international standard ISO 31000:2009 'Risk Management—Principles and Guidelines', which was published in the latter part of 2009, although some standards are better recognized than others, organizations should select the approach that is most relevant to their particular circumstances.

It is important to distinguish between a risk management standard and a risk management framework. A risk management standard sets out the overall approach to the successful management of risk including a description of the risk management processes, together with the suggested framework that supports that process.

In simple terms, a risk management standard is the combination of a description of the risk management process, together with the recommended framework. The key features of a risk management framework are described later. Table 28.1 provides a summary of the most widely used risk management standards and frameworks.

Table 28.1: Risk Management Standards

Standard	*Description*	*Reference*
ISO 31000	Standards published by the International Standards Organization (2009)	Figure 6.5
British Standard BS 31000	Standard published by British Standards Institution (2008)	Figure 6.4
Institute of Risk Management (IRM)	Standard produced jointly by AIRMIC, Alarm and the IRM (2002)	Figure 6.1
COSO ERM	Framework produced by the Committee of Sponsoring Organization of the Treadway Committee (2004)	Figure 6.3
Turnbull Report	Framework produced by the Financial Reporting Council (2005)	Chapter 6
Orange Book	Standard produced by HM Treasury of the UK Government (2004)	Chapter 6
CoCo (Criteria of Control)	Framework produced by the Canadian Institute of Chartered Accountants (1995)	Figures 31.4

One of the best established and most widely used risk management standard was produced by the IRM in 2002 in co-operation with AIRMIC and Alarm. The IRM Standard is a high level approach aimed at non-risk management specialists and it has been translated into many languages. The Australian Standard and the COSO standard/framework are designed for use primarily by specialist risk management practitioners. The IRM Standard is available as a free download from the IRM website, and the risk management process used in it is reproduced in Figure 28.1.

For organizations that are listed on the New York stock exchange, the approach outlined in the COSO Internal Control framework (1992) is recognized by the Sarbanes-Oxley Act of 2002 (SOX). The requirements of SOC also apply to subsidiaries of US listed companies around the world. Therefore, the COSO approach is internationally recognized and in many circumstances, mandated. It is worth noting that SOC requires the approach described in the COSO Internal Control Framework (1992). This is not the same as the COSO ERM framework (2004) described later, although the COSO ERM framework does contain all of the elements of the earlier Internal Control version.

The COSO Internal Control framework has become the most widely used internal control framework in the United States and it has been adapted and/or

Figure 28.1: IRM Risk Management Process (IRM/AIRMIC/ALARM, 2002)

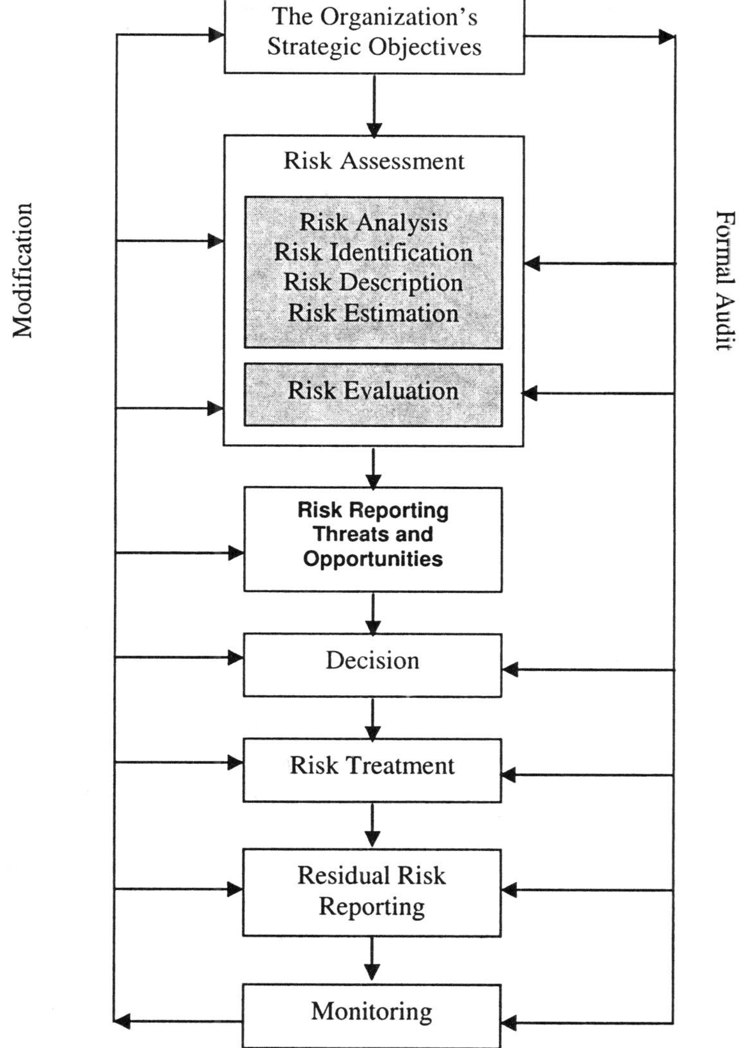

adopted by numerous countries and businesses around the world. An enterprise risk management (ERM) versions of the COSO framework was produced in 2004 and this has both risk management and internal control within scope.

Apart from the British, ISO and COSO standards, a number of others are also well regarded and in widespread use. The UK's Turnbull guidance was updated in 2005 and is considered by the Securities and Exchange Commission (SEC) in the United States to be an acceptable alternative to the COSO Internal Control framework for Sarbanes-Oxley compliance. The updated Turnbull guidance can be found as a free download from the website of the Financial Reporting Council.

As well as the established standards and frameworks, a considerable amount of guidance on risk management has been published by various government departments. HM Treasury in the UK has published the highly respected 'Orange Book', which contains a significant amount of useful information on risk management tools and techniques. Many of the ideas and concepts presented in the Orange Book are referenced throughout this volume.

Some of the available standards were developed by risk management professionals, while others were developed by accountants or auditors. There are three distinct approaches followed in the various standards:

- 'Risk management' approach followed by ISO 21000, British Standard BS 31100 and the IRM Standards.
- 'Internal Control' approach developed by COSO Internal Control framework and by the Turnbull Report.
- 'Risk Aware Culture' approach developed by the Canadian Institute of Chartered Accountants, known as the CoCo framework.

RISK MANAGEMENT PROCESS

The risk management processes and a similar process is contained in all of the established risk management's standards are found in all progressive organisations. Many of the standards distinguish between the risk management process and the framework that supports the process. However, this distinction is not always clear in many of the established risk management standards/framework.

The best-established risk management approaches are the IRM Standards, ISO 31000, BS 31100, and the COSO ERM framework. All four provide a description of the risk management framework, but more emphasis is placed on the risk management process in the IRM Standards, ISO 31000 and BS 31100. The COSO approach does not provide the same clear distinction between the framework and the risk management process itself and is mainly concerned with framework considerations.

Several countries have developed their own internal control and risk management standards as part of their requirements for being listed on a stock exchange. Typically, these are frameworks similar to COSO internal control in approach, and this is certainly the case with the Turnbull requirements that exist in the UK.

Although there are many ways of representing the risk management process yet the basis steps are all similar. There can be difficulties with the terminology that is used to describe the various steps, and Appendix A provides definitions of basic terms, as well as cross referencing the different terminologies that can be used.

RISK MANAGEMENT FRAMEWORK

There are many risk management standards and risk management frameworks that have been produced by various organizations. It is generally acknowledged that a standard is a document that produces information on both the risk management process and the risk management framework.

Within many risk management standards, risk management activities should take place within the context of the business environment, the organization and the risks faced by the organization. In order for the context to be described and defined, a framework is required to support the process. ISO 31000 places particular emphasis on context and states that consideration should be given to the internal context, external context and risk management context when undertaking risk management activities.

In supporting the risk management process, the risk management framework needs to facilitate communication and the flow of risk information. As the framework is a supportive structure, it is shown as a series of components built around and supporting the risk management process.

For example, an organization might decide to follow the structure of the IRM Risk Management Standards. The company would then have to set-up a framework that includes the structure, responsibilities, and administration, reporting and communication components of risk management. All of these procedures will then be recorded in a risk management policy.

Figure 28.2: Components of an RM Framework

Risk Architecture Risk architecture defines roles, responsibilities, communication and risk reporting structure	**Risk Strategy** Risk strategy, appetite, attitudes and philosophy are defined in the risk management policy
Risk Management Process	
Risk Protocols Risk protocols are defined in the risk guidelines for the organization and include the rules and procedures, as well as the risk management methodologies, tools and techniques that should be used.	

- *Internal environment*—The internal environment encompasses the tone of an organization and sets the basis for how risk is viewed and addressed.
- *Objective setting*—Objective must exist before management can identify potential events affecting their achievements.
- *Event identification*—internal and external events affecting achievement of objectives must be identified, distinguishing between risk and opportunities.
- *Risk assessment*—Risks are analyzed, considering likélihood and impact, as basis for determined how they should be managed.
- *Risk response*—Management selects risk responses—avoiding, accepting, reducing, or sharing risk.
- *Control activities*—Policies and procedures are established and implemented to help ensure the risk reponses are affectively carried out.
- *Information and communication*—Relevant information is identified, captured, and communicated so that people can fulfil their responsibilities.
- *Monitoring*—The entirely of enterprise risk managed is monitored and modifications made as necessary.

COSO ERM described the framework by stating: 'within the context of the established mission or vision of an organization, management establishes strategic objectives, selects strategy and sets aligned objectives cascading through the enterprise. This enterprise risk management framework is geared to achieving corporate objectives, set out in four risk categories"

- *Strategic:* High-level goals, aligned with and supporting its mission.
- *Operations:* Effective and efficient use of its resources.
- *Reporting:* Reliability of reporting.
- *Compliance:* Compliance with applicable laws and regulations.

FEATURES OF RM STANDARDS

The main risk management standards that have been developed are the IRM Standards, ISO 31000, British Standard BS 31100 and the COSO ERM Framework.

British Standards BS 31100:2008, entitled 'Risk Management—Code of Practice' was published in October 2008. It emphasized the requriemetns for a risk management framework to support the separately described risk management process. In particular, British Standards BS 31100 states that the risk management process. In particular, British Standards BS 31100 states that the risk management process should provide a systematic, effective and efficient way by which risks can be managed at different levels throughout the organization.

The risk management framework is described in the British Standard in some detail. In fact, most of the standard is made up of a description of the risk management framework, together with a detailed part on how to develop risk management activities. The risk management framework is continuous cycle of review and improvement. BS 31100 also processes a version of the risk management process and this is also presented as a continuous cycle of activities represented by the following five stages:

(i) Identify,
(ii) Assess,
(iii) Respond,
(iv) Report, and
(v) Review.

British Standards BS 31100 describes the risk management framework as a set of components that provide the foundations and organizational arrangement for designing, implementing, monitoring, reviewing and continually improving risk management processes throughout the organization.

CONTROL ENVIRONMENT APPROACH

The approach adopted by the Canadian Criteria of Control (CoCo) framework produced by the Canadian Institute of Chartered Accountants is based on the idea that the risk culture of the organization is the most important consideration. If the risk culture is correct, then the successful management of risks should follow. The CoCo framework states that:

> A person performs a task, guided by an understanding of its purpose (the objective to be achieved) and supported by capability (information, resources, supplies and skills). The person will need a sense of commitment to perform

> the task well over time. The person will monitor his or her performance and the external environment to learn about how to do the task better and about changes to be made. The same is true of any team or work group. In many organizations of people, the essence of control is purpose, commitment, capability and monitoring and learning.

The COSO ERM framework refers to the control environment as the internal environment. This can be considered to be equivalent to the control environment that is considered in the CoCo framework. CoCo provides a structured means of analyzing the control environment that enables a quantitative assessment of the control environment, so that the features for improvements can be identified.

The CoCo framework is considered in more detail in Part 6 of this book. Although there are different versions of the CoCo questions yet, the following are the headings that are normally used in order to evaluate the risk aware culture within an organization using a CoCo approach.

- Purpose, version and mission;
- Commitment to integrity and ethical values;
- Capability, authority and responsibilities; and
- Learning and development of competence.

29

Risk Management Responsibilities (Practices)

ALLOCATION OF RESPONSIBILITIES

Everybody working for the organization will need to be made aware of their risk management responsibilities, as will contractors and suppliers. There are many professional people in large organizations who have an understanding of risk and a substantial contribution to make to the successful management of the priority significant risks. Unfortunately, there is not always a common view of risk management or the issues that are important to the organization.

Ownership of core processes, key dependencies and risks is important, because it enables the risk management and audit committee to monitor actions and responsibilities. This ownership is important for all risks, although the audit committee will only monitor the priority significant risks.

Any confusion of responsibilities and reporting structure must be eliminated. There need to be clear statements of responsibilities for the following aspects of the management of each priorities significant risk.

- Setting required risk standards;
- Implementing risk standards; and
- Monitoring risk performance.

A detailed set of responsibilities is well ensure that the roles of risk owners, process owners, international audit, risk manager, specialist risk management functions, members of staff, contractors and outsourced operations as well as all other are clearly defined and understood.

ROLE OF THE RISK MANAGER

Historically, the risk manager has been involved in assessing overall risk policy with endorsement from the board. Decision on insurance risk management issues and the provision of statistical analysis of insurance losses have been part of these historical responsibilities.

The insurance risk manager needs to evaluate the current status of risk management and reflect on the current state of the insurance market. Increases in insurance rates and a more sophisticated approach to risk financing have effected the amount of insurance purchased by large organizations. In many cases, there has been less insurance purchase and this has led to a reduced premium spend and a lower budget for the insurance risk management department.

There is no single established reporting position in the structure of an organization for the risk manager. At present, risk manager may report to human resources manager, the finance director or the company secretary. Sometimes the risk manager is a report to the corporate treasure and occasionally, the chief executive officer (CEO).

There is still a need for a risk managements facilitator and co-coordinator in most large organizations. This will enable the organization to apply risk management tools and techniques to a wider range of issues. Risk have historically been divided into insurance able (pure) and non-insurable (speculative) risks, from a business success perspective, there are artificial divisions between types of risks.

Table 29.1: Historical Role of the Insurance Risk Manager

1. To establish the risk management strategy for protecting company property and people.
2. To co-ordinate the company insurance programme through the captive insurance company.
3. To work with the manager of the captive to maximize the contribution made by the captive insurance company.
4. To maintain key insurer relationships, monitor service providers and ensure cost-effective placement of insurance contracts.
5. To measures and monitor cost of risk performance of the group and individual group companies.
6. To ensure safe keeping and adequate retention of all insurance contracts and agreements.
7. To supervise the co-ordination of service provider activities and place the group and global insurances.
8. To co-ordinate the property survey programme, risk management procedures and incentive scheme.

The risk manager should be responsible for the corporate learning that has to take place so that the organization can understand the benefits of risk management. As guardian of the risk architecture, strategy and protocols (GRASP), the risk manager will be responsible for developing the strategy, systems and procedures by which the required risk management outcomes for the organization are achieved.

Historically, the insurance risk manager has probably not been involved in the strategic management and development of the organization. The broader role now required of a risk manager should lead to a greater involvement in project management and strategy formulation and delivery. The risk manager that enjoys a broad range of responsibilities will have a very challenging role within the organization. It will be a role that enables the risk manager to obtain a better level of understanding and involvement that most other roles or functions achieve.

CHIEF RISK OFFICER (CRO)

Perhaps, the title 'Risk Manager' has too many historical connections for it to be used as an appropriate description of what is now required. There is a need to find a new title and redefined the role of risk management at the same time.

Many organizations in the finance and energy sectors have identified the benefits of bringing the management of credit, market and operational risks together. It has been the case for some time in the finance sector that risk maganet has been separated from the purchase of insurance. The development of the role of Chief Risk Officer (CRO) reporting directly to the CEO reflects this fact.

Given that one of the key principles of risk management is that the approach to risk should be proportionate to the level of risk faced by the organization, it is unlikely that the majority of organizations will need to appoint someone of the seniority of a CRO. Nevertheless, organizations should, when reviewing their risk management architecture, decide the appropriator range of responsibilities and level of seniority of the risk manager.

The introduction of the job title Chief Risk Officer (CRO) is not universal, but it is becoming common in the specialist finance and energy sector. Guardian of the risk architecture, strategy and protocols (GRASP) is a superior description of the role that must be fulfilled.

For organizations where it is considered imperative for a CRO to be appointed, the contribution that can be made by that individual will be substantial.

As champion of the ERM process, the CRO plays a key part in bringing together disparate risk management processes to ensure that limited company resources are applied effectively. The COSO ERM Framework defines that role of the CRO as working with other managers to establish effective risk management, monitoring progress, and assisting other managers in reporting relevant risk information up, down and across the organization.

Internal auditors should work with the CROP as part of their risk management duties. In this role, internal auditors are responsible for evaluating the accuracy of ERM reporting and providing independent and value-added recommendations to management about its ERM approach. The IIA International Standards specify that the scope of internal auditors should include evaluating the reliability of reporting effectiveness, efficiency of operations and compliance with laws and regulations.

30

Risk Architecture and Structure (Practice)

RISK ARCHITECTURE

Figure 30.1 shows the risk architecture for a typical large corporate entity that is subject to the requirements of the Sarbanes-Oxley Act. This risk architecture should be set out in the risk management policy for the organization. Terms of reference of the various committees and a schedule of the activities should also be established, either in the risk management policy or in a calendar of risk management activities. This schedule of activities should be aligned with the other corporate activities in the organization.

For large organization with non-executive directors, the audit committee should also be shown in the risk management architecture. The role of the audit committee and the role of the head of internal audit are important in fulfilling the risk management strategy of the organization.

For organizations subject to the requirements of the Sarbanes Oxley Act, there will also a requriemetns to ensure that all information disclosed by the company is accurate. In many large organizations, this requirement has resulted in the establishment of a disclosures committee. The role of the disclosures committee is to check the source and correctness of all information that is disclosed by the organization. Sarbanes-Oxley requires that financial information is evaluated to a higher level of scrutiny.

The risk architecture of an organization sets out the hierarchy of committees and responsibilities related to risk management and internal control. In the structure shown in Figure 30.1, the corporate risk management committee focuses on executive risk management activities.

Risk management responsibilities for activities at divisional or unit level should be allocated to divisional management. Divisional management is responsible for co-

Figure 30.1: Risk Management Architecture for a Large Corporation

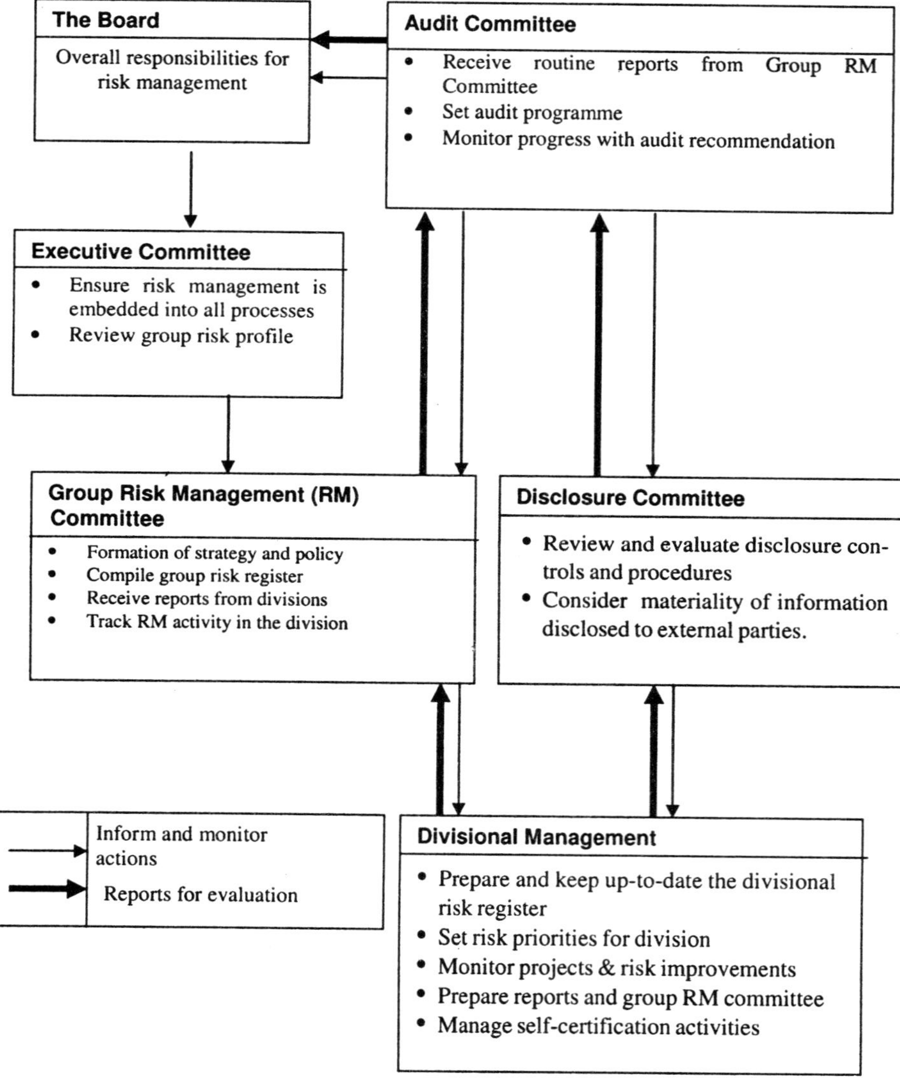

ordinating the identification of significant risk at divisional level, compiling the risk register for the division and ensuring that adequate controls are identified and implemented.

Divisional management should be provided with guidance from the group risk management committee. If there is a divisional committee, it should be required to send reports to the group risk management committee, so that the corporate or group overview of risk management priorities can be established.

For a public sector or charity organization, the risk architecture will be somewhat

Figure 30.2: RM Architecture for a Charity

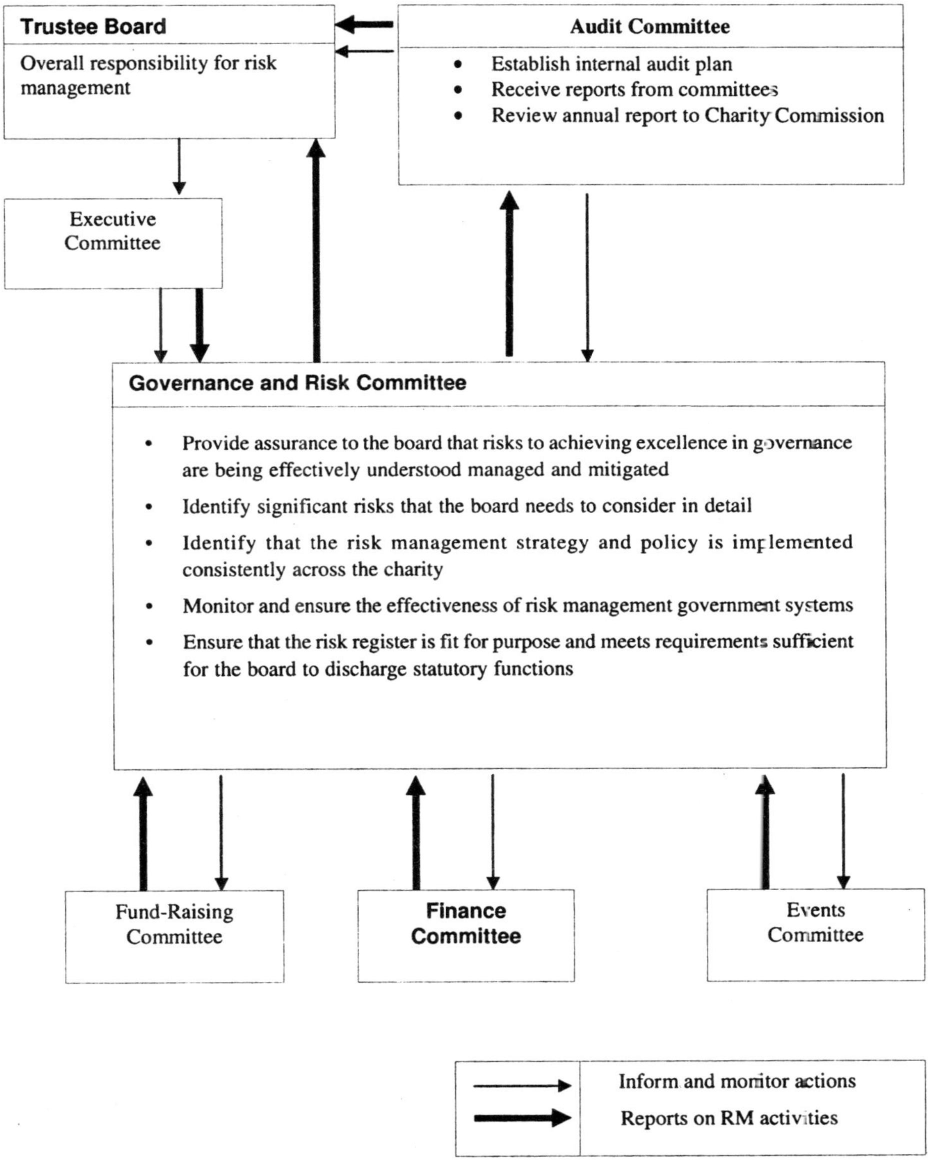

different. Figure 30.2 sets out a typical risk architecture for a charity. In this case, risk management activities are focused on the governance and risk committee. The flow of information and the control of risk management activities are illustrated by the arrows in Figure 30.2.

Corporate Structure

There are many ways for risk management reporting lines to be established. The reporting structure should be proportionate to the level of risk and the complexity of the organization. For high-risk organizations, such as those in the finance sector, the risk committee is likely to be a direct sub-committee of the board. In these circumstances, it is likely that the risk committee will be chaired by the group finance director and it will have other senior representation from the board.

In general, the risk management committee should be an executive committee made up entirely of executive directors with no non-executive director membership. This is because the management of risk is an executive function and non-executive directors are primarily responsible for audit and risk assurance. Typically, the risk management committee will send reports to the audit committee, and that will be the opportunity for non-executive directors to evaluate. Risk management committee will send reports to the audit committee, and that will be the opportunity for non-executive directors to evaluative risk performance and obtain risk assurance.

For organizations that are not operating in such a high-risk environment, it may not be necessary for the risk committee to report direct to the main board. In these circumstances, the risk committee may be a sub-committee of executive committee or the operations committee. In all cases, the corporate structure for the management of risk should be proportionate to the level of risk within the organization and the size, complexity, nature and risk exposure of the organization.

There are no specified correct structures for the risk architecture of an organization. Provided that the risk committee delivers the required outputs, the membership and terms of reference will be for the organization to decide. Nevertheless, the general point remains that management of risk is an executive function, whereas audit activities should be led by non-executive directors.

Risk Management Committees

Table 30.1 sets out typical responsibilities for a Risk Management Committee (RMC). Most large organizations will already have an audit committee, chaired by a senior non-executive director. An option considered by many organizations is to extend the role of the audit committee to include all aspects of risk management or to establish a separate risk management group chaired by an executive director.

There is a strong justification for the RMC to be an executive group, rather than part of any existing non-executive audit committee.

Some organisations have established the RMC as a sub-committee of the audit committee. In fact, establishing RMC as a sub-committee of the audit committee could impair the work of RMC because of increased bureaucracy and an unhelpful emphasis on auditing and compliance, rather than proactive management of risks.

Membership of the RMC is another question that needs to be addressed. The fundamental decision to be taken in large organisations is whether the risk management committee should be a small senior executive group setting strategy and policy or whether it should be a knowledge sharing group with representation from each of the units or departments within the origination. The answer will depend on the structure of the organization and the intended role of the committee.

Table 30.1: Responsibilities of the RM Committee

To advise the board on risk management and to foster a culture that emphasized and demonstrates the benefits of a risk-based approach to risk management.

To make appropriate recommendations to the board on all significant matters relating to the risk strategy and policies of the company.

To keep under review the effectiveness of the risk management infrastructure of the company, including:

- Assessment of risk management procedures in accordance with changes in the operating environment.
- Consideration of risk audit reports on the key business areas to assess the level of business risk exposure.
- Consideration of any major findings of any risk management review and the response of management.
- Assessment of the risks of new ventures and other strategies, project and operational initiatives.

To review the risk exposure of the company in relation to the risk appetite of the board and the risk capacity of the Company.

To consider the development of risk management and make appropriate recommendation to the board.

To consider whether disclosure of information regarding risk management policies and key risk exposures is in accordance with financial reporting standards.

The overall aim is to achieve a prioritized, validated and audited improvement in risk management standards in the organization. The RMC and the audit committee should, therefore, operate in a way that provides mutual support. However, combining the two committees into a single group, or placing one committee as superior to the other will not be the best way forward for most organizations.

RISK COMMUNICATIONS

Accurate communication on risk issues is vitally important. Internal communication within the organization will be undertaken through the risk architecture. This is the formal risk communication structure related to risk control activities and the collecting of information for external risk reporting purposes. For example, a road haulage company may wish to bring focus to the efficient operation of the organization and ensure that risk management receives appropriate attention.

RISK MANAGEMENT AS SUBJECT OF STUDY

The formal development of risk communication as subject began in the late 1970s with efforts by the nuclear and chemical industries in the United States to counteract widespread public concern about those technologies. It was believed that clear, understandable information was all that was needed to make people see that the risks were lower than many feared.

For many, this approach has failed, and most risk communication experts say it is inadequate. Perceptions of risk, and the behaviours that result, are a matter not only of the facts but also of our feelings, instincts and personal life circumstances.

Communication that offers the facts but fails to account for the effective side of our risk perception is simply incomplete.

Risk communication is also commonly thought of as what to say under crisis circumstances, but this is inadequate. It is certainly true that communication in times of crises is important in managing the public response. Countless examples have taught that a great deal of the effectiveness of risk communication during a crisis is based on what was done before hand.

RISK MATURITY

Table 30.2 sets out a system for determining the level of risk maturity within an organization with regard to risk management processes. This table sets out four levels of risk maturity, described as naïve, novice, normalized and natural (4Ns). The characteristics of each of these levels are described in the table. Clearly, it is better for an organization to seek a higher level of risk maturity. However, the approach to achieving risk maturity in the organization should be proportionate to the level of risk that the organization faces.

Nevertheless, achieving an improved level of risk maturity may be one of the strategic aims for risk management within the organization. If that is the case, an established framework for measuring risk maturity is required. It is important that the organization uses a risk maturity model that aligns with its own ambitious in relation to risk management maturity and provides a practical approach that can be embedded within the organization.

Several types of risk maturity approaches are in existence, including the Criteria of Control (CoCo) framework. The approach adopted by the CoCo framework focuses very heavily on the importance of risk maturity. The approach of this internal control framework is that if the risk culture and the risk architecture, strategy and protocols are correct then good levels of risk management and internal control will be achieved. Another risk maturity model that is frequently used is the European Foundation for Quality Management (EFQM) model.

Table 30.2: Four Levels of Risk Maturity

Level 1: Naïve Level 1 organizations are unaware of the need for the management of risk or do not recognize the value of structured caprices to dealing with uncertainty. Management processes are repetitive or reactive, with insufficient attempt to learn from the past or to prepare for future threats or uncertainties.
Level 2: Novice Level 2 organizations are aware of the potential benefits of managing risk, but have not implemented risk processes selectively and are not gaining the full benefits. The organization is either experimenting with the application of risk management or is operating a risk management process that has fundamental weaknesses.
Level 3: Normalized Level 3 organizations have built the management of risk into routine business processes and implement risk management throughout the organization. Generic risk management processes are formalized and the benefits are understood at all levels of the organization, although they may not be consistently achieved.
Level 4: Natural Level 4 organizations have a risk aware culture with proactive approach to risk management in all activities. As a result, the consideration of risk is inherent to routine processes. Risk information is actively used and communicated to improve processes and gain competitive advantage.

ALIGNMENT OF ACTIVITIES

Risk management activities and the risk architecture, strategy and protocols should be aligned with the business processes within the organization. Risk information flows around the risk management framework and (if successful) this will produce various outputs. These outputs have already been described as compliance, assurance, decisions and efficiency/effectiveness/efficacy (CADE3).

31

Risk Aware Culture Practices

DEFINITION OF RISK CULTURE

The culture of an organization is difficult to define. However, it is generally accepted that it is a reflection of the overall attitude or every component of management within a company. The culture of an organization determines how individuals will behave in particular circumstances. It will define how an individual feels obliged to behave in all circumstances.

A good risk culture will be the product of individual and group values and of attitude and patterns of behaviour. This will lead to a commitment to the risk management objectives of the organization. Organizations with a risk aware culture are characterized by communication founded on mutual trust and a shared perception of the importance of risk management. There also needs to be a sharing of confidence in the selected control measure and a commitment to adhering to the established risk control procedures.

Table 31.1 sets out the suggested components of a risk aware culture. These components were suggested only recently by the UK Health and Safety Executive (HSE) research as leadership, involvement, learning, accountability and communication (LILAC). This makes the acronym LILAC. Creating culture where effective risk management is an integral part of the way people work is a long-term aim for most organizations.

RISK MANAGEMENT TRAINING AND RISK CULTURE

As set out in Table 31.1, the risk culture of the organization can be defined by leadership, involvement, learning, accountability and communication (LILAC). The LILAC headings also provide an indication of the components of a successful initiative to embed risk management in the organization. The involvement, learning, accountability and communication components of a risk aware culture are all highly relevant to risk training and risk communication.

Table 31.1: Risk Aware Culture

A risk aware culture is achieved by LILAC:

Leadership	Strong leadership within the organization in relation to strategy, projects and operations.
Involvement	Involvement of all stakeholders in all stages of the risk management process.
Learning	Emphasis on training in risk management procedures and learning from events.
Accountability	Absence of an automatic blame culture, but appropriate accountability for actions.
Communication	Communication and openness on all risk management issues and the lessons learnt

Appropriate risk management documentation will provide managers and staff with information on the involvement that is required and the level of accountability that the organization expects. A good level of learning and communication can be established by adequate risk training and this will enhance the risk aware culture of the organization.

Consider the example of a publisher facing libel and slander risks. The company should prepare risk guidelines, including reference to awareness training for all staff. Comprehensive procedures for managing libel and slander risks should reflect the level of risk exposure. The level of attention paid to such risks will depend on each magazine title and the following framework may be appropriate:

- All journalists to be given basic libel and slander training;
- Specific review procedures introduced for political titles; and
- Legal evaluation of every issue of a satirical magazine.

Training needs to be provided for staff in the revised procedures, and information should be included on the company intranet site. Managers and staff need to be encouraged to comment on the new procedures, so that they may be improved further part of the learning culture within the company.

Risk training is a key part of the learning and communication and it is essential for managers, staff and other stakeholder engagement. It should cover a wide range of topics and achieve a greater understanding of all the risk-related issues, as well as providing information on the control measures that are in place and the vital role played by staff in the successful implementation of these controls.

Risk Information and Communication

Stakeholders will already have a perception of risks, so risk communication should be provided against the background of that existing perception. The guidelines relevant to risk communication should be followed, as depicted in Table 31.2. These guidelines seek to establish rules for communicating risk issues to a broad range of stakeholders.

Table 31.2: Risk Communication Guidelines

- Know the stakeholders, by identifying both external and internal stakeholders and finding out their interests and concerns.
- Simplify the language and presentation, although not the content if complex issues need to be communicated.
- Be objective in the information provided and differentiate between opinion and facts.
- Communicate clearly and honestly, taking account of the level of understanding of the audience.
- Deal with uncertainty and discuss situations where not all information is available and indicate what can be done to overcome these problems.
- Be cautious when putting risks in perspective, although comparing an unfamiliar risk with a familiar one can be helpful.
- Develop key messages that are clear, concise and to the point, with no more than three messages communicated at any one time.
- Be prepared to answer questions and agree to provide further information if it is not currently available.

These rules become more important when the communication about risk is with external bodies. Nevertheless, they provide a useful set of guidelines for risk communication with internal as well as external stakeholders. Internal stakeholders have additional reasons for being provided with risk information. There will normally be an expectation by the organization that managers and staff will play a role in the future management of the risk, whereas this may not always be the case for external stakeholders.

32

Future of Insurance

INTRODUCTION

A string of large and highly public organizational and Governmental failures over the past 10 years (Woolworths, Golden Wonder, Northern Rock, Citigroup, Enron and even the entire banking system of Iceland) has focused the attention of inventors, customers and regulators on the way in which directors, managers and boards are managing risk. This has led to a greater appreciation of the wider scope of risks facing organizations, which in turn has led to risk management becoming a core management discipline.

Risk is everywhere and derives directly from unpredictability. The process of identifying, assessing and managing risks brings any business full circle back to its strategic objectives: for it will be clear that not everything can be controlled. The local consequences of events on a global scale, such as terrorism, pandemics and credit crunches, are likely to be unpredictable. However, they can also include the creation of new and valuable opportunities. Many of today's households names were born out of times of adversity.

Risk management provides a framework for organizations to deal with and react to uncertainty. Whilst it acknowledges that nothing in life is certain, the modern practice of risk management is a systematic and comprehensive approach, drawing on transferable tools and techniques. These basic principles are sector independent and should improve business resilience, increase predictability and contribute to improved returns. This is particularly important given the pace of change of life today.

Risk management involves a healthy dose of both common sense and strategic awareness, coupled with an intimate knowledge of the business, an enquiring mind and most critically superb communication and influencing skills.

The institute of Risk Management's International Certificate in risk management is an introductory qualification, which reflects the changing and global nature of risk management. Recognizing both the enterprise-wide (for 'ERM') importance of comprehensive risk management and the growing use of international standards (such as ISO 31000), this qualification equips future professional risk managers with the fundamental knowledge and tools to make invaluable contributions to long-term organizational growth and prosperity.

RISK MANAGEMENT IN CONTEXT

We all face risks in our everyday lives. Risks arise from personal activities and range from those associated with travel through to the ones associated with personal financial decisions. There are considerable risks present in the domestic components of our lives and these include fire risks in our homes and financial risks associated with home ownership. Indeed, there is also a whole range of risks associated with domestic and relationship issues, but these are outside the scope of this book.

We are presently and primarily concerned with business and commercial risks and the roles that we fulfil during our job or occupation. However, the task of evaluating risks and deciding how to respond to them is a daily activity not only at work, but also at home and during leisure activities. Life Insurance can not be kept at bay or ignored. It is equally important to keep ourselves fully ensured as we live for happiness as the ultimate goal of life, for which we need to keep relationship at four levels—between 'self' and 'body', between our 'self' and other 'self'; between self and family; between self and society; between self and the nature and the rest of establishment. We also need to have prosperity (earning more than required to meet our expenditure), and all the four that is self, family, society and nature—for happiness in continuity, and relations also in continuity—not one time shot. Insurance will provide safety, security and provision for future and for those we love and leave behind at the time we make an exit from the world.

APPENDICES

ANNEXURE 1

Some Cases that are Integral to the Evolution of General Insurance

Case 1: Principles—Non-Disclosure

Joel *vs.* Law, Union and Crown Insurance Company, (1908) 99 LT 712, CA.

(Dispute on what should be disclosed and that would be treated as non-disclosure).

Finding: There is no duty on the insured to disclose facts which he could not reasonably be expected to know.

Fletcher Moulton, L.J. (at 718)

The duty is a duty to disclose, and you cannot disclose what you do not know. The obligation to disclose, therefore, necessarily depends on the knowledge you possess. If a reasonable man would have recognized that the knowledge in question was material to disclose, it is no excuse that you did not recognize it. But the question always is was the knowledge you possessed such that you ought to have disclosed it? Let me take an example. I will suppose that a man has occasionally had a headache. It may be that a particular one of these headaches would have told a brain specialist of hidden mischief, but to the man it was an ordinary headache indistinguishable from the rest. Now, no reasonable man would deem it material to tell an insurance company of all the casual headaches he had in his life, and if he knew no more as to this particular headache, there would be no breach of his duty towards the insurance company in not disclosing it. He possessed no knowledge that it was incumbent on him to disclose, because he knew of nothing which a reasonable man would deem material or of a character of influence the insurers in their action. (He) can not be held liable for non-disclosure in respect of facts which he did not know. Insurer are … (entitled) to full disclosure of all knowledge possessed by the applicant that is material to the risk.

Source: E.R. Hardy Ivamy, 'Casebook on Insurance Law', London, Butterworths, 4th Edition (pp. 5-6, 1984).

Case 2: Motor-Damage to Insured Vehicle

Seaton *vs.* London, General Insurance Company Ltd. (1932)43 LLL Rep 398.

[The engine of an insured lorry was removed for repair to the insured's workshop at a distance of nearly 150 yards away from the garage where the lorry was kept. There, the engine was destroyed by fire. Insure repudiated liability stating that the vehicle was covered only when it was in a complete condition].

Finding by the King's Bench Davison: Where a vehicle is dismantled into two pieces, and one piece is removed for the purpose of repair, it is still a vehicle for the purpose of a motor insurance policy.

Du Parcq J. (at 399)

(If) he had taken the whole of the vehicle into his yard or any other place to repair it, and then would have taken the engine for the purpose of repair, he would still have been insured in respect of the motor vehicle ... and any damage to it would have been covered. But he left the vehicle bereft of its engine in the garage and look the engine to another part of the premises ... the engine was burned. ... while it was in the carpenter's shop.

It is said ... (that the company) ... Did not insure against loss of two vehicles, and that if he is going to be allowed to divide up his vehicles in two or more sections, it seem hard on the company ... (if) seems to be almost beyond dispute that the mere fact that he has taken the engine out of the vehicle does not prevent the vehicle as a whole from being insured ... Therefore, ... in my opinion that at the time when the fire occurred. Mr. Seaton still had a motor vehicle although it was in two pieces.

I think, therefore, it is impossible to say that Mr. Seaton was not covered by his policy because he divided the lorry into two and took the engine to another part of the premises.

Source: E.R. Hardy Ivamy, 'Casebook on Insurance Law', London, Butterworths, 4th Edition (pp. 85-87, 1984).

Case 3

Yorkshire Insurance Co. Ltd. *vs.* Nisbet Shipping Co. Ltd. (1961) 2 (All ER 487).

[Whether under the doctrine of subrogation, an insurer can recover from insured any more than what they had paid].

Finding by the Queen's Bench Division: Under the doctrine of subrogation embodied in the Marine Insurance Act, 1905, S. 79 the insurer could not recover from the assured anything more than he has paid to the assured.

[A vessel insured for pound 72,000 became a total loss after colliding with a Canadian Government ship. The insurers paid pound 72,000 to the assured, who then claimed damages from the Canadian Government. Meanwhile, as the Pound Sterling had been devalued in 1949, the loss (when converted into English currency) came to nearly pound 127,000 which was paid by the Canadian Government to the assured. The assured repaid the pound 72,000 to the insurers, and claimed that they were entitled to keep the excess sum of pound 55,000.]

It follows that in my view the insurer's rights in this case were limited to recovering from the assured the amount overpaid, that is to say, pound 72,000. He is entitled to no more. The principle, I think, is a simple one, it renders irrelevant any consideration of the particular concatenation of circumstances which enable the assured to recover from the Canadian Government a sum in sterling in excess of the value of the ship at the time of the casualty. The fact that the policy was a valid policy, with, as it transpired, a policy value somewhat less than the real value is also irrelevant. The simple principle which I apply is that the insurer can not recover under the doctrine of subrogation now embodied in S. 79 of the Marine Insurance Act, 1906 anything more than he has paid.

Source: E.R. Hardy Ivamy, 'Casebook on Insurance Law', London, Butterworths, 4th Edition (p. 224, 1984).

Case 4: Householder's Comprehensive—Definition of Flood

Young *vs.* Sun Alliance and London Insurance Ltd. (1976) 2 Lloyd's Rep 189.

[Definition; the meaning of the word 'flood' in a Householder's Comprehensive Insurance policy covering storm, tempest or floods].

Finding of the Court of Appeal: 'Flood as used in the phrase in the policy referred to something that is violent and abnormal, and not seepage.

Lawton, L.J. (at 191)

[A house was insured to cover (*inter alia*) damage by storm, tempest or flood. Seepage of water from on underground water course damaged a lavatory on the ground floor of the house. The insured made a claim on the ground that the damage was caused by flood].

This appeal raises a semantic problem which has troubled many philosophers for centuries, and it can, I think, be expressed in the aphorism that an elephant is difficult to define but easy to recognize. I find difficulty in defining the word flood as used in this policy, I have no difficulty in looking at the evidence in this case and coming to the conclusion, as do, that the water in the lavatory was not a flood within the meaning of para 8 of this policy.

(Counsel) pointed out to the court that the phrase in the policy is storm, tempest or flood, and that the word flood is used as a word in ordinary English usage to cover a situation which may be very different from the situations to which the words flooded or flooding are appropriate. I agree. It is not without reference that Para 9 in the next paragraph in the policy, refers to the Escape of water from or frost damage to any water, drainage or heating installation, so flood is something different for the purposes of this policy from an escape of water.

I agree with Shaw, L.J. that the essence of flood is ordinary English is some abnormal, violent situation. It may not necessarily have to be sudden, but it does, in my judgment, have to be violent and abnormal. This seepage of water through a rise in the water level was not violent, and it was not all that abnormal, it was the sort of incident which householders sometimes have to suffer as a result of rising damp. I, too, would dismiss the appeal.

Source: E.R. Hardy Ivamy, 'Casebook on Insurance Law', London, Butterworths, 4th Edition, (pp. 266-67, 1984).

Case 5: Liability—Negligence and Fraud

West Wake Price & Co. *vs* Ching, (1956) 3 All ER 621.

[Whether a claim due to a mix of 'negligence a fraud' is covered under a liability insurance covering 'negligence'].

Finding of the Queen's Beach Division: The 'claim' was limited to an unmixed claim relating only to an 'act of neglect, default or error'.

Devlin, J. (at 831)

[A firm of accountants had affected a Lloyd's Accountants indemnity policy against claims arising out of an act of neglect, default or error on the part of the assured or their servants in the conduct of their business as accountants. One of the clerks employed by the insured converted a client's money to his own use. The client made a claim partly on the grounds of negligence and partly on dishonesty. The accountants firm, in turn, claimed any indemnity from their insurers, who repudiated liability stating that the loss was not covered under the policy].

I have reached the conclusion that there is in fact a simpler and more effective test, which is the correct one. It depends simply on the true construction of the policy. Businessmen often want to write into a document the words which they think will amplify its meaning, but which lawyers reject a superfluous, nevertheless, the writing in of superfluities sometimes helps to clarify questions of construction. If a layman wanted a phrase such as claim in respect of negligence only or claims in respect of the negligence but not in respect of fraud, a lawyer would tell him that his additions were superfluous, since negligence meant negligence and nothing else and did not include fraud ... if words such as these were there, however, they would serve to show that a claim in respect of negligence alone. Applying this test, which I think is the right one, the claim in this cause is outside the policy.

Source: E.R. Hardy Ivamy, 'Casebook on Insurance Law', London, Butterworths, 4th Edition (pp. 257-58, 1984).

Various Forms Prescribed by IRDA

Form IRDA/RI—Request for Registration Application

(1) Name of the applicant.
(2) Address.
(3) Date of incorporation as a company.
(4) Registration No. (issued by the Registrar of the Companies).
(5) Classes of insurance business for which registration is sought.
(6) Amount of authorized capital and face value of shares and their numbers.
(7) Amount of paid up capital and number of equity shares.
(8) Classification of shares.
(9) Voting rights of each class of shareholders.
(10) Details of shareholders.
(11) Background information on the applicant.
(12) Key aspects of the applicant company.
(13) Capital structure.
(14) Details of directors and key persons.
(15) Details of external auditors (Proposed).
(16) Details of business to be transacted.
(17) Details of proposed locations of insurance business.
(18) Distribution channels.
(19) Financial projections.
(20) Sensitivity analysis.
(21) Rural business.
(22) Obligations in unorganized sector and backward classes.
(23) Particulars of previous application.
(24) Conclusion viability of the operations.
(25) Certification and signature of the authorized person (with seal).

The form for applying for registration prescribed under IRDA, Regulations, 2000 is Form IRDA/R2—"Application for Registration". The composition of the form is as follows:

Form IRDA/R2—Application for Registration

(1) Existing or proposed geographic spread.
(2) Details of market research and analysis on market potential, etc.
(3) Description of products to be sold.
(4) Proposed distribution network.
(5) Proposed sales promotion.
(6) Underwriting approach proposed.

(7) Investment plan.
(8) Information technology plan.
(9) Proposed customer service standards.
(10) Retention limits and reinsurance.
(11) Approach towers recruitment and training.
(12) Internal control proposed.
(13) Expenses of administration.
(14) New product pricing.
(15) Information policy.
(16) Premium rates.
(17) Certification with signature of the authorized person (with seal).

IRDA has prescribed form IRDA/R3 for issuance of the Certificate of Registration to the Company. The specimen is given below:

FOR IRDA/R3—CERTIFICATE OF REGISTRATION

FORM IRDA/R3

Insurance Regulatory and Development Authority
(Seal of the Authority)
Certificate of Registration

Registration Number ....

This is to certify that (Name of Insurer and his address) has this day been registered in accordance with the provision of sub-section (2A) of section 3 of the Insurance Act, 1938 (IV of 1938) to transact the classes of business specified in the Schedule below:

Given under the seal of the Authority at New Delhi this .... day of .... two thousand and ....

INSURANCE REGULATORY AND DEVELOPMENT AUTHORITY

SCHEDULE

Classes of business which may be transacted:

(1) ....
(2) ....
(3) ....
(4) ....

For the purpose of issuing a duplicate copy of the certificate of Registration, IRDA has prescribed form IRDA/R4. The specimen is given on next page:

FORM IRDA/R4 ISSUE OF DUPLICATE CERTIFICATE OF REGISTRATION

To
Insurance Regulatory and Development Authority,
New Delhi.

Sub: Application for issue of duplicate certificate of registration.

We request you to issue a duplicate certificate of registration for which we give below the following details:

(1) Name of insurer
(2) Registration number
(3) Date of Certificate of Registration
(4) How original certificate has been lost, destroyed or mutilated?
(5) Particulars of remittance of fee

Place
Date:

Yours truly
Signature of the Principal Officer
(Name of the Principal Officer)
(Seal)

For applying for renewal of the Certificate of Registration, IRDA has prescribed Form IRDA/R5. The specimen is given below.

FORM IRDA/R5—APPLICATION FOR RENEWAL

Date:

From: (Name of insurer)

To Insurance Regulatory and Development Authority

Dear Sir,
As required by Regulation 20 of Insurance Regulatory and Development Authority (Registration of Indian Insurance Companies) Regulation, 2000, we hereby apply for renewal of registration for the year .... to ....

Our total gross premium written direct in India during the financial year .... to .... was Rs. ....

Accordingly, we enclosed a bank draft no. .... dated .... drawn on .... Hyderabad, for Rs. ....

Kindly issue the renewal of registration certificate.

Yours faithfully,

(Name of Signatory)
(Designation)

IRDA has prescribed Form IRDA/R6 for renewal of the Certificate of Registration of the company. The specimen is given below.

FORM IRDA/R6 CERTIFICATE OF RENEWAL OF REGISTRATION

Registration Number

Date of Renewal of Registration

The certificate of registration of (Name of Insurer) hereby renewed under Section 3A of the Insurance Act, 1938 for the year .... to ....

Issued at New Delhi on .... day of 2000

(Seal of the Authority)

(Authorized Signatory)

Forms relating to the intermediaries' licensing

As per various regulations of the IRDA relating to different intermediaries\all intermediaries in the insurance market have to file the necessary applications with IRDA.

Agents' Licensing: There are different forms prescribed for agents, which are listed below:

(1) Form IRDA—Agents-VA has been prescribed for individuals applying form/renewing a licence to work as an insurance agent.
(2) Form IRDA—Agents VC has been prescribed for firms or companies applying for/renewing a license to work as an insurance agent.
(3) The IRDA grants the license vide Form IRDA-VB.
(4) The IRDA grants identity cards to individual agents vide Form IRDA-VZ.
(5) The IRDA grants identity cards to corporate agents vide Form IRDA-VY.

Brokers' Licensing: There are different forms prescribed for brokers, which are listed below:

(1) Form A under the IRDA (insurance brokers) Regulation, 2002 has been prescribed for applying for/renewing a licence to work as an insurance broker.
(2) The IRDA grants the license vide Form B under the IRDA (Insurance Brokers) Regulations, 2002.

Third Party Administrators' Licensing: There are different forms prescribed for TPAs, which are listed below:

(1) From TPA-1 under the IRDA (TPA Health Services) Regulation, 2001 has been prescribed for applying for licence to work as a Third Party Administrator.
(2) The IRDA grants the licence vide From TPA-2 under the IRDA (TPA Health Services), Regulations, 2001.
(3) Form TPA-3 under the IRDA (TPA Health Services) Regulation, 2001 has been prescribed for renewing a licence to work as third Party Administrator.
(4) TPAs have to present their annual report as per Form TPA-4.

Bibliography

IRDA circulars on file and use guidelines & data collection post de-tariffing, website: http://www.irdaindia.org.

IRDA regulations, website: http://www.irdaindia.org.

Report of the Committee Reforms in the Insurance Sector by R.N. Malhotra and others.

Report of the K.P. Narasimham Committee on Provisions of the Insurance Act, 1938 by Mr. K.P. Narasimham (and 10 other members) submitted to the IRDA, (July 26, 2005).

Standing Committee on International Financial Standards and Codes Report of the Advisory Group on Insurance Regulation by R. Ramakrishana, T.G. Menon and others, DEAP, Reserve Bank of India (2000:30) (*ibid.*, 31-32).

The Actuarial Practice of General Insurance, D.G. Hart, R.A. Buchanan, and B.A. Howe, Institute of Actuaries of Australia Motor Accidents Authority (MAA), the regulatory body of the New South Wales State of Australia. Utah State Insurance Rules, Definitions, website http://www.insurance.utah.gov/rules/590-121.htm

The India Motor Tariffs Published by the TAC, website: http://www.tac.org.in

The Insurance Act, 1938.

The Insurance Act, 1938. All tariffs published by TAC, website http://www.tac.org.in. Website of Wikipedia.

The Sarbanes-Oxley Act of 2002 of USA, also known as the Public Company Accounting Reform and Investor Protection Act of 2002 and commonly called SOX or Sarbox.

Website of Agriculture Corporation of India Ltd., Website of General Insurance Corporation of India Ltd.

Website of Bajaj Alliance Insurance Co. Ltd.

Website of ICICI Lombard Insurance Co. Ltd.

Website of Insurance Information Institute http://www.iii.org

Website of International Association of Insurance Supervisors: http://www.iaisweb.org.

Website of IRDA http:///www.irdaindia.org

Website of National Insurance Co. Ltd.

Website of Oriental Insurance Co. Ltd.

Website of New India Insurance Co. Ltd.

Website of the Risk and Insurance Management Society (RIMS): ERM for Financial Institutions, Rating Criteria and Best Practices by Standard and Poor, website: http://www.mgt.ncsu.edu/pdfs/erm/sp_erm_busdevbk.pdf.

Website of United India Insurance Co. Ltd.

Website of Wikipedia: Website of the Committee of Sponsoring Organizations of the Treadway Commission.

Index